INDONESIAN COMMUNISM UNDER SUKARNO

Ideology and Politics, 1959–1965

BOOKS BY REX MORTIMER

Indonesian Communism under Sukarno: Ideology and Politics, 1959–1965

The Indonesian Communist Party and Land Reform, 1959–1965

Editor and contributor: *Showcase State: The Illusion of Indonesia's "Accelerated Modernization"*

INDONESIAN COMMUNISM UNDER SUKARNO

Ideology and Politics, 1959-1965

REX MORTIMER

Cornell University Press

ITHACA AND LONDON

First published 1974 by Cornell University Press.
Published in the United Kingdom by Cornell University Press Ltd., 2-4 Brook Street, London W1Y 1AA.

International Standard Book Number 0-8014-0825-3
Library of Congress Catalog Card Number 73-19372

Printed in the United States of America by York Composition Co., Inc.

For Mary, who understands, and Michael,
who may one day comprehend as we cannot,
that we are all victims

Contents

Preface

The history of Indonesian Communism has been fatefully consistent in its tragedy. In three distinct periods, the Indonesian Communist Party (PKI) has risen from obscurity to prominence with the amazing rapidity of that "prairie fire" whose image Mao Tse-tung evoked to describe the peasant upsurge in central China in 1925, only to be engulfed each time by a torrent of violence. The pattern of the period with which this book is concerned differs from the others only in the magnitude of the party's expansion and of its disaster.

Much of the fascination of this movement, for this writer at least, lies in the paradoxes associated with this extraordinary cycle of fortune and misfortune. The obligation to adopt a detached and balanced approach in analyzing the processes making up the Communist saga in Indonesia need not blind one to the poignant human implications of the party's fate. It is estimated, for instance, that somewhere between half a million and one million Communists and purported Communists perished in the reprisals which followed upon the "coup attempt" of October 1, 1965. Yet this ghastly massacre, visited alike upon Communist leaders and hundreds of thousands of followers whose only crime was that they found in the PKI sustenance for their needs and aspirations, aroused remarkably little notice and concern in the West. Viewed by many with relief and satisfaction as the removal of a baneful threat to Western interests, and by others as a regrettable and embarrassing, but understandable, resolution of a nonnegotiable political impasse, the killing of countless innocents has attracted far less humanitarian attention than other occurrences of considerably smaller dimensions in other parts of the world.

We find echoes here of that deep-seated feeling among Westerners that the taking of life in "the East" is of less consequence than in other contexts. Additionally, it is hard to avoid the conclusion that the bland unconcern shown over the Indonesian massacres was caused in no small degree by their occurrence at the height of the Vietnam war, when the interests of Americans, Australians, and Europeans in Southeast Asia appeared threatened as never before. I feel that the apathy evinced in prevailing attitudes toward the killings would have been less had their significance for those most closely involved, either as perpetrators or as close kin and neighbors of victims, been explored more thoroughly. Unfortunately, not only has this dimension been barely touched upon by scholars, but in addition, and regrettably, neither political scientists, sociologists, nor ethnologists have ever given the Western reader much insight into the world of the kinds of people the Communists appealed to and spoke for.

Academic attitudes toward the PKI have been affected in more direct ways by the climate of opinion created by the events of 1965–66. At the time I was gaining my first acquaintance with Indonesia and the PKI, in 1964, Western scholars were engaged in a debate about the character of Indonesian Communism and its prospects for gaining power. On the one hand there were those who, like Guy Pauker and Justus van der Kroef, saw the rapid progress in organization and influence of the PKI as presaging a likely Communist takeover in conditions of economic chaos, political instability, and a declining will on the part of the Indonesian elite to resist the Communist steamroller. Different estimates were made, notably by Donald Hindley and Ruth McVey, on the basis of an interpretation of Indonesian politics that stressed the determination of those in power, especially the army leaders, to keep the Communists out, the unsuitable nature of the large but loose Communist organization for engaging in any real struggle for power, and in Hindley's case the degree to which the Communist leaders had been "domesticated" by Sukarno. One attitude that most of the disputants shared, however, was a considerable respect for the qualities of the PKI leaders and cadres, for their political capabilities, attention to the interests of the workers and peasants, realistic assessment of the workers' situation, and relative freedom from the taint of corruption.

The events following the coup attempt resolved this controversy but at the same time gave rise to a tendency on the part of many Western academics writing about Indonesia to denigrate the PKI's role in Indonesian national life. As a result, certain stereotypes of Indonesian Communism have emerged that obstruct a balanced understanding of its political role. Of these stereotypes, three in particular are highly misleading.

The first comes close to suggesting that millions of Indonesians flocked to the PKI banner only to give expression to the cries of pain that they, as victims of social change, were impelled to utter. This explanation allots no significance either to any rationally conceived interests on the part of those concerned or to the character of the Communist movement in Indonesia. Considering that, even when Sukarno's protection offered some security, adherence to the PKI always involved risks, it seems far more likely that masses of workers, peasants, teachers, and low-level officials found in this movement the one significant political force displaying a devotion to their interests and seeking, under difficult circumstances, to give them an entrée onto a political stage dominated by the neotraditional elites and the swanky "modern" suburbs of Djakarta, Bandung, and Surabaja. However the contrast between the Old Order of Sukarno and the New Order of General Suharto may be drawn, the role of champion of the masses formerly filled by the PKI has now been eliminated, with the political vacuum thereby created being justified on the grounds that the lower orders constitute a "floating mass" to be insulated from the unsettling and potentially subversive effects of participation in party politics. In this respect alone, then, the immolation of the PKI has led to the reversal of an important trend of earlier postindependence politics; the impact on power concentration, social stratification, and in particular the position of the worker and peasant may well prove of the greatest consequence.

Nor, despite the seeming plausibility given to the argument by the PKI's stance over the 1963 economic stabilization plan, can the contention be convincingly upheld that the Communists deliberately promoted or connived at the economic chaos of the later years of the Sukarno era in order to rise to power on the wreckage. The point is dealt with specifically in the corpus of this study, but it is at least arguable from a more general standpoint that the PKI represented the most hopeful prospect for a reconstruction of Indonesian society that would have made possible sustained development combined with attention to mass social welfare and the elimination of the gross inequities and bureaucratic vices that plague the country. We can only speculate on the form these changes might have taken, and the sacrifices they would have involved, but the time is surely past when we must assume that Communist prescriptions for economic and social development are uniform or predictable in the degree of ruthlessness with which they are pursued. There is no doubt that the PKI leaders could be ruthless and singleminded in pursuing their objectives, and that many would have suffered intensely had they attained them. But ruthlessness was never a Communist monopoly. The ruthlessness of men in power exists in plenty in Indonesia today, in the methods employed to deal with critics and questioners in the arena of national politics, and above all in the burdens which misery and powerlessness lay daily upon the mass of the people. Only by comprehensively comparing the present with a hypothetical Communist future, or that part of it whose shape we can deduce from the clues that the PKI's ideology and actions provide, could we assess the relative benefits and costs of each for the bulk of the population.

Again, fears and prognoses expressed in the West that a Communist Indonesia would have ushered in an era of Chinese domination over Southeast Asia or gravely threatened the security of non-Communist nations in the area are open to serious question. The PKI did indeed promise, as did Sukarno, that "the lifeline of imperialism was destined to be cut in Southeast Asia"; but the examination of PKI nationalism and the roots of its jealously guarded independence undertaken in these pages will, I believe, show this fear of Chinese domination to have been in large part hyperbole. The impact of a Communist Indonesia on the future of the Southeast Asian region is a subject for judicious evaluation and debate, but apocalyptic judgments are as out of place as were the dire forecasts made only a few short years ago about the threat represented by China.

For obvious reasons, we have had very few opportunities since 1965 to balance the views of the present Indonesian government and those that prevail in Western writing with the PKI's own interpretation of events and its role in them. For this reason, mention should be made of one case where such comparison can be made for the light it throws on the appeal and characteristics of the movement. In a dignified and moving speech to the court that sentenced him to death in 1967 for his alleged part in the 1965 coup, Sudisman, general secretary of the party, admitted that he and a few other PKI leaders had become involved in the coup attempt because they feared that the army was intending to move against the Communists. He acknowledged that this action was "adventurist" and accepted full blame for it, just as he undertook responsibility for other mistakes that he said the PKI had committed prior to the coup. At the same time he averred that the PKI needed no defense:

Although the PKI is now shattered, I firmly believe that this is only for a time, and that in the process of history the PKI will eventually arise again, because the PKI is a child of the times, given birth to by the times. . . . Through many hardships and difficulties, the PKI will rediscover a way to rise again with men far fresher than the five of us. They will certainly make our failure the mother of their victory.

Hunted, in fear of enemy bullets, it [the PKI] is now compelled to lie low. But ultimately it will crawl back on hands and knees to take aim at the enemies of the People: the imperialists, the landlords and other reactionary groups within the country.

Sudisman refused to plead for his life, aligning himself instead with the fate of his fallen colleagues:

Why would I choose the path of the courts, when my beloved comrades, my colleagues in the party leadership, D. N. Aidit, M. H. Lukman, Njoto, and Sakirman, have taken the short cut of the path of death for the honor of the PKI? All four are dead, shot down without taking the path of the courts. The four of them are I, and I am the four of them. Communist solidarity demands that I unite my stance with theirs and choose the path of death. With the four of them I have been five-in-one. . . .

For this solidarity one must be ready to make sacrifices, since without this readiness to make sacrifices, and to subordinate personal interest to the interest of all, solidarity cannot be achieved.

Sudisman concluded his speech with a typically Javanese peroration:

I am a Communist who was born in Java; and therefore it is my duty, in accordance with the custom of the Javanese, to take my leave by saying: First: *matur nuwun*—I thank all those who feel that they have helped me in the course of the struggle. Second: *njuwun gunging pangaksomo*—a thousand times I ask forgiveness, above all of the progressive and revolutionary masses who feel that I have harmed them in the course of the struggle. Third: *njuwun pangestu*—I ask for blessings, especially from my family, my wife, and my children, as I leave to undergo the verdict of the law.

This statement demonstrates how in the PKI Communist ideas merged with indigenous strains of thought and feeling to create a message of profound appeal to a populace hungry for a vision of hope as well as relief from their material cares. Trenchant in its attack upon social and political ills, Sudisman's speech is at the same time infused with elements of Javanese mysticism; nowhere can this be seen more clearly than in the implied equation of the Communist leaders with the Pendawa, the five legendary brothers of the *wajang* plays, Java's most beloved hero figures and symbols of courage, steadfastness, and compassion.

This work tries to place the PKI in its setting, and so to probe its ideas and actions as they related to specific opportunities and constraints. With such an approach, I hope to avoid the pitfalls of hindsight judgments attuned to different circumstances, whether these judgments be idealized interpretations or sweeping disparagements.

My first and only direct contact with the PKI was in the latter part of 1964, when Indonesian Communism was at the height of its strength and influence. At that time, I spent many hours in conversation with PKI chairman Aidit and his central leadership team, interviewed leaders of PKI mass organizations as well as men prominent in government, party, and press, and studied at first hand the work of PKI committees at the provincial, district, town, and village levels in Central and East Java. I was impressed by the vitality and political acumen of Indonesia's Communist leaders, surprised by their ready accessibility and apparent frankness in discussing their views and problems, and attracted by their engaging and warm personalities. In an admittedly brief and limited contact with Indonesian political life, I could find no counterpart in other parties and organizations to the sense of purpose and dedication, the egalitarianism, and the combination of social vision and down-to-earth realism which animated the PKI. At the same time, I could not help but note evident paradoxes in the PKI's position—notably the contrasts between the militant flavor of the party's rhetoric and the studious moderation of its domestic policies, and between the self-confidence PKI leaders exuded when discussing their future prospects and the acute uneasiness they displayed at any sign of army movements. At lower levels of the organization, I was struck by the free-and-easy atmosphere that prevailed in discussions and activities, the undiscriminating devotion accorded Sukarno, and the confidence with which party members believed that following their leaders would assure a painless victory for their cause.

Yet the PKI remained an enigma. I was sufficiently well acquainted with the operations of other Communist parties to realize that there was something distinctive about Indonesian Communism at that time —a curious ambivalence in its ideology, a markedly more tolerant attitude toward competing currents in political life, and the seeming irrelevance of the size of its following to the problem of gaining power under Indonesian conditions. I resolved to learn the Indonesian language and probe more deeply into the puzzle, for, like many others, I had become intoxicated by the heady atmosphere of Sukarno's Indonesia after one exposure to it. Nevertheless, it is probable that my observations would have remained little more than formless impressions had it not been for the encouragement of Professors J. D. Legge and Herbert Feith of Monash University, whose interest and stimulation led me to embark on systematic political studies and the assimilation of a wealth of political and social material from and about Indonesia.

By the time I began detailed research into the ideology of Indonesian Communism the PKI as I had known it was no more. The October 1965 coup attempt and its aftermath had destroyed the organization; many of the individuals who were to have been the focus of my study had been killed, and direct access to Indonesian Communist ideas and activities was no longer possible. This necessarily affected the nature of my work and the research methods I could employ. While my major concern was still to analyze the manner in which an indigenous Communist movement arrives at an accommodation between its doctrinal heritage and its environment, and translates that accommodation into practical policies and actions, I could no longer hope either to explore all the nuances of this process with those directly involved or to examine at first hand the nature of PKI commitment at the grassroots level. To some extent, this handicap was overcome by contact with PKI expatriates, but much that I would have liked to pursue in depth had perforce to be treated in a limited fashion.

I have been most fortunate in the assistance I have received from many colleagues, of whom the following require special mention: Herbert Feith, who as my teacher, guide, and friend inspired, encouraged, and enlightened me at every stage, to an extent which no form of acknowledgment can adequately convey; J. D. Legge, J. A. C. Mackie, and other staff and student members of the Centre for Southeast Asian Studies at Monash University, in whose stimulating and critical company my ideas took shape and many of my grosser misconceptions were corrected; Ruth T. McVey, whose enormous range of knowledge and critical insight was with unfailing generosity placed at my disposal on the many occasions on which I sought it; W. F. Wertheim and the staff of the Anthropological and Sociological Centre on South- and Southeast Asia of the University of Amsterdam, who with cordial hospitality received a stranger at short notice and placed the full resources of the Institute at his disposal (Professor Wertheim in particular not only gave freely of his own time and scholarship, but made it possible for me to interview a number of persons who provided me with invaluable information and assistance); F. Tichelman, of the Institute of Social History, Amsterdam, who with great kindness and expertness guided me through the relevant materials in the Institute's possession; M. A. Jaspan and colleagues at the Centre for Southeast Asian Studies at the University of Hull, who invited me to make full use of the documents and facilities of the Centre and arranged discussions of my work in progress; George McT. Kahin, Benedict R. O'G. Anderson, and staff and students of the Modern Indonesia Project, Cornell University, who introduced me for all too brief a period to the warm community and documentary treasures at 102 West Avenue; Daniel S. Lev, of the University of Washington, who gave me unlimited access to his research files and the benefit of his incisive mind; and, finally, many Indonesian émigrés in Europe and Australia who must for good reasons remain unnamed but without whose willingness to discuss their experiences my understanding would have been much the poorer.

Needless to say, none of those mentioned has any responsibility for the deficiencies of this study; they are my contribution alone.

R EX M ORTIMER

Sydney

INDONESIAN COMMUNISM UNDER SUKARNO

Ideology and Politics, 1959–1965

Introduction

The Indonesian Communist Party (PKI) rose to its height of strength and influence during the first half of the 1960's, a period dominated in Indonesia by the charismatic figure of President Sukarno, who for a time mesmerized his own countrymen and attracted world attention by prodigious displays of grandeur and anti-imperialist bravado. During Sukarno's reign, and under his protection, the PKI became the largest nonruling Communist party in the world, and many inside and outside Indonesia believed it would usher in the next Communist state. Then, almost overnight, the party was destroyed in one of the great bloodbaths of modern history. In the wake of the bizarre and controversial coup episode of October 1965, it was swept off the political stage, to be followed soon after by its patron Sukarno.

The saga of the PKI raises interesting and complex questions about the dynamics of new states, and especially about the character and sources of the appeal of those vehicles for political and social development that struggle for dominance within them. In particular, the history of the party in this period directs attention to such issues as why a Communist movement had such widespread mass appeal in Indonesia, how it managed to contrive such a successful accommodation with the ruling elite of the country, and why, despite the prodigious gains it registered, it ultimately went under without offering more than token resistance.

At first sight, conditions might not seem to have been particularly favorable to the growth of Communism in Indonesia in the 1950's and 1960's. Aside from the ethnic and cultural diversity of the people and the nominal adherence of the great majority to Islam—both factors that have been accounted severe impediments to the development of Communism elsewhere—the PKI encountered powerful political obstacles to its rise. It had not only failed to gain the leadership of the national revolution between 1945 and 1949 but had been crushed in internecine Republican strife; when the rebuilding of the party began in 1951 under D. N. Aidit it suffered under the disabilities of numerical weakness, internal disunity, political isolation, and a reputation for having "stabbed the Republic in the back" during the independence struggle against the Dutch. Nevertheless, it quickly recovered and indeed thrived under the parliamentary system. In 1959 this path of advance was blocked by the inauguration of an authoritarian and avowedly antiparty system dominated by a Jacobin president and a strongly anti-Communist army leadership. Once again, however, the PKI rapidly reoriented itself to the new conditions and demonstrated an extraordinary capacity to turn the atmosphere and events of the period to its advantage.

The ability of the Communists to establish a strong foothold in the political life of Indonesia in the postindependence period was in large measure the product of factors which, on closer investigation, can be seen to have provided greater opportunities than such a simplified recital of events might suggest. Among the most important of these factors were the existence among politically activated lower strata of the population of a strong current of discontent with the fruits of independence and the performance of the dominant parties, and a vast reservoir of Javanese villagers awaiting a social and cultural champion. In addition, the party benefited from divisions within the ruling group. These divisions made it possible for the Communists to fashion an alliance with one part of the group while another part remained enemies of the party; thus the PKI could be an ally of the Nationalists (PNI) in the period when the PNI was wrestling for power with the Masjumi Muslims and the Socialists (PSI), and later could ally itself with Sukarno, whose strong and growing radical propensities heightened his need for a dynamic mass-based force to counteract the power of his irksome partners the army leaders.

But opportunities may be grasped or allowed to wither on the vine. In the case of the PKI, credit for taking full advantage of these circumstances must be given to the Communist leaders, who were able to keep their eyes fixed steadily on the goal of power while devising flexible tactics for reaching it. In responding to their unusual, in many ways unique, situation under Guided Democracy, they developed distinctive policies and political attitudes, original in their cast and unorthodox even in a period characterized by growing diversity in the ranks of international Communism. This book seeks to penetrate the logic of the distinctive approach of the PKI and its results by analyzing the ideology which informed its policies and the major influences which shaped this ideology.

Ideology will be discussed here as "a systematic set of ideas with action consequences serving the purposes of creating and using organization."[1] This is a useful definition for the analysis of a movement as an organized force for the achievement of political objectives rather than, say, as an organic grouping embodying discrete patterns of meaning animating its members. It follows that not only the systematized ideas themselves, but also their implications for action, are the objects of attention. Ideas as such are abstractions, and frequently they are meaningless or misleading abstractions for purposes of strictly political analysis, bearing little or no relation to a political body's aims and actions. The implications for action in any idea or group of ideas, then, can only be ascertained by tracing the effect of these ideas on the political body's practice and political orientation.

Consequently, the elucidation of the ideology of the PKI will necessitate a survey of the party's activities and of the events to which those activities were related. But the present work does not purport to be a history of the PKI, and still less a history of Guided Democracy. Events and actions are introduced only to the extent that they demonstrate how the PKI conceived of the action implications of its generalized strategy; the selection of pertinent actions and events is determined by what the author, having studied both the ideas of the party and its actions, takes to be the significant and politically crucial ideas it advanced.

As Schurmann has pointed out, the link between ideas and action may be either direct or indirect. Some ideas are advanced with the intention of providing the organization with a mode of apprehending its identity and aspirations—these are what he terms "pure" ideas. Others are designed to produce immediate action consequences, to mobilize and direct the members toward some feasible short-range objective—these may be labeled "practical" ideas.[2] The distinction is an impor-

---

[1] I have taken this definition from Franz Schurmann, *Ideology and Organization in Communist China*, 2d ed. (Berkeley, 1968), p. 18.

[2] *Ibid.*, p. 21.

tant one. Confusion about the role of a particular idea or group of ideas can easily lead to mistaken conclusions about how the organization intends to act. For example, as will be argued in Chapter 5, those writers who regarded early PKI denunciations of the Malaysia scheme as evidence of the party's decisive influence in bringing about Indonesia's subsequent confrontation of the Federation in effect mistook "pure" ideology designed to shape the general thinking of party members for "practical" ideology intended to produce immediate action by them.

It is not at all easy to distinguish between pure and practical ideology, especially since a strong tradition exists in Communist parties of combining the two in speeches, reports, and articles in order to fortify the link between belief system and proposed action. But it is important that the attempt be made, taking particular note of the total ideological and action context in any given instance.

The ability to fuse these two types of ideology into a dynamic action system is one of the strongest features of Communist political organization. Schurmann has commented that "nationalistic movements tend to generate only pure ideology."[3] In the Indonesian case, this was a hallmark of Sukarno's political rhetoric; while it provided his audience with symbolic meanings and hence shaped the general lines of their thinking, it did not give clear directions for action, except in relation to a small category of actions and events connected with the colonial past. On the other hand, parties in postcolonial societies which forswear militant or agitational nationalism—"parties of order" —often tend to generate only practical ideology and thus fail to provide those meaning-setting causes and cognitive maps which, in times of uncertainty and crisis, are sorely needed by large sections of the populace.[4] Again Indonesia provides an example, in the political behavior of the Masjumi and the PSI, whose parliamentary defeat in the early fifties was closely connected with their failure to govern in a style that quenched men's thirst for political meaning.[5] The strong combination of pure and practical ideology, it will be suggested, was

[3] *Ibid.*, p. 23.

[4] See Clifford Geertz, "Ideology as a Cultural System," in David E. Apter, ed., *Ideology and Discontent* (New York, 1964).

[5] Herbert Feith, *The Decline of Constitutional Democracy in Indonesia* (Ithaca, N.Y., 1962), pp. 114–20, 134–36.

one of the important factors contributing to the PKI's ability to win support and influence in the Guided Democracy period.

The PKI's ideology was not remarkable for its theoretical concerns or creativity. Like the Lao Dong Party of Vietnam, and unlike the Communist Party of China, the PKI was a practical party in that its programmatic statements were always concerned with the political tasks of the foreseeable future and in that it was seldom constrained by considerations of doctrinal fidelity from pursuing a course which its leaders felt were in its best immediate interests. There was always a strong flavor of Realpolitik about its guidelines. But it would be a mistake to conclude from this that the party was pragmatic or opportunist in any narrow meaning of those terms. If it was consumed by the down-to-earth problems of gaining political leverage, and ultimately power, certain definite parameters were nevertheless set by its Communist character within which it defined and pursued its goals. The parameters may have been broadly drawn and may have allowed policies that were unorthodox by traditional Communist standards, but they existed in the form of such principles as the party's obligation to represent as best it could the interests and dignity of the workers and peasants, opposition to racism, opposition to hereditary rank and title, and dedication to popular participation in government.

Ideology, in the sense in which it is being used here, is not a static set of ideas but an evolving body of precepts, programs, and policies. New ideas are added to the original stock to take account of new situations and tasks confronted by the organization. Additionally, the initial ideology of a specific leadership may be modified to one degree or another in response both to changes in circumstances and to the altered preceptions of the leaders with regard to their basic requirements. In the case of the PKI, changes of both kinds were extensive and highly significant. Attention has already been drawn to the flexibility the party displayed in pursuing its goals. Yet while on specific issues it may not always be easy to discern an underlying pattern in attitudes, a basic line of development in the evolution of its ideology is apparent. This has sometimes been described as a move away from Soviet strategic doctrine toward that enunciated with increasing vehemence in the early sixties by the Communist Party of China, but this analysis is misleading.

At first the Aidit leadership worked with a concept of the united national front strategy taken from Soviet sources, but by 1954 it had already begun to modify this strategy, principally by downgrading the role of class struggle and the significance of PKI hegemony over the front in favor of a top-level alliance with the PNI in which the PKI was prepared to accept a subordinate status for an indefinite period. In this it anticipated changes in both Soviet and Chinese policies which were later to encourage such a course for Communists in countries ruled by "neutralist" governments. This trend in the PKI's ideology continued throughout the period of the Aidit leadership, finding its most fully developed expression under Guided Democracy in the elaboration of a formula for gaining power which depended on the maintenance of a close alliance with Sukarno and the "progressive" wing of the national elite and expressly subordinated the party's claims to Sukarno's continued primacy in the political system. The ideological terms in which this strategy was formulated were original and unorthodox from a Communist standpoint, but they had some affinities with Soviet theories of "national capitalism" and at the same time used concepts adapted from Mao Tse-tung's ideological armory.

In aid of this strategy, the PKI increasingly projected its appeals and action slogans in a nationalist and populist frame, both to cement its alliance with Sukarno and to maintain a tempo of growth and influence in the climate Sukarno was sustaining. To the extent that Chinese revolutionary theses were capable of being adapted to these purposes the PKI incorporated them into its ideological framework, but without taking over those features of Chinese doctrine that conflicted with its peaceful and accommodating domestic strategy. In relation to the competing doctrines of the major Communist powers, then, the position of the PKI was an eclectic one; the unity of its ideology must be sought, accordingly, in terms not of these doctrines but of the Indonesian party's own perception of its requirements for attaining its goals.

This brings us to the question of the influences that shaped the PKI's ideology. An analysis of the actual evolution of the party's ideology, as manifested in the major spheres of its political work, reveals *how* the party perceived the attainment of its aim of assuming power and transforming Indonesian society. But only by seeking out the influences that shaped the evolution of this ideology can we understand *why* the evolution took the form it did. The isolation and ranking of these factors pose the most difficult problems for the researcher in this field, since he cannot base his conclusions on the content of ideological materials alone but has to arrive at them by relating the content and style of these materials to wider systems of meaning impinging upon the leading stratum of the party. In other words, significant influences have to be gauged in terms of recognizable "cultures" affecting those responsible for drawing up the ideological guidelines.

It is obvious, both from general premises and from what has already been said on this score, that Marxism-Leninism, the common set of ideological principles of the Communist movement, forms one major source from which the PKI's ideology was drawn. But this general body of doctrine is complex and multiform, and specific features of it have varying degrees of relevance in different social contexts. In any attempt to analyze influences on the ideology of the PKI, the relative importance of various components of Marxism-Leninism —the writings of Marx, those of Lenin, the current elaborations of the Soviet and (at a later stage) Chinese leaders—would have to be assessed. Limited attention was paid to the works of Marx, which contain little that the leaders of Indonesian Communism (and of Communism in the third world generally) found readily applicable to the conditions in which they operated. The political and organizational theories of Lenin, on the other hand, have found ready acceptance, not only by Communist parties such as the PKI but by all radical nationalist movements displaying a preoccupation with anti-imperialism and the virtues of statist economies. Insofar as any external Communist prescriptions held weight with the PKI leadership, however, they were above all the contemporaneous views of the leaders of the Soviet and Chinese parties. The success of these parties in gaining power is a major reason for the prestige their prescriptions have for nonruling parties, though their role as patrons, manipulators, and centers for training the cadres of the nonruling parties is also important.

Many students of Communism are so impressed by evidence of the influence of one or the other of these ruling parties upon the indigenous parties of other countries that they are largely content to characterize the latter as their ideological (and even organizational) offshoots. In the case of the PKI, no neat line can be drawn from the doctrines of either to the strategy of the Indonesian party. This is only one illustration of a more general argument. Communist parties—especially those of any size and influence within their own communities—cannot be dismissed as appendages of some external power. They emerge out of and develop through interaction with a specific socio-cultural environment which leaves its impress upon them and imparts discrete qualities to their ideologies. Thus influences from Communist authority centers compete with influences from the local environment to form a "mix" of varying proportions in particular parties.

The force of indigenous influences upon the PKI cannot be overestimated. For reasons that are examined in detail in the corpus of this book, the PKI leaders of the Aidit generation were unusually independent of spirit. They were lightly touched in the formative stages of their development as Communists by the hand of Moscow or Peking. And they acted out their political roles in a socio-political framework where identification with a national ethos, and with subnational cultures, was of tremendous political significance. There will be frequent occasion to emphasize the manner in which these identifications shaped crucial aspects of the PKI's ideology, including the stress laid upon nationalism, concepts of national "oneness," and the role of vertical rather than horizontal social cleavages as a frame for its united national front.

The specific life experiences of members of the PKI's leading stratum, it will be suggested, fortified their general identification with the national ethos and gave it a militant flavor. Still youths and young men at the time of the Japanese occupation and the war of national independence, their most deeply felt emotions at a decisive stage in their personal development were bound up with their participation in the chaotic, painful, and exhilarating events of those years. Out of it they acquired a powerful and lasting attachment to the mystique of national unity, an intense anti-imperialist feeling, and a conviction that only the spirit of revolution which the radical youth of the time embodied could make their country strong, united, and socialist. These were all themes that Sukarno was to make his own under Guided Democracy and that formed a strong bond of sympathy between him and the Communists of that period.

A central theme of this work, then, will be that Indonesian Communism can only be comprehended on its own terms, as a specific response by Indonesians to Indonesian conditions and aspirations. This does not mean, however, that Communism will be treated as nothing more than one among several political vehicles of Indonesian nationalism. Those writers who have tended to regard Communism in Asia as a movement created by intellectuals identical in composition and aims with other nationalist parties have done service in correcting the undue stress placed upon management from Moscow or Peking by "Kremlinological" analysts,[6] but in the author's view they underrate the degree to which Communism as a movement goes beyond the bounds of nationalism and is likely to come into conflict, as distinct from mere competition, with nationalism.

That Communists and non-Communist nationalists share many common goals and concerns is readily demonstrable. But the distinctions between them are as important as these similarities. We have already referred to Schurmann's argument that practical ideology is absent in nationalist movements. This absence reflects both the traditionally elitist character and the shallowness of commitment to egalitarian social change of such movements. The contrast may be sharpened by asserting that nationalists are mainly concerned to bring about a shift of power from foreign to national control, whereas Communists are equally preoccupied with creating a major shift in the social basis of power in the indigenous community itself.

This difference in ideology corresponds to differences in social status and political mobilization approaches between the Communists and nationalist elites. In most countries of Asia, and in Indonesia in particular, Communist leaders come from lower status circles than do the leaders of the nationalist parties,[7] and this helps to account for their more thoroughgoing social radicalism. It also affects their relations with the lower strata, and particularly the workers and peasants. Whereas most of the ruling nationalist parties of non-Communist Asia have only traditional patron-client links with these strata and customarily seek to mobilize the populace in an undifferentiated manner, often in purely demonstrative displays of allegiance, the Communists tend to have a capacity for and interest in promoting organization and self-activity among the workers and peasants.

[6] See for example, John H. Kautsky, "An Essay in the Politics of Development," in John H. Kautsky, ed., *Political Change in Underdeveloped Countries: Nationalism and Communism* (New York, 1962), pp. 3–119.

[7] See Richard Lowenthal, "Development Versus Utopia in Communist Policy," *Survey*, 74–75 (Winter-Spring 1970), 9.

Finally, there is a corporate dimension to the distinction between the two groups. Differences in social origin, ideology, and experience combine with organizational distinctness to create internal solidarities and codes that are in the long run mutually incompatible. The fact that the PKI was able to draw so close to the most prestigious nationalist figure in Indonesia, to accommodate so fully to his policies and influence his ideology so powerfully in his last years, and to propitiate all who showed a willingness to tolerate the party's advance, while never being able to dispel the mutual suspicion and consciousness of incompatibility that divided its leaders from most members of the ruling elite, is indicative of the gulf between Communists and nationalists.

Hopefully, then, a study of the ideological wellsprings feeding Indonesian Communism may do more than disclose how a major political movement faced its problems, registered its achievements, and demonstrated its weaknesses within a particular setting. It may contribute to a clearer understanding of the nature and role of Communism in societies readjusting after the colonial experience, and hence to the study of comparative politics generally.

1. The United National Front: Ideological Foundations of the PKI

In January 1951, the leadership of the PKI was assumed by a new group within the party headed by four young men: D. N. Aidit, M. H. Lukman, Njoto, and Sudisman.[1] The change was of great importance; under the stimulus and guidance of these four, the party was transformed within a few short years from a weak, divided, and dispirited organization on the periphery of national politics into a dynamic, rapidly growing, and powerful movement which, in the period covered by this study, was to play a crucial role in the Republic's affairs. The reasons for their success in overcoming the PKI's weaknesses, and the strategy they pursued in carrying it to national prominence, will be explored at length in the course of this book. First, however, it is necessary to indicate something of the backgrounds and formative experiences of the leading men of the party, since these were pivotal in determining their political orientations and the style that they brought to their political tasks. No assessment of the factors responsible for the meteoric rise of Communism in Indonesia in the fifties and sixties, or of its sudden and drastic eclipse in 1965, would be complete without some consideration of the cultural and political dispositions of those most responsible for the decisions which determined the general course followed by the organization.

In 1951 none of these four men was aged more than thirty. Aidit, first secretary and subsequently chairman of the PKI, was twenty-seven; Lukman, his first deputy, was thirty; Njoto, second deputy, was twenty-five; and Sudisman, who throughout the period of Guided Democracy occupied the post of general secretary, was thirty. In a

---

[1] For a brief account of the circumstances leading up to and culminating in the leadership change, see Donald Hindley, *The Communist Party of Indonesia, 1951–1963* (Berkeley, 1964), pp. 22–26.

historically remarkable fashion for a Communist, or indeed any other, party, these leaders' collectivity remained intact throughout the fourteen years of their stewardship, and no patent conflicts marked their relations. If the steady rise in the party's fortunes is invoked to explain this solidarity, it must also be recognized that the absence of splits and purges in the ranks of the top leadership contributed in turn, and in no small measure, to the reputation and organizational capability of the movement. To transcend this circularity, it is all the more necessary to explore the common experiences out of which their unity was initially forged.

Aidit, Lukman, Njoto, and Sudisman were in a very real sense products of the Indonesian national revolution, and particularly of the *pemuda,* or youth, upsurge which provided its dynamic thrust. Each had been drawn into political activity in his teens through involvement in one or more of the nationalist organizations that were active during the last years of Dutch colonial rule and the Japanese occupation. All were caught up in the wave of youthful political fervor and frenetic revolutionary activity that accompanied the collapse of Japan and the attempted reimposition of colonial power.

In a period of bewildering change and intense hardship, when the certitudes of both the old colonial order and the already attenuated traditional society were destroyed, first by a conqueror with a radically different political style from that of the colonial power and then by a bitter and prolonged struggle for nationhood, the future leaders of the PKI found their way to Marxism through immersion in underground activity, participation in the activities of insurgent youth groups, and exposure to the rhetoric of such nationalist ideologues as Sukarno and Mohammad Yamin. They were never to shed the nationalist commitment that gripped them at the verge of adulthood and provided them, along with so many of their generation, with a consuming cause and a sense of personal identity and meaning in a disintegrating social world. It was to become a central feature of their distinctive brand of Communism.

The Japanese occupation gave a great psychological shock to the Indonesian population, upsetting a centuries-old political order and destroying the myth of Dutch superiority which rising nationalist consciousness had by no means dispelled. In place of Dutch colonial methods and manners the Japanese implanted a vastly different myth and introduced a political style in violent contrast to that of the older colonizers. As Anderson aptly puts it, "Where the Dutch had relied on whiteness and the mystique of *zakelijkheid* [businesslike efficiency], the Japanese promoted a countermyth of violence, physical prowess and extraordinary spiritual power"; their style of rule was characterized by "political romanticism," embodying as elements "the dramatization of politics, the creation of massive rituals of state, the propagation of 'ideological' formulas of vague but patriotic content, would-be popular movements."[2]

Equally important, the Japanese for the first time provided Indonesian youth with a political role and an organizational identity. Whereas the Dutch had ignored the younger men, preferring to rely almost exclusively on the authority of regents and elders, the Japanese sought to mobilize the youth on a grand scale and to inculcate in them their own style and values. No doubt the Japanese were influenced by the exigencies of war and the possibility that Indonesian youth would be needed to defend Japan's new conquests; at the same time, the maintenance of order in difficult conditions suggested the advisability of giving the young carefully supervised outlets for their energies. Thus, scores of thousands of teenagers and young men were organized into a variety of military, paramilitary, and propagandist bodies, where they were subjected to intense physical and mental training and mobilized for all manner of ritualistic and expressive activities.

The Japanese may well have wrought more than they envisaged by their efforts to win the youth of Indonesia to their wartime cause. In analyzing the role of the *pemuda* in the national revolution, Anderson has stressed the crucial importance of traditional cultural experience and the manner in which Japanese organization and training replicated many central motifs of this experience. As he sees it, the traditional Javanese *pesantren* (religious or mystical school), in which initiate youths were inducted into the mores of Javanese life, constantly revitalized utopian, voluntarist, and transcendent elements of belief which in times of crisis provided a "source of leadership for the countless localized peasant uprisings in the last century of Dutch

---

[2] Benedict R. O'G. Anderson, "Japan: 'The Light of Asia,'" in Josef Silverstein, ed., *Southeast Asia in World War II: Four Essays* (Monograph Series no. 7, South East Asia Studies, Yale University, 1966), pp. 20–21.

colonial rule." By mobilizing young men in organizations accenting similar veins of thought, the Japanese inadvertently reinforced this strain in the Javanese tradition and prepared the *pemuda* for the catalytic role they were to play when, at the close of the occupation, the economic and social indicators of crisis were all too apparent and established politicians and officials had, by their complicity with the occupier, forfeited the prestige and will necessary for them to assume the initiative in social reconstruction.[3]

In considering the impact on the youth of this sudden propulsion into political life, involving as it did an entirely new respect for their importance, other social changes taking place at the same time need to be borne in mind. The defeat of the Dutch was only one psychological shock with which the youth had to cope. Traditional ties and values had also been undermined, in many cases shattered, by the disorganization, communication difficulties, and other by-products of the war and occupation. Thousands of young men were left to fend for themselves, not only because of physical separation from their families and elders but also because the startling events that had occurred had left traditionally respected older men as bereft of explanations and satisfactory solutions as were the youth themselves. All traditional authorities, as a result, lost a good deal of the awed respect they had formerly been accorded.

What took the place of traditional leaders was less the new foreign power, which, though feared, lost most of its hold on the youth particularly in the later years of the occupation both because of its brutality and because of its military defeats, than those leaders of local and national political organizations who by their daring, their nationalist fervor, or their ascribed mystical powers established themselves as heroes for young men and youth seeking to find new poles of meaning and certainty in troubled times. Ancient divisions of culture, religion, and ethnicity, fortified by Japanese tactics of rule, prevented the emergence of any single focus for the rising spirit of national passion among the youth, themselves divided into myriad groups, all with their own orientations and internal solidarities.

Economic crisis, especially after 1943, added its toll to the anguish, impatience, and intensity of the youth. Rampant inflation and unem-

[3] Benedict R. O'G. Anderson, *Java in a Time of Revolution: Occupation and Resistance, 1944–1946* (Ithaca, N.Y., 1972), especially pp. 1–34.

ployment, grave food shortages, epidemics, and the horrors of the
romusha system of forced labor accelerated the flight to the cities,
exacerbated class and status differences, and further undermined the
prestige of older officials.[4]

As the Japanese occupation drew to a close, in a situation of widespread social fragmentation and acute unrest, furious political conflict, and burgeoning apocalyptic fears and visions, the radicalized
youth pressed for decisive action to achieve independence and thereby
precipitated a major confrontation with the "collaborationist" nationalists who were anxious to avoid violence. The course of that
conflict, and its resolution in the reassertion of the power and authority of the older elite, has already been brilliantly described.[5] For our
purposes, it is sufficient to note two related characteristics of the
pemuda phenomenon. In the first place, the methods and style adopted
by the *pemuda* owed a tremendous amount to lessons imbibed from
the Japanese—a disposition toward bravado and violence, authoritarianism, an emphasis on *semangat,* or spiritual zeal. In the second
place, the characteristic political outlook of the youth tended toward
diffuse radicalism rather than rigorous social criticisms and programs,
which in turn promoted leader-worship and Messianic expectations
rather than disciplined political activity.

Aidit, Lukman, Njoto, and Sudisman were all part of this *pemuda*
efflorescence and shared its characteristic experiences. Unlike the
great majority of their fellows, they were attracted to the disciplined
and ordered ideology of Marxism instead of the diffuse and romantic
radicalism that was more symptomatic of the times. But, in the early
years of the national revolution particularly, this orientation represented not a sharp opposition to the *pemuda* outlook and style but
one of many variants among them. What united the radicalized youth
—common experiences in Japanese-sponsored organizations, commitment to the revolution, and an almost mystical belief in their cause—
far outweighed the ideological distinctions among them. So intensely
felt were these mutual experiences, and so closely linked to the goal
of complete national independence, that they were to color the political ideals of an entire generation. Sukarno's enormous success in appealing to the "spirit of 1945" in the failing years of constitutional

---

[4] Anderson, "Japan: 'The Light of Asia,'" pp. 12–16.

[5] In Anderson, *Java in a Time of Revolution.*

democracy forcefully confirmed the depth of these feelings among the *pemuda* generation.

Aidit was born in Medan on July 30, 1923, of Malay ethnic origin. His father had been a state official in the forestry service and at the time of Aidit's election as first secretary of the PKI in 1951 was a member of parliament for a minor party. In about 1934 the Aidit family moved to Djakarta (then Batavia), where the young Aidit attended primary school and later a commercial secondary school. His education came to an end with the Japanese invasion of the Dutch East Indies early in 1942, when he was 18 years old. In any case, he told an interviewer in 1964, he did not consider himself cut out for commercial life.[6]

In 1939 Aidit first became involved in nationalist activity as a leader of the Persatuan Timur Muda (Association of Youth of the East), which he said attracted him because it was not "racialist," including among its members Chinese, Arabs, and people of various other minorities. Not much later, he also joined the Barisan Gerindo (Gerindo Front), a youth affiliate of the most left wing of Indonesia's prewar nationalist organizations. Gerindo (Gerakan Rakjat Indonesia, Indonesian People's Movement) was reputedly under Communist influence; one of its principal leaders, Amir Sjarifuddin, who served as a prime minister during the revolution, claimed in 1948 to have been an underground Communist from the 1930's on.[7] It had an anti-fascist united front orientation, and Sjarifuddin offered the Dutch his cooperation in preparing the Indonesian people to resist a Japanese invasion. When this was imminent Amir received Dutch financial assistance to set up underground activity, but his network was quickly broken up and Amir himself was arrested in 1943. From the little that is known of its activities, it appears, like other underground bodies, not to have developed much beyond the stage of discussion and preparation of resistance.[8]

[6] I am indebted to Ruth T. McVey for this information and a great deal of the biographical data on Aidit and the other PKI leaders. Brief biographies of Aidit may also be found in D. N. Aidit, *Menempuh Djalan Rakjat* (Along the People's Road), 4th ed. (Djakarta, 1954), pp. 3–4; *Bintang Merah*, IX (Sept.–Oct. 1953), 479–80; *Review of Indonesia*, VII (July–Aug. 1963), 11–12.

[7] G. McT. Kahin, *Nationalism and Revolution in Indonesia* (Ithaca, N.Y., 1952), pp. 272–73.

[8] *Ibid.*, pp. 111–20; Anderson, *Java in a Time of Revolution*, pp. 37–39.

Aidit said in later years that he joined Gerindo because he felt attracted to the left; he was aware of Marxist influence in the organization but did not acquire any more than a vague notion of Marxism until the war years. In any case, it seems safe to assume that by the time of the Japanese occupation he already had some acquaintance with left wing ideas and, unlike a great many other Indonesians, was not strongly attracted by Japan's "Greater Asia" propaganda. Early in the occupation period his interest was quickened under the influence of Muhammad Jusuf, a Marxist with mystical tendencies who was to become the first postwar leader of the PKI and from whom Aidit borrowed a copy of Marx's *Das Kapital* in Dutch. In 1943 Aidit joined the illegal PKI.[9] At about this time he met Lukman, with whom he formed a close friendship and whose activities from this time onward were to parallel his own.

Among the organizations to which Aidit and Lukman belonged were several of more than ephemeral importance. One was the Angkatan Muda (Young Generation), described by Anderson as,

a Japanese device, established in mid-1944, for controlling undesirable elements among the youth. . . . Young men who were known or suspected of having "illegal" connections or who were persistently and openly hostile to the Japanese and at the same time influential among their comrades, were forced to assume leadership in the organization [10]

This suggests that Aidit may have been regarded by the Japanese as an actual or potential troublemaker and subjected to surveillance and indoctrination. The spirit developed by this organization in the closing stages of the war is indicated by the resolutions of a meeting held from May 16 to 18, 1945, in Bandung, where the members swore to face "freedom or death," called for the unification of all Indonesian nationalist groups under a single leadership, and demanded independence as early as possible.[11] Among the more notable of Aidit's companions in the Angkatan Muda were Sukarni and Chairul Saleh, both of whom were to become prominent in the Guided Democracy period.

Another important group to which Aidit was attached was the

[9] From notes kindly made available to me by Ruth T. McVey.
[10] Benedict R. O'G. Anderson, *Some Aspects of Indonesian Politics under the Japanese Occupation: 1944–45* (Interim Reports Series, Modern Indonesia Project, Cornell University, 1961), pp. 51–52.
[11] *Ibid.*

Asrama Angkatan Baru Indonesia (New Generation Hostel of Indonesia) in Djakarta, a political training school established by the Propaganda Department of the Japanese military administration, in which Sukarni and Chairul Saleh were again leading participants.[12] Aidit gained a good deal of his nationalist education at the Asrama, attending lectures by the most popular Indonesian ideologues of the age—Sukarno, Yamin, Hatta, and Amir Sjarifuddin. Aidit was to declare in 1965 that Sukarno had given him his first training in Marxism here.[13]

Finally, Aidit belonged to the Barisan Pelopor (Vanguard Corps), the activist arm of the Hokokai, the principal political organization formed by the Japanese in Java.[14] Members of the Barisan Pelopor were given drill instruction, patriotic lectures, and experience in the techniques of mass mobilization to train them as key political activists among the population.[15] In the later stages of the occupation a small band from this group emerged as the Barisan Pelopor Istimewa (Special Vanguard Corps), to which both Aidit and Lukman belonged and which formed Sukarno's special "bodyguard."[16]

The outstanding features of Aidit's occupation experiences, then, can be said to have included: adherence from 1943 to Marxism and the illegal PKI; exposure to concentrated doses of Japanese propaganda and culture; training in Japanese-style political activism; close relations with some of the most "radical" and fervent *pemuda* leaders; lessons in nationalism from its most prestigious ideologists, including Sukarno and Yamin whose myth-making and spellbinding capacities were legendary; and fairly intimate association with Sukarno. It is not suggested, of course, that Aidit reacted uncritically to these experiences. His Marxist convictions provided a strong antidote to Japanese propaganda, and his later conflicts with Sukarni and Chairul Saleh also reflect the overriding influence of his Communist attachments. On the other hand, an expressive nationalism and a critical

[12] Anderson, *Java in a Time of Revolution,* pp. 41–42.

[13] *Harian Rakjat,* March 13, 1965.

[14] On the Hokokai, see Anderson, *Some Aspects of Indonesian Politics Under the Japanese Occupation,* p. 13; Anderson, *Java in a Time of Revolution,* pp. 27–29; Harry J. Benda, *The Crescent and the Rising Sun* (The Hague and Bandung, 1958).

[15] Anderson, *Java in a Time of Revolution,* pp. 29–30.

[16] *Ibid.,* p. 48.

appreciation of Sukarno's qualities remained motifs of his career, at least from 1952 onward.

In the feverish days of the Japanese collapse and surrender Aidit and Lukman were active, with other *pemuda* leaders, in the intense discussion and activity surrounding the burning issue of when and how independence was to be declared. When it appeared that Sukarno and Hatta, in seeking to retain Japanese goodwill, were unduly delaying the proclamation of nationhood, an emergency meeting of *pemuda,* among whom was Aidit, was held on August 16, when it was decided to send a deputation to Sukarno immediately. Dissatisfied with the outcome of the discussions held with Sukarno, a further meeting was convened at which more decisive action was resolved upon; this resolution a group (which included neither Aidit nor Lukman) executed by kidnapping Sukarno and Hatta and pressing them to proclaim independence immediately. Sukarno then issued the proclamation on the following morning, though not in the fervently anti-Japanese form the *pemuda* had wanted.[17]

Living at the Asrama, Aidit and Lukman continued to act in concert with the others of the center. A fortnight after the proclamation of independence they took part in the formation of the Angkatan Pemuda Indonesia (Indonesian Youth Corps), which was led by Saleh and Wikana and had its headquarters at the building occupied by the Asrama. The new organization, whose aims included the seizure of arms and installations from the Japanese, aspired to coordinate and unite all *pemuda* underground organizations. Under its influence two other bodies, the Barisan Rakjat (People's Force, a peasant mobilization center) and the Barisan Buruh (Workers' Force), were set up shortly afterwards; Lukman played a leading role in the former and Njono, later to become chairman of SOBSI, the PKI's trade union federation, in the latter. Takeovers of railways, tramways, and broadcasting installations in the capital were in fact carried out at the instigation of these bodies.

Then, on September 19, the Angkatan Pemuda Indonesia organized a popular demonstration, at least partly to pressure the Republican leaders into taking a more forceful line against the Japanese. The same night Aidit and Lukman were arrested by the Japanese. Aidit escaped shortly afterwards but was then arrested by the British army

---

[17] For further details of this drama, see *ibid.,* pp. 70–78.

authorities and handed over to the Dutch, who held him captive for the next seven months.[18]

Aidit's incarceration kept him out of the struggle between the *pemuda* and the older generation nationalists for leadership of the revolutionary movement. By the time of his release, this struggle had been as good as won by the older men, and politics had entered a more orderly phase in which political parties and army formations played the decisive role. From the sketchy details available concerning Aidit's activities between 1946 and 1948, he appears to have devoted most of his time to work in the party organization. He was elected to the PKI Central Committee in 1947 and in the same year became a delegate to the Republican parliament and chairman of the party fraction in that body; in 1948 he was elected first a candidate member and then, in early September, a full member of the Politburo.

Within a few weeks of his elevation to the party's highest ruling body, it was no more. At Madiun, in East Java, there took place the most serious of a series of clashes between irregular armed units oriented toward the PKI and units of the Republican forces and allied irregulars. This time the government branded the incident the beginning of a Communist insurrection; battle was joined by the PKI leader, Musso, and within a few weeks the PKI was decimated in what rapidly developed into a bloodbath with strong cultural and religious overtones.[19] Escaping from the sanguinary aftermath of the "incident," in which most of the party's leaders lost their lives, Aidit and Lukman made their way via Singapore to China and then to Vietnam, returning to their homeland again in mid-1950.

Lukman, Aidit's first deputy secretary and close associate since 1943, was three years his senior.[20] His father, a Moslem *kijai* (re-

[18] Benedict R. O'G. Anderson, "The Pemuda Revolution" (Ph.D. Thesis, Cornell University, 1967), pp. 172–79.

[19] No satisfactory account of the Madiun incident exists. That in Kahin, pp. 286–303, contains much valuable background material but accepts the government version too much at face value. See also D. N. Aidit, "We accuse 'Madiun Affair,'" in Aidit, *Problems of the Indonesian Revolution* (Bandung, 1963), pp. 103–35. The communal aspects of the conflict are dealt with in Robert Jay, *Religion and Politics in Rural Central Java* (New Haven, 1964), pp. 96–97.

[20] Brief biographies of Lukman appear in *Bintang Merah,* IX (Sept.–Oct. 1953), 481–82, and *Harian Rakjat,* Sept. 7, 1955.

ligious teacher) in Central Java, had been active during the twenties
in the Sarekat Rakjat (People's Association), a Communist-led break-
away from the Sarekat Islam (Islamic Association), the first mass-
based nationalist organization. He was imprisoned by the Dutch after
the Communist anticolonial uprising of 1926 and in 1929 was exiled
to the notorious Boven Digul detention camp in West New Guinea.[21]
His family accompanied him, and so the young Lukman grew up and
received his schooling in a camp for political prisoners. In 1938 he
returned to his home area of Tegal where he worked as a bus con-
ductor until the Japanese occupation. He joined the illegal PKI in
Djakarta, possibly at the same time as Aidit.

Njoto, second deputy to Aidit, was born in 1925 in East Java;
different accounts of his life give Besuki, Djember, and Blitar as his
birthplace.[22] His father had been a professional PKI worker in Solo,
Central Java, but in 1925 fled to Besuki, where he settled as a trader.
(The father died in a Dutch prison in 1947). From the age of fourteen Njoto moved in PKI circles and thus gravitated naturally into
the party's orbit. No details are available concerning his education
or prewar occupations (he was of course only sixteen when the Japanese occupied Indonesia). During the occupation he took part in
underground activities in East Java. When Japan surrendered he was
active in seizing arms to prevent them falling into Dutch hands, and
later in 1945 he fought in the famous "battle of Surabaja" against
British occupation forces. In November 1945 he formed a PKI section committee in Besuki, from where he later rose to higher local
and then national positions in the PKI apparatus. Njoto was a leader,
with Aidit, of the Front Demokrasi Rakjat (People's Democratic
Front), a party alliance formed on PKI initiative in 1947, and in mid-
1948 was elected to the Central Committee and the Politburo of the
party.

Among some of those who knew him in Solo during the occupation
years, Njoto had the reputation of having been a somewhat dissolute
young man, and he is said to have had a penchant for high living
in later years.[23] It is interesting that his reputation for intellectualism

[21] On this formative period in the history of the PKI, see Ruth T. McVey,
The Rise of Indonesian Communism (Ithaca, N.Y., 1965).

[22] For brief biographies of Njoto, see *Bintang Merah,* IX (Sept.–Oct. 1953),
483–84, and *Harian Rakjat,* Sept. 7, 1955.

[23] Interview with "A" (Melbourne, June 1969); interview with "N" (Nov.
1968).

and possession of superior Javanese traits of gentility exceeds what one might expect on the basis of the scanty information we have about his social background.

The fourth member of Aidit's group in 1951, Sudisman, was born in Surabaja in 1920 and attended higher secondary school there.[24] After graduating from minor nationalist youth groups to Gerindo, he became a member of the illegal PKI shortly after the Japanese occupation commenced and took part in anti-Japanese student movements until he was arrested in September 1942. Released in September 1945, he fought in the battle of Surabaja and joined the East Java PNI. Moving to Jogjakarta, he served as secretary of the November 1945 youth congress; later he was secretary-general of Pesindo (Pemuda Sosialis Indonesia, Indonesian Socialist Youth) and a leader first of the Sajap Kiri, a "united front" of left wing parties which operated in 1946–47, and then of the People's Democratic Front. Reportedly a close associate of Amir Sjarifuddin, he became a member of the PKI Politburo in 1948. After the Madiun affair, Sudisman helped to revive the PKI and took part in anti-Dutch guerrilla activities until arrested by the Dutch in June 1949. He was released after the Round Table Conference agreement and in 1950 became the head of the PKI secretariat in Jogjakarta.

In a very real sense, then, the emergence of the Aidit group at the head of the PKI in January 1951 represented the capture of the organization by the *pemuda* generation; in this the PKI was to remain unique among the major political parties. Just what flavor this change gave the party, and what the implications were for its ideological cast and relations with other political groups, we shall have cause to consider more than once in the ensuing pages. One thing, however, is clear at the outset—the bonds forged among these four by their common experiences and common orientations during the revolution assured the PKI of an extraordinary cohesive leadership that was to persist intact until their deaths.

Identified with the Communist Party from the time of its reconstitution in October 1945, the four men had participated in its climb to

---

[24] For brief biographies of Sudisman, see Parlaungan, *Hasil Rakjat Memutih Tokoh-tokoh Parlemen* (The People's Success in Improving the Composition of Parliament) (Djakarta, 1956), pp. 295–96, and *Harian Rakjat,* Sept. 7, 1955.

influence and mass standing during the nationalist revolution, experienced the ebb and flow of its fortunes, and risen to prominence in its hierarchy.[25] They were present when, in August 1948, the veteran Musso, newly returned from long exile in the U.S.S.R, indicted the current leaders of the PKI for their failings and missed opportunities and advanced his *New Road* by which the Communists were to gain the leadership of the revolution.[26] The great impression made upon them by Musso's program was to be strongly reflected in their own subsequent policy formulations. Before the efficacy of Musso's prescriptions could be tested, however, the PKI was overwhelmed in the aftermath of the Madiun affair.

The PKI was allowed to surface again within a few months, but an enfeebled and uncertain leadership was able to do little more than hold the hard core of 10,000 surviving members together. Impatient with this lack of enterprise and vigor, and above all critical of the failure of those in charge of the party to respond to the growing dissatisfaction of the restless younger generation with the fruits of independence, Aidit and his group led an internal revolt, succeeding, in January 1951, in turning out the old guard and installing themselves in its place.

By 1954 they already had significant achievements to their credit. By adapting themselves skillfully to the antagonisms which had grown up between the major parliamentary groupings they had managed to secure a working alliance with the dominant wing of the PNI against its main competitors for power, the Masjumi and PSI. In 1953 the PKI's tactics had been rewarded by the formation of a government led by the PNI's Ali Sastroamidjojo that excluded representatives of the Masjumi and PSI.[27]

Aidit and his colleagues had steered the PKI through a difficult crisis in August 1951, when a renewed governmental crackdown threatened to isolate and crush the party once more.[28] They had built up the party's membership from a low of less than 7,000 members in

---

[25] On the history of the PKI during the national revolution, see Hindley, pp. 18–22; Ruth T. McVey, *The Soviet View of the Indonesian Revolution* (Interim Reports Series, Modern Indonesia Project, Cornell University, 1957).

[26] On Musso's New Road strategy and its implications, see McVey, *The Soviet View of the Indonesian Revolution*, pp. 58–66.

[27] Hindley, pp. 244–45.

[28] See Feith, pp. 187–92.

early 1952 to more than 150,000 in 1954, established its organization on a nationwide basis, and made its trade union federation, SOBSI, the largest in the country. Progress had also been made in expanding the other important party mass organizations, the BTI (Barisan Tani Indonesia, Indonesian Peasants' Front), Gerwani (Gerakan Wanita Indonesia, Indonesian Women's Movement), and Pemuda Rakjat (Workers' Youth). Opposition to the line of the new leadership, initially strong and based on the older membership, had been undermined and was to be dealt the coup de grace at the party's fifth congress.

THE FIFTH CONGRESS OF THE PKI

In the history of any Communist party, there is usually one central document or series of documents that serves to define a specific leadership phase of the organization. One set of documents may be appropriated by successive leaderships where the element of policy continuity is stressed over innovation. Alternatively, a new leadership may underline its break with past policies that are regarded as having been mistaken or deviant by embodying its own distinctive line in a founding document. A third variant occurs where a given leadership radically changes course at some point in its incumbency, discarding one repository of its strategy and substituting a new one to formalize the change.

Characteristically, the key document of any such phase is cast in Marxist-Leninist concepts and terminology and sets out the goals of the leadership and the manner in which it aims to achieve those goals. It serves a number of purposes in the organization. First, it legitimizes the leadership by establishing its fidelity to the principles of Marxism-Leninism. Secondly, it forms the point of reference for all future policy initiatives and elaborations by the leadership, whether in fact the relationship between them is symbolic or real. Thirdly, it is used to instruct the party following in the goals of the movement and so to enhance their organizational commitment and bind them to the leadership's interpretation of the appropriate application of Marxism-Leninism to national conditions. Finally, it acts as a weapon to be used against internal critics, who are commonly charged with departing from the agreed guidelines of the organization.

The founding document, then, is a key element in the organization's ideological armory, and as such supplies a useful starting point for a consideration of its character and behavior. In the case of the PKI during the period of Guided Democracy, the fount of indigenous doctrinal authority was unquestionably the program and resolution drawn up and adopted at the party's fifth congress in March 1954. This was the first congress convened by the leadership group that had assumed control in January 1951 and provided the occasion for a fully elaborated outline of both the leadership's analysis of Indonesian conditions and its policies for transforming those conditions in accordance with Communist objectives.

In a very real sense the congress marked the ratification of the new leadership and its line by the organization, and the great symbolic importance which the decisions of this congress had in the subsequent life of the party was due in no small measure to these circumstances. Later there will be occasion to mention other reasons for the resilience of the fifth congress deliberations. For an evaluation of the PKI's ideology during the Guided Democracy period, however, the importance of these documents lies as much in the revisions to which they were subjected over time as in the ritualistic power invested in them. For, despite the constant reiteration by the PKI leadership of the continued force of the fifth congress decisions, they were in fact radically amended and departed from in subsequent party theory and practice. Indeed, to a great extent the evolution of the PKI's ideology can be traced through the manner in which the 1954 analyses and prescriptions were modified in the light of later insights and exigencies. The direction of these revisions, and their significance, will be revealed most clearly if we begin by outlining the major contents of the fifth congress documents.

The decisions of the fifth congress were embodied in a program and a resolution, the latter consisting of a summary of the report to the delegates delivered by Aidit. They covered substantially the same ground and were identical in their analysis and prescriptions, and it will be convenient for the purposes of exposition to treat them for the most part as a unified declaration. Aidit's report, being the fullest elaboration of congress themes, is drawn upon most frequently in this outline. In these documents, the congress defined its political line in the context of an analysis of the socio-economic character of Indonesia after independence. The settlement negotiated with the Dutch at the Round Table Conference of December 1949 was depicted as an act of treachery that sacrificed the aims of the revolution and condemned the country to the status of a "semi-colonial and semi-feudal society." Responsibility was attributed to the mistakes of the PKI leadership during the revolution and the perfidy of the Masjumi-dominated Republican government that negotiated the settlement. The PKI's departure from its political, ideological, and organizational independence (a reference to its tactic of working through a number of parties instead of concentrating its strength) and the fact that "it did not place any importance on work among the peasants" so weakened it in an otherwise favorable situation that the "national bourgeoisie," under the impact of defeats suffered by the Republic, went over to the side of "the compradores and the imperialists" and "capitulated to imperialism by agreeing to the treacherous RTC Agreement created by Hatta, Sultan Hamid, and Mohammad Roem."[29]

As a result of the Round Table Conference agreement, said Aidit in his report,

> Dutch imperialism has succeeded in preserving its control over Indonesia, Indonesia has become a member of the so-called Indonesian-Dutch Union. Indonesia's foreign and foreign trade policies are controlled by the Dutch government. West-Irian, a legal part of the Republic of Indonesia, is still completely under Dutch domination. Vital economic resources still remain in the hands of imperialist countries. Dutch civil and military officials still remain in control of the Indonesian state machinery and the army.[30]

At the same time, the report indicated, the failure of the revolution to achieve its goal of a fully independent Indonesia had prevented the uprooting of survivals of feudalism that held back the development of the country by perpetuating backward productive techniques and keeping the peasants poor and without rights. Aidit did not undertake an analysis of rural social relations in the report, but in an article written in July 1953 he had already listed the following significant remnants of feudalism:

> the continued monopoly rights of the large landowners, with the result

[29] D. N. Aidit, "The Road to People's Democracy for Indonesia," *Problems*, p. 267.
[30] *Ibid.*, p. 245.

that the majority of peasants could not own land and were forced to rent land on the landowners' terms;

the payment of most of the crops as land rent in kind, so that the majority of the peasants were kept in poverty;

the payment of land rent in the form of work on the landlords' land, "which places the majority of peasants in the position of serfs";

the heavy debts of the majority of peasants, which placed them "in the position of slaves vis-a-vis the landowners."[31]

The conclusions Aidit drew from the analysis contained in his congress report were far-reaching. According to him "all talk of reconstruction, industrialisation and the prosperity of the country" was nothing but demagogy so long as the Round Table Conference agreement remained in effect and the power of imperialism and feudalism in the country was not broken.[32] This necessarily involved also the replacement of the Indonesian "state power," consisting of "feudal lords and compradores who are closely connected with foreign capital," by "a government of the people, of people's democracy."[33]

In order to realize this essential and fundamental change, the party program declared, the masses of the people must be aroused to bring about a shift in "the balance of forces between the imperialists, landlord class, and compradore bourgeoisie on the one hand, and the people on the other." In this struggle the working class must play the leading role, and accordingly,

must not only wage a struggle to improve its living standard, it must also . . . support the struggle of the peasantry for land, the struggle of the intelligentsia for its vital rights, the struggle of the national bourgeoisie against foreign competition, the struggle of the whole Indonesian people for national independence and democratic liberties.[34]

By acting in this way the working class would fulfill the most urgent political task confronting the party, namely the creation of a "united national front" of all anti-imperialist and antifeudal forces in the country, that is to say, "the working class, the peasantry, the petty bourgeoisie and the national bourgeoisie." Only such a broad front would be capable of bringing about the formation of a people's demo-

---

[31] Hindley, p. 33.
[32] Aidit, *Problems,* p. 245.
[33] PKI program; see *Problems,* p. 94.
[34] *Ibid.,* p. 95.

cratic government "formed on the basis of the alliance of workers and peasants under the leadership of the working class" and concerned to bring about "not socialist but democratic reforms." The program of such a government would be to unite all anti-imperialist and anti-feudal forces, transfer the land to the peasants without compensation, ensure the democratic rights of the people, defend national industry and trade against foreign competition, improve the material standards of the workers and abolish unemployment.[35]

In his 1953 article on the peasant question Aidit had repudiated previous party policy calling for "nationalization of all land," which he recognized as conflicting with peasant aspirations to own their own land. He admitted the PKI's ignorance of rural conditions and its lack of cadres in this sphere and called for greater attention to be paid to landless rural laborers and poor peasants, proposing as demands that could be popularized among them such issues as the lowering of land rents, interest rates, and taxes, the abolition of compulsory labor for landowners and authorities, the granting of unworked land to the peasants, provision by the government of improved seed and fertilizers, the establishment of agricultural schools, and improved irrigation. By patient organization around these demands, he claimed, the party would eventually be able to mobilize the peasants behind its radical policy of "land for the peasants."[36] Now, in his report to the fifth congress, Aidit stressed that in building the united national front primary importance must be attached to drawing the peasants into an alliance with the workers. Since the peasantry comprised "more than 70 per cent of the population," there could be no "real, broad and strong united national front" until they were organized and led by the working class to fight for their own interests. For this reason, "the agrarian revolution is the essence of the People's Democratic revolution in Indonesia."[37] But it was not to be an exclusively peasant revolution, Aidit made clear, and he criticized those PKI members who, on the basis of a superficial study and mechanical application of the lessons of the Chinese revolution, advocated that the Communists "must therefore leave the towns and work among the peasants" to the exclusion of other classes and strata.[38] Indeed he pointed out

[35] *Ibid.*
[36] Hindley, p. 161.
[37] Aidit, *Problems,* pp. 252–53.
[38] *Ibid.,* p. 254.

that not only could the national bourgeoisie participate in the revolution, because it too "is being oppressed by foreign imperialism," but in addition, "under even more specific circumstances, when the Party's policy at a given time is only directed against one particular imperialism, a part of the compradore bourgeoisie can also be an additional force in the struggle against that particular imperialism."[39]

The principal form of struggle to achieve the united national front, it was laid down in the PKI program, was to be mass action and mass organization. Parliamentary and election work were of subsidiary importance, but nevertheless not to be neglected; indeed, "the PKI has taken and continues to take a most active part in the parliamentary struggle [and] treats parliamentary work with the utmost seriousness."[40]

Both the program and the report clearly implied that, because of the weakness of the working class and poor connections with the peasantry, the basic tasks before the party would only be accomplished after a long, patient accumulation of strength. "The people can count on victory," stated the program, "only when the working class of Indonesia becomes an independent, conscious, politically mature and organized force capable of heading the struggle of the whole people, only when the people will see in the working class their leader."[41] So far as the peasants were concerned, the party's work would have to proceed by way of organizing them around their everyday demands and gradually educating them on the basis of their experience to go on to demand full liberation through the confiscation of landowners' holdings.[42]

At the present time, said Aidit, the imbalance in the development of the united national front posed dangers for the party:

unity with the national bourgeoisie is getting closer and closer . . . [but] the alliance of workers and peasants is still not strong. In other words, the party does not have strong foundations. At this stage, the party must fight resolutely against the right deviation which gives exaggerated significance to unity with the national bourgeoisie and underestimates the significance of the leadership of the working class and of the alliance of workers and peasants. There is danger of losing the Party's

[39] *Ibid.*, pp. 268–69.
[40] *Ibid.*, p. 97.
[41] *Ibid.*, p. 95.
[42] *Ibid.*, p. 253.

independent character, the danger of its merging itself with the bourgeoisie. Side by side with this, of course, the Party must also resolutely
prevent the "left" deviation, prevent sectarianism, that is, the attitude
which places no importance on the policy of a united front with the
national bourgeoisie; the Party must preserve this united front with all
its might.[43]

Despite these words of caution Aidit pointed to favorable political
developments that he claimed had already been achieved by the implementation of united national front tactics and that therefore
showed the correctness of the party's current strategy. By forming
blocs of cooperation with other organizations and parties, even in conditions where these were unable to be consolidated into firm alliances,
important victories had been won, among them "defeating the Suki-
man August mass arrests in 1951 . . . frustrating the attempted
coup of the right-wing socialists and militarists on October 17, 1952
. . . forming the Wilopo Cabinet in 1952 and . . . forming the Ali
Sastroamidjojo Cabinet in 1953."[44]

The decision to support the Ali government was defended with
special vigor, and a principle was enunciated to cover future PKI
relations with parties in office:

The CPI will give any government the opportunity to work on condition
that it gives the chance to the people's movement to develop. . . . It
would be adventurism if the CPI, because it hoped for the formation of
a better cabinet, were to withhold its support from the present Ali
Sastroamidjojo Government which could result in the government falling
into the power of the ultra-reactionary Masjumi and PSI parties which
would certainly fiercely suppress the people's movement. But the CPI
does not regard the present Ali Sastroamidjojo Government as a united
national front government or as a truly progressive government.[45]

As well as stressing the importance of the formation of a united
national front, the congress also proclaimed one of the party's basic
tasks to be the building of a PKI organization "nationwide in scale
which has a broad, mass character and which is fully consolidated in
the ideological, political and organisational spheres."[46] This aim had

[43] *Ibid.,* p. 268.
[44] *Ibid.,* p. 253.
[45] *Ibid.,* p. 256.
[46] *Ibid.,* p. 97.

been discussed earlier at a national conference called by the leadership in 1952, where it was resolved to wage a campaign to increase the size of the party's membership to 100,000 in six months. Suggestions that what was needed was quality, not quantity, had been met with the argument that "from a large quantity it is far more possible to achieve higher quality," but assurances were given that strict conditions of admission would be maintained. Furthermore, much greater emphasis than previously would be placed on ideological and political education, to ensure that all members were reared in a thoroughly proletarian and internationalist spirit.[47] In his congress report Aidit treated his concept of the mass party as equivalent to the creation of a party "of the Lenin type." He also reported on the considerable progress already made in expanding the PKI's membership; whereas at the beginning of 1952 the number stood at only 7,910, and organization existed only in Java and Sumatra, by the end of that year, as a result of the concerted drive launched by the 1952 national conference, "it was possible to increase membership to over 100,000, to expand the Party to Madura, Sulawesi, Kalimantan, the lesser Sunda Islands and the Moluccas, and to win the sympathy and support of broad sections of the democratic elements outside the Party."[48] By the time of the congress the membership had grown to more than 165,000. The main task in future party building was to overcome the isolation of the PKI from the peasantry, who constituted "less than 50 percent of the total Party membership."[49]

In retrospect, one explanation of the long-lasting influence of the 1954 program is apparent: it embodied, in a fairly generalized form, most of the agreed propositions of the time concerning Communist strategy in the "underdeveloped" countries while leaving largely undetermined those questions that were later to become the focus of acrimonious argument between the Soviet and Chinese parties and their respective supporters. By the time of the PKI's fifth congress, both the Soviet and Chinese parties had abandoned the extreme hostility which they had manifested toward the independent states of Asia and Africa over a number of years and were embarking on that cultivation of the "neutralist" countries which found its most dramatic

[47] Hindley, p. 74.
[48] Aidit, *Problems,* pp. 262–63.
[49] *Ibid.,* p. 264.

manifestations in the Bandung Conference of 1955 and Khrushchev's Asian tour of the same year. Accordingly, both the Communist giants were disposed to tolerate, even recommend, tactics of moderation and alliance with non-Communist parties and groups by indigenous Communist movements in those countries.[50]

Policies based on a united national front, people's democratic alliance, and the like, which had doctrinal precedents both in Eastern Europe and in China, were now being advanced as appropriate to a wide range of conditions in the colonial and ex-colonial world. To be sure, the trend was not yet definitive, but the signs were there to be read. The PKI program, while harmonizing with this general tendency, at the same time took a strictly orthodox position on those issues—such as working class hegemony, the primacy of the worker-peasant alliance, and a consistent stand against imperialism—which were of long-standing importance for a correct "Leninist" position but which were later to be watered down considerably in the concept of "national capitalism"[51] advanced by the Russian party (CPSU).

In addition, an issue that was to become the major focus of ideological contention at a later date, the question of armed struggle, was handled at the congress in an evasive way sanctified by long usage and therefore thoroughly reputable for its time: the PKI sought a peaceful path to a people's democratic government, the program indicated, but as experience had shown that the reactionaries would not allow their power to be undermined by parliamentary methods the issue would be decided by mass struggle.[52]

The PKI may have been influenced to some extent in the positions it took by trends in the wider Communist movement, which reached it via publications and the interchange of Communist delegations; but the basic lines of its strategy were evolved well in advance of these overseas tendencies and from the Aidit leadership's own reading of the Indonesian political situation. The most important direct influence on the PKI leaders' strategy was unquestionably Musso's *New Road.* This 1948 report, which bore the stamp of Moscow's thinking at the time, foreshadowed many of the propositions contained in the congress

[50] See Charles B. McLane, *Soviet Strategies in Southeast Asia: An Exploration of Eastern Policies under Lenin and Stalin* (Princeton, 1966), pp. 450–70.
[51] This point is discussed in more detail in Chapter 3 below.
[52] *Program PKI* (Departemen Agitprop, PKI, 1954), p. 19.

decisions. In particular, it proclaimed the necessity for the PKI to grasp the hegemony of the national revolution through the agency of a united national front alliance based upon the unity of the workers and peasants; envisaged the possibility of the party achieving power through peaceful means (Musso had expressly labeled his program a "Gottwald Plan" after the successful seizure of power in Czechoslovakia in February 1948); and defined the tasks of the united national front alliance in terms of national democratic, rather than socialist, objectives.[53]

At the tactical level, however, the influence of Chinese Communist experience was also apparent in Aidit's report, even while the Chinese strategy of armed agrarian revolution was rejected. Thus he recommended the Chinese party's methods of combating such ideological errors as "subjectivism" and revealed that Chinese theoretical publications were occupying pride of place in the PKI's educational program.[54] It also seems virtually certain that Aidit's argument that it was possible under certain circumstances to ally temporarily with one group of "compradores" against another was derived from Chinese theory.[55]

In this connection, it should be born in mind that the CPC had inaugurated, early in 1952, study courses in China for Communists from the Asian area. Judging by the testimony of other Communists who attended these courses, it seems more than likely that Indonesian students returning at this time communicated a sense of the greater relevance, flexibility, and practicality of Chinese revolutionary theories in comparison with the more scholastic and doctrinaire teaching at Moscow training institutes.[56]

The importance of Chinese, or any other foreign Communist, influence on the PKI should not be overestimated, however; the Aidit

[53] McVey, *The Soviet View of the Indonesian Revolution*, pp. 58–65.

[54] Aidit, *Problems*, pp. 273–74.

[55] I base this on personal experience of Chinese Communist Party (CPC) education in 1957 and discussions with Communists who attended political courses in China in earlier years. CPC instructors especially stressed the tactics used in 1937–41 in obtaining support from other "imperialists" for strikes against Japanese city enterprises.

[56] Again this assessment is based on discussions with Australian and Indian Communists who attended these courses. See also Keith McEwan, *Once a Jolly Comrade* (Brisbane, 1966), pp. 26–50.

leadership at this time and later was working out its approach to Indonesian political life in a predominantly pragmatic fashion, borrowing freely from those overseas experiences it considered of value but subservient to none and confident that no one outside Indonesia had very much to teach it about how to work in the Indonesian situation. The PKI leaders were certainly operating within the context of an international movement, with its classic texts, pronouncements, and authoritative decisions; and by conditioning and orientation they regarded these sources as valid and binding. But at the same time they took with the utmost seriousness the proposition that each Communist party had to apply the general theories of Communism to its own particular conditions. In their own case, this application was frequently to involve curious and intricate exercises in reconciliation but never the mechanical adoption of a course of action that appeared to be contradicted by their own requirements.

The program makes clear that great significance was attached to the Round Table Conference agreement and survivals of feudalism and imperialism in Indonesia. Few Indonesians would have argued at that time that the Round Table Conference agreement was other than a wretched compromise that imposed severe and humiliating restrictions upon Indonesian sovereignty. A very wide circle of nationalist opinion also resented continued Dutch political prerogatives and regarded the domination of Dutch capital over the modern sector of the economy as a major hindrance to the growth of indigenous enterprise and the development of a national economy. Many among them, including the president, viewed the removal of these foreign influences as the main requirement for the country's self-assertion and progress. But the PKI program and Aidit's congress report went well beyond these viewpoints. They treated imperialist control and the remnants of feudalism (about which opinion was much more varied) not merely as grave impediments to economic development and material improvement but as insuperable barriers without whose destruction no progress whatsoever was possible, all claims to the contrary being but outright deception. Such an approach did more than put the PKI in the camp of those who placed nationalist demands and goals before all others; it assured the party of a position in the van of nationalism's most extreme exponents.

Taken literally, the fifth congress theses would have had extraordinary and far-reaching implications. It followed from them for example, that PKI leaders would not be justified in putting forward any proposals for social betterment other than in the context of campaigns against imperialism and feudalism. Similarly, the party would be obliged to evaluate other parties and groups, and the government of the day, according to one criterion alone—their resolve to supplant imperialist and feudal power—and to treat any proposals for economic construction or social amelioration outside these spheres as illusory and dishonest. Needless to say the PKI did not adopt such an absolute posture, the effect of which would have been to limit seriously its appeal and influence. Nevertheless, the "purity" of the party's nationalism, and the overwhelming significance it attached to the question of foreign influence in particular, will become apparent in the course of this work.

The emphasis given to this aspect of the PKI's analysis must be understood in the light of prevailing political and social conditions. The Communist leaders had discovered in the course of the previous two years that, whereas class agitation was not only of limited appeal but also highly dangerous for the party's survival, the appeal to nationalist sentiment struck a powerful chord with a wide segment of opinion, particularly among the ex-revolutionaries of little education and the lower urban strata who represented the party's most immediate hope of further growth and influence. Equally important, it was a line of approach promoting accord between the PKI and the elite groups with whom its best hopes for political alliance lay—principally the PNI and the president. An approach that answered many of their own inclinations and aspirations, as well as the orientation of a large part of their actual and potential supporters and the requirements of their alliance strategy, was hardly to be denied. A desire to obliterate past suspicions about their patriotism and to demonstrate their unrivaled devotion to the national interest probably explains the extreme position adopted by the PKI's leaders in their presentations to the congress.

The program was unmistakably aimed at consolidating cooperation with the president and the PNI leadership, both of whom since 1952 had shown an increasing disposition to respond to urban discontent with postindependence conditions by emphasizing radical nationalist slogans at the expense of routine governmental tasks. Further, in order to overcome their more conservative competitors, the Masjumi and the PSI, they had indicated a willingness to accept PKI support and in return to sponsor its credentials as a legitimate political party. But the PNI was by no means a socially radical party. It rested heavily for support upon the *prijaji,* the bureaucratized gentry of Central and East Java, where the PNI's strength was concentrated. The *prijaji,* whose ways of life and thought derived from the sophisticated civilization of the ancient kingdoms of precolonial Java and its latter day descendants, had been consolidated in their prerogatives of authority by incorporation into the Dutch administration, and the PNI was accordingly entrenched among the civil bureaucracy inherited by the new Republic. With the aid of this bureaucratic lever, the PNI reached out through traditional channels to tap the support of the *abangan,* that majority of ethnic Javanese whose nominal adherence to Islam only lightly concealed a deep-seated aversion to the dispositions of more orthodox Moslems. In the face of Islamic zeal, the *abangan* jealously defended their *agama Djawa,* a syncretic religious and cultural value system blending Islamic, Hindu, and animistic strains and representing the "little tradition" in the distinctive culture of the great kingdoms of fact and legend, Madjapahit and Mataram. By shared attitudes and the conditioning of a long-established habit of deference to authority, the *abangan* were the clientele of the *prijaji.* In terms of contemporary problems, the nature of the PNI inclined it toward a statist society, defense of the importing interests of Java, an assertive nationalism, the preservation of an entrenched social hierarchy, and a permissive attitude toward religious variety.

The full implications of the PKI's de facto relationship with the Javanese bureaucratic elite would become manifest only at a later stage. So far as the 1954 congress formulations were concerned, it is significant that neither the president nor the PNI was mentioned by name as an adherent of the "progressive" camp. Rather, their roles were indicated negatively, by the absence of any reference to them in the passages describing the betrayal of the revolution and the misdeeds of past governments with which they had in fact been associated. Obviously the PKI leaders were not yet sufficiently confident of the trustworthiness of these allies to give them an outright endorsement; though their past involvement in forays against the PKI was not mentioned, neither was it forgotten. However, the party was prepared to make substantial concessions to their standpoints and susceptibilities in order to assure their goodwill.

One major concession to the PNI and Sukarno was on the question of the struggle against imperialism. Prior to the congress the PKI had attacked Dutch and American imperialism with equal fervor, the one because it had the greatest direct influence in Indonesia, the other because, by common agreement among the Communist parties, it was the most powerful and active anti-Communist nation and the greatest source of the "neocolonialist" threat. Within the PNI, however, a different view prevailed, to which President Sukarno also adhered to some extent. This view was that the United States had been partly instrumental in inducing the Dutch to concede independence to Indonesia and could still be of assistance to the Republic in recovering West Irian. Furthermore, Indonesia would need economic aid in its development, and the Americans were the most obvious source for both loans and private investment. The PKI leaders, anxious to remove a source of friction between them and their allies, altered their approach to accommodate this view. At the congress, Aidit declared:

The main enemy of the Indonesian people, from the viewpoint of the extent of its domination in various spheres, particularly in the economic sphere, is Dutch imperialism. Therefore, the united national front must be directed, in the first place, at liquidating Dutch imperialism and not at liquidating all foreign imperialisms in Indonesia at one and the same time. . . . But, in the event of American and other imperialisms giving armed support to the Dutch colonisers and their Indonesian hirelings, then the struggle must be directed at all imperialisms in Indonesia.[57]

The PKI had no intention in fact of abandoning its attacks on U.S. imperialism, which it saw as more dangerous than the Dutch in the long run, but considered it expedient to make a tactical retreat on the issue until such time as events gave it more favorable opportunities to strike at the Americans.

The structure of the program was such as to draw a sharp line between the PKI and its allies on the one hand and the leaders of the Masjumi and the PSI on the other. The PSI was a relatively small party, whose core consisted of Westernized intellectuals of considerable ability and influence espousing a social democratic philosophy.

[57] Aidit, *Problems*, pp. 254–55.

The much larger Masjumi, on the other hand, was a federative political organization of variegated composition. Its main appeal was to the various strands of committed Islamic belief. Islam had found its most devoted adherents among the trading elements in Indonesian society, and the Masjumi tended to attract and represent the entrepreneurial sector, the urban traders and some of the more innovative and well-to-do peasants and landowners, the religious teachers, and indeed all those for whom Islam acted as a challenge to the social inertia and hierarchy sanctified by the values of the Javanese bureaucratic caste. In East and Central Java the party membership had originally embraced two strains among the *santri* (the orthodox Islamic element, which forms with the *abangan* the two competitive streams, or *aliran,* in this society): a small but dynamic reformist grouping centered on the urban trading strata, and a larger and more conservative rural Islamic following which in 1952 broke away from Masjumi and established itself an as independent party, the Nahdatul Ulama (Religious Scholars). By 1954 Masjumi's greatest strength clearly lay in the Outer Islands, where Islam's conquests had been more decisive and where thriving smallholders' production of such export crops as rubber and copra sustained a more vigorous entrepreneurial spirit and a more flexible social pattern than in Java. In terms of practical policy, Masjumi's leaders gravitated toward liberal economic policies, the defense of the exporting regions outside Java, a pro-Western and anti-Communist bias, and the establishment of an Islamic state.

The PKI's attitude toward the Masjumi-PSI grouping was determined by its political rather than its socio-economic characteristics. Being pro-Western and anti-communist, it represented the major political threat to the Communists' safety and prospects. Accordingly, the program accused its leaders—men such as Vice-President Hatta, Natsir, and Dr. Sumitro—of deprecating radical nationalist propaganda as divisive and diversionary and being "demagogic" advocates of development within the semi-imperialist, semifeudal integument and defenders of foreign concerns (the "Dutchified" element in society, as Sukarno was later to call them). No pains were spared in Aidit's report to depict them as agents of imperialism, traitors to the nation, and deceivers of the people. The odious title of "compradores," redolent of Mao Tse-tung's denunciations of the "Chiang Kai-shek clique" and the wealthy Soong and Kung families who buttressed it, was applied to them. The Round Table Conference agreement was depicted as a deliberate sell-out on their part to their Dutch masters. Every reactionary and unpopular measure of the post-1949 period was attributed to them and them alone. In opposing the parties these men led, therefore, the PKI presented its stand not merely as a political battle against conservatives and anti-Communists but also as a patriotic struggle of the whole people; not political advantage or self-protection motivated the party, but the national interest.

The line of the congress clearly spelled out the PKI's intention of working through the existing political system to achieve its goals, the central element of this strategy being the united national front. This option had been chosen by the leadership from the time of their accession in early 1951. Even at that time, when the uncompromising "Zhdanov" doctrine was dominant in the world Communist movement and guerrilla struggles were being waged in Vietnam, Malaya, and the Philippines, the Aidit group had shown no liking for the path of armed struggle. That there were elements in the PKI that were influenced by the example of the Chinese revolution and favored such a course was indicated by Aidit himself.[58] But he took pains to point out that conditions in China and Indonesia were different; some years later he stressed that Indonesia lacked China's great hinterland and her "friendly rear" across the Sino-Soviet border.[59]

Equally important in Aidit's mind, however, must have been the weakness and division in the PKI in the first years of his leadership. As he told a Chinese audience in 1963, in explaining why armed struggle had been out of the question:

The Party membership was small, and in many areas the Party organisations were paralysed. . . . Some members of the Party's leadership were opposed to carrying out the *New Road* resolution concerning the merging of the Socialist Party and the Indonesian Workers' Party into a single Marxist-Leninist Party [and] no identity of views had been reached within the Party even on basic questions of the Indonesian revolution.[60]

The party's outside influence was also small. As Hindley observes,

---

[58] *Problems*, p. 254.

[59] See, for example, "Indonesian Society and the Indonesian Revolution" (1957), in Aidit, *Problems*, pp. 7–8.

[60] *The Indonesian Revolution and the Immediate Tasks of the Communist Party of Indonesia* (Peking, 1964), pp. 18–19.

"Communists had a loose control of the higher echelons in the largest trade union federation SOBSI, but little organization among the peasantry or youth."[61] In extending its mass appeal, the PKI faced a number of obstacles, including the stigma of having "stabbed the Republic in the back" at the time of Madiun, religious antagonism from Moslems in particular, and a low level of political or class consciousness among the workers and peasants.

Within the party, there was a strong emotional disposition to favor a united front strategy rather than a resort to armed struggle, deriving from the experiences of the younger generation in particular in the years of the national revolution. From the perspective of 1954, the revolution lay only just around the corner, and its outcome, while unsatisfactory, was not lightly to be set aside. The struggle had been protracted, desperate, and traumatic, issuing in a united Republic which few outside a core of fanatics on the right and the left, and remnants of Dutch-supporting groups, would see exposed to jeopardy. President Sukarno, who articulated both the deep yearning for national unity and the desire to "complete the revolution" felt by a large segment of the political public, was the symbol of nationhood against which no outsider group could hope to prevail by armed subversion. The new PKI leaders belonged within and not outside this tradition; they too had fought for the same ideals, experienced the same pride mingled with disappointment and disillusion, and continued to see as their principal enemy the same force as they had confronted in the revolutionary years, the Dutch. Their experiences had prepared them for a struggle *within,* not for one *against,* the constituted Republic. They conceived of themselves as the heirs of what had been accomplished, not as its destroyers.

Finally, as Aidit was again to emphasize in 1963 in Peking, "Since the party's legal status acquired after the Round Table Conference had been won through armed struggle [that is, through the party's participation in the fight to repel the last Dutch offensive in late 1948 and early 1949] it would be a great error to give it up voluntarily."[62] The Chinese Communists, after all, had taken to the mountains after legal channels had been closed to them by Chiang Kai-shek in 1927;

[61] Hindley, p. 49.
[62] *The Indonesian Revolution,* p. 19.

the PKI on the other hand had its open means of struggle, and Aidit could see nothing to be gained, and a great deal to be lost, by ceding them.

Given the adoption of a united front policy, the PKI leaders were obliged to resolve the problem of how the party would gain ascendancy over its allies in order to reach its objective of a people's democracy. Initially they had followed Musso in assuming that by espousing a vigorous national policy the PKI would be able to draw into its sphere on an individual basis all those who shared its immediate aims and on this basis to overshadow all other parties and groups in the political arena. Their experiences in 1951 and 1952 had demonstrated, however, that this was not a feasible expectation in the prevailing conditions. The party was too vulnerable to challenge the major power groups openly, and these groups would certainly not willingly stand by and see their members attracted away to the PKI. Even formal top level party alliances had proved disappointing at the parliamentary level because they tended to fall apart when the fluid state of elite politics offered the PKI's allies greater advantages elsewhere; worse still, the PKI found that when the anti-Communist crackdown took place in August 1951 its allies promptly deserted it and left it to its fate.

Consequently, the PKI leaders modified the Musso program in a crucial respect. Instead of attempting to construct an alliance under their own leadership they opted in the short term to settle for a good deal less—principally, protection from further persecution and freedom to build their own independent organization without hindrance. If they could obtain reasonable guarantees on these points, they were prepared to play a junior and subordinate role in any parliamentary coalition and to defer to their major alliance partner, the PNI. The problem of hegemony was therefore deferred until such time as the PKI's own organizational strength should give it the leverage required to claim greater prerogatives.

Despite the gains made by the PKI by the time of the fifth congress, no theoretical answer to the problem of hegemony was advanced. The omission is striking since the united front strategy only made sense in Communist terms if it was seen as a means of placing the party in a commanding position in relation to its allies and so enabling it to implement its basic goals of completing the national revolution and then making the transition to a socialist system. Yet at the same time the absence of such a transitional concept is not altogether surprising. Quite apart from the PKI leaders' propensity to solve problems as they arose, and to show little concern with hypothetical questions, the problem was one for which no precedent existed in Communist experience. The only Communist parties at that time to have won power largely through their own unaided efforts— those of the Soviet Union, Yugoslavia, China, and North Vietnam— had never faced a problem of this kind, and prescriptions for such an eventuality were suitably vague. In all four cases where Communist parties had come to power as the result of a domestic revolution they had done so by a violent assault upon the prevailing social and political system and had drawn support from other quarters mainly on the basis of their demonstrations of independent power. The PKI was of course in no position to emulate them and had resolutely rejected such a course, pinning its faith on a strategy of peaceful struggle utilizing parliamentary methods combined with the cultivation of mass support. It had accumulated considerable strength, but only by adopting an attitude of subordination to those in power. To date it had not won even a minor place in any government, and any attempt to force its way into positions of real power would assuredly have thrown its united front into disarray and prompted attacks upon the party from several political parties as well as the feared army.

Did the PKI leaders, then, have any idea at all how they were to obtain a purchase on the levers of power? The generalities of the fifth congress documents permit no more than inferences. It is clear that the united national front was aimed initially at isolating and rendering powerless the main anti-Communist parties, Masjumi and the PSI, and so weakening the forces most implacably opposed to the PKI. The party counted on being able to obtain decisive mass support among the workers and peasants, on the basis of which it would be a strong contender for national power. Its main competitor within the united national front spectrum was the so-called national bourgeoisie —in other words, the PNI and the social forces sustaining it. The strategy of the PKI leaders appears to have been to avoid a breach with this social and political grouping while at the same time building up its own independent strength to the point where it could take over the running from the bourgeois nationalists without having to resort to an armed struggle. Basically, this approach to the problem of hegemony was similar to the concepts that were to gain endorsement for application on a world scale at the twentieth congress of the CPSU in February 1956 and the meeting of world Communist parties in December 1957.

There were two obvious deficiencies in the strategy, and these were to make themselves abundantly felt in succeeding years and occupy a great deal of the PKI leaders' attention. First, by treating the PNI as a party representing entrepreneurial interests, which the PKI correctly estimated as being socially and politically weak, the party program greatly underestimated the significance of the bureaucratic social base upon which the PNI rested; as the trend toward concentration of economic and political power in the central state apparatus grew in the late fifties and early sixties, so did the strength and ambitions of the political-bureaucratic strata become enhanced and their desire and capacity to block the PKI's aspirations accumulate. Secondly, and equally importantly, the fifth congress proceedings ignored the political role of the leaders of the armed forces, who had repeatedly demonstrated their determination to carve out a place for themselves in the political system and who were overwhelmingly anti-Communist in outlook.

Other points covered in the program adopted by the fifth congress can be summarized briefly.

State power.   There was a clear contradiction on this point between the program and Aidit's report. The program described Indonesian state power as consisting of feudal lords and compradores; but Aidit regarded the Ali government, which the PKI was supporting, as something else—though precisely what is not clear. It was not a truly progressive government, he declared, but neither was it a reactionary one; at any rate the PKI could hardly throw its weight behind a government of compradores and landlords. In Marxist terms, of course, the state power consists of much more than the government; it embraces all those who carry out functions of domination over the society—members of parliament, civil servants, the army, police, etc.[63] Aidit could still have regarded the state power *as a whole* as

---

[63] V. I. Lenin, "The State and Revolution," in *Selected Works* (Moscow, 1947), II, especially 145–49.

controlled by feudal lords and compradores, but even then some discrimination between the government and other organs of state would have had to be made. This problem of defining the state was, as we shall see, to bedevil the PKI in later years.

The working class.   No reference was made in the report to the congress of the economic grievances or demands of the working class, and indeed the entire emphasis of the congress was upon the self-abnegating role of the workers and their political responsibilities toward other classes and the nation as a whole. This was in line with the position adopted by the Aidit leadership following the anti-Communist measures taken by the government in August 1951, which had been prompted in part at least by industrial unrest. Recognizing the party's vulnerability to governmental and army power in the urban centers, and aware too that to foment strikes would damage relations with the national capitalists whom it proposed to woo under the united national front formula, the PKI had resolved to moderate its class policies in favor of nationalist slogans and campaigns. Nevertheless, such total neglect of the immediate interests of the workers, of which this instance was to become symptomatic of the party's general orientation, was, to say the least, unusual in a Communist party and especially so in one that had gained control of the major trade union federation.

Mass struggle.   The insistence of the program on mass struggle as the primary means of creating a united national front, and the corresponding playing down of top-level alliance and parliamentary activity, is one of several stands taken by the congress that might be described as militant, in contrast to the overall tendency to emphasize a moderate, patriotic, and alliance-oriented approach. There are several possible explanations: the PKI was still feeling its way from the more orthodox and uncompromising formulations of Communist theory on this question to the position it subsequently adopted; these emphases (and the stress on the danger of right deviation) were included to reassure the party faithful that the new strategy was not so heretical as its critics alleged; or, the alliance with the PNI being still brittle and of uncertain duration, the PKI leaders wished to be cautious about the possibilities of top-level unity and to encourage members to do their utmost to establish wider influence at the grassroots level. Even so, as the report makes clear, the type of mass struggle intended was not of a large scale and "adventurist" kind, but small scale and of a welfare character. This did not in any sense detract from the essentially defensive nature of the policy line of the congress, most clearly revealed in Aidit's statement of reasons for supporting the Ali Government, these being to secure "the chance to the people's movement to develop" and to prevent "the government falling into the hands of the ultra-reactionary Masjumi and PSI parties which would certainly fiercely suppress the people's movement."

The peasantry.   Another radical item was the demand that land be confiscated from landlords without compensation and given to the peasants. This goal requires another kind of explanation, since it was to remain a prominent feature of the party's program and agitational demands throughout the Aidit period. The PKI apparently felt safe in putting forward such a demand at this time partly because it obviously remained a question for the future and partly because the party did not regard those whom it was wooing as allies as having any stake in the perpetuation of the existing agrarian social structure. On the contrary, it considered the national bourgeoisie to have an objective interest in the abolition of remnants of feudalism inasmuch as this would result in the release of peasants' purchasing power.

Both the program and Aidit's report spoke of the party's weakness among and lack of knowledge concerning the peasantry. The fact that the social structure in the countryside and the peasant struggle generally were not enlarged upon, despite the characterization of the Indonesian revolution as "above all an agrarian revolution," is to be explained by this weakness. Aidit's 1953 article on the survivals of feudalism in Indonesia remained for the time being the best that could be managed in this field.

The bourgeoisie.   The terms "national bourgeoisie" and "compradore bourgeoisie" as used in the program and report clearly bore little relation to identifiable socio-economic groups. The PNI, with its base among the Javanese bureaucracy and petty nobility, and with little entrepreneurial orientation, was by implication equated with the national bourgeoisie because its behavior most clearly conformed with what Communist texts ascribe to that class and, more to the point, because it was the elite group that showed most signs of being prepared to enter into an alliance with the PKI against other party competitors. The Masjumi and the PSI, the former with a strong entrepreneurial bias and the latter being predominantly a party of Westernized intellectuals, were allocated the role of the compradore bourgeoisie, not on the basis of the support they enjoyed among big subsidiaries of foreign enterprise but because they were pro-Western and most strongly anti-Communist. There were no indigenous Kungs or Soongs in Indonesia; there were smaller firms dependent on foreign principals, and some, but by no means all, of these were Masjumi and PSI supporters.

In making such categorizations, the PKI was dependent upon the general stock of Communist jargon but was manipulating it to fit the party's own situation. At the same time, these terms involved the party in some confusion, since they were frequently used as if the political groups to which they referred were motivated by economic interests appropriate to bourgeois formations in industrial societies, with consequent misreadings of the facts. The PKI's expectation that the PNI would fall in with the party's radical agrarian program because of its capitalist ambitions was an instance of such confusion.

The party. Although presented to the congress as a thoroughly Leninist concept, the idea of a "broad mass party" was anything but Leninist; it was in fact very close to the kind of approach Lenin condemned fiercely in his polemics with the Mensheviks.[64] Nor does Aidit's stress on the need for ideological, political, and organizational consolidation of the party's ranks alter the picture dramatically, since a body growing at the rate the Party had achieved (and was to exceed in the future) was incapable of achieving the kind of monolithic cohesion Lenin demanded. Aidit may have believed that his views were reconcilable with those of Lenin, but the conclusion is irresistible that for him numbers were the decisive thing if the party was to obtain the protection and prestige crucial to his strategy. His recognition that "Indonesia is a petty bourgeois country" with a wide prevalence of small scale industry and petty bourgeois ideology[65] would logically have called for careful selection and ideological training of the party's

[64] "The organizations of revolutionaries must consist first, foremost and mainly of people who make revolutionary activity their profession. . . . Such an organization must of necessity be not too extensive and as secret as possible" (Lenin, "What is to be Done?" *Selected Works* (Moscow, 1950), I, pt. I, 323).

[65] Aidit, *Problems,* p. 271.

members, strategies that were incompatible with the leadership's stated membership targets and standards.

Socialism.   It was an extraordinary feature of the congress that, although its major function was to outline and ratify the strategy of the new leadership, and therefore to confirm that leadership's ability to map out the road to attainment of the goals of Indonesian Communism, neither the program nor the general report contained any indication of how the transition from a people's democratic government to a socialist state would be effected. The people's democratic government, we have noted, was to confine itself to national and democratic tasks, in which the interests of the national bourgeoisie would be protected and advanced. Thus it was only a step along the way to the realization of the party's ultimate goal. But how the transition to this ultimate goal was to be made remained unspecified; indeed the word "socialism" was barely mentioned in either the program or the report. The PKI leaders were apparently interested only in immediate objectives; those that lay beyond their conceivable reach were set aside. Perhaps they saw no need to elaborate a utopian vision of a Communist future; or perhaps they preferred not to alarm their allies by referring to the changed status that would await the national bourgeoisie under a socialist system.

PROGRAMMATIC ADAPTATIONS, 1954–1959

The strategy of the united national front adopted at the fifth congress presumed the continued existence of the constitutional democratic system then in force. It was, as we have noted, a program for a political alliance cast in the terminology of a class alliance, and the key units of the alliance were political parties and their followings. Within five years, however, the constitutional system had been overthrown, the role of political parties had sharply declined, and a radically different distribution of power was being shaped under the more authoritarian Guided Democracy regime. The change was preceded by a succession of events that posed a multitude of problems for the young and relatively inexperienced Communist leaders: general elections in 1955; a severe crisis in the parliamentary system in 1956, accompanied by moves from a number of quarters, including the president and army leaders, to impose a new political format on the country; regional disaffection and revolt outside Java; the declaration of martial law in March 1957; bitter interparty controversy about the permanent constitutional basis of the state; the nationalizaion of Dutch enterprises in December 1957; and a massive intrusion by the army into all major spheres of society.

Throughout these tempestuous and dangerous years, the PKI hewed steadfastly to its course of allying itself with the PNI and the president, supporting them from attack from whatever quarter, and at the same time building up its own mass base of support. As President Sukarno came more prominently to the fore as the arbiter of politics, so did the PKI place its emphasis more decisively upon establishing close relations with him. Not without evident misgivings, the party leaders subordinated every other consideration to that of winning his favor and protection, and to this end they endorsed the drastic overhaul of the political system he sponsored that resulted in the demise of parliament and the concentration of power in the hands of himself and the army leaders.

It was a bitter pill for the PKI leaders to swallow. The parliamentary system had served them well on the whole. In the 1955 elections they had emerged as the fourth largest party in parliament, polling 16.4 per cent of the national vote.[66] Two years later, in local elections, they had done better still, increasing their total vote by 2,036,940 and eclipsing the PNI as the first party in Central Java. One feature of these elections was that they revealed the PKI to be, in terms of support, the most Javanese of all political parties, not excluding the PNI. In the 1955 elections, for example, no less than 88.6 per cent of the PKI's vote came from Java, the overwhelming majority of it from the centers of *abangan* strength.[67] With the PNI and the NU also gaining most of their votes from ethnic Javanese (the NU more from the *santri* stream), and the Masjumi demonstrating its predominance in the Outer Islands, the regional and religio-cultural elements in political conflict were starkly exposed.

Part of the PKI's parliamentary success was due to the willingness of its leaders to court popularity at the expense of doctrinal rigidity. In November 1954, for example, they announced their adherence to the Pantja Sila, the five principles defining the foundations of state

[66] See Hindley, pp. 222–29.

[67] *Ibid.* The implications of *santri-abangan* schism are elaborated in Clifford Geertz, *The Religion of Java* (Glencoe, 1960).

philosophy enunciated by Sukarno in 1945 and subsequently adopted by all parties and groups opposing the aspirations of committed Moslems to the establishment of an Islamic state.[68] This decision among other things obliged the PKI to accept "Belief in One God" as one of the political bases of the Republic, a substantial ideological concession and one that was to involve the party in a great deal of controversy and circumlocution in later years.

Not long afterwards, and again in the context of the campaign for the general elections, the party leadership simply cast aside one of the major propositions of the fifth congress with an eye to accommodating its allies in the government parties. It will be recalled that the congress conceived of the united national front as leading to the formation of a people's democratic government. This term, of course, was well known as one used by the governments of the Eastern European socialist states and China to describe their systems. Any prospective ally of the PKI with any degree of sophistication would also have known that, whatever the participation of other parties in them, these governments were firmly dominated by Communist parties. The use by the PKI of the same term, therefore, implied that it too foresaw a similar relationship within its united national front, a fact not calculated to encourage parties and non-Communists to put themselves at the PKI's disposal. Once again demonstrating his concern for immediate advantage over doctrinal rigidity, Aidit rewrote the election platform, substituting a national coalition government as the party's goal.[69] The change signified something more than a mere alteration of wording. Use of the term "coalition" clearly indicated that the PKI was prepared to settle for an equal, or even a minority, role in the government; indeed in the absence of such an intention, the change was meaningless.

Thus was the concept of the party's leading role in the united front abandoned, at least for the immediate future. Aidit and his fellow leaders may have had their own ideas of how such a coalition would ultimately turn out, of course; they are not likely to have cast away the belief that the PKI would one day be the decisive political force

---

[68] Feith, p. 359.

[69] Both terms continued to appear in party formulations, but the "coalition" formula and its successors, a *gotong rojong* and a Nasakom cabinet, steadily displaced the original concept.

in society. More important, however, was the long term effect of these and other compromises upon the character of the party as a whole, as well as on its relations with other political groups. Once new and more accommodating positions had been adopted, they had to be upheld consistently to avoid damaging charges of deception. Gradually they became part of the party's general framework of ideas, albeit alongside other and contradictory propositions. In the course of time, the party membership was to become accustomed to a "liberal" interpretation of its role; new members were won to the party on the basis of its tolerance and moderation, and all manner of relationships between the party and other groups and individuals were formed and cemented on the basis of this understanding of its purposes. The overall effect could only be a weakening of the party's militancy, diminishing that sense of being set apart and representing something essentially different from other groups that long formed part of the revolutionary dynamic of Communist parties.

The flexibility of the PKI, and the moderate patriotic stance it adopted during and after the elections, brought organizational gains along with electoral backing. Between 1954 and 1959, the party's membership grew from 165,000 to 1.5 million, and the membership of its labor, peasant, youth, and women's organizations also expanded greatly.[70] The PKI had good reason to defend a system under which it was faring so well. Yet between 1957 and 1959, the party's leaders elected to accept the overthrow of parliamentary democracy and its replacement by the Sukarno-army dominated regime of Guided Democracy, effected by a return to the presidential constitution of 1945.

An examination of the party's statements and actions during this transition period strongly suggests that its approach was governed, not by ideological predispositions or any long term analysis of Communist prospects and perspectives, but by immediate political concerns. The overriding consideration of the party leaders was to protect the party and its gains from destruction and to retain such freedom of maneuver as could be negotiated with those who had acquired decisive positions in the changed political constellation. They estimated that, in view of the many pressures working toward the downgrading of parliamentary institutions, these could not be preserved in their

[70] Aidit, *Problems*, pp. 386–87.

established form and any attempt by the party to assume the task of their outright defense would be fatal to it.

The other parties could no longer be counted on to act in concert with it in such a venture, and in any case their unpopularity and demoralization made them weak allies. Not much could be expected of the political public either, in whose eyes the paraphernalia of the parliamentary system was deeply discredited and lacking in any grand vision. Even the members of the party and its mass organizations were doubtful quantities; reared on a moderate political diet, with no deep commitment to constitutional norms and no substantial material gains to be defended, they were not likely to follow their leaders out on a limb in opposition to a president to whose charms they were addicted and an army they had good reason from past experience to fear. Aidit and his colleagues could envisage only isolation and defeat from such a foolhardy course, and the ashes of past defeats were too fresh on their palates for them to relish another meal of the same kind.

The main hope rested on Sukarno's growing partiality toward the PKI and his competition for political dominance with his army partners, with whom he had little in common apart from a desire to strengthen centralized government. Beyond a belief in their own qualifications to govern and a conviction that socially "disruptive" elements such as the Communists must be suppressed, the generals had no very clear ideas, and certainly no consensus, on the objects of the state.

Sukarno saw things in quite a different frame. Governmental efficiency as such meant little to him, especially in its more routine aspects; a government was fulfilling its role if it was uniting the nation behind meaningful displays of its prestige and grandeur. For him, the symbolic aspects of strong nationhood were all-important—the public demonstrations of identity, the pulling together of all political and social groups in support of bold and imaginative policies, the setting aside of petty interests and disputes in a common endeavour to put the country on the world map. In the *konsepsi* (concept) he advanced in February 1957 as the solution to the nation's ills, he deemed it essential to find a place in the political system for the Communist Party, since it was obviously there to stay and any attempt to keep it beyond the pale would perpetuate a major source of national disunity. Moreover, PKI participation had become a key element in the strategy by which he sought to gain a position of greater control over

the destinies of his country. Lacking a political party or mass movement of his own, Sukarno's pre-eminence came in time to depend
upon the maintenance of a political balance that prevented any one
group gaining ascendancy over him, a balance so delicately poised
that he could tilt it this way or that according to the prevailing winds
or the requirements of his ambitions. Without the PKI, he recognized,
none of the other political forces was capable of standing up to the
army; if the PKI were to be excluded, therefore, he would face in the
long run the repugnant prospect of becoming the gilded prisoner of
generals whose orientations he distrusted and many of whose actual
persons he disliked. His problem at this stage was to utilize the huge
following, the dynamism, and the organizational skills of the PKI
to erect a counterbalance to the army without driving Nasution and
his fellow army leaders into the arms of the regionalists, and so to
preserve for himself a considerable area of freedom and maneuver.

In many ways Sukarno would have preferred to rely on the PNI,
but that party's leaders had disappointed him sorely by their lack of
energy and militancy, their self-seeking, and their ideological flabbi-
ness, and they were badly demoralized. In the meantime, he was convinced that the Communists represented no serious threat; they had
amply demonstrated their support for him and had adopted a genuinely nationalist position, and he believed they could be induced
to resist foreign dictates. He knew the PKI leaders well and could
trust them not to abuse his favor in ways that would embarrass him
with the army. In any case, if it came to a showdown they would be
no match for his own power combined with the physical might of the
armed forces. Sukarno had still not abandoned the idea of creating
his own mass organization, but the question did not appear to him to
be one of urgent moment, whereas the opposition any move in this
direction was certain to arouse among all parties would represent a
problem.

The PKI leaders, for their part, badly needed the protection of the
president against the army and were delighted by the emerging possibility that they could make themselves indispensable to him. His
every pronouncement and intervention was greeted with unrestrained
enthusiasm, and to ensure that Sukarno understood the strength that
lay behind their support the party mobilized huge demonstrations

and rallies to greet his *konsepsi* and extol his role. At the same time, the Communists were by no means sure of their hold upon the president. They feared both his partnership with the generals against the parties and his close association with various radical nationalists, particularly from the small but influential Murba Party, who aspired to manage a presidentially patronized state party. The PKI, in fact, had no firm guarantee either that the president would not desert them at some stage in favor of some other political combination, or that he would not establish a personal dictatorship. For this reason it could not afford to rely exclusively on him to advance and defend its interests. While keeping its main eye on Hatta and the forces seeking to bring him back as prime minister, the party was obliged also to guard against moves from the president or his allies to force them off the political stage. Accordingly, it adopted a number of policies designed both to protect itself to the utmost in case of the worst, and to put it in the best bargaining position in the political contest taking shape. The Communist leaders were stubborn and undeviating in their defense of parliament and the parties, not so much because they respected these institutions (about which they were in point of fact ambivalent) but to shore up their own right of existence and keep power dispersed as much as possible. Their most prominent slogan of the transition period, "Realize the *konsepsi* 100 per cent" was in fact quite deceptive in its meaning, as indeed were all their protestations of complete backing for Guided Democracy; what the slogan implied was the party's demand for inclusion in a *gotong rojong* (mutual cooperation) cabinet, as promised under Sukarno's *konsepsi,* a position that would give them prestige and added protection and, so they believed, place them in a better position to preserve parliamentary and party prerogatives. For the same reason they continually defended the cabinet against extreme attacks and attempts to downgrade it while reserving to themselves the right to make measured criticisms of its performance. Whatever the deficiencies of the parliamentary system, they had shown their capacity to compete on more than equal terms there with their rivals, and they had no desire to see it destroyed by more formidable opponents.

Simultaneously, the PKI pressed ahead vigorously with the expansion of the party and its mass organizations, on the principle that the stronger the PKI was, or appeared to be, the less the army was likely to risk an all-out attack on it, and the less President Sukarno would sanction any such serious fracturing of the nation's unity.

In a sense, the PKI wanted the best of both worlds, the liberal political system and Sukarno's Guided Democracy. On the one hand they favored greater authority for their protector the president; a system defining the permissible limits of political behavior in such a way as to exclude their most inveterate enemies; greater stress on nationalist and anti-imperialist issues; and a *gotong rojong* cabinet. On the other hand they desired the army to be confined to its military role; a guarantee against attempts to suppress the party or incorporate it into some wider body under the control of others; a reasonable diffusion of power that would inhibit ganging-up against the communists; and the opportunity to use public forums such as parliament and the press to advance their cause. In six years they were to gain a good deal of what they sought, but in the shorter period under consideration they were obliged to settle for much less, lacking even the assurance of their unfettered survival.

The fundamentally defensive character of the PKI's tactics at this time are borne out in Aidit's report to the party's sixth congress, which met in September 1959. Explaining and defending the party's decision to support a return to the 1945 constitution, Aidit did not claim that the party had gained any advantages from the change but in his references to it, the very briefness of which suggested his unease, spoke of the necessity "to save the country from the disaster of a further split in the national forces," "to avoid a shameful compromise between those middle-of-the-road forces in favour and those against the 1945 Constitution," and "to prevent the return to power of a military dictatorship." At the same time Aidit was at pains to emphasize, if not exaggerate, the subservience of the Guided Democracy system to the rule of law.[71] These brief comments suggest that the party leaders feared two possible developments, one a compromise between the PNI and Masjumi on a more pro-Western and anti-Communist policy, and the other a military takeover. Frequently, indeed, in this period the choice was presented as one between Guided Democracy and "fascist dictatorship."

[71] *Ibid.,* pp. 328, 333.

Doubt and disagreement continued in the party, however, and prompted a major article by Politburo member Ir. Sakirman which was published in two succeeding issues of the party's periodical, *Bintang Merah,* in mid-1960.[72] Admitting that "it is not at all easy to understand clearly the political line followed by the party up to now and especially since the party decided upon its agreement to a return to the 1945 constitution," Sakirman nevertheless attributed such confusion to "subjectivism," which led many members to see only the negative sides of the party's work and of Guided Democracy and, on the other hand, only the positive aspects of parliament and general elections.[73]

The main thrust of Sakirman's article was to dampen expectations among party members of the possibility of the organization either going it alone or achieving rapid victories. The Russian and Chinese revolutions were surveyed in order to show that the Indonesian revolution had to pass through the "bourgeois democratic" stage before it could proceed to workers' power and socialism, and that the united national front embracing differing classes and strata was an essential element in the strategy for carrying through the national democratic revolution. To make the lesson still clearer, Sakirman emphasized that in several key respects the Indonesian revolution suffered from greater problems than either the Russian or the Chinese ones: both the proletariat and the national bourgeoisie were weaker; the party was less experienced; and religion was a powerful force that could be used to manipulate backward strata of the population.[74] Finally, before turning to immediate past events, the dangers of the party's isolation were stressed by reference to the negative results of the policies followed by the PKI leadership in 1950.[75]

Turning to the question of Guided Democracy, Sakirman stated that the party accepted the return to the 1945 constitution because the Constituent Assembly could not agree upon a constitution, and at the same time threats to the existence of the parties were becoming very menacing. A quick decision was forced upon the party because,

[72] *Bintang Merah,* XVI (May–June 1960), 194–291, and (July–Aug. 1960), 320–40, 348.
[73] *Ibid.,* p. 194.
[74] *Ibid.,* pp. 207–8.
[75] *Ibid.,* p. 213.

if the Constituent Assembly had met again without reaching a decision, there was every possibility that the pro-Pantja Sila and anti-
Pantja Sila parties would have arrived at a compromise harmful to
the people's interests. The PKI had only two effective alternatives: to
ally itself with the anti-Pantja Sila reactionaries; or to unite with the
democratic forces led by Sukarno. The latter was the only possible
choice, not only because it was essential for the party to go along with
the middle forces but also because of the great popular support for
the president's *konsepsi*.[76] Sakirman did not claim that the decision
had resolved the party's problems. Without a mass movement of
struggle from below, he warned, the reactionaries could use the 1945
constitution as "an instrument to oppress the people." The Communists must therefore fight determinedly for democratic rights, an executive power comprising President Sukarno and a cabinet representative of the people, the democratization of state power by the inclusion
of people's representatives, state planning on a national and democratic basis, and the fostering of a spirit of independence, unity, devotion, and awakening. At the same time, the movement from below
had to be assisted by efforts from above—that is, by a political alliance
between the party and "democratic" elements.[77]

Here again the defensive character of the party's position, and an
intimation of lingering doubts about the outcome of what had occurred, is apparent. Sakirman does not claim that the PKI was an
enthusiastic partisan of Guided Democracy from the outset. Once
having decided to swallow the pill, however, it was incumbent on the
party leaders to do so with the best possible grace. There were always
enemies waiting to undermine their standing with the president by
seizing upon every manifestation of party half-heartedness or "hypocrisy"; and indeed the PKI's continued defense of the parties did
in fact evoke such attacks. The only possible tactic to pursue in the
circumstances was to respond eagerly to every step in the transition to
the 1945 constitution, while at the same time striving to obtain the
concessions that would preserve the party's freedom of action.

It is conceivable that the PKI leaders might have taken a different
standpoint had their commitment to constitutional democracy been
deeper. But in point of fact neither their early experiences as na-

[76] *Ibid.*, pp. 325–26.
[77] *Ibid.*, pp. 321–22.

tional revolutionaries nor their ideological adherence to Communism had led them to such a commitment. The revolution had virtually equated democracy with nationalism, with mass action, and with the "spirit" of organizations and leaders, but not with the norms of a constitutional process. The part played by Aidit and Lukman in the 1945 proclamation crisis had demonstrated their passionate attachment to the goals of the national struggle and their belief that the rightness of these goals justified direct revolutionary measures by a minority if these were necessary to achieve what they regarded as the aspirations of the people. Communist doctrine reinforced such attitudes in so far as it tended, especially in its vulgarized Stalinist form, to dismiss constitutional forms as mere "shams" and to place overwhelming emphasis on democracy as a struggle, more or less violent, to impose the standpoint of one or another class on the rest of the population, with parliament and other institutions merely ratifying the decisions arrived at in a wider arena. This approach found an echo in Aidit's fifth congress report where, as already noted, mass action was regarded as of considerably greater importance than parliament or elections as means for realizing the party's aims. In Sakirman's article, a multiparty system was defended not as inherently basic to the democratic process but as essential to the defense of democracy in a "capitalist class society."[78]

The experience of the party under the constitutional regime of the previous ten years was not likely to have strengthened its commitment to parliamentary institutions as such; alongside the general bickering, nepotism, political trafficking, and corruption with which the system was redolent, it had been marked by a persistent and united opposition by the elite to any share in government for the PKI. The party leaders undoubtedly shared the popular disgust and impatience with parliamentary standards, although they had been capable of defending corruption in the second Ali government when this seemed necessary to the party's united national front tactics. Equally important, they shared the widespread enthusiasm for Sukarno's style—his revolutionary rhetoric, his radical dynamism, and his projection of lofty goals for national awakening. They were drawn toward him by the logic of their situation and the stirrings of their national spirit; and they were to take the plunge with him into Guided Democracy. It is

[78] *Ibid.,* p. 219.

apparent that they did so, however, without any clear appreciation of whether the united national front strategy could be applied under the new conditions, and if so how this could be done. The concept had been tailored to a constitutional system in which parliament and political parties played the dominant roles and in which the PKI itself could operate under relatively free conditions. Before the Communist leaders could determine whether, and in what form, the basic elements of their strategy were viable under a more authoritarian order, they had to wait for the outlines of the system to become more clearly defined and at the same time probe and assess its characteristics in order to discover the avenues open to them. This meant, in particular, obtaining greater experience in handling the two main centers of power in the new dispensation, the president and the army.

2. The PKI and the
Political System

Once having committed themselves to underwriting Guided Democracy, the leaders of the PKI turned their attention to devising ways of overcoming the obvious disadvantages for them in the more authoritarian climate and seeking avenues to advance party interests within the terms set by the new dispensation. It was by no means an easy task. They had given their imprimatur to, and sworn loyally to uphold, a system in which they were at most junior, insecure, and controversial participants. They had undertaken to propagate an ideology created outside their own ranks and to bring their social and political program into line with that of the regime. They were beset with enemies only too anxious to strike them down and turn their protector, the president, against them.

No clear precedent for their predicament existed in Communist history, and hence the PKI leaders could find little if any guidance from texts or the experience of other Communist parties. Consequently their policies could not but be indigenously derived, however much they might draw upon the general strategic content of the international movement's doctrines. If they were to survive and prosper it would have to be by their own efforts. Understandably, for some time after the introduction of Guided Democracy the Indonesian Communists were feeling their way toward a comprehensive understanding of their position and its implications. Only after a considerable amount of practical political experience under the new conditions, during which their situation improved and they gained greater confidence in the future, did they attempt a total appraisal and prospectus in doctrinal terms.

Initially it was imperative for the PKI leaders to define their tactics toward the major repositories of power. Guided Democracy had simplified the political structure by concentrating decisive power in two agencies—the president and the army. The PKI, as the largest and most dynamic political party, could claim to represent a third force, but one immeasurably weaker than either of the other two. In terms of the triangular shape of the political structure, then, the PKI's objective was to change the configuration by enlarging its side of the triangle. Since it could not hope to do this at the expense of both of its more powerful competitors at once, it resolved to aim first for an isosceles form, with Sukarno and itself in some kind of paramount parity in relation to the army.

To enhance the president's role in the political system and, under his patronage, to gain the freedom and respectability necessary to strengthen its own independent position thus became one aspect of the PKI's strategy. The other, complementary, aspect was to work for a reduction of the army's prerogatives and standing. The general scheme was straightforward, but its application required infinite patience and skill, and considerable ideological concessions. In return for the president's support, the party was obliged to defer to his guidelines and policies, and diminish its own distinctive philosophy and aims; as we shall see, this resulted in a marked reformulation of its basic strategy. On the other hand, the military's power and the eagerness with which most generals anticipated a crackdown against the Communists meant that opposition to the army had to be conducted with great delicacy and indirectness. In this sphere, the PKI became involved in a tense race against time, the length of which could not be predicted.

The Communist leaders did not neglect subsidiary but important centers of power in the president's court circle, the political parties, state institutions, and the bureaucracy. Negatively, they were concerned to counter intrigues and policies harmful to the party emanating from these quarters. Positively, they aimed to woo influential figures among the political and bureaucratic elite by demonstrating the PKI's patriotism, its energetic support for government policies, its problem-solving capabilities, and, not least, its capacity to make life difficult for those who opposed it. In this way, the party would enhance its value as an ally of the president and create an impression of being the wave of the future that others might strive to stem only at their peril.

In large measure owing to the mobilizing strength it developed behind the West Irian and Malaysian campaigns, the PKI succeeded by the latter part of 1963 in overcoming the defensive posture it was obliged to assume in the early years of Guided Democracy and laying the ground for a more forceful assertion of its claim to be considered a major contender for national power. It consolidated its alliance with the president, helped to weaken the political role of the army, and exacted respect, if not affection, from a sizeable segment of the elite. At this point the party leadership came forward with a theory that attempted to conceptualize its practice by defining the character of the Indonesian state system in Marxist terminology and indicating the lines on which it could be transformed in a socialist direction. The nature and implications of this highly novel theory will be analyzed at the conclusion of this chapter, but first it is necessary to trace the interactions between the PKI and the various forces encompassed in the political system out of which the theory was constructed.

THE PARTY AND THE PRESIDENT

By 1959 President Sukarno had come to look favorably on the PKI as the most energetic and consistent supporter of his militant nationalist creed, a useful counterweight to the army in the political system, and the most effective mass mobilizer behind the patriotic campaigns he held dear.

At the party's sixth congress in September 1959, he took the unprecedented step of addressing the closing reception, after first intervening with the army to allow the congress to be held, and publicly expressed his pleasure at the PKI's attitudes, particularly its stress on national unity. Hailing the Communists as "fighters for Indonesian independence, fighters against imperialism," he adapted a Javanese proverb to express his identification with them: "You are my blood relatives, you are my brothers, and if you die, it is I who shall be the loser."[1] On the PKI's part, Aidit had declared in his report to the eighth plenum of the Central Committee, held just before the congress, that one of the two indispensable conditions for the Guided Democracy system was Sukarno's leadership of the state.[2]

---

[1] *Bintang Marah,* XV (Sept.–Oct. 1959), 376.
[2] *Ibid.,* XV (July–Aug. 1959), 292.

This was a far cry from the days of Madiun, when Sukarno had called upon the people to choose between himself and the Communists, and from the early fifties, when the PKI had publicly denounced the president as a "Japanese collaborator" and a "false Marxist." Yet there were factors besides political convenience that had drawn these two political forces toward each other and that both facilitated and fortified their relationship. As early as 1926 Sukarno had recognized Marxism as a legitimate strain in the nationalist movement and had advocated cooperation between nationalists, Moslems, and Marxists in the common struggle against colonialism, at the same time appealing to the Communists to abandon the dogmatic and sectarian ideas that hindered such cooperation.[3] And this stress on the unity of different ideological *aliran* in the national movement was but a part of a complex of ideas that made the president susceptible to the appeals of Communism.

Sukarno was a man of intensely romantic temperament, who viewed life as an unfolding drama, or a series of dramas, in which satisfaction for the revolutionary was to be found not so much in the attainment of perceived objectives but in the expectation, excitement, and tension of the struggle itself. In his own often repeated phrase, he was "infatuated by the rhythm of revolution."[4]

His nationalism, conditioned by the strongly Javanese culture in which he was reared, was both past- and future-oriented. On the one hand, he wished to see Indonesia strong in the symbols and technology that the world regarded as the hallmark of greatness. On the other, his national pride was fostered by the idealized picture of the Javanese past that he found in the *wajang* plays and the myths of the more traditionally minded nationalists. This envisioned past, with its emphasis on harmony, its conflicts mediated by consensus practices, and its sense of order, fused with his modernist ideas into a dynamic conception of a future harmony based on modern social organization but recreating the values of a distinctive past national identity.

He was never wholly captivated by the West, unlike many of his

[3] Sukarno, *Nationalism, Islamism, and Marxism* (1926) (Translation Series, Modern Indonesia Project, Cornell University, 1970).

[4] Similarly he said "I want to go on being in tune with the waves of the Revolution" (*Like An Angel that Strikes from the Skies: The March of Our Revolution,* address on Aug. 17, 1960 [Djakarta, 1960]).

contemporaries who studied in Europe; he understood the need to borrow its ideas and to adapt to its all-conquering techniques, but this, he felt, should lead not to imitating its ways but, rather, to combining them into an Indonesian-flavored amalgam with the traditional values. Nor was he entirely a slave to tradition; the stasis of old Javanese society had no appeal for a temperament in which tranquility was boredom. He leaned to a politics in continual and exhilarating flux, controlled by one whose vision was "in tune with the cosmos" and thus capable of bringing to society peace, prosperity, and harmony.

To his devotion to the cause of national emancipation and uplift, Sukarno had added in the late 1920's a basically Marxist-derived analysis of colonial and national oppression and a strongly held belief that the different streams of anticolonial thought could be and must be united to throw off the imperialist yoke. The differences between various ideologies, he contended, were subsidiary to their common objective.

Sukarno did not take over the class concepts of Marxism, however. He divined that social demarcations in Indonesia did not lie principally along class lines and that the class consciousness even of the small proletarian nucleus was at most incipient. Nationalism, he believed, should appeal to most strata in the society, and their differing interests were not of a character to prevent cooperation among them. He developed a "populist" social philosophy, according to which the archetypal citizen was the *marhaen,* the small peasant or artisan who owned his own plot of ground or tools, and was therefore nominally an independent producer, but was ground into abject poverty by the operations of imperialism.[5] We may read into this concept a sociologically-based argument justifying the leadership of the little people by their historically determined leaders, the higher status intelligentsia from which Sukarno sprang, without discounting the sincerity with which the analysis was propounded or the genuine insights it contained into Indonesian society.[6]

---

[5] Sukarno, *Marhaen and Proletarian* (1953) (Translation Series, Modern Indonesia Project, Cornell University, 1960).

[6] Similar concepts have been advanced in many underdeveloped countries, suggesting that they form a legitimizing ideology for nationalist elites. The question is discussed in Peter Worsley, *The Third World* (London 1967), pp. 118–75.

Sukarno regarded himself as a socialist; his socialism, however, was not programmatic in form but rather a reaction against imperialism and capitalism, a re-evocation of the "village communism" of traditional Java, and a reflection of the bureaucratic gentry's revulsion against trade and commerce. In a striking passage in his "autobiography" that demonstrates among other things the typically Javanese pride he took in his eclecticism and his ability to fuse ancient and modern symbols, Sukarno declared that socialism was nothing more nor less than social justice:

Our socialism does not include extreme materialistic concepts since Indonesia is primarily a God-fearing, God-loving nation. Our socialism is a mixture. We draw political equality from the American Declaration of Independence. We draw spiritual equality from Islam and Christianity. We draw scientific equality from Marx. To this mixture we add the National Identity: Marhaenism. Then we sprinkle in *gotong rojong,* which is the spirit and the essence of working together. Mix it all up and the result is Indonesian Socialism. These concepts . . . don't fall neatly into a box according to the Western mind, but, then, you must remember I do not have a Western mind. . . . I always work in terms of Indonesian mentality.[7]

In Sukarno's romantic view of the nation's crisis in the late fifties, what was needed most to overcome the failings of the parliamentary system was not a more efficient apparatus of political direction, allied with a planned attack on the problem of economic development, but the inculcation of a spirit, a will, a sense of dedication. This required an apparatus, but one specializing in the determination of grand objectives and the dissemination of unifying guiding concepts. Once the whole nation was pulling together in a spirit of mutual dedication, economic problems would solve themselves; and in any case the real determinants of a nation's fiber were not the quantity of goods it produced but the extent to which it realized its own identity and projected its image to its citizens and the wider world.

As he himself put it in one of his famous Independence Day addresses, "I am not saying that we do not need technology. . . . And yet, more than those skills, we need the spirit of a nation, the spirit of freedom, the spirit of revolution. . . . What is the use of taking

[7] Cindy Adams, *Sukarno: An Autobiography* (Indianapolis, 1965), p. 75.

over the technology of the Western world if the result of that adoption is merely a state and a society à la West . . . a copy state?"[8]

The most important task of a political leader, as he saw it, was to rally the country against the enemy preventing it from realizing its identity and its world role. It was an old enemy: at one level of meaning the perennial giants of the *wajang* who stood in the way of the attainment of the just kingdom; at a more immediate level, the imperialists who had held Indonesia down for 350 years and were still occupying part of her territory (West Irian), dominating her economic resources, scheming with dissident rebels to dismember her, infecting her national culture with "cosmopolitan" depravity, and even capturing the souls of many of her ("Dutchified") political leaders. All energies must be mobilized to defeat this enemy and to realize the nation's destiny; for this, a trustworthy and strong leadership was required, everyone must be compelled to put the national interest before his own selfish concerns, and all departures from the goals formulated by a far-sighted leadership must be suppressed as forms of "Western liberalism."

The analysis and prescription were pertinent enough to have a wide appeal. Their implicit authoritarianism was if anything welcomed by a great part of the political public for whom the novel practices of Western-style democracy had proved deeply disenchanting and who were ready to follow a leader with charisma and a panacea. Not that the president's solution was anything like universal in its attraction. It gave little satisfaction to the Outer Islands elite, who sought greater consideration of regional interests and tough restrictions on Communism. By resolving the Constituent Assembly's long debate on whether Islam or the Pantja Sila should be the foundation of the state in favor of the latter, it deeply offended the susceptibilites of the politically organized Moslems. And it was distasteful, too, to that large number among the country's intellectuals who valued Western learning and Western democracy. In essence, it was a formula that promoted Indonesian unity on Javanese terms; that accorded first place in politics to "symbol wielders" as opposed to "administrator types"; that strengthened the bureaucracy at the expense of entrepreneurs; that depreciated efforts at economic development in favor of radical

[8] *Tahun "Vivere Pericoloso"* (A Year of Living Dangerously), address on Aug. 17, 1964 (Djakarta, 1964).

nationalist objectives; and that promoted the credentials of "native sons" above those of the "Westernized." As such, its most pronounced appeal was to the alienated political public and the *abangan* Javanese who read into it (with Sukarno's aid) a sign of the return of a strong and just ruler who would restore the stability of the realm and make of the *kraton,* or palace, a center of power and attraction. It had a strong attraction for those with traditional (especially Javanese) orientations and those with modern notions of progress, but above all for those suspended in the uneasy land between past and present and responsive to the echoes of each. It laid little stress on tangible benefits to any public (save the vague promise of a "just and prosperous society" in the future) but embraced millions in the psychological rewards of integration in the national crusade and the struggle to achieve utopia. Additionally, in power terms it gave the army a strong stake in the regime, held out sufficient hope to the party elites (other than the Masjumi and the PSI) that they would be accommodated in some fashion, and offered no threat to the extensive civil bureaucracy.

Sukarno's professed Marxism, which he expressed more and more strongly after 1959, would not in itself have facilitated a partnership with the PKI, any more than the adherence to Marxism of both Communists and social democrats elsewhere has made cooperation between them any easier. Communists tend to be jealous of their rights over the title of Marxists, and the accusations of "false Marxism" made against Sukarno in the early fifties were typical of the reaction of many Communists to those who claim to share their philosophy but disagree with their practices and their claims to exclusive power. Far more important to the cooperation of Sukarno and the PKI than such shared views were the changes wrought in PKI ideology and policy by the Aidit leadership, the combined effects of which were to emphasize national unity and nationalist goals over class agitation and Communist claims to hegemony over the national movement.

When Sukarno said at the Party's sixth congress in September 1959, "I have been very pleased with the PKI, especially during the recent period . . . because the PKI clearly states that it is indispensable to have national unity,"[9] he was placing his finger on the factor that made it both possible and desirable for them to combine

---

[9] *Bintang Merah,* XV (Sept.–Oct. 1959), 377.

their political efforts. He went on to describe the implications of the party's changed tactics, as he understood them, in crystal-clear terms:

Even though throughout history there will always be a class struggle [and] class contradictions. . . . we must not during a national revolution sharpen the class conflicts and the class struggle within our national revolution. On the contrary, we must all build national unity, build all revolutionary forces, into one powerful wave to sweep away our main enemy, political imperialism and economic imperialism.[10]

This was precisely the implication of the party's program, with its emphasis on the united national front and the primacy of the struggle against imperialism. It was to be made more explicit at the end of 1960, when the PKI openly proclaimed the necessity of subordinating the class struggle to the national struggle. The party leadership had, in fact, taken lengthy strides towards a "populist" position, and in the increasing stress it was to place on the *aliran* aspect of national unity (as distinct from the class alliance aspect) and the revolutionary qualities of the whole Indonesian population (excluding only the compradores and the feudal landlords) it was incorporating a good measure of Sukarno's *marhaenist* philosophy into its own ideology.[11]

More specific aspects of Sukarno's outlook were also attractive to the PKI, in particular his rejection of the demands of the regional rebels and of Moslem extremists, as well as his anti-Westernism. Of equal significance were the implicit elements common to both ideologies. Though the PKI would have indignantly rejected accusations of Java-centricity, nevertheless it was a fact that the overwhelming bulk of its membership and its cadre force was drawn from that island, and policies that favored Java's place in the political constellation were bound to give the party greater influence and protection. Thus, although it supported greater autonomy for regional and ethnic groups, the PKI also emphasized the necessity for a strong central government. Similarly, the PKI gave an important place to the na-

---

[10] *Ibid.*

[11] This does not mean that the PKI abandoned class analysis and class appeals. Rather, there was set up within the party's ideology and practice an uneasy tension between the class approach and the nationalist approach, with the emphasis varying with circumstances but with no satisfactory resolution ever being achieved on the ideological plane. See Chapter 3 for more discussion of this issue.

tional bourgeoisie in its united national front and from time to time advocated policies beneficial to the entrepreneurs. But the weight of its policies was on the side of strengthening the state sector of the economy, and hence would result in the enhancement of bureaucratic rather than entrepreneurial power. Again, its emphasis on the fact that no economic or social progress was possible in Indonesia until imperialist influence had been destroyed strongly inclined the party to identify itself with nationalist crusading and to avoid pressing too hard against internal impediments to social improvement. Finally, the PKI leaders shared Sukarno's detestation for the PSI administrator types, although for different reasons. With the PKI, it was not the style of the administrators but their political outlook that was unacceptable. The PKI leaders themselves took pride in their expertise and sought to impress the governmental elite with their prowess in problem solving, but they insisted that those appointed to administrative positions must be "both expert and patriotic."[12] Nevertheless, given the lines of cleavage in the elite, the party could not avoid strengthening the general tendency to prefer loyalty and solidarity-making skills over administrative competence.

The similarity of orientation between Sukarno and the Aidit leadership also reflected their mutual dependence on a common public. Sukarno, as we have suggested, struck his most powerful chords among the lower urban strata caught between the influences of tradition and modernity, and, more extensively, among the *abangan* of Central and East Java. The former supplied the bulk of PKI activists and the latter its massive electoral support. It is not stretching things too far, therefore, to suggest that Sukarno and the PKI were each seeking to define and articulate the needs and interests of these strata, providing for the political public a utopian vision to counter its psycho-cultural disorientation and for the *abangan* an assurance that their cultural values would be defended against the challenge of orthodox Islam. By mobilizing these strata behind national symbols, the PKI was supplying Sukarno with the "troops" he needed to maintain his supremacy against the army and the Moslems and fortifying his ambitions for the nation with an organized base of support. Nor was it a one way benefit. Sukarno's identification with the PKI assuredly

---

[12] Cf. Aidit's remarks on the appropriate qualities for members of the National Planning Council in his "Report to the Seventh Plenum of the PKI Central Committee," *Review of Indonesia*, V (Dec. 1958, Supplement), 11–12.

gave heart to the party's members and supporters and strengthened their belief in the rightness of their cause and the wisdom of their leaders.

The ideological affinities between Sukarno and the PKI might never have proved of great significance if the course of events between 1956 and 1959 had not generated political need by each for the backing of the other. Close ideological affinities, after all, can add bitterness to the differences of political rivals with divergent interests. On the other hand, however, political cooperation is obviously facilitated if, in addition to a strong common bond of interest, there exists also a disposition to view large areas of politics in substantially similar terms. The mutual interdependence of the president and the PKI inclined both to emphasize and develop those aspects of their larger views that they shared, particularly since these shared ideas had to be maintained against opponents who threatened each of them to differing degrees. Consequently, by the closing stages of Guided Democracy, there was little in the general ideological propositions of Sukarno and, say, Aidit that distinguished one from the other, although their political styles were poles apart. Theirs was truly a marriage of convenience in which the partners in the course of time came to acquire strong characteristics in common.

It was very much in the PKI's interest to maximize the president's role as against that of other non-Communist forces, both because he was the most favorably disposed toward the party and because his concept of the nation's goals best accorded with its own. Accordingly, Aidit had insisted in December 1958 that the president's pre-eminent place in the political system was vital to the party's acceptance of it, and thereafter the PKI went out of its way to emphasize the uniqueness of his contribution to the revolution. An early example of this was the occasion of the party's opposition to new regulations on regional government promulgated in July 1959, which strengthened the powers of appointed regional heads at the expense of elected assemblies. Answering arguments that regional executives ought to be entrusted with the same "guiding" functions in their spheres as those exercised by Sukarno nationally, the party replied curtly, "there is only one Sukarno."[13]

The dependence of the PKI on the president was great. Through-

[13] Aidit, in an interview with *Berita Indonesia*. See *Review of Indonesia*, VI (June–July 1959), 9.

out the Guided Democracy period the party's leaders looked to him for protection from the army, and he seldom failed them. They also counted on him to secure their entry into the institutional network of the political system, and here too he seems to have done his best, although he was unable to obtain for them those seats in the inner cabinet that were their main stated objective. Beyond protection and integration into the political system, however, the president, by his frequent praise of the party and bestowal of favor upon it, made it acceptable as a genuinely national and revolutionary party to a large proportion of the population. The value of his support in aiding the growth of the party's organization and influence, or obtaining for it tolerance by authority, is impossible to measure but must have been very substantial.

In return, the PKI gave Sukarno unswerving devotion and support. In the early days of Guided Democracy there were clear differences between the party and the president, especially concerning the role of the political parties and parliament; but the PKI leaders never allowed these to grow into sources of acute friction. Later the party was at times critical of the president's stance in the Malaysia dispute, and objected to his statement early in 1965 that Indonesia was then entering the socialist stage of development. But these were minor flaws in the alliance between the two on major policy questions. The party vied with other political groups in showering praise and honors on the president, extolling his contribution to revolutionary thought, and hailing him as the country's savior. By 1963 the party's worship was becoming almost idolatrous. Despite the president's notorious disdain for, and ignorance of, economic affairs, it declared that the solution of economic difficulties could safely be left in his hands, with the people's backing.[14] In the same year, in his analysis of the Indonesian political system, Aidit virtually identified Sukarno with the "pro-people's aspect" of the state power.[15] In 1964 Aidit was exculpating the president from all past anti-Communist offensives: if Sukarno had held the reins of power in 1948, he declared, there would have been no "Madiun provocation."[16] A short time later he bestowed the

[14] Aidit, *Dekon dalam Udjian* (Dekon on Trial) (Djakarta, 1963), pp. 6–8.
[15] Aidit, *The Indonesian Revolution*, p. 42.
[16] *Revolusi, Angkatan Bersendjata dan Partai Komunis* (The Revolution, the Armed Forces and the Communist Party) (Djakarta, 1964), p. 15.

final accolade by describing the president as his first teacher in Marxism-Leninism.[17] At this stage, Aidit was emphasizing that the PKI's conception of a people's democratic government was not inconsistent with the continued acceptance of leadership by Sukarno.[18] Whatever its disagreements with government policies, and these were often deep and sharply enunciated, the PKI almost invariably excused Sukarno from blame and attributed responsibility to reactionary or corrupt ministers and officials, thereby strengthening the traditional disposition to believe that the "king" could do no wrong and that all the failings in the realm were attributable to evil or incompetent advisers.

Privately, leading circles within the PKI were not so uncritical of the president. A number of party officials were critical of his private life—his polygamy, sexual licence, luxurious and wasteful expenditure, and demand for servile *kraton*-style deference.[19] There was condescension toward him for his inability to come to grips with economic problems.[20] Above all there was a feeling that Sukarno's ideology, while potent in its mass appeal, was formless and demagogic in comparison with the "scientific" ideas of the party. Few except a small group of persistent critics in the party would have argued against the policy of alliance with the president, however, since the benefits that had accrued to the party were obvious. Below the top personnel of the organization, most of the members seem to have been ardent admirers of the Great Leader and to have derived a good deal of their confidence in the party from its standing in his eyes.[21]

President Sukarno occupied unchallenged pride of place in two areas of the political system: in the articulation of national symbols, and in the fashioning of the country's foreign policy. The latter sphere lies outside the scope of this chapter, but the state ideology, made up of the president's prescriptions and compulsorily imposed upon all participants in public life, illustrates the advantages and disadvantages

[17] *Harian Rakjat,* March 13, 1965.

[18] *Revolusi, Angkatan Bersendjata dan Partai Komunis,* p. 30.

[19] Gerwani members were particularly disapproving of his marriages and sexual behavior. (Interview with "B," an expatriate PKI member, July 1968.)

[20] Karel Supit, a member of the PKI Central Committee and head of its International Department, was most scathing on this subject in an interview with the writer in November 1964.

[21] This estimate is based on the writer's observations in Oct.–Nov. 1964, as confirmed by other and better qualified scholars who have studied the PKI.

accruing to the PKI from its interaction with the dominating force in the political system.

Symbolic activity in tune with Sukarno's slogans and precepts provided scope and opportunity for those political groups such as the PKI which sought to advance their interests through, rather than outside, the officially sanctioned political system. The parties and office-holding cliques secured their existence and place in the sun primarily by identifying with the state ideology. Other criteria for acceptability were of secondary importance, and many prominent figures were able to cover their manifest deficiencies and vices by the clamor of their declarations of loyalty.

Identification with common symbols enhanced solidarity among the elite-sanctioned groups but at the same time provided a vehicle for competition among them. Since each was endeavoring to advance its interests at the expense of the others, but was inhibited from giving free play to this drive by the compulsory obeisance exacted in favor of national unity and the Nasakom formula,[22] open competition was largely restricted to claims to represent the truest, most consistent, and most wholehearted commitment to the ideology of the state.

The PKI had a number of advantages when it came to ideological competition on these terms. It was a party of great proselytizing zeal and consequently paid indefatigable attention to ideological warfare; and in the long international experience of the Communist movement it possessed a redoubtable armory of formulations and doctrines with which to fight. Its organizational power was immeasurably superior to that of any other political party, so that when it came to public demonstrations of loyalty it could put on an unrivaled show of mass devotion. Finally, since the party's leaders continued to be excluded from the top circles of power and confined largely to the window-dressing apparatus, they were least subject to the temptations of corruption, to which in any case their discipline and the puritanical strain in Communism helped to make them resistant. Whereas the sudden acquisition of wealth by other competitors undercut their protestations of dedicated and disinterested service to the nation, the PKI leaders were able to present themselves as the unsullied cham-

---

[22] Nasakom, an acronym combining Nas (nationalist), A (*agama,* religion), and Kom (Communist), became the accepted term denoting PKI participation in government from 1961.

pions of self-sacrificing zeal. This combination of advantages meant that, so long as rivalries and antagonisms were fought out within the terms of official ideology, the PKI generally fared well and advanced its prospects.

At the same time, there were considerable drawbacks for the party in being bound by the prescriptions of an official ideology, no matter how much in tune this may have been with its own. Still very much an out group so far as elite status and official power positions were concerned, the dynamism of the PKI depended very much on its ability to distance itself from the failings of the regime and keep alive a sense of being an independent entity with a unique contribution to make to the resolution of the problems facing the nation. Should it come to be regarded as merely another link in the chain of Guided Democracy, then its sense of mission would decline and it would stand less chance of forcing its claims to be considered the indispensable agent of effective rule. In other words, the party required an identity of its own—an ideology, policy, and organization.

This was not easy to achieve in the ideological sphere, owing to the president's prior rights. However the difficulty was not as intractable as would appear at first sight. Commentaries on the state ideology were permitted, provided they did not derogate from its basic content; and in this way many groups, including the PKI, obtained some latitude in interpreting the Great Leader's bequests, a latitude that they used to inject their own distinctions into the credo. There were limits to the effectiveness of this technique, especially as care had to be taken not to offend the president's susceptibilities or to give political competitors the chance to brand interpretations as deviant. The PKI probably enjoyed greater freedom in this respect than most, because Sukarno was the ultimate arbiter in all things to do with ideology, and he became increasingly inclined to view politics in terms scarcely distinguishable from those of the PKI. By 1964–65, in fact, the PKI seems to have acted as a *creator* of the state ideology, as the president's ideological tendencies moved further to the left and he came to lean more upon the Communists for ideological ammunition against his enemies or those who resisted his innovations. In this later period it became difficult to trace the origin of ideas, so alike did the themes of the president and the PKI become.

The PKI's relation to the state ideology, and the problems that

beset it in endeavoring to combine general conformity with distinctiveness, are well brought out in its handling of the two central ideological
catechisms of the regime, the Pantja Sila and the Political Manifesto.

The philosophical foundations of the state were contained in the
Pantja Sila, the five-point summation of national values advanced by
Sukarno in 1945. The five points comprised Belief in One God, Nationalism, Humanity (or Internationalism), Democracy, and Social
Justice.[23] The Aidit leadership, as previously noted, accepted the
Pantja Sila in November 1954, "while suggesting improvements"
which were not specified but which without doubt referred to the first
principle. Then, in 1957, when the question of the ideological foundations of the state became crucial, creating deadlock in the Constituent Assembly, the PKI dropped its reservations in order to cement
its alliance with the opponents of an Islamic state against the Moslem
political groups. This obliged the party to accept "Belief in One God"
as part of its own ideology, and this delicate spot was quickly detected
and probed by the party's opponents under Guided Democracy.

The PKI leaders could claim to be tolerant toward religion; however, they could hardly abandon fidelity to dialectical materialism,
the philosophical basis on which Communism rests, and hence their
atheism was strictly speaking in contradiction to the requirements of
the state ideology. The object of the PKI's enemies was to expose its
"hypocrisy" on this point, and thus to brand it as disloyal and drive
a wedge between the president and the Communists, or at least make
it difficult for Sukarno to pursue his attempts to bring the PKI into
the government over the opposition of Moslem and Christian groups.
The army leadership used this line of argument in July 1960 to justify
restrictions on the party, including a ban on its activities in three
Outer Island provinces. Sukarno rejected the charge, however, stating
that the Communists supported Pantja Sila and were not against
religion.[24]

The issue assumed greater proportions in 1962, a year of improving PKI fortunes following a series of lean years between 1959 and
1961. In his report to the seventh congress in April 1962, Aidit re-

[23] This English rendering, though adopted in official Indonesian publications, does poor service to the traditional associations and complexities of the
Indonesian terms, but it will suffice for our present purposes.

[24] *Review of Indonesia,* VII (Sept.–Oct. 1960), 8.

ferred to rumors being spread about by reactionaries in an unnamed political party that the PKI was two-faced in its attitude to the Pantja Sila.[25] In meeting the attack, Aidit skillfully seized upon Sukarno's statement that Pantja Sila was an instrument of unity to deny that the PKI was being unfaithful to the Panja Sila philosophy; rather, those who sought to use the state ideology as a means of sowing disunity in the national forces were guilty of violating Pantja Sila's essence and spirit.[26] He thus evaded the ticklish question of religion and shifted the argument on to ground favorable to the PKI and popular with the president.

Despite Aidit's dexterity, however, the matter did not rest there; the religious issue remained unresolved, and leaders of the Nahdatul Ulama, the conservative Javanese-based Moslem party, began to show an inclination to use it against PKI claims for inclusion in the cabinet. So, in a speech in November 1962, Aidit returned to the subject. His manner of doing so, however, was not likely to propitiate his opponents. He began with a highly devious argument, the aim of which was to reconcile adherence to dialectical materialism with acceptance of Pantja Sila, but again without facing the religious question squarely:

Materialism is the world outlook that starts from objective facts. . . . It is undeniable that if viewed from the situation obtaining in Indonesia and the process of development of Indonesian history, the influence of religion is great in Indonesia, and it is an objective fact that, viewed from the angle of religion, the majority of those professing a religion in Indonesia adhere to the belief of there being One Divine Omnipotence or monotheism (believing in one God) and not polytheism (believing in more than one God).

Therefore, Aidit concluded, "belief in One God" is an objective fact in Indonesia, and Communists, as materialists, must accept this objective fact![27] He then moved to safer ground:

The Communists recognize that accepting the Pantja Sila, one of the silas of which is One Divine Omnipotence, includes the understanding of not being allowed to make anti-religious propaganda in Indonesia. This

[25] Aidit, *Problems,* p. 510.

[26] *Ibid.,* pp. 210–11.

[27] *Ibid.,* pp. 210–13. For a similar statement later the same year, see *Harian Rakjat,* Nov. 22, 1963.

we do accept because we Communists have indeed no interest in carrying out such propaganda. But on the other hand, the Communists do also demand that because of the other silas, religion may not be imposed on people, since this is not in line with humanitarian feelings, not in harmony with democracy and justice.[28]

This was as far as the PKI went in trying to surmount the difficulty about religious belief. Thereafter it concentrated on the more favorable issue of unity, using the argument that those who attacked the party on the Pantja Sila issue (or any other issue for that matter) were violating Nasakom, and it was impossible to accept Pantja Sila without accepting Nasakom and vice versa.[29] But on two occasions the party came under fire for allegedly distorting Pantja Sila or decrying its significance. The first was in mid-1961, when the party daily published a version of the Pantja Sila omitting "Belief in One God"; in all probability this was an oversight (or at most a Freudian slip), but naturally enough it was hailed as evidence of the PKI's disparagement of religion.[30] The other occasion followed a speech by Aidit in 1964 in which he was accused of saying that once Indonesian socialism was achieved, Pantja Sila would no longer be needed as a unifying philosophy. This was a different pattern of attack, since it was designed to arouse the suspicions of the president and of those nationalists who feared the Communist alliance because it might lead to their own destruction. Aidit vehemently denied the charge, and a full-blown polemic ensued between *Harian Rakjat* on the one hand and a number of newspapers that shortly afterwards supported the anti-Communist Body for Promoting Sukarnoism on the other. Eventually the government had to step in and put an end to the debate, but not before the PKI had counterattacked by linking the furore with alleged imperialist plans for a coup against Sukarno.[31]

[28] *Problems*, pp. 212–13.

[29] See Aidit, *Revolusi, Angkatan Bersendjata dan Partai Komunis*, p. 13.

[30] J. M. Van der Kroef, *The Communist Party of Indonesia* (Vancouver, 1965), p. 162.

[31] The PKI published an account of the polemic, under the title *Aidit Membela Pantjasila* (Aidit Defends Pantjasila) (Djakarta, 1964). For an account of the heated exchanges of this period and their background, see Guy J. Pauker, "Indonesia in 1964: Towards a 'People's Democracy,'" *Asian Survey*, V, no. 2 (Feb. 1965), 88–97, and J. M. Van der Kroef, "Indonesian Communism's 'Revolutionary Gymnastics,'" *Asian Survey*, V, no. 5 (May 1965), 217–32.

It is hard to estimate the effect of the Pantja Sila controversies upon the PKI's acceptability. In all probability the party lost no ground over this question, particularly since the president repeatedly came to its rescue by reiterating that those who used Pantja Sila as a divisive weapon were distorting its function. Most of the political elite, while not averse to seeing the PKI embarrassed on the religious issue, had no interest in Moslem efforts to impose strict conformity in this sphere. Among the devout Moslem community, however, where the atheistic beliefs of the PKI were a real affront as well as a useful weapon, accounts of the controversy were probably retailed to intensify anti-Communist passions, particularly in 1964 when the land reform question became a focus of antagonism between the Communists and Moslem rural interests.[32]

Sukarno's Independence Day speech of August 17, 1959, was elevated by Indonesia's Supreme Advisory Council into the Political Manifesto of the Republic, commonly referred to as Manipol or Manipol-Usdek and subsequently schematized into a series of propositions on the nature, tasks, social supports, enemies, etc., of the Indonesian revolution.[33] This document presented no difficulties for the PKI to match those associated with the Pantja Sila. In the first place it was a thoroughly secular document devoted to political, economic, social, and cultural issues; and in the second place Aidit himself had participated in the formulation of its schematic version—and judging by the contents had not been without influence in the drafting committee. Rather, the PKI's problem here was a different one: how to identify with Manipol and at the same time maintain the independence and standing of the party's own program.

The Political Manifesto in its schematic form offered a justification of the steps taken to establish Guided Democracy and an elaboration of Sukarno's ideological themes of that time. On the political plane, its most important features were: a statement that the objective of the nation was the attainment of Indonesian socialism, which was to be

[32] PKI publications in the second half of 1964 and in 1965 repeatedly referred to the distribution of "illegal" leaflets "slandering" the party on the religious issue. See Chapter 9 below for more coverage of this issue.

[33] Usdek represents an acronym for the five central ideas contained in the Manifesto: the 1945 Constitution, Indonesian Socialism, Guided Democracy, Guided Economy, and Indonesian Identity.

achieved in two revolutionary stages, the national democratic stage followed by the socialist stage, with the target of the first stage being defined as the elimination of imperialist and feudal influences; an outline of the alliances to be followed to achieve these aims, namely a national front of all anti-imperialist and antifeudal forces; a description of the workers and peasants as the pillars (*soko guru*) of the revolution; and an elaboration of the means to be adopted in achieving national goals, chief among them retooling the apparatus of the state and simplifying the party system.

The substantial areas of common ground shared by Manipol and the PKI program need not be labored. The PKI immediately hailed Manipol as a document of basic importance, and on the first anniversary of the speech of Sukarno's that inspired it Aidit declared that it "delineated a new road for the completion of the demands of the August 1945 revolution, a revolutionary road for the achievement of a society free from imperialism and feudalism, an Indonesian society which is national and democratic, the unconditional way to a socialist Indonesia."[34]

The Political Manifesto was to prove very useful as a weapon of ideological struggle for the PKI. In the first place, the ideals it expressed could be used as sticks to beat the government, individual ministers, and the bureaucracy for their acts of commission and omission. In this way Manipol not only kept open an avenue for legitimate PKI criticisms of the power-holders but also enabled the party to represent itself as the only force thoroughly and consistently behind Manipol, and consequently the force that ought to be entrusted with greater responsibility for its implementation. Secondly, indoctrination of officials and others in the themes of Manipol helped to incline more people toward a revolutionary socialist outlook; further, the close similarity between Manipol and the party's program was calculated to orient those who responded to the indoctrination more benevolently toward the party. Although there is no evidence to support the hypothesis, it seems likely that Manipol indoctrination aided PKI recruiting efforts, particularly among lower government employees who were most affected by the political courses, because it combated anti-

[34] "Untuk Pelaksanaan Jang Lebih Konsekwen dari Manifesto Politik" (For the More Consistent Implementation of the Political Manifesto), *Bintang Merah*, XVI (July–Aug. 1960), 302.

Communism and helped to establish an image of the PKI as "Bung Karno's party."

On the other hand, the very closeness of the two programs was a source of uneasiness for the party leaders, particularly when they had overcome the disabilities they suffered in the early years of Guided Democracy and were aiming to force their way more decisively into positions of political power. If Manipol and the PKI program were virtually identical, how was the party to justify clinging to and seeking support for its own particular platform? The PKI could argue, as it did, that it would be a better practitioner of Manipol than the current government, but the distinct identity and sense of mission the party required to maintain its pressure for recognition as the nation's savior demanded in addition a program that marked it off from its rivals in the establishment. Communists, party doctrine taught, were people of a special mould with the only genuine and scientific ideology of social revolution; to accept that others were operating with exactly the same concept would blur distinctions between Communists and non-Communists vital in maintaining the party's surge toward national leadership.

Aidit seems first to have become aware of this dilemma whilst in China in September 1963; possibly his Chinese hosts had queried a situation in which a Communist party accepted the ideology of a "bourgeois state" as its own. At any rate, whereas in April 1963 Aidit had told a school of air force officers that "the implementation of Manipol is the same as the implementation of the PKI program itself,"[35] in a lecture at the Higher Party School of the Central Committee of the CPC in Peking on September 2 he entered a caveat. Although the two programs had many "close links," he said, and Manipol had been "tempered in the crucible of the Indonesian people's struggle against imperialism and feudalism," which, "under the leadership of the PKI has clarified the contents of the Political Manifesto and ensures its scientific interpretation and resolute implementation," still there were certain differences between the two documents:

The Program of the CPI clearly points out that to achieve the aims of the Indonesian revolution the leadership must be in the hands of the working class. It is impossible to expect that the question of working-

[35] *PKI dan AURI* (The PKI and the Air Force) (Djakarta, 1963), p. 15.

class leadership should be included in the Political Manifesto. The Political Manifesto only points out that the workers and peasants are the pillars of the revolution and its says nothing about which class shoulders the historic task of leading the revolution.

Nevertheless, he reiterated, "the resolute implementation of the Political Manifesto is tantamount to implementing the Programme of the CPI."[36]

There were two assurances contained in this explanation: first, that the PKI was exercising decisive influence on the interpretation and implementation of the Political Manifesto; and secondly, that the party had not abandoned its struggle for hegemony of the Indonesian revolution. Both, in point of fact, were exaggerations. The PKI may have had much to say on the schematization of Manipol and have been the most vociferous and effective manipulator of Manipol as a symbol, but it was far from having a decisive influence on the way it was applied, as its constant criticism of the government on this point demonstrated. Again, while it had not forsaken the hope of establishing working class (i.e., party) hegemony of the national front, it had, as will be discussed below in more detail, markedly subordinated the question in its ideological propaganda out of consideration for the requirements of its political alliances.

This point was to be heavily underlined little more than six months later, when Aidit effectively destroyed the point of the argument he had put in Peking. Addressing another school of military officers on March 17, 1964, he referred to "people who make the accusation that the PKI cannot recognize one national leadership if it proposes the leadership of the working class." This was not so, he replied:

The PKI certainly stands for the leadership of the working class, that is, *the leadership of working class ideology,* the revolutionary ideology opposing exploitation of man by man. On the other hand, what is meant by one national leadership is a leadership animated by Manipol. Because implementing Manipol thoroughly is the same thing as implementing the PKI program, then *the proposal of working class leadership does not conflict with the PKI accepting the necessity of one national leadership and the Manipolist leadership of Bung Karno.*[37]

[36] *The Indonesian Revolution,* pp. 34–37. See also *Harian Rakjat,* Feb. 25, 1964.

[37] *Revolusi, Angkatan Bersendjata dan Partai Komunis,* p. 30 (emphases added).

Thus, what had formerly been represented as a crucial difference turned out to be no difference at all. If the only distinction between Manipol and the PKI program was the question of working class leadership, and if "working class" referred not to class origin or occupation but to *ideology*, then it follows that supporters of Manipol ideology could implement the PKI program. In formal terms, at least, Aidit had surrendered the PKI's claims to be the only repository of working class ideology.

Once again, Aidit's ventures into the ticklish field of the relationship between state and party ideology had failed to resolve the crucial point at issue. The fact was, of course, that no resolution was possible—belief in God could not be reconciled with atheism, and PKI hegemony could not be reconciled with the continued acceptance of Sukarno's leadership. On each occasion, Aidit was forced into the field by pressures from outside, which may or may not have been accompanied by pressures from within the party. In neither case could he frankly outline the PKI's distinctive attitude without risking its alliances and inviting ostracism; and in both cases he chose to give up specifically PKI positions. The party had to rely for the maintenance of its momentum not on the distinctive appeal of its concepts but on more dynamic activity around the ideas that (nominally at least) it had in common with the political elites in power. It was not a stance to prepare the party for an independent bid for power; the PKI appeared rather to be bidding for acceptance by the elite, or a significant section of it.

The president was the inventor of several novel organs in the Guided Democracy structure, and it was in these that the PKI was accorded the closest resemblance to a *gotong rojong* role. However, with one exception, the new institutions to which the party was admitted on something like equal terms with other political groupings were nothing more than advisory or consultative bodies, their ceremonial trappings notwithstanding. They were of importance to the party in elevating its status and giving it an opportunity to impress upon the elite its constructiveness and expertise, but they did not enable it to participate in executive decisions or exercise executive powers.

Nevertheless, the party welcomed the establishment and constitution of the new bodies, both for the advance they represented and also, no doubt, in the hope and expectation that they would prove precursors of more substantial gains. Thus, following the establishment on July 30, 1959, of the Supreme Advisory Council (successor to the National Council set up in 1957 to give advice on state affairs) and the National Planning Council (charged with drawing up a national construction plan), on both of which the PKI was represented, the party newspaper greeted them as "arousing new hopes among the people" that Sukarno's *konsepsi* would be fully implemented.[38] In the event, neither body came to have more than secondary significance, and they rapidly faded into the background of PKI concerns. A similar attitude was taken toward the People's Consultative Assembly (MPRS)—an appointed "superparliament" charged with electing the president and deciding the "broad lines of national policy" but required to meet only once every five years—which Mackie has aptly described as no more than "a quasi-plebiscitary sounding-board."[39]

Of greater importance was the National Front, formally inaugurated at the first meeting of the Supreme Advisory Council in August 1959. This body was seemingly intended by Sukarno to become the main instrument for mass mobilization, superseding the army-sponsored National Front for the Liberation of West Irian. It got off to a rather inauspicious start, partly owing to its undistinguished leadership and the suspicions of the political parties that its purpose was eventually to swallow them up. The PKI expressed these misgivings in February 1960, when it stressed that the National Front would only be effective if it functioned democratically,[40] and again in May, when Aidit, giving a lecture on the fortieth anniversary of the foundation of the party, stated:

The National Front is not a political party. It is not a class organisation. It is a cooperation body of various classes, various groups and various revolutionary and democratic political trends. . . . The idea of "putting an end to the parties and groups" by means of the National Front is a deviation from the real purpose of the National Front and, because of this, if an attempt is made to force this through, it will definitely meet with the opposition of the people.

Aidit blamed efforts to transform the National Front into a state

[38] *Harian Rakjat,* July 31, 1959.
[39] J. A. C. Mackie, "Indonesian Politics under Guided Democracy," *Australian Outlook,* XV, no. 3 (Dec. 1961), 265.
[40] *Review of Indonesia,* VII (Feb. 1960), 17.

party on "fascists and adventurers," by whom he presumably meant both army officers and the Murba group.[41]

By August 1960 it was clear that Sukarno had abandoned the idea of forming a single state party, and the fears of the PKI and other political parties were allayed. When the names of the sixty-one members of the Central Board of the National Front were announced on August 15, the PKI was reasonably represented, directly by Aidit and Njoto, and indirectly by Asmu (BTI), Munir (SOBSI), and Sukatno (Pemuda Rakjat). The aims of the Front were declared to be "the gathering together of all revolutionary forces to guide them in completing the national revolution" and "organizing the closest cooperation between the Government, the people and other state bodies." The Front had a pyramidal organization reaching down from the center to the suburbs and villages, with steering committees at all governmental levels.[42] The question of whether the Front should have individual membership only (thus opening the way to replacing the parties) or should also incorporate whole groups was argued for a long time. Eventually fears that it might turn into a monster and devour the parties were laid to rest when, in January 1962, political organizations as well as individuals were allowed to join the Front; the PKI promptly signed up.[43]

The mass organization of the National Front was slow to expand initially, partly because the right obstructed the formation of committees in the provinces but possibly also because the PKI had not thrown its full weight behind the body.[44] The heightening of the West Irian campaign gave it a shot in the arm, however, and from 1962 it began to develop considerable strength, channeling mass demands and arranging demonstrations to back up government policies. The PKI supplied most of the popular constituency of the Front, and the party came to exercise strong influence in the leadership councils (though not in its permanent executive). In March 1964 the standing of the National Front was raised further when the committee chairman at each governmental level was added to the body of key functionaries

[41] *Ibid.*, VII (June 1960, Supplement), 14.

[42] *Ibid.*, VII (Sept.–Oct. 1960), 12.

[43] *Serba-serbi Dokumen Partai 1962* (A Collection of Party Documents 1962) (Djakarta, 1964).

[44] Mackie, p. 275.

in each province, regency, and municipality known as the *Tjatur Tunggal,* or quadrumvirate of governor (or regency head or mayor), army commander, police chief, and public prosecutor.[45] Many of these committee chairmen were PKI members or nominees, and the results of the reorganization of local executive powers gave the party a voice inside a key unit of regional government.

THE PARTY AND THE ARMED FORCES

If President Sukarno was the PKI's guardian and protector in the Guided Democracy period, the army was its scourge. The army's sense of having a vital role to play in politics and society, fostered during and after the revolution when it was almost continually engaged in campaigns to defend the Republic's integrity against armed dissidents of various kinds, inclined it strongly against all political parties; indeed, in its view, it was the parties' incompetence, corruption, divisive self-seeking, and meddlesomeness toward the armed forces that was responsible for much of the strife afflicting the country. But a special animus was directed toward the PKI, especially on the part of the officer corps. The party stood condemned in the eyes of most officers for the blow it had dealt the embattled Republic at Madiun in September 1948, an act which, moreover, it had been able to perpetrate through its penetration of a substantial section of the army. To these officers, the PKI remained treacherous, an antinational party committed to international goals and controlled by a foreign power. To a minority of the higher officers, including the defence minister, General A. H. Nasution, the PKI was additionally an atheistic party abhorrent to their religious convictions. The party was seen as a threat, too, in that it possessed the very qualities of organization and dedicated discipline that constituted the army's claim to superiority over most civilian groups—both parties and bureaucratic segments—and that the officers had used to build up those vested social and political interests they had no desire to relinquish to the PKI. The officers understood very well that the PKI's intense commitment to its own goals would lead it to do its utmost to win over people inside the services and thus undermine their cohesiveness and potential as a political instrument.

[45] Herbert Feith, "President Sukarno, the Army, and the Communists: The Triangle Changes Shape," *Asian Survey,* IV, no. 8 (Aug. 1964), 969–80.

Unlike the president, most army leaders were reluctant to accept that the PKI could be incorporated into the political system and induced to conform to common national objectives. They shared Sukarno's passion for national unity, his emphasis on social discipline, and his patriotic slogans, but only a minority had his revolutionary romanticism or his confidence in Indonesia's ability to merge different ideological streams into a single national effort. At least one of the officers' motives in agitating for the overthrow of the parliamentary system was to block any further progress by the PKI. About this they made little secret, and a crucial feature of Guided Democracy politics was the struggle between the president and the army over the Communist issue.[46]

The army was a difficult entity for the PKI to treat in its political schema. Quite apart from the inhibitions and circumlocutions forced upon the party by the army's power, the military organization did not lend itself to any neat characterization within the class or united national front categories generally employed by the Communists. In terms of Leninist analysis, the armed forces were an instrument of the state and so their leaders were assimilated to the class in power. But this concept, while it may have been adequate in systems where service chiefs were not accustomed to playing a distinctive political role, fell a long way short of the requirements of Communist analysis in Indonesia. The Indonesian army leadership not only took up political positions independent of the government, but so far as the PKI was concerned these positions were overwhelmingly reactionary. On the other hand, however, the army had unassailable revolutionary origins and credentials, and the loyalty of most of the officers to the ideals of a united and independent Republic had been demonstrated over many years. The officers could not, therefore, be lumped in with

[46] For interpretations of the major political trends in the army high command, see Feith, *Decline*, especially pp. 394–405; George McT. Kahin, "Indonesia," in Kahin, ed., *Major Governments of Asia*, 2d ed. (Ithaca, N.Y., 1963), pp. 640–43; Guy J. Pauker, "The Role of the Military in Indonesia," in J. J. Johnson, ed., *The Role of the Military in Underdeveloped Countries* (Princeton, 1964), pp. 185ff.; Daniel S. Lev, *The Transition to Guided Democracy: Indonesian Politics, 1957–1959* (Monograph Series, Modern Indonesia Project, Cornell University, 1966), especially pp. 59–74, 182–201; Lev, "The Political Role of the Army in Indonesia," *Pacific Affairs*, XXXVI, no. 4 (Winter 1963–64), 349–64; Feith, "Dynamics of Guided Democracy," in Ruth T. McVey, ed., *Indonesia* (New Haven, Conn., 1963), pp. 327–50.

the Masjumi and PSI as "compradore" and therefore "alien" forces. The national character of the army leaders had to be conceded, but when, after 1957, officers became heavily involved in economic administration (including the management of state enterprises) the PKI developed a new term to indicate their antipopular character, dubbing them "bureaucratic capitalists."

The army rank-and-file, in contrast to its officers, was treated as belonging to the people, being frequently described in PKI literature as "peasants in uniform." Their conditions of life and status amply justified this attribution; more importantly, the PKI regarded the common soldier as susceptible to its appeals and therefore the Achilles heel by which the anti-Communism of the officers could be countered. The party claimed to have received no less than thirty per cent of the votes of members of the armed forces in the 1955 elections for parliament and the Constituent Assembly, a much higher proportion than in the country at large.[47] Although this vote could be assumed to have come overwhelmingly from the ranks, it held out hopes for the party of extending its influence vertically as well as horizontally. This was another reason for treading carefully in categorizing the army. Any overt appeal to the lower ranks against their officers would bring certain retribution against the party; it might also lead to a witch hunt against Communist agents and sympathizers inside the force. The best tactic for the Communists, and the one they came to use more often in the course of time, was to direct their propaganda against those generals who either opposed the president or were exposing themselves to criticism by their luxurious way of life.

In the early years of Guided Democracy the PKI was forced very much on to the defensive in relation to the army, carefully angling its attacks so as to make the most of differences between the army generals on the one side and the president, the political parties, civil authorities, and the other armed services on the other. Only in 1963, when political conditions gave the party greater freedom and greater prospects of making inroads into the officers' domain, did it attempt a more rounded analysis of the role of the armed forces in the "Indonesian revolution."

The introduction of martial law in March 1957 provided the

[47] D. N. Aidit, *Pilihan Tulisan* (Selected Works) (Djakarta, 1959–60), II, 127.

army with a political and economic charter that it was quick to employ on an extensive scale to restrict the parties, impose its conception of social discipline, and establish its right to a prominent and guaranteed place in the political system. The martial law powers remained in force until May 1, 1963, although some modifications made during the intervening years lessened the ambit of army authority to some extent. During the whole of this period the PKI, with intermittent support from other parties, waged a constant campaign to have the army's powers drastically scaled down or withdrawn.

During the greater part of 1959, attention was focussed mainly on army claims to representation in the political organs of Guided Democracy. By early 1960 this matter had been disposed of, but by this time martial law authorities had earned a good deal of unpopularity by the heavy-handed and in some cases corrupt manner in which their powers were exercised. The PKI felt encouraged to take the attack. The party's traditional New Year message argued that the arbitrary powers in the hands of army men were leading to demoralization. The statement contended with some force that the maintenance of a full state of emergency throughout the whole country was unjustified, considering the wide disparity of security conditions in different regions, and called for its repeal in East and Central Java, where security conditions were good, and a graduation of emergency powers in other regions in accordance with the actual threat to national safety posed by rebel groups.[48]

This statement followed the parliamentary budget debate of the previous month, in the course of which Politburo member Sudisman had delivered the most trenchant and wide-ranging criticism of the army leadership that the PKI was ever to make, and in which he called for drastic modifications of the state of emergency. Sudisman not only attacked the size of the army's budget, and its uses, but singled out Defense Minister General Nasution for special attention. Quoting extensively from Nasution's writings "when he was non-active" (a reference to his removal from the post of Armed Forces Chief of Staff in October 1952), in which he had warned against the army becoming too deeply involved in matters outside its own field, Sudisman commented: "How fine it would be if the things he said while non-active were borne in mind today when Lieut. General

---

[48] *Review of Indonesia,* VII (Jan. 1960), 4.

Nasution is not only back in service but is also a member of the Inner Cabinet."[49]

In the prevailing conditions, with party activities closely circumscribed by the army authorities and its press repeatedly suspended under the martial law regulations, this outburst was courageous, if not rash. It signaled a new militancy in the PKI's approach, militancy that was not reduced when, later in January, the government eased the stringency of martial law regulations. Commenting on the change in these regulations, Lukman grudgingly conceded that it was an advance, but it still fell "far short of what the people demand" and could be considered no more than "an incentive to the people to continue with their struggle for the complete implementation of what they demand."[50]

In May, Njono, secretary-general of SOBSI, entered the lists against "military regulations and measures which restrict the right to assemble, to hold meetings and to express opinions either in oral or in written form, the freedom of the press and other democratic liberties." Njono gave the issue a theoretical cast by raising and answering the rhetorical question of whether army-worker conflicts still represented "a contradiction among the people."[51] The answer was in the affirmative:

The SOBSI maintains its viewpoint that the Armed Forces of the Republic is [sic] still the true son of the Popular Revolution of 1945, and that therefore the majority of its members, from officers down to NCO's and soldiers, cannot be dragged into actions which are treacherous to the Republic. Besides, President Sukarno, who identifies himself with the people, possesses a strong influence over the members of the armed forces, and he refuses to be a military dictator.

The implications were clear: the PKI was not aiming at an all-out confrontation with the army but was relying on "progressives" in the armed forces, and the influence of the president, to keep it in check. At the same time the party had to maintain its own momentum if it

[49] *Ibid.,* VII (Feb. 1960), 12–15.

[50] *Ibid.,* 9.

[51] The PKI had adopted Mao's concept distinguishing between "nonantagonistic" and "antagonistic" contradictions, the former being "contradictions among the people" and therefore soluble by peaceful means (Mao Tse-tung, *On the Correct Handling of Contradictions among the People* [Peking, 1957]).

was to attract the support and protection of these forces. Another problem, according to Njono, was whether mass actions would sharpen the contradictions between the workers and the army. The answer was no, according to him, as long as the actions

remain natural, with just, reasonable and know-the-limit demands, and are conducted under capable leadership. The daily experiences of the workers teach us that each natural action is not only strongly supported by the working masses and gains the broadest public sympathy, but it will also serve as a means to check the Government from taking further measures detrimental to the workers and the people; measures which, if not checked in time, may sharpen all the more existing contradictions.[52]

In July the army seized on the publication by the party of a statement containing a wide-ranging attack on government policies to ban the distribution of the statement and summon PKI leaders for long interrogations by the Djakarta war administrator. Somewhat surprisingly, the action was not pushed further in the capital, but in three provinces regional commanders took the opportunity to outlaw all activities by the PKI and its front organizations. The PKI protested vehemently, and President Sukarno was obliged to step in and relieve the crisis. At a top-level conference at the palace, the president defended the patriotic outlook of the PKI and chided the regional commanders in "the three Souths" (South Sumatra, South Sulawesi, and South Kalimantan) for their unilateral action; to avoid a humiliating retreat for the army, he ordered a temporary ban on *all* political parties, but the PKI was put on "good behavior" probation until April 1961[53] and its publications, with the exception of *Harian Rakjat,* were suspended for three years. The regional bans remained in force, and the PKI suffered severe restrictions in these provinces for up to two years.

The July 8 Affair, as it was known, had ended indecisively for the PKI. As was often his way, Sukarno moderated the collision between the two parties, demonstrated his authority over both, and left the power balance relatively undisturbed. The party could take no great heart from the outcome, and for the next eighteen months its criti-

---

[52] SOBSI May Day reception speech, May 2, 1960, as reported in *Review of Indonesia,* VII (June 1960), 28–29.

[53] For a lengthier discussion of the July 8 Affair, and its aftermath, see Van der Kroef, *The Communist Party of Indonesia,* pp. 229–40.

cisms of the army were cautious and muted, in keeping with the general retreat from militancy that it felt obliged to undertake at this time. The final indication of its feelings toward the army leaders was given in the last issue of its English-language monthly, in a poem allegedly written at the time of the party's sixth congress in 1959:

Generals, it's we that adorned
Your chests with medals
Wrested from landlords' and usurers' torturous hands,
We now demand of your medals, where's our land?

Generals, it's we that adorned
Your chests with medals
Out of the sweat of a seven-hour that became a ten-hour day,
We now demand of your medals—where's our pay?

Generals, one after another we fell
Arms in hand against the Dutch.
We now demand of your medals—where's our Irian?

Generals, certainly it's not you
Who will give land, wages and Irian.
What we want is: let us build one mighty corps
And above all, give us freedom to speak.[54]

With the surrender of the major remaining groups of regional rebels in 1961, the PKI felt that the time had come to press the issue of martial law powers once again. In his report to the party's seventh congress in April 1962, Aidit declared that the conditions making the state of emergency necessary had passed and that,

If in one or several regions the State of Emergency is utilized to paralyse the implementation of Guided Democracy and Gotong Rojong, to foster one-man dictatorship and bureaucrat capitalism, to persecute the progressives and outlaw the activities of the CPI and the revolutionary mass organisations, this is completely out of keeping with the purpose for which the State of Emergency was declared. To borrow the words of President Sukarno: this is solely because the "gun" wants to lead the Manipol, and not the Manipol lead the "gun."[55]

[54] *Review of Indonesia,* VII (Aug. 1960), 46. The poem, which was introduced as one that "very well conveys the feelings of the Indonesian people on the present situation of democracy," was written by Agam Wispy.

[55] Aidit, *Problems,* p. 461.

These and similar protests brought no immediate result, but in November 1962, with the West Irian campaign victoriously concluded, the president announced that martial law powers would expire on the following May 1. In the following months the PKI concentrated on propaganda against the danger that military powers would be restored by other means.[56]

After all-out confrontation against Malaysia began in September 1963, the party warned against the use of this crisis to reinvoke martial law powers,[57] and implied that the generals were seeking to extend hostilities in order to provoke a situation that would facilitate "Bonapartist" solutions to domestic problems. A security regulation was in fact introduced in September 1964, when fears existed that British forces might strike at Indonesian bases in retaliation for attacks against Malaysia, but the PKI expressed itself satisfied with safeguards requiring army authorities to consult with civilian officials before invoking their powers.[58] In fact the new regulation seems to have been used sparingly and never became a political issue. Sukarno was more than ever unsympathetic to army harrying of the Communists, and the focus of army concerns had in any case shifted to post-succession politics.

In the 1957–63 period, army leaders recognized that martial law powers could be revoked at any time and so were casting about for alternative ways to maintain a decisive role in political life. One idea to which they gave special attention was that of "functional groups," bodies notionally representative of major occupational, ethnic, and religious strata which under Sukarno's *konsepsi* were to be given direct political representation. Consequently, when the outlines of the Guided Democracy system were being drawn in 1959 they claimed for the armed forces recognition as a functional group entitled, along with other functional groups, to representation in the parliament and other state bodies. After considerable negotiation and dispute it was decided that the armed forces as a whole should have thirty-six appointed seats in parliament, with the preponderant share going to the army.

Having conducted a rearguard campaign against this proposal by

---

[56] See, for example, Aidit's report to the PKI Central Committee of Feb. 10, 1963: *Dare, Dare and Dare Again!* (Peking, 1963), pp. 7–8.

[57] *Harian Rakjat*, Nov. 8, 1963.

[58] Text in *Harian Rakjat*, Sept. 17, 1964.

army leaders, the PKI recognized the inevitable but argued, vainly, that these representatives should be elected by members of the armed forces in the same way that other functional group delegates were to be elected by the population at large. The point turned out to be an academic one, however, since no elections of any kind were ever held under Guided Democracy. Nevertheless, the PKI's argument that members of the armed forces were being denied their democratic rights may have found some support among the lower ranks.[59] The party may also have reckoned that the introduction of political campaigning into the armed forces would help to break down the internal solidarity of the corps, a factor no doubt equally operative in the generals' successful resistance to its proposal. In any case, the PKI could take some comfort in the fact that the army's representation in parliament remained far less than army leaders had aspired to, with their early hopes of functional representation under army control completely replacing party representation.

The first Sukarno cabinet, formed in July 1959, was a disappointment for the PKI since the party did not obtain the representation promised under Sukarno's *gotong rojong* concept. The case was otherwise with the armed forces: of thirty-seven ministers in the cabinet, twelve were officers or ex-officers, counting the chiefs of staff of the army, navy, air force, and police, who were made ex-officio members. Although the presence of the armed forces in the cabinet was to remain a feature of governmental composition, never again were the services to enjoy such substantial representation.

In his report to the eighth plenum of the Central Committee in August 1959, Aidit avoided a direct attack on the presence of so many military men in the cabinet but made the party's viewpoint plain in challenging the officers to prove themselves in the public eye. Their newly won posts, he said, "can be either positive or negative, depending on what these military men do in their ministerial posts." The people had had no previous experience of a cabinet with military men in it, he went on, and so it was natural that they should have expressed doubts and queries. Now the ministers from the armed services had the opportunity to demonstrate their goodwill "by putting the welfare of the people before their own interests . . . by holding high the basic democratic rights of the people . . . [and] . . .

[59] *Review of Indonesia,* VI (June–July 1959), 4.

by consulting with the people's representatives."[60] In speaking thus, Aidit again gave the impression that he anticipated that the armed forces ministers would prove unequal to the task he set them, thereby undermining the attractiveness of the military as an alternative to civilian rule and enhancing the PKI's claims to be the only political force in the country unsullied by the corruptions of power.

Coincident with its drive to gain purchase on the state institutions, the army had undertaken strenuous efforts to pre-empt the political parties at the grassroots level by enrolling mass organizations of youth, women, veterans, etc., into its "fronts" and cooperation bodies. But in the face of opposition from the political parties and the president the army proved incapable of establishing these fronts as vigorous entities under its own leadership. Only among the veterans were its efforts successful. By mid-1959 the PKI had already declared that its subsidiaries were unwilling to have anything more to do with the army-controlled fronts, but the battle dragged on. President Sukarno gave grist to the party's mill in his Independence Day address in 1959 by criticizing the army's most ambitious body, the National Front for the Liberation of West Irian, for its failure to advance its stated aim effectively. (By this time, the president had begun to inaugurate his own National Front.) Thus encouraged, the PKI, through the person of Sudisman, used the occasion of the budget debate in parliament to turn the screw on the army by questioning the allocation of funds for the National Front for the Liberation of West Irian: "We have a National Front for the Liberation of West Irian," he said. "We have a West Irian Bureau. The only thing we don't yet have is a struggle for the liberation of West Irian!"[61] Two months later the army received a further setback when an all-Indonesian youth congress rejected its plans for a merger of youth organizations into a single youth front and voted instead for a federation. Army-sponsored delegates thereupon walked out of the congress, putting an end to what the PKI termed "efforts to militarize the youth."[62]

[60] *Bintang Merah,* XV (July–Aug. 1959), 295–96.

[61] *Review of Indonesia,* VII (Feb. 1960), 13.

[62] The congress is reported in *Review of Indonesia,* VII (March 1960), 34–35. The comment is cited from Pemuda Rakjat leader Sukatno's speech to the seventh congress of the PKI in April 1962; see *Madju Terus! Dokumen-dokumen Kongres National ke-VII (Luarbiasa) PKI* (Ever Forward! Docu-

The only other notable army foray into mass organization was its sponsorship of SOKSI, a corporative union established late in 1961 on the initative of army and ex-army managers of state enterprises; centered on the nationalized firms, SOKSI aspired to break SOBSI's domination in the trade union field. For a year or more the new organization fared well, making heavy inroads into SOBSI's following in the state enterprises, partially owing to its ability to channel government subsidies to workers. By the latter part of 1963, however, it had lost steam and began to fall apart. The PKI, needless to say, had campaigned vigorously against the federation and had received a fair degree of support from other labor bodies in its undermining efforts.[63]

The army also played a part in protecting and encouraging parties and groups that were hostile to the president as well as to the PKI. Members of the Masjumi and the PSI received "a degree of sympathy and protection from the military," even after these parties were banned by Sukarno in August 1960.[64] The Democratic League, formed in March 1960 to protest Sukarno's dissolution of the elected parliament and fight Communist influence, also enjoyed the active support of some army leaders and the tolerance of a wider circle, including Nasution. Initially formed by some Masjumi and PSI leaders in cooperation with IPKI (Ikatan Perdukung Kemerdekaan Indonesia, League of Upholders of Indonesian Independence, an army-connected party) and the two Christian parties (Roman Catholic and Protestant), the League waxed strong during Sukarno's absence abroad in the second quarter of 1960 and, with the support of the army's chief of intelligence, Colonel Sukendro, attracted the involvement of several PNI and NU officials. When the president returned, however, he insisted that the army withdraw the support it had lent the organization and thereafter it rapidly declined, until a year later Sukarno was able to ban it with hardly any reaction.[65]

The Democratic League was the forerunner of several attempts by

---

ments of the Seventh [Extraordinary] National Congress of the PKI) (Djakarta, Oct. 1963), pp. 183–92.

[63] See Everett D. Hawkins, "Labor in Transition," in McVey, ed., *Indonesia,* pp. 248–71.

[64] Feith, "Dynamics," pp. 342–43.

[65] On this affair see Feith, "Dynamics," pp. 343–44; Lev, "The Political Role of the Army in Indonesia," p. 357; Mackie, pp. 272–74; Arnold C. Brackman, *Indonesian Communism: A History* (New York, 1963), p. 275.

army and political groups to sink their differences in a common front against the PKI, the last and most concerted of which was the formation in August 1964 of the Body for Promoting Sukarnoism. On this occasion the Murba Party, which had repeatedly tried to advance the "one party" proposal as a means of heading off PKI advances, played a prominent part, in association with a number of army officers. Once again, however, President Sukarno's refusal to countenance anti-Communist sallies proved decisive; after a tense political struggle in the latter months of 1964, the Body for Promoting Sukarnoism was outlawed in December, and a few weeks later Murba itself paid the price for its too blatant attempt to circumvent the Nasakom code by being suspended from further political activity.[66]

The minor constituents of the armed forces—the navy, the air force, and the police—never represented a great threat to the PKI. The air and naval forces were much weaker than the army and much less involved in general administration. Interservice rivalries centered particularly on the efforts of these two services to obtain a greater share of expenditure and to raise their status to one of greater parity with the army. For this reason the heads of both services, and particularly the air force, tended to lean toward President Sukarno in his competition with the generals, and, following his policies more closely, to give greater allegiance to the Nasakom principle. The police also, although frequently coming into collision with PKI-led groups agitating on industrial and peasant issues, were led by men less influential in national politics and more inclined to accept official policies. From 1963 onward, Aidit paid some attention to relations with the police, in an attempt to avoid open clashes between them and the party's mass activists. He stressed the common interests of the police and the people[67] and used the slogan, "For civil order, help the police!"[68] When clashes became frequent during the land reform campaign of 1964, he appealed to both sides to avoid violence.[69]

Taking their cue from the president, who sought to build up the air force and navy as services loyal to him and who, when army leaders

---

[66] For a brief account of this episode and its background see Van der Kroef, "Indonesian Communism's 'Revolutionary Gymnastics,'" pp. 217–32.

[67] *Harian Rakjat,* Feb. 25, 1963.

[68] *Ibid.,* July 1, 1964.

[69] *Ibid.,* June 2, 1964.

obstructed his policies, went out of his way to praise the other services, PKI leaders assiduously wooed these rivals to army dominance. Thus, in his budget speech of December 1959, Sudisman made much of the fact that "well over half the amount devoted to security as a whole was allocated to two items alone, the land forces and the Department of the Minister for Security, Lieut. General A. H. Nasution." Referring to a large proposed allocation of special (secret) funds for the army, which he alleged were devoted to internal political surveillance activities that fostered dangers of military dictatorship, Sudisman asked whether it would not be better "to transfer some of these special funds to the Navy," which, he argued, was inadequately catered for.[70] Similarly, in his lectures to the armed forces in 1963 and later, Aidit went out of his way to stress the equality of all branches of the services in a manner calculated to please air force and navy officers.

In 1963, however, the PKI seems also to have decided that the time had come to make more determined efforts to increase its leverage within the army. The decision was a logical one, considering the extent of army power and the obstacle it represented to the party's political aspirations. But the timing may also have been stimulated by developments enhancing its opportunities in this respect. In May 1963 martial law came to an end, and while in many cases army officers continued to exercise strong influence in regional government the weight of the army in political affairs overall was considerably reduced. Observers noted at about this time, too, that there appeared to be a general "softening" in the officer corps. As Feith expressed it:

Four years of sharing hegemony have tended to blunt the army's sense of a separate political purpose. Much of the army's drive to power has become spent as officers have become involved in a host of relatively small political, administrative and managerial tasks. Material comfort has frequently mellowed these officers' reforming zeal, and the experience of responsibility has tended to lessen their confidence in the army's capacity to solve the country's problems. Finally, the 1958–62 period has seen the growth of an increasingly vigorous popular dislike of the army, thus making it more and more difficult for the army to bid for top power on the moral claim of championing reform.[71]

[70] *Review of Indonesia,* VII (Feb. 1960), 13.
[71] Feith, "Dynamics" p. 357.

One sign of the changed atmosphere in 1963 was that an invitation was extended to Aidit to take part in an indoctrination scheme for armed forces personnel sponsored by Sukarno, in order to explain to them the outlook and policies of the Marxist strain in the national revolution. In his lectures Aidit mainly concentrated on expounding PKI policies, in order to remove misapprehensions among his listeners and indicate to them the congruence between PKI doctrine and that of the state ideology. On several occasions, however, he also dealt specifically with the role of the armed forces in the revolution.

Thus, in a lecture to the army staff and command school in 1963, Aidit was at pains to stress three things: that the armed forces as a whole were an instrument of the people; that their function was solely to implement the Political Manifesto and not to take political initiatives; and that all four services were of equal importance and one should not be emphasized at the expense of the others. Those elements in the services that did not side with the people, he stated, were a "foreign substance" against whom all patriotic servicemen had a duty to struggle.[72]

In a second lecture to army staff school trainees on March 7, 1964, Aidit referred rather optimistically to "the feeling of mutuality and unity [that] daily grows stronger between all the armed forces of the Indonesian Republic . . . and the various groups of the Indonesian people, including the Communists" and emphasized that it was impossible genuinely to support Pantja Sila without also supporting Nasakom.[73] The following month, at the Naval Academy in Surabaja, he went a step further and developed what he termed a concept of "national defense":

National unity and national defense can become two united weapons if both are loyal to one and the same policy, namely the Political Manifesto. . . . If national defense is loyal to the general strategy of the Indonesian revolution, then every one of the armed forces must serve the revolution, serve the struggle of the Indonesian people . . . If all the armed forces are inspired by this doctrine, the doctrine of the oneness [*dwitunggal*] between the armed forces and the people, then we can speak of the doctrine of national defense, that is, the doctrine of serving

[72] D. N. Aidit, *PKI dan Angkatan Darat* (The PKI and the Army) (Djakarta, 1963).

[73] *Revolusi, Angkatan Bersendjata dan Partai Komunis,* pp. 5, 13.

the revolution, serving the people. . . . The above doctrine must not only play a role in great patriotic actions, national and international, but must also become the guide in daily work, for example in carrying out small operations, in training and also in study.[74]

The import of these lectures is not difficult to discern. Aidit was in effect arguing against the idea of the armed forces having a distinct and separate political role in the life of the country; all were subject to the ideological directives of the state, which meant the doctrines of the president. Aidit was urging members of the armed forces to draw a line between the "patriotic" elements in their ranks who subscribed to this understanding of their function and "alien elements" and potential "counterrevolutionaries" who did not.

At the same time, Aidit began to urge all PKI members to rid themselves of sectarian attitudes giving currency to the idea that the party was antiarmy.[75] At the PKI's conference on revolutionary art and literature on August 28, 1964, he launched an appeal to all left wing artists and writers to make the "soldier masses" the subject of art and literary works in order to stimulate rapport between the troops and the "popular forces."[76]

Another prong of the PKI's attack on the problem of the armed forces, and probably the most important in the party's eyes, was the attempt to gain official influence in the military sphere. One facet of this tactic was of long standing—the proposal, made repeatedly since the time of the anti-Darul Islam campaigns of the mid-fifties, that workers and peasants should receive military training so as to assist the armed forces in their campaigns and help guard the security of the state.

The first breakthrough on this issue came during the West Irian campaign, when some tens of thousands of youth and students were given rudimentary experience in drilling and maneuvers. But the army as far as possible excluded Communist-influenced youth from the

[74] D. N. Aidit, *Marxisme dan Pembinaan Nasion Indonesia* (Marxism and the Construction of the Indonesian Nation) (Djakarta, 1964), pp. 40–45.

[75] *Harian Rakjat,* Nov. 27, 1964.

[76] D. N. Aidit, *Tentang Sastra dan Seni jang Berkepribadian Nasional Mengabdi Buruh, Tani dan Pradjurit* (Concerning a Literature and Art with a National Identity Serving the Workers, Peasants and Soldiers) (Djakarta, 1964), pp. 30–31.

program and kept a firm hand on the guns. As Pemuda Rakjat leader Sukatno reported to the PKI's seventh congress in April 1962, a quarter of a million Pemuda Rakjat members registered for training but the greater part of them were not inducted.[77] In the course of the Malaysia campaign, the training scheme was greatly expanded and extended to factories, workplaces, and schools, and the role of Communist youth and student organizations became greater; but again most of those who took part in the regular drilling and marching were armed with nothing more lethal than sticks.[78] A more threatening attack on the army's near monopoly of the instruments of violence emerged in 1965 when the PKI began to urge the appointment of political cadres to units of the armed forces and the formal establishment of a "fifth force" of armed workers and peasants, the latter signifying separation of the volunteers from army control.

THE "POPULAR" ORGANS OF GOVERNMENT:
POLITICAL PARTIES, PARLIAMENT, ELECTIONS

The PKI's efforts during the transitional period from 1957 to 1959 to preserve as much as possible of the democratic aspects of the overthrown parliamentary system were continued, with some qualifications, in the succeeding years. The party was concerned not only with its own freedom of action, narrowly defined, but with the maintenance of all those institutions and popular rights that would assist it in any degree to oppose trends toward army rule or other forms of right wing authoritarianism. It is not altogether surprising, then, that the party should have been on occasion accused of "liberalism" by those who favored one party government or other forms of authoritarianism.[79]

The crux of the PKI's argument in defense of representative institutions and popular liberties was that the evils of liberalism had been cured by the concentration of executive power in the hands of

[77] *Madju Terus,* pp. 185–86.

[78] In a month spent in Java during the height of the training program, in Oct.–Nov. 1964, the writer did not observe one group bearing arms. Discussion with PKI leaders bore out my personal observations. However, some PKI-influenced volunteer units were armed and dispatched to the Kalimantan border area.

[79] See, for example, Aidit's rejection of a charge along these lines made by *Kalimantan Berdjuang* in *Harian Rakjat,* Sept. 18, 1962.

President Sukarno and the adoption of a binding guideline for all
state and political activities—the Political Manifesto. It insisted that
Guided Democracy was still democracy, and that encroachments upon
the rights of "Manipolist" parties and organizations were not only
inimical to the achievement of the goals of the state but also calculated to encourage "adventurers" and "fascists" who were only trying
to use the antiliberal trend to establish their own dictatorship.

The defence of the parties that the PKI had undertaken during the
transitional stage continued into the debate on the future of the
parties in the latter half of 1959 and throughout most of 1960. When
the issue of simplifying the party system was raised—the object of
such a simplification being to reduce the considerable number of
small parties, which were said to have helped make previous parlia-
ments unworkable—the PKI took the attitude that, while it made
sense to exclude from parliament those parties that had failed to obtain a certain percentage of votes ("perhaps 2 per cent, 3 per cent or
more," in Aidit's words), these parties should nevertheless retain
their right to exist:

The role of small parties outside parliament is important; they can exercise control over the parties sitting in Parliament. If the parties in Parliament act against the wishes of the people, then it is quite possible that as
a result of subsequent general elections, they will no longer have the
right to sit in Parliament, and the parties formerly outside the Parliament
may get in.[80]

The law on parties, as promulgated by the president on January
12, 1960, gave the executive wide discretion in licensing or prohibiting
parties. Among other things, it required parties desiring to continue in
operation to accept the state philosophy, to confine themselves to
peaceful and democratic methods of attaining their objectives, and
to register their membership with the state. Only parties with a minimum of 150,000 members spread over a stipulated number of provinces would be licensed.[81] In commenting on the law, Lukman indicated the PKI's opposition by arguing that "the most proper and
democratic method of simplifying party life is through general elec-

[80] Address to PKI May Day gathering, May 3, 1959; see *Review of Indonesia*, VI (June–July 1959), 4.
[81] See Mackie, p. 273n.

tions." He said he could not approve or disapprove of the law as promulgated until the party had had an opportunity to see it in operation.[82] In August 1960 ten political parties, including the PNI, NU, and PKI, were approved under the law; the remainder, including Masjumi and the PSI, were ordered to wind up their affairs.

In June 1960, in a speech on the occasion of the PKI's fortieth anniversary, Aidit gave a theoretical defense of parties. "The forty years of the PKI are the clearest evidence of the correctness of the party system for the Indonesian people," he said. "Were the party system not an objective need of the people, were it not supported by the people, parties would not have lived on for such a long time." The people were divided into classes and groups and, along with economic organizations, each class and group required a political organization to struggle for its interests. The collaboration and competition of the parties reflected the cooperation and conflict between these classes and groups, which rested on objective interests which could not be ignored. The parties had played a vital role in the struggle against colonialism, and still did so, as "centres of activity to raise the consciousness of the people against imperialism, to give democratic education to the people, to raise the national consciousness of the people, to increase their consciousness of the unity of the nation and of the Republic of Indonesia." There were those who claimed that the parties were corrupt, nests of position-seekers: "Were the persons who say such things not themselves corrupt and not themselves position-seekers, there might be some point in considering their opinion." Similarly, there were those who tried to charge all the parties with responsibility for the counterrevolutionary activities of the Masjumi and the PSI, but they conveniently forgot that had there not been "such 'non-party' individuals as Achmad Husein, M. Simbolon, V. Sumual, and others . . . in control of the armed forces, they [the Masjumi and the PSI] would never have dared to rebel. . . . It is therefore incorrect to blame the party system for this."

Aidit's attitude on whether the Masjumi and the PSI should continue to be legal parties was ambivalent. On the face of it the party had no reason to be interested in preserving the political rights of these inveterate enemies; yet there were suggestions in Aidit's speech

[82] *Review of Indonesia,* VII (Feb. 1960), 16.

that he did not welcome the ban on them that was shortly to be announced. He was careful not to defend their right to exist, saying
that "if the Government is courageous enough to withdraw the rights
of these parties to exist, we would not only not obstruct such a measure, we would agree to it and support it." At the same time he stressed:

What is even more important is to destroy the source of these parties, to
destroy their social basis . . . [in] imperialism and feudalism. As long
as these sources . . . have not disappeared the Masjumi and PSI will
continue to exist, perhaps with different names, or perhaps the compradores and landlords or their agents will join legal parties and make
them the centre of their activities, which would mean in essence these
parties becoming the new Masjumi and PSI.[83]

It would seem, in fact, that Aidit preferred to have the right wing
parties out in the open, where their activities could be kept under
observation and they could be maintained as a target (especially now
that they were stigmatized by their links with the regional rebels),
rather than underground, where they would tend to establish illicit
connections with the army and other anti-PKI groups that would be
harder to attack publicly. Additionally, with the PKI itself under constant harassment from the army, he feared that the proscription of
parties would set a dangerous precedent. There was considerable
discussion along these lines at the time, and one of the reasons why
the army leaders went along with the ban on Masjumi and the PSI
was their hope of being able to proscribe the PKI soon thereafter.

After the August simplification, Sukarno apparently decided against
any further measures against the parties. Having eliminated the representative institutions that nourished them, and secured their vows of
loyalty to the state ideology, he seems to have decided that the anti-
parties swing had gone far enough. His major concern henceforth was
to use the parties to combat army attempts to monopolize the mass-
based structures of Guided Democracy.

The PKI's defense of the elected parliament in 1959 and early
1960 was conspicuously less successful than its efforts on behalf of
the parties. It labored under the disadvantage that at this time Sukarno was still experiencing the full flush of excitement about his
Guided Democracy edifice, and angry with critics. He felt that if the

83 Aidit, *Problems,* pp. 162–66.

parties were permitted to restore parliament to its former powers, or anything resembling them, then the whole point of the Guided Democracy changes would have been lost. The Communist leaders chose to ignore this fact. Parliament had been their major public platform inside the state apparatus, a forum where they could expound their policies and inveigh against threatening trends in political life; given general elections, they envisaged strengthening their position considerably, possibly even securing an absolute majority. They must have had serious doubts about their ability to preserve this sanctum, but they labored to rescue what they could of its former status. It was a brief struggle, over to all intents and purposes by March 1960.

Under the 1945 constitution, the government was not answerable to parliament, and in 1959 Sukarno and his ministers made very broad use of presidential decrees, passed laws without reference to parliament, and even amended or repealed laws which that body had earlier passed. This drew sharp protests from the PKI. In a press statement on August 28, 1959, on the occasion of a two month recess in parliamentary sittings, Lukman, as chairman of the PKI faction in parliament, contended that every legislative act of the government must have a clear legal basis in parliamentary approval. The 1945 constitution did not authorize government by decree, he argued; once the initial decree restoring it had been issued, all future laws had to be adopted by parliament in accordance with the constitution's provisions.[84] On October 2, in a comment on the resumption of parliament, the party's newspaper made much the same point, while also defending parliament's role under the new constitution in more general terms.[85]

During the debate on the budget shortly afterwards, PKI and other party representatives vigorously asserted parliament's prerogatives, particularly in regard to levying taxes.[86] Sukarno was unimpressed; when parliament threatened to reject the budget, he summarily dismissed it and a few weeks later announced the composition of a new appointed parliament, a *gotong rojong* parliament. The PKI protested the decision; in a telegram to Sukarno (one of the very few occasions

[84] *Review of Indonesia,* VI (Sept.–Oct. 1959), 18–19.
[85] *Harian Rakjat,* Oct. 2, 1959.
[86] For the statements of PKI speakers see *Review of Indonesia,* VII (Feb. 1960), 10–14.

on which the PKI directly attacked an action of the president) Aidit described the dissolution of the elected parliament as "an event which seriously endangers democratic life in our country" and called for general elections before the end of the year.[87]

When the composition of the appointed parliament was announced, it was clear that the PKI had fared reasonably well, obtaining thirty seats in its own right and another twenty to thirty-five seats if the political affiliations of functional group representatives were taken into account.[88] The party's reception of the announcement was anything but enthusiastic, however; Aidit described it as "better than having no parliament at all" but added that if democratic elections were held, "the PKI would receive more seats than it commanded now." More important than the party's actual representation was the blow that had been delivered to the standing of parliament and the obvious prospect that the new appointed assembly would be around for a good while. Aidit repeated his call for elections, but it must have been a forlorn gesture.[89]

Parliament was never again to gain any initiative in the political system, and within a short time, as the realities of the situation impressed themselves upon the party, it came to occupy a relatively minor place in PKI concerns. The agitation for elections continued, however; at one stage the party even drew up proposals for a new election procedure to meet objections that holding a nationwide poll would be too expensive.[90] But, despite the establishment of a parliamentary committee in 1962 to draw up a new election law, reasons were always found for postponing actual measures to prepare for a vote. The interest of the other political parties was at best half-hearted; they were occasionally frustrated by the clique pattern of political trading in the capital, but on the whole they had adapted themselves to it. Above all, they feared that general elections would be a gift to the Communists.[91]

The role of the cabinet under Guided Democracy was much less

[87] *Review of Indonesia,* VII (April 1960), 9.
[88] On the composition of the new parliament see Mackie, pp. 271–72.
[89] *Review of Indonesia,* VII (April 1960), 11–12.
[90] *Harian Rakjat,* May 14, 1965.
[91] For some later PKI comments on the elections issue see *Harian Rakjat,* March 19 and May 24, 1962, and Aidit, *Problems,* pp. 462–63.

of a popular one than under the superseded parliamentary system, since it was no longer responsible to parliament and became essentially a presidential instrument. However, so long as First Minister Djuanda lived there were at least gestures of respect for the principle that the government ought to have a general mandate from parliament for its policies.

The expectations of cabinet representation held out to the PKI in the president's *konsepsi* speech of February 1957 failed to materialize. The party's most constant refrain throughout the ensuing six years was its demand for the formation of a *gotong rojong* cabinet, later given more specific meaning, in an attempt to overcome mere token overtures to a barren slogan, in the formulation "a Gotong Rojong Cabinet with Nasakom as its core." Although bearing varying emphases at different times, this slogan may justly be described as the central motif in the party's political propaganda after 1957. It represented in a new form the goal of achieving a united national front government enunciated in the 1954 program; and, although it was stressed on occasion that the establishment of such a government would not in itself solve the country's problems, it was equally emphasized that no important problems could be solved until it had been achieved and that the entire political situation would be transformed once it had.

In an early comment on the first Guided Democracy cabinet Aidit declared that "not only in other countries, but in Indonesia too, there are no state affairs that can be solved by any government as long as the proletariat and the working people in general, whose true representative is the PKI, are being ignored." He excused Sukarno from blame for the failure to form a *gotong rojong* cabinet, arguing that the president had sincerely sought such an instrument; the fault lay rather with leaders of the "middle forces," the "right wing of the nationalists and the reactionaries in the religious groups," who played upon fears that "if the Communists are in the cabinet, Indonesia would be plunged into catastrophe as a result of an attack from the U.S.A." Nevertheless, the aim would be achieved in time:

The forces of the working people, the left wing of the nationalists and the progressive religious leaders are still in a process of growth. As the democratic forces grow, the centrists among the middle forces will be drawn into supporting a *gotong rojong* cabinet. . . . There is no power that can prevent the formation in the future of the cabinet that the people yearn for.[92]

At the sixth congress of the party in September 1959, the call for a *gotong rojong* cabinet was repeated, but Aidit apparently felt it necessary to caution members against excessive optimism concerning what could be expected from including Communists in the cabinet:

"Participation of Communists is not to be looked upon as a cure-all, since the ability or inability of a government to solve the pressing problems of the country very much depends on the composition of the government as a whole and on its policy. Nevertheless, letting Communists participate in the government would be a positive sign, a sign, that is, that all democratic and patriotic groups are deeply aware of the gravity of the situation; and a sign that they sincerely wish to overcome this grave situation. It is thus clear that a cabinet including Communists would be sure to arouse new hopes, create new possibilities, and stimulate fresh enthusiasm among the broad masses of the people.[93]

Was Aidit's cautioning an indication that the PKI leaders expected their demands to be granted shortly, at least in part? Conceivably it was, for in a press interview a few months later he declared that "there is still the possibility" of a *gotong rojong* government being formed, as a result of mass pressures and President Sukarno's continued efforts.[94] A few weeks later he was demanding the party's immediate admission to the cabinet.[95] These expressions of optimism, and the unaccustomed intensity of the PKI's campaign against the government, may indicate that the PKI was encouraged in its demand by the president himself—in which case the army's clampdown on the party in July 1960 can perhaps be seen as its response to a joint bid by the president and the PKI to bring the latter into the government.

In any case, the July 8 Affair put the *gotong rojong* cabinet issue on ice for a time, and although Sukarno was to raise the idea again, late in 1960, in mid-1961, and in early 1962, he never succeeded in gaining more than token agreement to it. As Aidit had remarked in

[92] *Bintang Merah, XV* (July–Aug. 1959), 297–302.
[93] *Ibid.,* XV (Sept.–Oct. 1959), 350.
[94] *Review of Indonesia,* VII (Jan. 1960), 8–9.
[95] *Ibid.,* VII (Feb. 1960), 6.

1959, opposition came not only from the army but also from the so-called middle forces in the PNI and the NU. As anti-Communists saw it, entry of the Communists into the government would alienate the West, make it more difficult for Indonesia to obtain foreign aid from the United States, and increase the country's dependence on the Communist bloc.

The PKI made its strongest bid for a *gotong rojong* cabinet late in 1962 and early in 1963. The party unleashed a full scale mass campaign behind the demand, and Aidit went so far as to talk of the possibility of civil war should the people's expectations be frustrated.[96] On this occasion the PKI's vehemence was almost certainly provoked by fears that the government was about to take a decided swing to the right in a bid to obtain U.S. credits for economic stabilization. Its premonitions proved justified, and its campaign failed. According to report, Sukarno was at that point encouraging the right wing trend and compelled the party to call off its offensive.

It is more than possible that the party did not in fact expect to win entry into the cabinet on this occasion; halting or limiting the rightward trend was almost certainly its principal concern. More generally, some observers have expressed doubts that the PKI ever really wished to participate in the cabinet, as distinct from obtaining posts for more party sympathisers. Such a view holds that the party would have had nothing to gain except a share in the responsibility for the deteriorating economic situation.[97] The point is certainly arguable, but it is this writer's view that, generally speaking, the PKI leaders were more concerned about the respectability, influence, and protection that cabinet posts would have afforded them. A major limb of their strategy was to secure their acceptance by the elite and increase its dependence on their skills and mobilizing power; for this, participation in the cabinet would have been of considerable importance. The PKI could still have argued, as Aidit did in 1959, that its minority position in the government prevented it from initiating the measures it regarded as necessary, and this in turn would have provided the cornerstone for a new campaign to have the party entrusted with key

[96] Hindley, pp. 296–97; Guy J. Pauker, "Indonesia: Internal Development or External Expansion?" *Asian Survey*, III, no. 2 (Feb. 1963), 71.

[97] See in particular Van der Kroef, *The Communist Party of Indonesia*, pp. 277–78.

responsibility for national affairs. Whatever else they may have lacked, the PKI leaders do not appear to have been wanting in confidence in their ability to put the country to rights. In any case, the issue was made more real for the PKI by the vociferousness of the anti-Communist response and the effect that the contest itself must have had on party cadres. If they had their doubts at the beginning, Aidit and his Politburo colleagues must have come after a short time actually to want a *gotong rojong* cabinet.

The most the president was able to obtain for the PKI, however, was the appointment in March 1962 of Aidit and Njoto as special ministers without portfolio, positions involving neither specific policy responsibilities nor participation in the work of the inner cabinet. While pointing out the symbolic importance of this development, Aidit was quick to add that it did not represent the fulfilment of the *gotong rojong* demand and that, since the Communists were not represented in either cabinet consultative sessions or cabinet working sessions, the PKI could not in any way be held responsible for the government's failings.[98]

The Nasakom cabinet campaign received new impetus after Indonesia launched its all-out confrontation of Malaysia in September 1963, by which time the argument against offending the United States had less force. By 1964 the PNI leadership appeared to be more receptive to proposals to admit the PKI to the cabinet, but the NU remained stubbornly opposed, as did the army and the Murba group. Sukarno was either unable or unwilling to surmount this resistance, and the PKI's ambitions remained unfulfilled. In August 1964 Njoto was admitted to the enlarged cabinet as one of three ministers appointed to supervise land reform,[99] but this was a mere token gesture toward the concept of a Nasakom cabinet.

THE GOVERNMENTAL BUREAUCRACY

Guided Democracy brought with it a substantial augmentation of bureaucratic power, a not surprising development in view of the fact that the inauguration of the system represented a victory for bureaucratically oriented factions over commercial and entrepreneurial groups. It also produced a rapid and marked reversion to centralizing

[98] Aidit, *Problems,* pp. 451–54.
[99] *Harian Rakjat,* Sept. 23, 1964.

tendencies in government, in contrast to the trend of the mid-fifties when the regions got more and more control over their own affairs.

The decline in the importance of the political parties as channels for the articulation and bargaining of social interests further enlarged the role of the bureaucracy; ceasing to be subject to any weighty outside pressures and controls, it arrogated to itself many of the political functions of interest representation and decision-making. Politics at the center became increasingly a matter of rivalries and conflicts between politico-bureaucratic cliques, in which the prizes were prestige, influence, and the spoils of office. Inordinate overregulation, corruption, and arbitrariness was the result.

At the local level, the experiments in autonomous self-government that had gathered momentum throughout the constitutional phase were brought to a sudden and drastic halt by the promulgation of new local government regulations in September 1959. With the regional rebellion defeated, a Java-dominated centralism was triumphant, and the rebels' weakness enabled the change to be effected with speed and thoroughness. It was no longer necessary to make concessions to groups asking for regional autonomy, and the democratic sentiment that had helped sustain the autonomists was now superseded by proleadership sentiment which served the cause of the *pamong pradja,* the administrative corps which combined within itself the cultural ethos of ancient Javanese aristocratic rule and the bureaucratic techniques introduced by the Dutch. Rescued from threatened dissolution under proposals for enlarged regional autonomy introduced early in 1957, the *pamong pradja* now found its powers confirmed and strengthened.[100]

The PKI's attitude to the bureaucracy was necessarily ambivalent. The party had contributed, for reasons connected with wider political issues, to the demise of the major political representatives of private business and to the concomitant growth of bureaucratic influence. But the PKI now found itself caught in a contradiction: on the one hand it was committed to the defense of the interests of the "national bourgeoisie," and frequently outlined proposals for the advancement of the interests of indigenous commercial and industrial groups; on

---

[100] On the trend in the fifties, and its reversal in 1959, see J. D. Legge, *Central Authority and Regional Autonomy in Indonesia: A Study in Local Administration, 1950–1960* (Ithaca, N.Y., 1961).

the other hand it was even more strongly committed to the notion that the state sector must occupy the primary role in the economy, on the assumption that this was a necessary and important foundation for the establishment of socialism. In practice, the strengthening of the bureaucratic element in society, running parallel with the country's increasingly insecure trading conditions, was making it well-nigh impossible for entrepreneurs to stay in business except as clients of the bureaucrats. To have highlighted this trend effectively, and urged measures to combat it, would have opened the PKI to the charge of favoring a "liberal economy." Neither political conditions nor the party's ideological commitments to state ownership and control would allow it to take this course, and its proposals on behalf of the national bourgeoisie became little more than abstract generalities.

The PKI first drew pointed attention to the dangers of enhanced bureaucratic power in connection with the ban imposed in July 1959 on high civil servants belonging to or joining political parties. The party strenuously opposed the measure, its daily newspaper commenting that it would weaken outside control over the civil service and that dictatorship and liberalism thrived on bureaucracy, corruption, cliquism, and nepotism.[101] A week later Aidit issued a press statement in even stronger terms. The ban would not solve the problems being faced in the civil service, he said:

These problems cannot be solved so long as "favoritism" and the "family system" are not eradicated from the service. . . . This new regulation may give birth to an artificial elite of the type of government corps in colonial times, a corps that was completely divorced from the masses of the people and that fawned on its superiors but treated its inferiors like servants.[102]

The government stood firm, however, and the PKI campaign faded away. Generalized attacks on the bureaucracy as a social group were rare thereafter, being replaced by more specific and sustained campaigns against officials in particular departments who were allegedly sabotaging national policies or who took up an antagonistic attitude toward PKI-led actions. In other words, the pattern of attack shifted to the *political* outlook of officials, as part of the PKI's effort to

[101] *Harian Rakjat,* July 29, 1959.
[102] *Ibid.,* Aug. 6, 1959.

weaken all elements in the political and administrative apparatus that stood in the way of its aspirations. In the later years of Guided Democracy, "retooling" campaigns against unpopular, corrupt, or "reactionary" officials became a pronounced feature of the struggle among the contenders for power, with the Communists using their organizational weight to the full in an attempt to strengthen their leverage in the central and provincial governing apparatuses. The only social group among the bureaucracy that came in for generalized denunciation by the PKI was that of the "bureaucratic capitalists," or managers of state enterprises, whose army links made them particularly dangerous opponents of the Communists. Since their role was concentrated in the economy, their place in PKI concerns will be dealt with in that context.

In the local government sphere, the PKI had vigorously agitated for and supported all moves toward elected self-government and autonomy in the fifties. The party was intent on enlarging its area of political freedom and drawing the masses more effectively into the political process by reducing the effects of authority-deference relationships. It continued its struggle for popularly elected forms of local government during the Guided Democracy period; in many ways local democracy was more than ever important to it as a means of reducing the powers of local war administrators, compensating for the moderate role the party had to play in capital city politics, and facilitating its campaign to build a large organized mass base among the peasantry which it launched seriously in 1959. On the other hand, the PKI toned down its advocacy of regional autonomy, partly because this demand was viewed with disfavor by the president and his entourage and partly because it recognized that central power was more likely than local legislative bodies to protect the party organizations in the Outer Islands. This compromise appears to have provoked some criticism within party ranks that the party was neglecting regional problems and interests and thus missing valuable opportunities for extending its influence in areas outside Java.[103] It is difficult, however, to see how the PKI could have gone far toward meeting this criticism without placing its general strategy in jeopardy.

A presidential edict of September 1, 1959, suspended the crucial provisions of a 1957 law providing for elected regional heads (*kepala*

---

[103] Interview with "X," an expatriate PKI member, July 1968.

daerah) and for regional executive councils responsible to their legis-latures. From this date on these officials were once more to be ap-pointed by the central government; at the same time, a new type of executive council was appointed, responsible not to the elected re-gional assembly but to the *kepala daerah* himself.[104] Of all the politi-cal parties, the PKI most vigorously opposed the new regulation, which threatened to negate the effects of its victories in the 1957 re-gional elections in Java. While the regulation was still only being rumoured, Aidit, in an interview with *Bintang Timur,* attacked the proposal emphatically, correctly anticipating that it would mark a resurgence of the *pamong pradja,* whose loyal service to the Dutch he was at pains to stress, and commented bitingly on those who thought they could play the role of "Sukarnos in miniature." He defended the elective system then in operation and rejected the idea that what the regional system needed was greater expertise: "their [the bureaucrats of colonial times] expertise is as useless as colonialism itself."[105] With the promulgation of the regulation on September 1, the party's agita-tional apparatus was called into full operation, and protest delegations, telegrams, and resolutions poured in to the minister for the interior. SOBSI called on its members and the entire people to "prepare for actions to resist" the regulation.[106]

Sukarno listed the issue for discussion by the Supreme Advisory Council on October 20. In what was obviously a bid to impress upon the president the strength of its feelings, the PKI Politburo, on the day following the session and prior to the announcement of the presi-dent's decision, issued a statement warning that if the regulation was confirmed the party would continue its struggle against it. Even if the president modified the regulation, the party added, it would continue "to use all parliamentary and democratic methods to convince the public of the correctness of the PKI's point of view." It called on the people to continue their struggle but to beware of "provocations" (presumably because these might invite military reprisals). In the event the president made only minor concessions to the opposition: the party was obliged to exaggerate the significance of these conces-sions and bow its head to the inevitable, at least for the time being.[107]

[104] Legge, pp. 61ff.
[105] *Review of Indonesia,* VI (June–July 1959), 9.
[106] *Ibid.,* VI (Sept.–Oct. 1959), 9–10.
[107] *Ibid.,* VI (Nov.–Dec. 1959), 14–15.

Despite martial law, the PKI maintained a discreet pressure for the democratization of local government in the succeeding years, adding to its demands for the restoration of the rights lost in 1959 pressure for the extension of election provisions to the village level.[108] As part of its preparations for celebrating the fifteenth anniversary of independence, the PKI daily newspaper published in August 1960 a feature article tracing the history of the struggle for regional autonomy from the revolutionary days onward; but, in contrast with the agitational vehemence with which the 1959 regulation had been greeted at the time of its promulgation, on this occasion the appeal for greater local democracy was couched in such moderate terms as to be almost indiscernible.[109] The party felt in no position to take a strong stand so soon after the July 8 Affair; perhaps, too, it had been temporarily mollified by Sukarno's appointment of Communist deputy governors in Central Java, West Java, and Djakarta, the selection of Communists as mayors in a number of important cities and towns in Java (Tjirebon in West Java, Surabaja in East Java, and Surakarta, Magelang, Salatiga, and Bojolali in Central Java),[110] and the reconstitution of regional assemblies along *gotong rojong* lines, which excluded the Masjumi and the PSI.[111]

In the first half of 1961 the party resumed its pressure, through deputations and propaganda, for regional assembly elections, but the campaign, never very vigorous, made little headway and petered out later in the year. Aidit made a strong point of regional democracy in his report to the party's seventh congress in April 1962, stating that the functioning of regional assemblies left a great deal to be desired and placing the blame on the highhandedness of regional heads and the "dictatorship of one-man bureaucratic capitalists" (i.e., army war administrators and governors). He called for the repeal of the regulations of 1959, the disbandment of the *pamong pradja,* and the convening of elections from the provincial down to the village level.[112]

These demands continued to form the basis of the PKI's campaign for regional democracy in the following years, but from 1963 onward they were overshadowed by agitation for the "retooling" of local

[108] See for example the article by Asmu in *Suara Tani* of March–April 1960.
[109] Nungtjik, A. R., in *Harian Rakjat*, Aug. 11, 1960.
[110] *Review of Indonesia*, VII (March 1960), 9, 31.
[111] *Ibid.*, VII (Sept.–Oct. 1960), 16.
[112] Aidit, *Problems*, pp. 458–62.

government officials, from governors and regional heads down to village *lurahs* (headmen). The main targets of PKI attacks were officials who had attempted to remove squatters on government lands, interfered with the party or its mass organizations, obstructed land reform measures, or in some other way come into conflict with the PKI. Some successes were scored, but usually only when the party's agitation coincided with the efforts of more powerful interests to remove the incumbent; and, with perhaps a few exceptions, the changes did little to alter the general structure of local government or the outlook of local officials.

In 1964, in two major statements touching on village government, Aidit recognized that more than personnel was involved. Many villagers, he noted, still held fatalistic attitudes toward the authorities, and even in cases where "progressive" village heads had been elected they often succumbed to the pressures of the mighty and ended up as "servants of the landlords." The only remedy, he concluded, was a thoroughgoing renovation of rural social relations leading to the destruction of all "feudal survivals."[113]

A NOVEL THEORY OF THE STATE

Prior to 1963 the PKI had shown little interest in presenting a global characterization of the Indonesian state as such. Its concern was rather to test the reactions of each branch of the political structure to its activities and policies and to model its attitudes accordingly. At the fifth congress in 1954, as was noted in Chapter 1, the party leadership was apparently undecided as to whether the national bourgeoisie had replaced the compradore bourgeoisie in effective control of the state machine, although its appreciation of the Ali government tended to suggest that this was the case. Five years later, at the sixth congress, Aidit was more explicit, if somewhat succinct: "the national bourgeoisie . . . has been holding state power for a short while," he stated. Presumably this comment referred to the decisive exclusion of the Masjumi and the PSI from power, since these two parties were

---

[113] "Kaum Tani Djawa Barat Mengganjang Setan Desa" (The Peasants of West Java Crush the Village Devils), a report on rural research conducted in West Java, *Harian Rakjat,* May 11–16, 1964; *Revolusi Indonesia, Latarbelakang, Sedjarah dan Haridepannja* (The Indonesian Revolution, its Background, History, and Future) (Djakarta, 1964), pp. 52–55.

identified with the compradore bourgeoisie. What the brief statement failed to do was to recognize and evaluate the new distribution of power occasioned by the decline of parliament and the cabinet and the emergence of two new and decisive centers of power, the president and the army.

At this stage the PKI leadership concentrated on welcoming the "shift to the left" that had taken place as a result of the isolation of the Masjumi and the PSI and the enhancement of the position of the president. It was still hoping to preserve many of the essentials of the constitutional system much as they had operated previously, and, perhaps partly because of this, its general pronouncements tended to treat this system as being still largely intact, despite the fact that PKI responses to specific developments in the political sphere revealed a more realistic awareness both of how fundamental the changes were that had taken place and of the illusoriness of much of the leftward shift. The PKI gradually adjusted its analyses to the new realities of power, but changes were acknowledged in practice long before they were encompassed in a new theoretical appraisal of the balance of forces within the state system.

Early 1963 marked the point at which PKI leaders began to give public expression to their attempt to reach a new understanding of the distribution of power under Guided Democracy. In February of that year Aidit gave a lecture to students at a police training school, where he first essayed a tentative outline of a novel theory:

In the political power of our country now there are not only compradores, bureaucratic capitalists, and landlords, but also people who are pro-people, who are supported by the workers, peasants, democratic intellectuals, and other democrats. Thus, political power in our country has two aspects, that is, a pro-people's aspect and an anti-people's aspect.[114]

The theory of a "state with two aspects" was elaborated in the lectures Aidit gave in Peking the following September. In a report delivered at the Higher Party School of the Central Committee of the CPC on September 2, he introduced the subject by outlining the Marxist proposition that the state, as part of the "superstructure" of society, is a reflection of the "economic structure or production relations." In the Indonesian case, he said:

---

[114] *Harian Rakjat,* Feb. 25, 1963.

The economic structure (basis) of the Indonesian society today is still colonial and feudal in character. But there also exists a struggle of the people to resist this economic system and to establish a national and democratic economy. Hence the existence of two kinds of forces: the forces of the colonial and semi-feudal system, and the forces which are fighting for the establishment of a national and democratic economy. . . . These realities pertaining to the basis also find their reflection in the superstructure, including state power and chiefly the cabinet. In the state power, a policy against imperialism, feudalism, bureaucrat-capitalists, and compradors is reflected alongside the policy which defends imperialism, vestiges of feudalism, bureaucrat-capitalists and compradors. A sharp conflict exists between the two policies in the state power of the Republic of Indonesia. . . .

The state power of the Republic of Indonesia is a contradiction between two opposing aspects: The first aspect is that which represents the interests of the people. The second aspect is that which represents the interests of the people's enemies. The first aspect is embodied in the progressive attitude and policy of President Sukarno. . . . The second aspect is embodied in the attitude and policy of the rightists and diehards. . . .

Today the popular aspect has become the *main aspect* and plays a leading role in the state power of the Republic of Indonesia, *meaning that it guides the course of the political development in the state power.* . . . On the other hand the anti-popular aspect has ceased to be the main aspect and no longer guides the course of development in the contradiction. *However it is still the dominant aspect.* . . . But in any case the state . . . as a whole is now led by the forces which represent the interests of the people, or in other words *it is led by the popular aspect.*[115]

In his second lecture in the same series, Aidit made only a brief reference to the state power as "still dominated by those forces which defend imperialist and feudal interests."[116] In a third lecture, repeating the same theme, Aidit added:

The CPI's struggle with regard to state power is to enable the popular aspect to grow increasingly strong and to take a dominant position and, on the other hand, to exclude from state power the forces which oppose the people. Such is the content of the people's demand for the reorga-

---

[115] *The Indonesian Revolution,* pp. 40–43 (all emphases except the first added).

[116] *Ibid.,* p. 57.

nization (of the state organs), and for a Gotong Rojong cabinet with NASAKOM as the fulcrum.[117]

The same general analysis was retained in a presentation by Aidit to the army staff school in March 1964.[118] But in a series of lectures arranged by the National Front and delivered over three months, from September to November 1964, he took the matter a step further: the existence of two aspects of state power meant, he said, that "the important problem in Indonesia now is not to smash the state power as is the case in many other states, but to strengthen and consolidate the pro-people's aspect . . . and to eliminate the anti-people's aspect."[119] Finally, in his report to the Central Committee in May 1965, he spoke of state power in these terms: "The anti-people aspect of the state power is increasingly under pressure, while the pro-people aspect is increasingly on top and government policies are more in accordance with the demands of the people."[120]

The most immediately striking thing about this analysis is that it was not cast in class terms. The contending social forces in Indonesia were given class labels, and the state was said to be a reflection of class relations, but the actual depiction of the two aspects of state power used not class terminology but the vague categories of "pro-people" and "anti-people" persons and forces. Any attempt to equate the "pro-people" aspect with the national bourgeoisie is made more difficult by the fact that Aidit tended to slide from state power as such to society at large when trying to specify more precisely the nature of the forces involved. Thus, in his 1963 lecture to army officers, he said in reference to the two aspects: "The task of revolutionaries is to develop those forces which represent the interests of the people and which in the cabinet are led by President Sukarno, and in which the workers and peasants form the main revolutionary contingent." Of the forces referred to, some were obviously part of the state power while others were not; but the distinction is confused. Overall, Aidit appeared to be deliberately avoiding using the term "national bourgeoisie" to describe Sukarno and other "progressives"

[117] *Ibid.*, pp. 85–86.

[118] *Revolusi, Angkatan Bersendjata dan Partai Komunis*, p. 38.

[119] Aidit, *Revolusi Indonesia, Latarbelakang, Sedjarah dan Haridepannja*, p. 80.

[120] *Harian Rakjat*, May 12–14, 1965.

and thus to be implying that they had moved beyond the class bound position of that social grouping to one substantially in accordance with the outlook of the workers and peasants, led by the PKI. To put it another way, Sukarno and his followers were regarded now as belonging firmly on the side of the "people," not on the side of the national bourgeoisie as a class.

There was, then, an implicit rejection of class characterization as applying to those ruling groups that aligned themselves with the PKI's immediate policies and goals. Class analysis had become intertwined with a more populist theme. Each aspect of the state power was supported by and to a degree representative of class interests (the pro-people aspect acted on behalf of the workers and peasants, "the people"; the anti-people aspect on behalf of the bureaucratic capitalists and compradores, imperialism, and feudalism), but neither could be reduced entirely to class categories. The "middle forces," often synonymous in PKI statements with the national bourgeoisie, had tended to disappear in the analysis—a tacit recognition perhaps of the polarization of politics that was developing between 1963 and 1965.

There was also in this formulation confusion about which aspect of the state power was "on top." The way in which terms such as "main aspect," "dominant aspect," "the aspect which guides development" and "the aspect which leads" were combined and counterposed led nowhere except to uncertainty, giving the impression that the uncertainty was in Aidit's own mind. The methodology was clearly derived from Mao's article on contradiction, in which the "main contradiction" in any dialectical unity refers to the side that is developing and growing stronger, while the "dominant" aspect is the one that is strongest at a given point of time but already giving way to the main aspect. Aidit was suggesting something of the same kind, but it is hard to see how an aspect that already led the state power could be other than dominant. The difficulty obviously arose in 1963 as a result of the government's swing to the right and adoption of an American-inspired stabilization scheme, to which Aidit directly referred in this context. In endeavoring to reconcile this fact with the "progressive" character of Sukarno and his followers, he found himself obliged to play with words in a meaningless way.

It was Aidit's conclusion in his analysis of state power that in Indonesia's circumstances it would not be necessary to smash the state machine; because of its dual character, it would be sufficient to strengthen the pro-people aspect and weaken the anti-people aspect to the point where the state as a whole bore a pro-people imprint. In other words, the state could be transformed peacefully as a result of "action from above and below"—the efforts of progressives in the state power, assisted by mass pressures from without. This was a major departure from mainstream Communist theory. Marx had emphasized the necessity for the Communists in most cases to smash the bourgeois state power by violence and to establish the dictatorship of the proletariat; Lenin had treated such propositions as the very hallmark of the Bolshevik, as distinct from the social democratic, interpretation of Marxism. In China, where Aidit was propounding his new theory of the state, the notion of peaceful revolution had become anathema. Aidit was sensitive to the argument that his theory, and the tactics of the PKI as a whole, smacked of revisionism and reformism. In a thoroughly unconvincing attempt to distinguish the PKI's concept from the Italian Communist Party's not dissimilar strategy of "structural reform," he insisted that the Indonesian Communists' plans were "revolutionary," but the appeal to this magic word could not alter the essentially "revisionist" nature of the concept.[121]

Aidit's concept of a state with two aspects was quite novel in Communist history. Lenin had used the term "dual state power," but in quite a different sense, to refer to the temporary and inherently unstable confrontation that developed in 1917 between two opposing organs, the parliament and the Soviets, both seeking to represent the sole legitimate state force. Yet Aidit's approach did have a wider frame of reference in the theory of state capitalism elaborated by Soviet theoreticians in the 1960's. This theory also conceived of the possibility that the Asian national bourgeoisie might in certain instances take the road to socialism after establishing a strongly state-centered economy. Unlike the PKI, however, the Soviet theorists attached key importance to the role of Soviet aid in strengthening the state sector, drawing the rulers of the state concerned out of the orbit of Western alliances and inducing them to complete the tasks of socialist development. Common to both concepts was the supposition that the national bourgeoisie could in certain circumstances transcend its class role and act as a representative of the people. Both theories represented positions far removed from the Marxist insistence on class as a determi-

[121] *The Indonesian Revolution*, pp. 86–87.

nant of ideology. The main difference between them lay in the fact that the PKI saw itself as fulfilling the dynamic pacemaking and watchdog role whereas in the Soviet version this was allotted to the socialist states. Both were primarily rationalizations of interest. In the Soviet case, national interest and foreign policy requirements dictated support for neutralist and Soviet-leaning polities irrespective of their social composition, and the theory of national capitalism acted to justify Soviet policy and discourage local Communist parties from upsetting the apple cart by "revolutionary" actions. In the case of the PKI, the logic of its situation advised alliance with the Sukarno group and reliance on it to accept the party as the prime instrument for a social transformation.

The Chinese Communist Party, by contrast, was by this time relying for the expansion of its influence not on friendly non-Communist governments (with many of whom it had already broken or was shortly to break relations) but on disrupting the bipolar world division by armed agrarian revolutions led by groups that it hoped would look to China for guidance. The very conditions which the Soviet party saw as leading, via national capitalism, to socialism (for example, in India) the Chinese party depicted as "bureaucratic capitalism" allied with feudal and compradore elements.[122] The Chinese position was by no means consistent, however, and nowhere was the inconsistency more apparent than in relation to Indonesia. Relations between the governments of China and Indonesia grew steadily closer from 1963 onward, and the Sukarno regime was favored with praise and cooperation to a degree shared by no other non-Communist country. Similarly, the PKI, the strongest Communist party in the Chinese orbit, was recognized as a staunch anti-imperialist and antirevisionist party, the thoroughgoing reformism of its domestic policies being overlooked in the greater interest of strengthening Chinese international influence.[123]

Thus it was that the PKI found no open opposition to its theory of

[122] For a discussion of the conflict between Soviet theories of "national capitalism" and Chinese theories of "bureaucratic capitalism," see W. F. Wertheim, "Communist Views of State Capitalism, with Special Reference to South and Southeast Asia" (unpublished paper delivered to a seminar at the Center for Southeast Asian Studies, University of Hull, June 1968).

[123] See the articles by David Mozingo and Ruth T. McVey in Tang Tsou, ed., *China in Crisis* (Chicago, 1968), vol. II.

the state from either camp in the international Communist movement. Only after the fall of Aidit and the destruction of his organization were pro-Chinese refugees from the PKI to recognize the "state with two aspects" as the quintessential manifestation of the PKI's revisionism and ideological degeneration in the period of the Aidit leadership.[124]

In summary, the PKI between 1959 and 1965 carefully studied and probed each of the significant repositories of power under the Guided Democracy system in order to assess its political potential. Initially, the party sought to combine the tactics of allying itself closely with the president, preserving as much as possible of the parliamentary edifice, and chipping away at the authoritarian institutions least responsive to its influence or pressures (especially the army and the state bureaucracy). In other words, it was still trying to reconcile the strategy of the fifties with the political realities of the sixties.

By 1963, however, the party had come to comprehend the political system in terms of two political blocs, one clustered around the president and one around the army. The other constituents of the system (party factions, mass organizations, bureaucrats, etc.) were perceived as divided in their allegiance. The power strategy of the PKI from that time onward turned on augmenting the strength of the presidential bloc, and enhancing Communist influence within it, and weakening the army bloc.

In theoretical terms, the two-bloc concept was assimilated to a highly modified version of the united national front strategy originally elaborated in depth at the 1954 congress. Whereas the decisions of that congress had conceived of the front at least notionally in class terms, the theory of the state with two aspects unmistakably, and with few residual concessions to class theory, conceived of it in terms of a political alliance between the PKI and the Sukarnoist wing of the national elite. While the party still spoke of this alliance as amounting in effect to a partnership between the workers and peasants (represented by the PKI) and the national bourgeoisie (represented by Sukarno and his loyalists), the impact of this formulation was heavily undercut by the substitution of an alliance concept centered on top-level negotiation and agreement for one which had laid the most important

[124] See *Indonesian Tribune* (Tirana), vol. I, no. 1 (Nov. 1966).

stress on mass struggle as the means by which the united national front would be forged.

A consequence of the new theory was that the problem of proletarian or Communist hegemony of the front was further than ever from being solved. The PKI was agreeing to accept the state leadership of President Sukarno and a position of parity for the national bourgeoisie. Transition to national democracy was to take place peacefully, without that smashing of the existing state which had hitherto been a fundamental requisite of the Marxist-Leninist concept of revolution. All that could be inferred from the theory so far as future Communist leadership was concerned was that it would emerge by gradual accretion.

In point of fact, however, the PKI leaders were not quite as modest in their aims or expectations as this analysis would imply. They realized that more than deference and negotiation would be necessary to persuade the "progressive" wing of the elite to admit them to an equal share in governmental power. Pressure from the party's mass membership and organizations would also be required, and the years 1964–65 were to witness a variety of tactics by the Communists to apply that pressure, notably an "encircling of the cities by the countryside" in the form of a PKI-led land reform campaign.

But this is to anticipate. So far we have examined only those features of PKI ideology and practice that related directly to the state political system. It is necessary to trace the evolution of its theories and activities in wider spheres in order to grasp the whole skein of the strategy that was to reach its culmination in 1965. The next step in this project is to examine how the party's analysis of Indonesian society and its potential for socialist transformation evolved in unison with its delineation of the political superstructure.

3. The Social Order and Its Transformation

In the Marxian schema, socio-economic class is the basic determinant of political behavior and class struggle the means by which human actors realize the potentialities for revolutionary change inherent in the productive system underpinning their social relationships. The leaders of Indonesian Communism, faithful to this doctrinal heritage, sought to comprehend the political process and devise a strategy for transforming it in accordance with their revolutionary aspirations within the framework of a class analysis founded upon categories well established in Communist theory. Increasingly, however, they found it difficult to define their situation or model their strategy in terms of a strictly class categorization, and especially one originally extrapolated from the dynamics of industrialized countries.

The class schema was too much a part of their ideological inheritance, too great a symbol of their hegemonic aspirations, for PKI leaders to think of abandoning or supplanting it altogether; but as their political prospects advanced and the responsibilities of decision-making assumed greater importance they became more conscious of the need to adapt the abstract criteria derived from foreign texts and declarations more closely to the social and cultural conditions they faced.[1]

In the course of time, PKI political practice diverged more and more from the doctrinal terms in which it was cast, and in turn the patterns of practice were assimilated to an "Indonesianized" version of Marxism-Leninism. In this way the myths of dogma were displaced

[1] The PKI was not alone of course in finding class conceptualization inadequate for its purposes. In fact a striking feature of revolutionary doctrine in our time has been its departure from the "deterministic" aspects of Marxism. See the discussion of this question in Hélène Carrère d'Encausse and Stuart Schramm, *Marxism and Asia* (London, 1969), especially pp. 108–12.

in order to take account of perceived political necessity, but without creating a clear and unambiguous break with received doctrine. On the other hand, the residues of doctrinal conformity continued to operate in some areas to impede empirical analysis and the adoption of appropriate lines of action, particularly in cases where the party leadership came up against problems they had not yet managed to interpret satisfactorily.

Overall, the evolution of PKI social doctrine took the form of downgrading class in favor of other cleavage patterns, all of which tended to pose conflict in nationalist terms and so facilitated the orientation of the party toward a strategy hinged on an alliance with Sukarno and those who followed him in regarding Indonesia's national concerns and anti-imperialist stance as of overriding importance. The party's social theory, in other words, worked in harmony with other aspects of its ideology to advance the course that the leaders saw as the only one capable of preserving it and guiding it to power.

THE APPLICATION OF MARXIAN CLASS THEORY

The first comprehensive PKI attempt to formulate a class analysis of Indonesian society was made by Aidit in 1957, in a document used as a training manual for party cadres.[2] This therefore offers an appropriate starting point for an examination of the social theory of the PKI and its evolution during the period under study.

In the manual, Indonesia is depicted as having passed through several of the stages of historical development generally treated as universal in Communist historiography of the time—from primitive Communism through slavery to feudalism. The transition to each phase was marked by changes in the means of production that rendered the established social structure obsolete and generated a revolutionary transformation in it. The latter two stages were accompanied by sharp class struggles between slave and slave owner, peasant and feudal landlord.[3]

Colonial domination disrupted the "normal" evolution and transformation of feudal society, stifling developments toward capitalism, superimposing Dutch oppression upon feudal exploitation, and stimu-

---

[2] "Indonesian Society and the Indonesian Revolution," *Problems*, pp. 5–61.
[3] *Ibid.*, pp. 12–13; cf. *The Indonesian Revolution*, pp. 2–3.

lating more intense resistence by the peasantry. By introducing a money economy, the Dutch undermined the closed feudal system, but feudal exploitation remained and became interwoven with the exploitation of foreign capital, compradores, and moneylenders.[4] The resulting amalgam was described by Aidit as "a semicolonial, semifeudal society." The independence revolution had as it principal task the elimination of colonial and feudal domination, but owing to the treachery of the compradore capitalists in signing a capitulatory treaty with the Dutch in 1949, these goals were not realized and the country remained trapped in the socio-economic stage arrived at in the late colonial period.[5]

The early struggles against the Dutch were led by feudal nobles, but in the twentieth century new forms of anticolonial struggle developed as a result of the emergence of the working class and the national bourgeoisie under the stimulus of Dutch imperialist methods of exploitation. Both these newly formed classes had an interest in ridding the country of imperialist oppression, but their aspirations for the future differed, the national bourgeoisie wanting to create an indigenous capitalist system and the working class, under the leadership of the Communist Party, to advance towards socialism.[6]

The PKI took the lead in the anticolonial struggle in the 1920's, being the first to raise the standard of revolt against Dutch colonialism; owing to the party's weakness and mistakes, however, the uprising of 1926–27 failed and the national bourgeoisie thereafter assumed the leading role.[7] Again during the armed struggle between 1945 and 1948 the PKI had the opportunity to win the leadership of the revolution, but once more its inexperience and failings robbed it of its chance.[8]

The defeat of the social "program" of the national revolution, by denying the aspirations both of the working class and the national bourgeoisie, provided the basis for their alliance in the postindependence period. Each class had an objective interest in eliminating survivals of colonialism and feudalism, but because of their disparate

[4] *Problems,* pp. 23–33; *The Indonesian Revolution,* pp. 3–4.
[5] *Problems,* p. 43.
[6] *Ibid.,* pp. 39–41.
[7] *Ibid.,* pp. 41–42, 68–72.
[8] *Ibid.,* pp. 79–90; *The Indonesian Revolution,* pp. 6–7.

aspirations a struggle was bound to take place between them for hegemony of the revolutionary forces. With correct tactics by the party, this struggle need not undermine cooperation between the working class and the national bourgeoisie; the essential thing was for the working class to represent the interests of the entire nation, confine itself to national democratic (not socialist) tasks, and defend the legitimate interests of the national bourgeoisie against imperialism and feudalism.

The PKI held that the ongoing revolution must end in the victory of the "progressive" forces favoring socialism. The October Revolution in Russia had marked the onset of the general crisis of capitalism-imperialism and the era of socialist revolution, and thereafter there was no room for precapitalist countries to take the path of capitalist development. The revolution in Indonesia was objectively part of the worldwide socialist revolution leading by way of national democracy to socialism.[9] In political terms, the road to capitalism was blocked to the national bourgeoisie by both the imperialists and the working class. The former, by reason of their domination of basic Indonesian resources and the world market, prevented the national bourgeoisie from developing into a fully-fledged capitalist class; the latter, because of its organized strength and determination to achieve a socialist society, compelled the national bourgeoisie to accept its blueprint for the future.[10]

Aidit distinguished six main strata in Indonesian society: the feudal landlords, the compradore capitalists, the national bourgeoisie, the urban petty bourgeoisie, the peasantry, and the proletariat.[11] The attitudes of each class "are completely determined by their economic and social position." The upper strata of the bourgeois and landlord classes "are the classes that govern."[12] Both classes represented inveterate enemies of the national democratic revolution and hence were

---

[9] *Problems,* p. 58; *The Indonesian Revolution,* pp. 14–15.

[10] *The Indonesian Revolution,* pp. 16–17.

[11] He also mentioned "the loiterers and vagrants" (including "thieves, robbers, gangsters, beggars, prostitutes") who were waverers and might be either bought up by the reactionaries or, in some cases, brought into the revolution; in the latter case, "they become the ideological source of roaming destructive elements and of anarchism." *Problems,* pp. 56–57.

[12] *Ibid.,* p. 50.

"targets" of that revolution, excluded from the united national front and destined to be destroyed as social classes.

The national bourgeoisie—the smaller industrialists and other entrepreneurs—exhibited a "dual character," which determined its role in the national revolution:

As a class that is also suppressed by imperialism and whose development is also stifled by feudalism, this class is anti-imperialist and anti-feudal, and in this respect it is one of the revolutionary forces. But on the other hand, this class does not have the courage fundamentally to fight imperialism and feudalism because economically and politically it is weak and it has class ties with imperialism and feudalism.[13]

Enlarging in 1959 on the weakness of the national bourgeoisie, Aidit stressed that it was predominantly a commercial bourgeoisie; even in this sphere its position was weak, but "even more striking is their weakness in the sphere of industry." While this weakness and dependence upon a commercial market dominated by the imperialists caused the national bourgeoisie to vacillate and show political cowardice, "on the other hand the weak economic position of the national bourgeoisie does not provide a strong material basis for sharp contradictions between the national bourgeoisie and the working class in general," and as a class it could fairly easily be won to the side of the proletariat. At the same time, Aidit acknowledged to some extent that the strength of the national bourgeoisie did not lie wholly in its economic basis: it exerts "a significant ideological and political influence among the intellectuals and within the state apparatus."[14] Lukman developed this aspect somewhat more strongly in an article written in the following year; the strength of the national bourgeoisie, he stated, lay not in numbers or the power of its organizations but in its political and ideological influence throughout the society.[15]

The petty bourgeoisie other than the peasantry—that is, "the urban poor, the intellectuals, the small traders, the independent workers and so on"—was classified as "a reliable ally of the proletariat" because its members "also suffer from the oppression of imperialism, feudalism and the big bourgeoisie and are every day pressed further

[13] *Ibid.,* pp. 51–52.
[14] *Ibid.,* pp. 317–18.
[15] M. H. Lukman, *Tentang Front Persatuan Nasional* (Concerning the United National Front) (Djakarta, 1960), p. 19.

towards bankruptcy and ruin." The petty bourgeoisie could only achieve its emancipation at the hands of the proletariat.[16]

The peasantry, being the biggest class and the one upon whose alliance with the proletariat both Lenin and Mao had placed great strategic importance, occupied a place of very special significance in the policies of the PKI. In his training manual Aidit described its role in these terms:

The peasants are basically divided into the rich peasants, the middle peasants and the poor peasants. There are indeed some persons among the rich peasants that lease out a part of their land, carry out money lending and brutally exploit the peasant-labourers, and they are by nature semi-feudal, but besides this, they themselves generally participate in labour, and in this sense they make up a part of the peasantry. Their productive activities will continue to be utilised for a certain period to come, and they can also help the struggle against imperialism. They can adopt an attitude of neutrality in the revolutionary struggle against the landlords. That is why we cannot consider them as part of the landlords.

The middle peasants are independent economically, they generally do not exploit others, and do not earn interest on money, on the contrary, they suffer from the exploitation of the imperialists, the landlords, and the bourgeoisie. Some of them do not own sufficient land for them to work it themselves. The middle peasants can not only become part of the anti-imperialist revolution and the agrarian revolution, but they can also accept Socialism. This is why they are one of the important forces pushing the revolution forward and are a reliable ally of the proletariat. Their attitude towards the revolution is a decisive factor for victory or defeat, because the middle peasants comprise the majority in the country-side after the agrarian revolution.

The poor peasants together with the agricultural labourers comprise the majority in the villages in our country, prior to the agrarian revolution. The poor peasants do not have any land or do not have sufficient for them to work it themselves, they are the village semi-proletariat, they are the largest force pushing the revolution forward and it is natural for them to be the most reliable of the allies of the proletariat and a basic part of the forces of the Indonesian revolution.[17]

[16] *Problems*, p. 52. Hindley's comment (pp. 42–43) is pertinent: "The groups that comprise the petty bourgeoisie as defined by Aidit vary greatly in social status and in political behavior. To put the Indonesian urban poor and fishermen in the same category as the high-status and wealthy doctors and lawyers is almost ludicrous."

[17] *Problems*, pp. 53–54.

However the peasants too "can only attain their emancipation under the leadership of the proletariat."[18]

Finally, the proletariat, the key social class in revolutionary transformation, was analyzed in these terms:

> The Indonesian proletariat consists of about 500,000 workers in modern industry (transport workers, factory-workers, repair-shop workers, mine-workers, etc.). The workers in small industry and the handicrafts in the towns number more than 2,000,000. The agricultural and forestry proletariat and other groups of workers make up a very large number. All this amounts to about 6,000,000 or, together with their families, some 20,000,000, which is about 25 per cent of the entire population of Indonesia. . . .
>
> As is also the case in other countries, the Indonesian proletariat has very fine qualities. Their work makes them unite in the most advanced economic forms, it gives them a strong understanding of organisation and discipline, and because they do not own any means of production, they are not individualistic by nature and apart from this, since the Indonesian proletariat is exploited by three forms of brutal exploitation, that is, imperialism, capitalism and feudalism, they become more firm and thorough-going in the revolutionary struggle than the other classes. Since Indonesia is not fertile soil for social-reformism, as is the case in Europe, the proletariat in its entirety is very revolutionary indeed.[19]

Aidit recognized that the Indonesian proletariat "contains within it some unavoidable weaknesses, such as its smallness in numbers in comparison with the peasants, its young age by comparison with the proletariat in capitalist countries, and the low level of its culture by comparison with the bourgeoisie," but, nevertheless, "the Indonesian revolution will not succeed unless it is under the leadership of the Indonesian proletariat."[20]

The major doctrinal sources of Aidit's social analysis are not difficult to trace. His dissertation upon Indonesian historical development was a transposition of the universalist theses contained in Stalin's short work, *Dialectical and Historical Materialism,*[21] the most popular

---

[18] *Ibid.,* p. 54.

[19] *Ibid.,* pp. 54–55.

[20] *Ibid.,* p. 55.

[21] Originally published in *The Short History of the Communist Party of the Soviet Union (Bolsheviks)* in 1936, the essay on Marxist philosophy was subsequently reproduced many times in pamphlet form.

and most highly simplified exposition of Marxian historical theory used in Communist education programs from the time of its appearance until after the Soviet leader's fall from grace.

Whatever its relevance to the Western European societies from which Marx drew his analysis, the theory, especially in the form in which Stalin cast it, fitted poorly with conditions of social development in Indonesia. The very approach adopted by Aidit of treating the historical past of Indonesia as an entity, with uniform features, was itself anomalous, and the stages of development that he outlined cannot be accommodated to what is known of the early history of Indonesian societies.[22] Of greatest significance for Aidit's political strategy, the notion of a feudal society existing prior to colonial occupation and characterized by class warfare between landlords and peasants is denied by historical scholarship. In Java, for instance, the social structure was much more akin to Weber's patrimonial model than to the Western European feudal one, the relations between rulers and ruled being characteristic of a political-bureaucratic authority structure rather than a landholder-serf one. Differentials of land ownership at the village level were generally of a low order and of relatively minor social significance.[23]

In devising a framework for analyzing contemporary Indonesian social structure, as shaped largely by the colonial experience, Aidit drew heavily upon a basic work written by Mao Tse-tung in 1939, "The Chinese Revolution and the Chinese Communist Party."[24] In fact many passages in Aidit's manual were taken almost word for word from Mao's article. Superficially, there was a good deal in common between the circumstances of China and Indonesia, and consequently Aidit's account carried conviction beyond the ranks of the PKI. In a number of respects crucial for Aidit's political strategy, however, the Indonesian case was significantly different from the Chinese.

In comparison with China, class formations were less pronounced and consequently operated less as determinants of political behavior and action. This applied particularly to the working class and the

[22] The general body of knowledge on the early history of the Indonesian archipelago is set out in B. H. M. Vlekke, *Nusantara* (The Hague, 1965), Chapter 1.

[23] See Rex Mortimer, "Class Social Cleavage and Indonesian Communism," *Indonesia,* no. 8 (Oct. 1969), 1–2.

[24] *Selected Works of Mao Tse-tung* (London, 1954), III, 72–101.

peasantry; the former was, indeed, as Aidit conceded, young and inexperienced (even by comparison with China), while the latter constituted the vast bulk of a relatively undifferentiated rural population among whom large landownership was highly exceptional. In Java, particularly, acute land shortage rather than its unequal distribution defined the peasants' predicament. Again, where in China the greater part of the population was ethnically and culturally homogeneous, in Indonesia socio-cultural cleavages related to and reinforced by ethnic and religious differences were all-pervasive and potent, cutting across incipient class solidarities and affecting the political process in a decisive manner.[25]

Aidit's figure of 500,000 for the number of workers in large or medium scale enterprises in 1957 agrees with estimates arrived at from official figures, although there was probably some decline in the number during the Guided Democracy period.[26] But in adding on a further four million "agricultural and forestry proletariat and other groups of workers" Aidit undoubtedly exaggerated the total; in 1959, SOBSI made the more realistic claim that the Indonesian workers, from all sources, constituted with their families ten per cent of the Indonesian population, as against Aidit's twenty-five per cent.[27]

Estimates of the degree of unionization vary widely owing to the absence of reliable figures, the tendency of Indonesian workers to join more than one union and to change their union allegiance rather frequently, and the exaggerated claims made by the different union federations. By the late fifties SOBSI was claiming a membership of three and a half million, a figure which it adhered to thereafter. Outside observers have challenged this claim, but most agree that the communist federation contained between fifty and sixty per cent of all union members.[28] Despite the moderation of SOBSI policies, its member unions were considerably more active on their workers' behalf than were their competitors, many of which were either little more than company affairs or primarily religious associations.[29]

[25] Mortimer.

[26] Douglas Paauw, "From Colonial to Guided Economy," in McVey, ed., *Indonesia*, pp. 178–79.

[27] Quoted in Hindley, p. 315, n. 2.

[28] *Ibid.*, pp. 135–36.

[29] See Lance Castles, *Religion, Politics and Economic Behavior in Java: The*

The Indonesian working class, consisting largely of "peasants in overalls," had not acquired a solidarity consciousness and a sense of its own specific economic and political interests as a class sufficient to enable the Communists or any other political agency to base itself on the proletariat as a self-acting and self-orienting force. PKI strategy, whatever its formal cast, took full account of this fact, and the party after 1951 largely confined its work among the unionists under its leadership to campaigns that would not tax their political loyalty too far by involving them in serious clashes with the authorities.

The peasants were even less of a force to count on for the promotion of class-based policies. Generally, as we have said, large landlordism was the exception rather than the rule in the countryside, and in many places the persistence of communal village customs combined with traditional values stressing social harmony and deference to authority to inhibit militant solidarity among the peasant poor.[30] It will be recalled that at the 1954 party congress, Aidit acknowledged the absence of Communist organization in the countryside; while this weakness was remedied to a considerable extent during the fifties, PKI allegiance among the peasantry was won largely on the basis of the party's welfare work and its political moderation and tended to rest on the prestige of wealthier village strata attracted to the party by its championship of *abangan* values or its modernist image. Only among the squatters on government and foreign estate lands did the PKI obtain a militant following in the wake of official efforts to remove the interlopers.

Social restlessness and dissatisfaction there was in the postindependence period, largely as a product of the high expectations aroused in the course of the national struggle and of the breakdown of traditional forms of social integration; but this dissatisfaction was mobilized by political parties and their mass organizations not along class lines but in conformity with ethnic, religious, and cultural lines of cleavage. The political elites themselves competed with one another in terms that owed a good deal to the cleavage factors operating in the society at large, something to differences in political style, and something again to divergent interests. The nature of the dominant interest

Kudus Cigarette Industry (Cultural Reports Series no. 15, South East Asia Studies, Yale University, 1968), pp. 81–84.

[30] Mortimer, pp. 5–6.

conflict, however, expressed in the struggle for power between the Masjumi, with its following among the *santri* businessmen and Outer Islands export producers, and the PNI, based to a considerable extent on the Javanese civil bureaucracy, coincided with, rather than cut across, more traditional cleavages and so reinforced the character of the contest as a value confrontation.

In this contest, the PKI occupied a somewhat anomalous position. On the one hand, it sought to mobilize the working class and peasantry behind it and to utilize class factors to strengthen its bargaining power; but on the other hand, it recognized its inability to command sufficient commitment along these lines to stand up against the combined hostility of the civilian political elites and the army, neither of which was disposed to tolerate activities that they saw as threatening social stability and their own political supremacy. Lacking a sufficient concentration of power to tackle economic problems or social reorganization effectively, the governments of the fifties foundered in deadlock between the values and interests of antagonistic elite groups. The PKI, by deciding to seek a political alliance with the PNI and to construct the biggest political apparatus it could muster from as wide a spectrum of the population as possible, was obliged to downgrade class appeals and utilize the dominant cleavages affecting the political process to advance its position. Increasingly, it emphasized radical nationalism as a political vehicle that appealed to its own supporters and the PNI and structured situations so as to place its pro-Western opponents at the greatest disadvantage in the political struggle.

At the same time it was important for the PKI to keep alive and nourish a sense of radicalism and of ideological and organizational distinctness among its members and followers, in preparation for the time when it would have to press the political elite harder for a greater share in power. The inculcation of class consciousness played some part in sustaining this distinct identity, but since class agitation and struggle were virtually ruled out the party had to rely mainly on educational techniques. The PKI had considerable success in securing identification with its goals and policies through its educational work, although the results always lagged a good way behind objectives.[31] It is doubtful that there was any great rise in class consciousness, however, considering the nature of the party's policies and the

[31] Hindley, pp. 76, 81–82, 89, 94–95, 99.

absence of any pronounced experiential factors promoting a shift in value orientations.

Thus, while Aidit in his 1957 manual described socio-economic class as virtually the sole determinant of political behavior, this claim was not only at odds with the observable facts about Indonesian society but also conflicted with the political practice the PKI was following even by 1954. By then, as the report of the fifth congress indicates, policy declarations had already begun to deviate from a strictly class-determined base, and in 1957 only the abstract formulations characteristic of the manual retained a doctrinal purity. The gap between theory and practice was too pronounced to continue indefinitely, and indeed before long the Communist leaders had moved to bring the two closer into line by modifying the theory.

THE DILUTION OF CLASS IN PKI IDEOLOGY

By the time of the 1954 congress, as has been noted, the notion of class in the united national front had begun to bear a stronger relationship to political outlook than to socio-economic position. If a political grouping acted in accordance with the prescriptions laid down in the united front program, then it was assimilated to the class to which these characteristics notionally belonged. So, instead of attitudes being determined by class, the opposite was the case—class was determined by political attitude. This transposition was maintained and intensified in succeeding years.

Following well-established Communist precedent, the party itself was identified with the workers and peasants, and particularly the proletariat. Thus, in one of his 1963 lectures in China Aidit made this easy transposition: "Since the Indonesian revolution is a new type of bourgeois democratic revolution, it is the historic task of the *proletariat* to contend for its leadership. . . . In other words, to win the leading position in the revolution, the *Party* must fulfill the following conditions."[32]

This identification of the party with class, a common Communist tendency that Trotsky dubbed "substitutism,"[33] in the PKI's case obscured the fact that its all-important cadre composition was anything

[32] *The Indonesian Revolution*, p. 15 (emphasis added).
[33] See Isaac Deutscher, *The Prophet Armed, Trotsky: 1879–1921* (London, 1954), especially at pp. 89–97.

but proletarian. Its leading cadres were drawn predominantly from the urban lower intelligentsia, and, according to a report to the party's seventh congress in April 1962, 28 per cent of the congress delegates were from the working class while 72 per cent were from the petty bourgeoisie including the peasantry. Since the PKI was prone to interpret the term "working class" very generously in this kind of context, it is highly probable that the real proportions were a good deal less favorable to its proletarian image. Further, the information in the report concerning educational qualifications suggests that the petty bourgeois majority was predominantly nonpeasant: of the delegates present, 68 per cent had been educated to secondary school level or beyond.[34] Since few poor peasants would have received such schooling, the petty bourgeois delegates must have been overwhelmingly urban or higher status villagers. Consequently, the "proletarian" features of the PKI were more an act of conscious ideological representation than a matter of direct working class influence on the party's policies.

Substitutism of another kind found explicit expression by the mid-sixties in the adoption of a Maoist identification of the peasantry with "proletarian" qualities no longer considered to reside in the actual proletariat of many countries. In part this ideological transition was induced by the PKI's decision to concentrate on the peasants in its search for a militant base of strength, in part it flowed from the party's estrangement from the European Communist countries (with the exception of Albania) and the Communist parties of most industrialized countries after 1963. A graphic illustration of the new trend is a speech by Aidit to a PKI New Year reception in early January 1964, in which he said:

We Indonesian Communists must cast far away the ideas of dogmatists and revisionists who think that there cannot possibly be a good Communist party if it is not based on a strong proletariat. There are many experiences in the world, and also in Indonesia, which show that the peasantry plus Marxism-Leninism can constitute a strong proletarian force. But there is also much experience in the world that the proletariat plus social democracy and the proletariat plus revisionism constitute a bourgeois force which is also strong.[35]

[34] *Madju Terus,* p. 168.
[35] *Harian Rakjat,* Jan. 6, 1964.

The contradiction between class as an objective category and as a subjective or ideological category is inherent in the structure of Marxism, inasmuch as it is at the same time both an analytical and an activist creed. Marx the bourgeois intellectual saw himself as epitomizing the will of the proletariat; Lenin went a step further by insisting that only a tightly organized band of professional revolutionaries drawn from the intelligentsia could carry socialist ideas to the working class and interpret its aspirations; Mao, and now Aidit, completed the disassociative exercise by substituting the peasantry for the proletariat as the mass recipients of the revolutionary legacy.

In relation to other groups and strata, too, the PKI came to be influenced more in its characterizations by political and ideological criteria than by socio-economic position. From the time of the 1954 congress, and even before, the PNI (or, on occasions, its "progressive" elements) was equated with the national bourgeoisie, and during the Guided Democracy period this identification was extended to all those among the political elite who followed policies more or less in accordance with President Sukarno's guidelines.[36] Usually the attribution to the PNI was implicit rather than openly stated, but there were occasions when it was made explicit, as when Lukman referred to the PNI as "the main representative of the national bourgeoisie."[37]

In this case, the assimilation of political role to class basis was strikingly at odds with socio-economic reality. The PNI, as has been observed, had its significant social base among the Javanese bureaucracy, which by tradition and the logic of its role was not attracted to entrepreneurial activity or values. Some entrepreneurs did support the PNI, particularly Javanese ex-politicians and ex-bureaucrats who had established themselves in importing and other forms of business by obtaining generous protection and government credits, especially in the constitutional period. In addition, a considerable portion of the Chinese merchant and manufacturing class looked for protection to the PNI, seeing it as less likely than any other of the established non-Communist parties to be swayed by anti-Chinese passions. But neither

[36] Here, as elsewhere, the PKI was merely echoing common Communist practice. As Ruth McVey has pointed out, "Communists almost invariably identified the national bourgeoisie with the non-Communist nationalist movement" (*The Soviet View of the Indonesian Revolution,* p. 26).

[37] *World Marxist Review,* vol. II, no. 8 (Aug. 1959).

of these groups was a major determinant of PNI policies; their position was rather one of dependence upon politico-bureaucratic patronage. After the introduction of Guided Democracy, with its nationalization of Dutch, and later British and American, firms and the extension of state controls over the economy, the position of entrepreneurial groups vis-a-vis the political and bureaucratic apparatus weakened considerably.[38]

Since the PKI's strategy largely hinged on the dynamics of radical nationalism, the use of a political determinant of class in this instance accorded with its requirements. The "national bourgeoisie" so defined did "create" a national economy by means of the confiscation of foreign enterprises. On the other hand, as a congeries of groups concerned to exercise political power, with its attendant perquisites, rather than a class with an entrepreneurial urge, the PNI and the Sukarno circle showed little interest in the development of this economic base but viewed it rather as a complex of appanages to be managed in such a way as to promote the interests of particular factional groupings. If the PKI had really assumed that this national bourgeoisie would stimulate economic development in its own interest, then it was doomed to disappointment.

One by-product of equating the PNI with the bourgeoisie manifested itself in relation to the "antifeudal" program of the PKI. Aidit had argued in 1954 that the national bourgeoisie had an interest in undermining feudal exploitation in order to liberate the peasants from penury and so create a market for its own manufactured products and trade. This was an instance of drawing a straight line from presumed economic interest to political response. By 1959, however, he felt compelled, by the experience of clashes between peasant squatters and the government and the latter's failure to introduce land reform, to revise his estimate. Speaking to the party's sixth congress, he declared that "the national bourgeoisie, and even the advanced elements among them, are in general evading the revolutionary way of transforming landlord ownership of the land into direct ownership by the

[38] See Feith, "Dynamics," pp. 373–75, 395–400. For a penetrating analysis of the relations between bureaucracy and enterprise in underdeveloped economies that is highly relevant to Indonesia, especially in the Guided Democracy period, see Fred W. Riggs, *The Ecology of Public Administration* (Bombay, 1961).

peasants who till it." He attributed this unsympathetic attitude toward peasant aspirations to the fact that "the bourgeoisie is still closely connected with the survivals of feudalism."[39]

In any semideveloped economy, entrepreneurs are likely to be connected with landed interests by family and social ties, and often to own land themselves, and any absolute distinction of interest between the two classes is therefore bound to be a considerable oversimplification. But the significant fact overlooked in Aidit's analysis was that, irrespective of economic interest, large segments of the PNI had a *political* interest in the rural status quo since they depended on bureaucratic and traditional networks in the villages to deliver peasant acquiescence (in the fifties in the form of votes, under Guided Democracy in more passive forms of allegiance). Put another way, most PNI leaders had no desire to present the PKI with a stronger mass base that it could use to undermine their social and political privileges.

It is unlikely that PKI leaders were unaware of the true causes of their problems with their allies over land reform, especially after the bitter furore in the PNI aroused by Communist election gains in Java in 1957, but they were unable to assimilate their knowledge into their ideology without doing too much violence to the class schema to which they were devoted and raising awkward questions about the real character of their allies.

To complete the class spectrum of the united front concept, the PKI equated its hated and feared political opponents, the Masjumi and the PSI, with the "compradore bourgeoisie." Here again, the attribution had a political foundation in that both parties were pro-Western and anti-Communist. But it lacked any convincing socio-economic basis. The PSI was a small cadre party based primarily upon the Western-educated intelligentsia. The Masjumi was a more heterogeneous party; it was strongly supported by the national businessmen (other than those of Chinese origin) and the Outer Islands exporting interests, and in addition it was *the* established party in several ethnic regions, being in some ways the social equivalent there

[39] *Problems,* p. 311. After the failure of the government to implement the 1960 land reform laws to PKI satisfaction, Aidit again referred to the national bourgeoisie's opposition to land reform, saying that the "national bourgeoisie is still young and has many family ties with the landlords. One of its legs is capitalist while the other is feudal;" see *Set Afire the Banteng Spirit! Ever Forward, No Retreat!* (Peking, 1964), p. 22.

of the PNI in East and Central Java. If any party could be described as representative of the national bourgeoisie, it was Masjumi, and the political history of the first years after independence in Indonesia is to some extent the history of the defeat of the ambitions of this class in its struggle with the bureaucratic gentry of Java.

In the Guided Democracy period, with the political eclipse of Masjumi and the PSI, the compradore bourgeoisie all but disappeared from PKI speeches and writings, the term only occasionally appearing as a euphemism for PSI advisers sheltered by political and military officials. Its place as the major internal enemy of the Indonesian people was taken by the bureaucratic capitalists, a grouping whose title better fitted its socio-economic role. But even here the term as used by PKI leaders was not limited to its socio-economic connotations; sometimes it referred to the army officer group, sometimes to all anti-Communist officials, and only occasionally was it strictly confined to state enterprise managers.

Another way in which the emphasis on political criteria of demarcation became embodied in PKI doctrine was through the adoption of a Maoist formula that divided actors into left, middle, and right (or diehard) forces.[40] The PKI took over this categorization in the latter fifties and employed it commonly thereafter. The "left" forces comprised the PKI detachments and its stauncher allies within the political elite (or, in class terms, the workers, peasants, and the "progressive" sections of the national bourgeoisie); the middle forces referred to the "waverers" among the people in power, those who identified themselves with the Sukarno regime but showed reservations about cooperation with the PKI (in class terms, the national bourgeoisie other than its progressive section); and the right or "diehards" consisted of all those opposed to the PKI (the compradore bourgeoisie, the bureaucratic capitalists, landlords, etc.). In accordance with Mao's tactical formulation, the PKI's task was conceived as one of consolidating the left forces, winning over the middle forces, and isolating the diehard forces.

The dichotomy of left, middle, and diehard forces was so flexible that it could be given almost any meaning required in a specific political context. Although it was sometimes assimilated to a class spec-

[40] See, for example, Mao Tse-tung, *Selected Works,* III, 194–203.

trum, this spectrum was itself predicated upon a definition of class by political outlook.[41] Beyond this, however, the formula was capable of being further subdivided along the same lines. Thus, while the political complex as a whole was divided into left, middle, and diehard forces, the same division could be applied to any constituent force within it. This was done especially with regard to the middle forces, so that we find that there were left, middle, and diehard sections of the middle forces! The resulting panorama may have been a more accurate reflection of the complexity of political attitudes found in society, but it left little room for the operation of class analysis.

Inevitably, the PKI had to concern itself with the relationship between class and *aliran,* or cultural-cum-ideological stream. Lukman tackled the problem frontally in 1960 by arguing that the united front essentially took the form of an alliance between the three main ideological streams: nationalism, Islam, and Communism. In this way he assimilated Sukarno's concept of the unity of these three, first enunciated in 1926, to the united national front strategy. But Lukman argued that nevertheless the alliance expressed a class content which would in the course of time come to have greater weight: "Attachment to *aliran* does not make it any the less true that finally the identity of material interests of the masses forms a connection that is stronger than the connection according to political *aliran.*"[42] At about the same time, Aidit expressed much the same view, but with rather less qualification:

We must wave on high the banner of the national front, because only in this way can we concentrate national strength as widely as possible. And waving high the banner of the national front must mean especially supporting the cooperation of the Islamic, nationalist, and Communist political *aliran,* as well as arousing the peasants, the largest group in our country, to take part in the political struggle.[43]

Four years later Aidit expressed the *aliran* concept of national unity even more unambiguously:

Based on the traditions of the national independence struggle in Indo-

[41] See, for example, *Problems,* pp. 314–27.
[42] *Tentang Front Persatuan Nasional,* pp. 34–35.
[43] "Untuk Pelaksanaan Jang Lebih Konsekwen dari Manifesto Politik," *Bintang Merah,* XVI (July–Aug. 1960), 308.

nesia, there exist three political streams that opposed Dutch imperialism
—that is, the nationalist political stream, the religious political stream,
especially that of Islam, and the Communist political stream. For that
reason it is natural to say that national unity in Indonesia can be said to
exist if these three political streams are united in political cooperation.[44]

The acknowledgement and forecast contained in Lukman's 1960
presentation was not followed up. He had obviously envisaged the
alliance based on *aliran* as a temporary expedient forced on the PKI
by the weakness of class factors in Indonesian society; in the course of
time, he intimated, class as a determinant of political action would
gain in weight and so come to exercise the major influence on party
strategy. In this light, the analytical stress on class in PKI material
could be taken as being *projective* rather than *actual*. How precisely
the Communist leadership saw their situation in these terms is, however, unclear. Certainly no answers were given to the questions raised
by Lukman's statement: over what period of time could class be expected to replace *aliran* as the basis of political behavior? Could the
conscious acts of the party assist the formation of class consciousness
without transgressing the bounds of the national front alliance? Was
it feasible for the party to think in terms of achieving state power before class factors had acquired predominant weight in the political
process? On the practical plane, the PKI's answers were what we
might expect from any aspirant group of political leaders, namely a
determination to use every opportunity to advance their claims to
power by the shortest possible road.

The centrality of radical nationalism in the party's political work,
especially after 1960, encouraged a tendency to conceive the political
struggle more and more within the framework of a polarity between
the *rakjat,* the people, on the one hand, and foreign-paid or -inspired
enemies on the other. As Aidit expressed the position, "The form of
the class struggle in Indonesia at the present time . . . is a struggle
of all the Indonesian people who are revolutionary against imperialism
(monopoly capitalism) and feudal remnants."[45] The same attachment
to a mystique of national "oneness" had been present earlier in
Aidit's description, in his 1957 manual, of the historical evolution
of Indonesian society, in which he conceived of "the ancestors of the

---

[44] *Revolusi Indonesia, Latarbelakang, Sedjarah dan Haridepannja,* p. 72.
[45] *Harian Rakjat,* Aug. 20, 1964.

Indonesian nation" as having originated "from one stock," "become dispersed for a time, but in the struggle for national independence and a new Indonesia . . . become reunited."[46]

Based on this dichotomy, all who supported the government's foreign policies and the Nasakom concept formed part of the people; all who opposed them were enemies of the people. Just as the Masjumi and the PSI were identified with foreign interests, so too were the landlords frequently labeled "unpatriotic" and the bureaucratic capitalists accused of acting on behalf of imperialist masters. All reactionaries were said to be conscious or unconscious tools of foreign powers. This frame, which all but eliminated class from consideration, had two notable precedents. It had, in the first place, very close resemblances to Sukarno's *marhaenist* concept, although retaining vestigial deference to class distinctions. Again, it is identical with Mao's conceptualization, in which the whole Chinese people was seen as waging a revolutionary struggle against a combination of foreign imperialists and domestic traitors.[47]

This same populist strain is a general feature of ideology in the new states. By minimizing the significance of internal social distinctions and clashes of interest and emphasizing the common aspirations of "the nation" in the face of hostile foreign powers, it undoubtedly seeks to foster the sense of nationhood that it takes for granted but that is only weakly established. It is thus an important element in the process of nation-building. At the same time, of course, it helps to legitimate the role of those leaders who articulate national symbols most radically, projecting them as the patriots who resist foreign ways and foreign domination.

The most striking instance of the PKI's departure from a class approach was provided at the end of 1960, when Aidit explicitly argued that the party should subordinate class tasks to national tasks. Two years previously, in an article written for an international Communist journal, he had somewhat plaintively pointed out "how difficult it is for the Indonesian working class and Communist Party to combine its class obligations with its national obligations."[48]

By the latter part of 1960, with the growth of army power and the

---

[46] *Problems,* pp. 6–9.
[47] See Stuart Schramm, *Mao Tse-tung* (London, 1966), pp. 54, 216.
[48] *World Marxist Review,* vol. I, no. 1 (Sept. 1958).

insistence of President Sukarno that the PKI abandon class agitation in return for his protection, it had become more difficult still. Following the storm over the party's July 1960 evaluation of the Sukarno cabinet, the party apparently reviewed the tactics that had led it into a dangerous confrontation with the army and concluded that the balance of forces was such that the party must avoid militant class agitation. Reminding members of the Central Committee of the fact that imperialism was the main enemy, Aidit declared that "our class struggle takes the form of a national struggle," and went on to say:

The basic principle which we must stand by in pursuing the national struggle is that the class struggle is placed below the national struggle. Only by placing the interests of the class and the Party below the national interests, that is, the interests of the entire revolutionary people, and by preserving within recognized limits the class and Party interests, will our cooperation with other classes and groups be beneficial and will it be possible to achieve such a cooperation.[49]

One effect of this policy was to aggravate the tension within the party over the priorities that ought to be accorded to unity with the peasantry and with the national bourgeoisie. If the peasantry was the main ally of the proletariat, and, according to PKI theses, the realization of the alliance between the two classes demanded the ending of remnants of feudalism, then it followed that class factors demanded greater emphasis in the party's strategy. If, on the other hand, the national bourgeoisie occupied the main role in the alliance, then it was of primary importance to keep within bounds acceptable to the power-holders, which certainly did not include the promotion of class struggle.

The decision to subordinate class interests to national interests would seem to have involved a recognition of the supremacy of the alliance with the national bourgeoisie. But on the other hand, the party did not desire to become totally dependent on its bourgeois allies. Therefore it essayed several policy approaches to the problem. One way, as the passage quoted above suggests, was to accept that class struggle must be confined but not totally abandoned.[50] Thus

[49] *Ever Forward to Storm Imperialism and Feudalism* (Djakarta, 1961), pp. 19–20.

[50] Aidit spelt out this interpretation a year later: "It is erroneous if placing the interests of the class beneath national interests is taken to mean that class

attempts were made to introduce class demands in the context of the national crusade by claiming, for example, that the struggle against imperialism could only be waged effectively by arousing the enthusiasm of the workers and peasants through improvements in their livelihood.[51] Another way, which will be considered at greater length in connection with the peasant question, was to exempt the peasantry from the ban on class agitation and apply it only in relation to the working class in the cities, where the PKI felt more constrained by army power.

On occasion, there were signs of open disagreement within the PKI leadership on the specific question of the respective importance to be attached to the national bourgeoisie and the peasantry in the united national front. In October 1958 Njoto stated unambiguously that the most decisive question was unity between the proletarian and bourgeois parties.[52] Other party spokesmen were not inclined to this view, and in an article that appeared in August 1959, Hutapea, a Central Committee member and the newly appointed director of the Aliarcham Academy, the PKI's theoretical school, specifically denied that the alliance with the national bourgeoisie could be regarded as of primary importance.[53] That this difference reflected wider currents within the party on this question was brought to light in a report given by Hutapea to the party's seventh congress in April 1962. He referred to views "which have been found among cadres" to the effect that the party had gone "too far and given in too much in following the policy of the national united front," that the party must bear some responsibility for the decline in living standards, and that "it was losing its independence."[54]

In general, the party leaders tried to steer a middle course on the issue, ascribing to both alliances equal importance for the strategy

---

interests cease to exist. . . . Therefore the struggle to improve the conditions of workers (and peasants) must continue. . . . But these struggles must serve the cause of the struggle against imperialism. . . . These struggles are part of the national struggle"; see *Strengthen National Unity and Communist Unity* (Report to the 3rd Plenum of the Central Committee of the PKI, end of 1961 [Djakarta, 1962]).

[51] This approach was especially featured during the confrontation against Malaysia. See, for example, *Harian Rakjat,* Sept. 18, 1964.

[52] *Review of Indonesia,* V, no. 10 (Oct. 1958), 30.

[53] *Ibid.,* VI, no. 8 (Aug. 1959), 30.

[54] *Madju Terus,* pp. 248–49.

of the party. Sometimes the role of the national bourgeoisie was definitely downgraded, on occasion being referred to in somewhat patronizing terms, as when Aidit in September 1963 conceded only that "the national bourgeoisie may take part in the [national democratic] revolution."[55] On other occasions however, the importance of relations with the national bourgeoisie was emphasized strongly.[56]

In 1964, under the stress of the peasant land reform actions, the issue seems to have come to the fore once more and prompted at least a momentary division of opinion in the party's leading core. In May, Aidit had expressed the fairly well-established view that:

Though unity with the national bourgeoisie is not so important as unity with the peasants, it is nevertheless true that the success or failure, the completeness or otherwise, of working class leadership of the revolution will be decided by the extent to which unity between the workers and the national bourgeoisie is built or not.[57]

Two months later, Lukman spoke at a national conference of the party in much sharper vein:

Although our party must with all its strength tug at and cultivate the national bourgeoisie so that it remains in the united front with the working class, nevertheless, at no time can it sacrifice the unity of the worker and peasant. This means that whatever the reaction, and however great the violence, attending the work of the party among the peasants, we cannot be in the least vacillating in our vanguard role of protecting and leading the peasants.[58]

If this contrast indicated the existence of a basic difference of approach among the PKI leaders, subsequent events suggest that this difference did not give rise to clearcut factionalism in the predenouement period, and a short time later Aidit was repeating a stand that

---

[55] *The Indonesian Revolution*, p. 68.

[56] See, for example, *Problems*, p. 90.

[57] "Djadilah Komunis Jang Baik, dan Lebih Baik Lagi" (Become Good and Still Better Communists) (speech delivered at the PKI forty-fourth anniversary meeting in Surabaya, May 23, 1964), *Harian Rakjat*, June 11–12, 1964.

[58] M. H. Lukman, *Untuk Perbaikan Pekerdjaan dalam Front Persatuan Nasional* (For the Improvement of Work in the United National Front) (Djakarta, 1964).

remained the basic position of the party. Pointing out that some class struggle between the workers and the national bourgeoisie was unavoidable, he stressed that, "This class struggle must not be sharpened; both the Indonesian capitalists and the Indonesian workers still have the same enemy, that is, imperialism and the remnants of feudalism."[59]

Some of these changes of emphasis may be attributable to the need to stress certain aspects of the party's policy before particular audiences at particular times. Two things are clear, however. One is that, until 1963, the general line of the PKI was to avoid trying to promote class struggle in deference to the need to maintain a firm relationship with Sukarno and the groups he influenced. The other is that, in attempting to reconcile this requirement with its doctrinal commitment to a class strategy, the party was compelled to bend and substantially abandon the latter, its ideological formulations coming to express a complex interweaving of disparate and often conflicting strands, among which unambiguous class analysis and appeals constituted a secondary motif.

The overall struggle concept which provided the basis for the united national front and justified the PKI's downgrading of class factors was the thesis that Indonesia was a semicolonial country. This terminology was derived from Mao Tse-tung's definition of China's status in 1939[60] and was considered by the PKI leaders to be equally applicable to Indonesia's condition following the Round Table Conference agreement.

The PKI was far from being alone in resenting Indonesia's continuing dependence on Dutch economic and political power after 1949, and its semicolonial thesis therefore was both consonant with widely held perceptions and appealing in so far as the conclusion was drawn from it that the major political objective of the times must be to rid the country of residual foreign control. Its thrust was indeed identical with that of Sukarno, whose constantly reiterated theme throughout the fifties and sixties was the need to "complete the national revolution." And, just as Sukarno derived from his concept his emphasis on national unity and later Nasakom, so the PKI leaders

[59] *Harian Rakjat,* Aug. 20, 1964.

[60] "The Chinese Revolution and the Chinese Communist Party," *Selected Works,* III, 76–82.

spelled out from theirs the necessity of the bloc of four classes whose common aims were served by a joint struggle against imperialist influence.

From this statement of the central political problem flowed the structuring of the political struggle in terms of a contest between "the people" and all who represented in some way or another "foreign" interests, which in turn promoted the alliance of all radically minded nationalists against those who gave priority to orderly development in association with Western aid and enterprise.

As militant nationalism gained the upper hand in the fifties, and the agreements perpetuating Indonesia's dependence on Holland were successively repudiated, the semicolonial thesis began to lose a good deal of its substantive basis. By the end of 1958, the political and military links between the two countries had been severed, and all Dutch capital (with the exception of an interest in the international consortium, Royal Dutch Shell) had been taken over, to be nationalized later.

Until this time the PKI had maintained the validity of its thesis largely on the basis of Dutch economic power.[61] With this foundation removed, the formulation became more difficult to sustain in the terms in which it had been stated. That Aidit for one was not completely unaware of this is shown by the questions he raised in a speech early in 1959:

We often say that Indonesia is already independent. If we don't include West Irian, this is indeed true. No one can say that Indonesia is still a colonised country. But how far does our independence go? Is our independence at the same stage as, for example, the independence of Malaya, of India, of the USA, of Britain, of the Soviet Union, of People's China, and so on? Are we politically really independent? Are we economically independent? How about our national culture in present-day independent Indonesia?[62]

Whatever the limitations of the thesis as an accurate depiction of Indonesia's economic and political status relative to Holland and the West in general, however, it remained politically indispensable to

----

[61] See Aidit's statement commenting on the abrogation of the Round Table Conference agreement and the repudiation of Indonesia's debts to Holland in *Problems*, p. 35; and the resolution of the Central Committee of the PKI in November 1958 in Hindley, p. 35.

[62] *Review of Indonesia*, VI, no. 2 (Feb. 1959), 37–39.

the party. The Communists were not engaged in academic exercises but in a struggle for supremacy—and survival. Not the analytic force, but the credibility and political potential of the analysis determined their retention of it in the new conditions created by the severing of Dutch political and economic influence. The radical nationalist wing of the political establishment did not regard the revolution as completed, especially so long as West Irian remained under Netherlands control. But more fundamental than this issue, the notion of the unfinished revolution was as vital to Sukarno as was the semicolonial thesis, with its similar connotations, to the PKI. It supplied the central dynamic of the Guided Democracy regime, legitimizing the role of leaders whose credentials had been established by the part they had played in the independence struggle, focusing political attention upon symbols that fortified the claims of central power over regional demands, and diverting attention from issues (such as economic development) that contained the seeds of acute interest conflict.

The nationalist issue was the hinge upon which the PKI-Sukarno alliance hung. Abandonment of the semicolonial thesis would have been difficult without the substitution of a new "basic contradiction" in Indonesian society centering on internal class cleavages and laying greater stress on economic policy. The united national front policy would have been jeopardized, and the PKI would have been faced with the threat of isolation, something it had striven hard to avoid. The PKI leaders may not have reasoned the problem out quite in these terms, but they were in no doubt about the necessity of eschewing class conflict and preserving the alliance based on nationalism. In these circumstances, Indonesia had to remain a semicolonial country come what may.[63]

It was not difficult, in the heady nationalist atmosphere of the late fifties and the Guided Democracy sixties, for the PKI's leaders to convince their followers that the view of Indonesia as "semicolonial" was still valid. Until, in late 1962, agreement was reached through the United Nations for the transfer of West Irian to the Republic, this immensely popular and volatile issue formed one of the lynchpins supporting the thesis. In addition, the PKI frequently underlined

---

[63] The ideological attraction of the concept is demonstrated by the fact that after the destruction of the PKI, émigré groups, while critical of many aspects of Aidit's policies, still adhered to the "semicolonial semifeudal" thesis.

economic aspects of Indonesia's dependence—the fact that Dutch capital still operated in the oil industry, that private and governmental capital from other foreign sources was still entering the country, and that Indonesia's exports depended upon the "capitalist world market."[64]

However, from 1959, the party began to shift the weight of its emphasis toward the threat of United States penetration in the economic, political, and cultural spheres. It was well aware that for a number of reasons the government was looking to the United States for economic aid and diplomatic support. Many among the political elite looked on the United States as the primary source for financial and military aid, and they wished to preserve the advantages of an independent foreign policy that gave them an opening to both America and the Communist bloc. A strong body of opinion, recalling the experience of the independence struggle, felt that the United States could be induced to lend support to Indonesia's claims to West Irian. Until the Malaysia confrontation finally ruptured relations with the United States beyond repair, Indonesian foreign policy oscillated between two poles, one focusing on the enticements of American aid and an independent and active foreign policy and the other on a radical anti-imperialist stance backed by the Communist states.

Gravitation toward the American sphere of influence held great dangers for the PKI, since United States aid could be expected to be made contingent on moves to limit the party's influence. Its concern to fend off this threat readily led to the incorporation of the United States in the semicolonial framework. As early as December 1958, in a report to the PKI Central Committee, Aidit began the process. While stating that Dutch imperialism was still the first enemy of the Indonesian people, he added that United States imperialism was "increasingly occupying important positions in Indonesia in the economic, political, and cultural spheres," maintaining military bases in West Irian, controlling right wing parties and individuals to promote its interests, carrying out cultural infiltration via films and education, and assisting the rebels in Sumatra and Sulawesi. It followed, he said, that "US imperialism already constitutes a constant danger threatening Indonesia's sovereignty and independence."[65]

---

[64] See, for example, Aidit's report to the PKI Central Committee in February 1963, *Dare, Dare and Dare Again!* pp. 35–45.

[65] Hindley, p. 35. It is perhaps symptomatic of the confusion obtaining with

At the party's sixth congress in September 1959, Aidit went a step further:

Dutch imperialism is still the enemy number one of the Indonesian people . . . [but] US imperialism is the most dangerous enemy of the Indonesian people since this imperialism is the most aggressive, the most capable of carrying out its criminal intentions, since the amount of US capital invested in Indonesia is growing, and since there are still quite a number of persons who naively believe that US imperialism is not so very criminal.[66]

Once the Irian issue had been resolved satisfactorily, the PKI felt the time had arrived to move the United States up into the position of both number one enemy and most dangerous enemy of the Indonesian people. The timing was by no means inappropriate; once the shutters were down on West Irian, economic problems assumed greater prominence and the government for a time showed every sign of putting through an American-financed scheme of economic stabilization. The PKI became acutely alarmed at the possible political implications of this policy orientation, but the cloud was finally dispersed in the winds of Malaysian confrontation. Under the impact of this campaign, as will be recounted in a later chapter, the PKI's indictment of the United States at last won decisive elite and mass approval and was translated into a vigorous and at times violent assault on various facets of the United States' presence in Indonesia.

Thus the semicolonial thesis was rescued and fortified by the dynamics of Indonesia's foreign policy, preserving a frame in which the basic form of struggle could be projected as one of the *rakjat* versus the alien enemy. During the early period of Guided Democracy, when the PKI was tightly restricted by army power, it used the concept as a defensive argument against those who sought to swing the political struggle back on to the home front. In the context of the West Irian campaign, for example, the party was at pains to stress that "our

---

regard to the semicolonial thesis by this time that Aidit here speaks of Indonesia's sovereignty and independence as if they were accomplished facts.

[66] *Problems*, pp. 286–87. It may be recalled that after mid-1958 government policy in Indonesia had taken a temporary swing to the right, and overtures from the United States were being favorably received. In July 1959 the PKI had made the foreign minister, Subandrio, and other ministers targets of strong criticism for their "antinational" policies.

enemy is still imperialism . . . not nationalism, not religion, not Communism. . . . Let us guard against all national dissension."[67] At the conclusion of the campaign, similar warnings were sounded against those who were said to be spreading the view that now the national struggle had been achieved it was time to settle accounts with enemies at home.[68]

However, from about mid-1963, when the PKI took the political offensive, it was itself vulnerable to the charge that by stimulating peasant actions and waging campaigns to remove anti-Communists from positions of political influence it was violating the terms of the national alliance against imperialism. With Sukarno's aid, the party was able to fend off this attack by the device of identifying all anti-Communists with the foreign enemy, leaving its opponents, no doubt, to regard with some bitterness and envy the success with which it operated its double standards.

THE TRANSITION TO SOCIALISM

The ultimate goal of the PKI—the establishment of a socialist order in Indonesia—received remarkably little attention from the party leaders. The 1954 program contented itself with setting as the party's main objective the formation of a people's democratic government based on a fully developed united national front; the reform program of such a government was outlined, and it was held that the achievement of this program would constitute the material prerequisites for socialism.[69] But the nature of the transition, its social effects, and the features of socialism in Indonesia, were left unclarified. Later statements added little by way of substance to this vague outline, and in subsequent years the people's democratic government itself faded from prominence in favor of the more modest immediate target of a Nasakom cabinet.

In their published speeches and writings, the PKI leaders sedulously avoided indulging in utopian forecasts about the socialist future. Their political style was an eminently practical and down-to-earth one, in striking contrast with that of the president. It may well be that they allowed themselves greater latitude when touring the villages,

---

[67] *Harian Rakjat,* May 10, 1961.
[68] See, for example, *Harian Rakjat,* Sept. 18, 1962.
[69] *Program PKI,* pp. 11–22.

and it seems unlikely that the strong Messianic strain in Javanese culture would have failed to find expression in the lower ranks of the party. On the other hand, the delicate political path the PKI leaders were treading may have led them to discourage the antidisciplinary trends associated with utopianism.[70]

There were sound tactical reasons for the party to avoid speculation about what was to follow the cementing of the Nasakom alliance. To pursue the issue could be divisive, in that it would raise the delicate question of hegemony. In order to conform with Communist orthodoxy, the leadership would have had to emphasize the primary role of the proletariat and the Communist party in the transition to socialism, as Aidit did, for example, in his lectures in China in September 1963.[71] But if it did this at home, the party would be open to the challenge that it did not fully accept the leadership of President Sukarno, who himself proclaimed the aim of his government to be "socialism à la Indonesia"; so it was necessary to backtrack on the assertion of Communist hegemony and concede that the country could take the socialist road under the aegis of the president and others of his circle.

The problem was made more difficult by occasional assertions by some officials of the Guided Democracy system that Indonesia had already entered the socialist stage. These claims aroused the indignation of the PKI for two reasons: as the party said, the equation of socialism with a situation in which standards of living were falling, bureaucratic capitalists dominated the state enterprises, and the peasants were still subject to "feudal exploitation," could only disparage the whole concept of socialism in the eyes of the masses; of equal importance, though not publicly stated, was the fact that these claims implied that Communist leadership of the state was not necessary in order for Indonesia to attain socialism. The vehemence with which

---

[70] Interpretations of Javanese Messianic movements may be found in J. M. Van der Kroef, "Javanese Messianic Expectations: Their Origin and Cultural Context," *Comparative Studies in Society and History,* I, no. 4 (1959), 299–323, and in Sartono Kartodirdjo, "Agrarian Radicalism in Java," in Claire Holt, ed., *Culture and Politics in Indonesia* (Ithaca, N.Y., 1972), pp. 71–125. For an interesting account of a recent Messianic movement deriving inspiration from Communism, see David Mitchell, "Communists, Mystics and Sukarnoism," *Dissent* (Melbourne), no. 22 (Autumn, 1968), 28–32.

[71] *The Indonesian Revolution,* pp. 16–17.

PKI leaders attacked "demagogic socialists" is explicable in the light of these considerations.[72]

The importance the PKI attached to emphasizing that the socialist stage had not yet been reached is shown by the fact that this issue occasioned one of the very few direct and open conflicts between the party and Sukarno. In the Manipol declaration Sukarno had accepted the Communist interpretation of the two-stage revolution, but in April 1965 he suddenly declared that the country was then entering the stage of socialist construction. The PKI protested in a number of press editorials and statements, and the president backed down.[73] However on September 25, 1965, he reverted to his earlier position, stating that "we are now about to enter the second stage of the Indonesian revolution, namely the implementation of socialism." Perhaps Sukarno was carried away by the spell of his own visions, or perhaps he felt it necessary to placate the anti-Communist army leadership, with whom he had been feuding, by demonstrating that he was still no creature of the Communists.

When they did refer to the eventual attainment of socialism, PKI leaders were inclined to present it as a distant objective having little bearing on current political questions. Thus, in early 1958, Aidit declared that a socialist state was not feasible before the end of the century.[74] In 1964 he remarked more generally that socialism was "not yet on the agenda" because the necessary conditions—the expulsion of all foreign capital, the elimination of remnants of feudalism, and industrialization—did not exist.[75] At the same time, the party was at pains to stress that the transition would not be marked by a violent struggle between the workers and the national capitalists; the absorption of private capital, it argued, could be settled by *musjawarah* (collective deliberation) and *mufakat* (consensus).[76] No theoretical quibble was to be allowed to harm the continued cooperation of the Nasakom constituents.

---

[72] See, for example, *Problems,* pp. 154–60; *Revolusi Indonesia, Latarbelakang, Sedjarah dan Haridepannja,* pp. 57–58.

[73] *Harian Rakjat,* April 29, May 6 and 21, 1965. (The last of these contains the text of a speech to the party's Central Committee by Anwar Sanusi refuting Sukarno's statement.)

[74] *Review of Indonesia,* V (Feb. 1958), 7.

[75] *Revolusi Indonesia, Latarbelakang, Sedjarah dan Haridepannja,* p. 57.

[76] *Ibid.,* pp. 61–62; *Harian Rakjat,* Aug. 20, 1964.

In 1956 the PKI had endorsed the "peaceful road to socialism" proclaimed by Khrushchev at the CPSU twentieth congress as suitable for Indonesia.[77] This in fact marked no new point of departure for the party, which had been proceeding for some time on the assumption that it could rise to power under the wing of the national elite. Consequently when, in 1960, regulations governing political parties were introduced that required them, among other things, to affirm that they would pursue their aims by peaceful means, the PKI experienced no difficulty in complying, and did so by writing a specific clause to this effect into its constitution at the seventh congress in April 1962.[78]

Aidit spoke on several occasions of the favorable conditions in Indonesia for a peaceful transition to socialism. In 1960, for instance, a Western correspondent reported him as saying that "the prospects for a peaceful transition to socialism, as laid down by Khrushchev at the Twentieth Soviet Party Congress, are the brightest and the opportunities most bountiful in two countries, namely, Cuba and Indonesia."[79] In 1964 he elaborated these prospects in another interview with a foreign correspondent:

When we complete the first stage of our revolution, which is now in progress, we can enter into friendly consultation with other progressive elements in our society and, without an armed struggle, lead the country towards Socialist Revolution. . . . The chastening effect [of the present stage of the revolution will] maintain a kind of revolutionary pressure on Indonesia's national capitalists. . . . There will be no armed struggle unless there is foreign armed intervention on the capitalists' behalf and, when we successfully complete our present national democratic revolution, the chances of any foreign power interfering with Indonesia's internal affairs will become extremely remote.[80]

A short time later, in discussing the factors guaranteeing that the transition to socialism would be made, Aidit cited the existence of the workers and peasants as pillars of the revolution, the commanding position of the state sector in the economy, Indonesia's position

[77] D. N. Aidit, "Tentang Perlawatan ke-empat Negeri" (Concerning a Visit to Four Countries), *Bintang Merah,* XII (June 1956), 214–16.
[78] *Madju Terus,* pp. 89–95 (report by Lukman on the changes in the party's constitution).
[79] Brackman, p. 302.
[80] S. M. Ali in *Far Eastern Economic Review,* Apr. 16, 1964.

among the "new emerging forces" in the world, and the influence of socialist ideas among the people.[81] This was not a particularly convincing itemization, considering that the workers and peasants had not been prepared for action as an independent revolutionary force, that the state sector was (as the PKI never tired of pointing out) the preserve of its most dangerous enemies, and that socialist ideas among the people derived as much from the official ideology, with its muddied concepts, as from the "pure" notions that the PKI may have held but was obliged to play down.

As has been observed in our discussion of Aidit's theory of the state, the PKI was compelled by the logic of its circumstances to propound a variant of the Soviet theory of national capitalism, with its implication that "progressive" states in the third world could "grow" into socialism without decisive intervention by indigenous Communist parties. That the PKI was far from happy with this concept is shown by its intermittent theoretical concern with the hegemonic role of the proletariat and the party. But it was too hemmed in by the terms of its alliance with the national elite, which held superior power resources, to break from the restricting bonds of the concept. It was obliged to slur over the question of socialist transition, to bind itself to the peaceful road, and to emphasize the element of continuity rather than change in the process of the transformation.

Two potent and interrelated factors, then, contributed to the PKI's tacit subordination of class bases of action in the formulation and implementation of its political strategy. The first was the relative weakness of class in comparison with other lines of social and political cleavage in Indonesia; especially important from the Communist point of view was the lack of class consciousness among the numerically small proletariat and the numerically predominant peasantry. The promotion or encouragement of urban-centered class activity by the workers, in particular, had proved detrimental to the party's interests and security, first in 1951, and again in 1960 when it was engaged in "reality testing" to determine how far it could assert itself without running foul of the military authorities.

The other, and equally important, factor was that any attempt by the PKI to represent the class interests of its constituents in any mili-

[81] *Revolusi Indonesia, Latarbelakang, Sedjarah dan Haridepannja*, p. 78.

tant fashion threatened the basis of its relations with those sections of the political elite to which it looked for succor and advancement. Sukarno's attitude in the early Guided Democracy years was clear: national interests took first place, and it was upon the PKI's acceptance of this fact that his patronage of it depended. Since he was not only the most powerful of the party's allies but also the most well-disposed toward it, this was enough to convince the PKI leaders about where their best interests lay.

The dilution of class in PKI ideology was not simply a matter of pragmatic opportunism, however. From the start of their political careers, the Communist leaders had been involved in the nationalist struggle, and the mystique of the national cause had a great hold on them. Perceived organizational interest thus coincided with their own disposition and that of the majority of their followers, who found in a nationalism invested with Sukarno's charisma and panaceas a sense of identity and a source of hope in circumstances of painful national social adjustment.

Nationalism, in fact, was to prove a powerful force which the PKI could harness, as the next two chapters will illustrate. At the same time, class as an analytical political device and a potential base for action clung on in the PKI's strategic elaborations. It may be suggested that, whereas the dilution of class represented the PKI's reconciliation to the prospect that, for the foreseeable future, it could hope for no more than a share in political power, the retention of class symbolized the aspiration of the party leadership to transcend this limitation and obtain power in its own right in accordance with the Marxist prescription. The promotion of class struggle in the countryside in 1964 was, as we shall see, an indication that the PKI had not completely abandoned it as an action principle.

4. Nationalism:
The West Irian Phase

If nationalism was to sustain an alliance between the president and the Communists and act as a political spearhead for both, as the trajectory of their policies in 1959 suggested, then it required a specific focus of action and general ideological concepts that would channel politics in the desired direction. As it happened, an answer to the first requirement was ready to hand, in the form of the West Irian issue, a piece of unfinished business left over from the 1949 settlement of the Dutch-Indonesian conflict.

As for the second requirement, a theory of international relations justifying the primacy of nationalist concerns in Indonesia already existed in embryo in the orientations of both Sukarno and the PKI and was to achieve full bodied expression in the course of the campaign to liberate West Irian that began to assume a militant form at the beginning of 1961. Though they started from somewhat different premises, both partners in the nationalist crusade shared the view that the struggle against imperialism constituted the central objective of Indonesia's national policies. Sukarno's formulation of this objective, in terms of a life-and-death engagement between the "new emerging forces" and the "old established forces" in the world, became the official doctrine encompassing the nationalist tendency. The PKI was quite content, during the West Irian phase, to rally behind this concept and elaborate upon it in keeping with its own analyses. In the first place, the doctrine was in harmony with the characterization of world developments the party had adopted under the influence of theses advanced by the Chinese Communist Party. In the second place, the PKI was not at this stage in a position to seize the initiative in propounding guidelines for the nation. That point was reached only later, during the confrontation against Malaysia.

For the PKI, the purposes for which nationalism could be used were, as has already been suggested, overwhelmingly domestic. Nationalism provided a framework within which agitational politics could be conducted with relative safety and that was both conducive to the promotion of the united front strategy, as conceived by the PKI leaders, and favorable to party growth. The PKI always endeavored to keep nationalist euphoria within bounds that would serve the party's major aim of enhancing its power prospects; and in this it was substantially successful.

THE BIRTH OF AN IDEOLOGY

The future of West Irian had been a bone of contention between Indonesia and Holland since the Round Table Conference agreement, which had left its status to be determined by negotiations between the two countries.[1] Each side interpreted the vague terms of the agreement in line with its own interests, and the dispute over the territory became a running sore in their relations throughout the fifties. All currents of Indonesian opinion were united in demanding that the last remnant of Holland's East Indies empire be ceded to the new Republic. But while the moderate governments of the early fifties had regarded the issue as secondary to the normalization of the country's external relations and its domestic situation, Sukarno and his radical nationalist allies saw it as central to the "completion of the revolution" by which alone that national unity and sense of pride necessary for the surmounting of Indonesia's problems could be achieved.[2] In the second half of the fifties it became a major source of political conflict and agitation, leading in the foreign policy sphere to deteriorating relations with the Netherlands and a more anti-Western orientation by Indonesian governments.[3]

The West Irian issue played its part too in preparing and consolidating the alliance between the PKI and the radical nationalist wing of the elite. In December 1950, a dispute over West Irian policy

---

[1] The course of the West Irian dispute up to 1958 is traced in Robert C. Bone, Jr., *The Dynamics of the Western New Guinea (Irian Barat) Problem* (Interim Reports Series, Modern Indonesia Project, Cornell University, 1958), and Justus M. Van der Kroef, *The West New Guinea Dispute* (New York, 1958).

[2] Feith, *Decline,* pp. 155–164.

[3] *Ibid.,* pp. 450–56, 583–84.

in the PKI had been a principal issue causing Aidit and his followers to challenge the established leadership of the party. In repudiating the "plague on both your houses" attitude of the previous leadership and coming out strongly behind the radical approach to the issue, Aidit and his group were not only announcing their own attachment to the nationalist cause but were also signaling, to the PNI in particular, that the PKI would be a staunch ally on this question.[4]

From this time onward throughout the constitutional democracy period, the PKI acted as a staunch supporter of the PNI and President Sukarno in all their major initiatives regarding West Irian and other foreign policy issues. At this stage, the party was concerned above all to demonstrate its reliability as an ally and to avoid isolating itself or exposing itself to attack; as a result it was content to leave all of the pacemaking to its more respectable partners. Its agitation over West Irian, for example, was in no significant way different from that of other radical groups, except perhaps that, carefully but persistently, the PKI sought to have a greater share of the odium of "neocolonialism" attached to the United States, in line with the prevailing international Communist emphasis on America as the main bastion and most aggressive exponent of imperialism.

With the advent of Guided Democracy, the liberation of West Irian became not only a matter of great moment to Sukarno personally but, now that he had assumed a more direct role in government, also something of a test of his leadership capacity. He had made it a priority issue; now it was incumbent upon him to deliver the goods. Beyond this, however, he also sought a more prominent role for his country and himself in world affairs. There were a number of reasons for this: Sukarno's desire to demonstrate the historic importance of the national revolution he had led; his belief that Indonesia could win the respect and prestige to which it was entitled only by bringing its distinctive viewpoint to bear upon world affairs; the personal satisfaction it gave him to cut a figure on the international stage; his realization that this area of politics peculiarly suited his style and talents, and so enhanced his political role at the expense of that of the generals and other potential competitors; and his appreciation of the fact that concentration on goals and enemy targets external to the state

[4] Hindley, pp. 25, 50.

helped to unify the nation and divert attention from the internal failings and stresses of the government.

Circumstances also combined to steer Sukarno toward a radical anticolonial and anti-imperialist stance in world politics. So far as West Irian was concerned, the most readily available allies for an assault on a "colonial bastion" were, as the experience of the previous few years had indicated, the Communist states and the more militant Afro-Asian countries. The West was cool toward Indonesia's claim; nevertheless, if it could be demonstrated, to the United States in particular, that the problems that would arise from denying the nationalist claims of an aroused Indonesia would be greater than those that would develop if its demands were met, then some favorable intervention from that quarter might eventuate. On both counts, then, radicalism had its political logic.

Sukarno was casting around for a formula to express his activist approach to the anti-imperialist struggle. His ambition to make Indonesia the centre of Afro-Asian solidarity and militancy had led him to undertake a series of world tours in an effort to win friends and gauge the climate of opinion in various countries. He was also lobbying for the convening of a second Afro-Asian conference to carry on the traditions established at Bandung in 1955.

His plan for a permanent Afro-Asian body reflected his impatience with the outlook and leadership of the nonaligned bloc of nations headed by Yugoslavia, India, and the United Arab Republic. For some time he had been aware of the conflict between his view of world problems, which focused on the destruction of the vestiges of imperialism, and that of Tito and Nehru, who were mainly concerned to avoid involvement in great power conflicts and saw the peace issue as their most appropriate means of playing a world role. Whereas the latter argued that big power conflicts should be moderated so that greater attention could be given to the developmental problems of the new states, Sukarno and some of the West African leaders saw the whole concentration on European questions and Soviet-American relations as a denial of the primacy of their demands upon the international political system. To the radicals, the very concept of nonalignment underwrote the supremacy of the great powers and treated the problems of the new states as the outcome of unfortunate clashes of interests among the giants instead of as the necessary result of deliberate imperialist machinations.

The trend of Sukarno's thinking was apparent in his speech to the United Nations in September 1960, although at that time he did not clearly distinguish himself from the "third force" advocates. He spoke as a representative of the "third world," thereby accepting the notion of a tripartite world division, but at the same time he insisted that colonialism-imperialism, not coexistence or disarmament, was the main problem in international relations; in this he took issue with the preoccupations that had led Khrushchev to take the unprecedented step of inviting the world leaders to appear in person before the international forum.[5]

A year later, in Belgrade, at a meeting of nonbloc powers assembled at Tito's invitation, Sukarno made clear that his position had diverged decisively from that of the neutralists. The fact that in the intervening year Indonesia had moved a few steps closer to the use of force against the Dutch in West Irian, and had entered into closer military and political relations with the Soviet Union, may help to account for the change in Sukarno's outlook. At any rate, he once again stressed that colonialism-imperialism, not cold war issues, was the crux of international politics, but on this occasion he added an explicit attack on neutralism. In place of big power conflict as the gravamen of world attention, he advanced an embryo version of what was to become his celebrated theory of confrontation between the "new emerging forces" (NEFO) and the "old established forces" (OLDEFO). The significance of this concept was that, in place of the imperialism-Communism dichotomy, or the threefold division of the neutralists, he advanced a new bipolar line of demarcation centered on problems of colonialism and imperialism.[6]

Sukarno did not carry the Belgrade Conference, and in particular he got only weak support for Indonesia's West Irian claim. But his challenge was to be followed by persistent efforts on Indonesia's part to undermine the nonaligned grouping and to establish a new international bloc in keeping with the NEFO-OLDEFO concept. For the time being, however, Indonesia's concern to get American support over West Irian acted as a restraint upon Sukarno's radical adventures abroad.

[5] See George Modelski, *The New Emerging Forces: Documents on the Ideology of Indonesian Foreign Policy* (Canberra, 1963), pp. 1–33.

[6] *Ibid.*, pp. 33–43.

Among the PKI leaders, a militant anti-imperialism accorded with deeply held beliefs about the course of revolutionary political strategy. Communist doctrine held that worldwide imperialism, headed by the United States, represented the greatest threat to world peace and the independence of nations. The defeat of imperialist schemes to attack the socialist countries, impose neocolonialist exploitation and oppression on the newly liberated states, and crush the workers' movements in the capitalist countries, was a necessary prelude to the complete destruction and overthrow of the imperialist system and the ushering in of world Communism. However, in current world conditions, as interpreted by the Soviet Communist leaders in an analysis still, in 1959, outwardly accepted by all contingents of the international Communist movement, the main task of the Communists was to "impose peaceful coexistence on the imperialist warmongers" by promoting a broad movement for peace embracing all social strata to whom this objective could be made to appeal. In the struggle for peace, the neutralist states and their leaders occupied an important place, and their efforts were to be encouraged and supported by the Communists.

The theory behind this policy, which Khrushchev had made the lynchpin of his political strategy, was that, if world war could be prevented, socialism would inevitably establish its superiority to capitalism in peaceful economic competition; more and more states would be encouraged to take the socialist path; and the overthrow of capitalist regimes could be accomplished in many cases by peaceful means without the danger of foreign intervention by the imperialist powers.[7]

This analysis and strategy were already under challenge by the Communist Party of China, which made its opposing standpoint clear with the publication in April 1960 of the article *Long Live Leninism,* a powerful polemic against Soviet concepts of peaceful coexistence and peaceful transition.[8] The crux of the Chinese argument was that war was inevitable so long as imperialism existed, and that if Com-

---

[7] The authoritative statements of this strategy were contained in Khrushchev's report to the twentieth congress of the CPSU in February 1956, and in the declaration of the meeting of Communist and workers' parties held in Moscow in November 1957.

[8] Originally published in *Hongqi* (Red Flag), the fortnightly magazine of the Central Committee of the CPC, on April 16, 1960, *Long Live Leninism* was reproduced in book form and became the first basic text of all supporters of China in the Sino-Soviet dispute.

munists allowed their revolutionary aims to be accommodated to the necessity of avoiding war then they were merely guaranteeing the status quo in pursuit of a chimera; therefore the thrust of Communist endeavor must be concentrated, not on the maintenance of peace, but on the destruction of imperialism. Such a strategy would render world war less likely, by weakening imperialism, but if war should come, then it would spell the doom of imperialism and the worldwide triumph of socialism. The Chinese Communists rejected the possibility of peaceful transition to socialism, and stressed that the struggle against imperialism must be carried on by violent means; in particular, nothing must be allowed to stand in the way of Communist leadership of and support for the liberation struggles of the people of the colonies and neocolonies who, in a period of relative capitalist stabilization, had come to occupy first place in the revolutionary movement. However, the Chinese did not reject cooperation with the nationalist leaders of newly independent states, so long as they were prepared to carry on a resolute struggle against imperialism.

It is possible, particularly in the light of present-day perspectives, to see a goodly measure of state interest behind the ideological formulations of the two Communist giants. For the Russians, concerned above all to preserve the international preeminence and national security conferred on them by the bipolar world division that emerged after World War II, new revolutions and Communist breakthroughs had become a goal of secondary importance. Peaceful coexistence and peaceful transition were ideological expressions of the Soviet's determination to pursue détente with the United States—a détente acknowledging defined spheres of interest. The Chinese, on the other hand, who considered themselves to be the greatest sufferers under the bipolar system and believed that Russia might well be prepared to sacrifice their security and international interests on the altar of détente, were intent on disrupting the emerging Soviet-American relationship, though with minimum risk to their own safety. With such an aim, their best policy seemed to be to champion the nationalist tide in the third world, which, they expected, would upset relations between the big two, and so prevent them combining against China, while at the same time pinning down substantial American forces and tarnishing Russia's image in the eyes of Communists and other revolutionaries.

It is probable that by 1959 the PKI leaders had some knowledge of the differences between the two major Communist parties, but it is doubtful that they were aware of the full import of these differences, let alone the lengths to which they would be taken in the following years. Certainly the Indonesian Communists at this stage showed no inclination to come down on the side of either of the disputants. Nevertheless, although in 1959 their formulations on foreign affairs still owed a great deal to the strategic lines pioneered by Khrushchev, there had taken place since 1954 a significant shift in emphasis away from the peace theme to one placing greater accent on Indonesian nationalist and anticolonial issues.

By 1963, the PKI leaders were to come down on the side of the CPC standpoint on international policies, arriving at this position largely as a result of the impetus and policy direction flowing from their nationalist bias. In 1959, however, the trend was still a recent and not necessarily definitive one. It became more pronounced because Soviet preoccupations seemed to take little account of the goals that were central to Indonesian nationalist sentiment and because fear of atomic warfare was not an important issue in Indonesia.

Of paramount importance, a radical nationalist orientation best met the all-important requirements of the PKI's domestic strategy. It strengthened the party's accord with the president, had potent appeal for wide sections of the political public, and was a relatively safe and popular focus for agitational politics.

The changed accent of PKI formulations on international affairs can be gauged from a comparison of Aidit's reports to the fifth and sixth congresses of the PKI, held respectively in 1954 and 1959. Although at the time of the fifth congress the party had already embarked on the path of collaboration with the radical nationalists, and was as a consequence elevating national issues to prominence in its work, the PKI leaders had not yet clearly spelled out the implications of this course in conceptual terms. The report, where it touched on the international scene, reflected the common line of the world Communist movement, which had begun to stress the centrality of the peace struggle and the importance of friendly relations between Communist and neutralist states. Aidit's treatment of world problems, in fact, might easily have emanated from any one of a score or more of Communist parties at this time, and there was little in it that related specifically to Indonesian national orientations. The report argued that the main contradiction in the world was between the socialist and imperialist camps, that the struggle for world peace must occupy first place in the work of all Communist parties, and that all international disputes could be solved peacefully by negotiation.[9]

By 1959 a new orientation could be discerned, although the report of the sixth congress still owed a good deal to the general approach of the international Communist movement as expressed, for example, in the 1957 declaration of Communist parties. As distinct from the priority obligation to the worldwide struggle for peace, the 1959 report emphasized first that "the foreign policy of the Republic must categorically serve the interests of winning victory for the August Revolution," and only secondarily that it "must also serve the interests of peace among nations."[10] The importance of the peace struggle and peaceful coexistence was still affirmed, but, significantly, within the context of the anticolonial struggle, the report stating that "we love peace because we love independence."[11] Mass involvement in the implementation of the country's foreign policy was said to be essential for its success (a populist approach that the PKI leaders fully shared with Sukarno), and the government was urged to direct its search for international alliances toward the Communist and Afro-Asian states.[12]

The Indonesian Communists, in keeping with the international Communist movement, had long excoriated "third force" concepts. But from 1958 on domestic considerations lent a new urgency and vigor to their denunciations, which were aimed first and foremost at President Tito of Yugoslavia. On the surface, the idea of emerging countries standing aside from the great power blocs and seeking to bring pressure to bear on each of them to relieve international tensions might seem to have had some potential appeal to a Communist party concerned above all to keep its government from gravitating

---

[9] Aidit, *Problems*, pp. 226–44.

[10] *Ibid.,* p. 340.

[11] *Ibid.,* pp. 370–71. The slogan is a variant on one coined by Sukarno during the nationalist revolution: "We love peace, but we love independence more." The original slogan had already begun to be revived (see, for example, Njoto in *Bintang Merah*, XI [July–Aug. 1959], 286) and would shortly oust Aidit's version entirely.

[12] *Problems*, pp. 364–85.

into the American orbit. But the PKI did not view the matter in this light at all. Yugoslav revisionism had been trenchantly criticized at the world meeting of Communist parties in November 1957, and although it is doubtful that Yugoslavia's departures from the Soviet model for building socialism were of great intrinsic concern to the PKI leadership, it was otherwise with that country's foreign policies and foreign relations. The most important consideration from the point of view of the Indonesian Communists was that Tito was accepting United States economic aid, the very instrument they saw as threatening their own political position in Indonesia. So far as the party leaders were concerned, acceptance of imperialist aid was incompatible with the pursuance of an independent foreign policy, a proposition that, for them, followed axiomatically from the policies of the Masjumi and the PSI.[13] Since 1954, Indonesia had been moving hesitantly toward closer relations with the Communist camp, and a third force stance would represent a denial of the trends that offered the PKI an opportunity to consolidate its alliance with the Sukarno ruling faction. Further, the notion of subordinating the anti-imperialist struggle to considerations of détente cut right across the PKI's political strategy.

Domestic reactions to Yugoslavia and her third force concepts did nothing to allay the PKI's apprehensions. The nonbloc posture had proved dangerously seductive for many among Indonesia's political elite, some of whom regarded it as an alternative to falling into the Communist camp, and some of whom went further and hinted that with such a foreign policy approach a pronounced PKI role in the political system would be a hindrance rather than an asset. In 1960 the PKI had suspected Subandrio of harboring such ideas and had bitterly assailed him for allegedly conniving with Tito to convene a "little summit" of non-aligned nations.[14] In another sphere, PSI-leaning intellectuals were making Yugoslav concepts of economic organization a useful talking point in opposition to the central planning emphasis of the PKI's developmental program that had found some echo in the president's Political Manifesto.[15] Yugoslav heresies were thus of considerably more than abstract significance for the

[13] See Aidit's characterization of the "sham independent" policies of Sjahrir and Hatta in his 1959 congress report; *Problems*, pp. 374–77.

[14] *Review of Indonesia*, VII (July 1960), 19.

[15] I am indebted to Herbert Feith for drawing this point to my attention.

party; they not only stood in the way of the policy of fostering closer identification with the Communist states, but also provided a focus for anti-PKI maneuvers on the Indonesian political scene.

Tito was repeatedly and bitterly attacked by the Indonesian Communists on various grounds—his alleged complicity in United States plans in the Balkans, his failure to condemn imperialist acts of aggression, his lukewarm attitude on the West Irian issue—but above all for his attempts to strengthen the third force bloc. On occasion, both Nasser and Nehru were rebuked too for lending weight to Tito's designs.

The PKI had preceded the Belgrade Conference with a series of attacks on neutralism, and the "sham neutralism" of Tito in particular.[16] It is apparent that the party leadership was apprised in advance of the tone Sukarno would seek to set and fully approved it. Aidit, moreover, was included in the presidential party that went to Belgrade, as he had been in several previous delegations, including that which accompanied Sukarno to the UN in 1960. Sukarno's speech was hailed by the PKI as a new stage in the development of the national independence struggle and an exposure of the bankruptcy of neutralism. Indonesia's "free and active" foreign policy, which clearly recognized the need for a militant fight against imperialism and colonialism, was contrasted with the spurious "impartiality" of the Tito and Nehru brand of neutralism. A statement issued by the International Department of the Central Committee stressed that only a vigorous opposition to imperialism could advance the cause of world peace.[17]

The PKI was not slow to appreciate that the NEFO-OLDEFO concept was fully consistent with its own international views, and at the seventh congress of the party in April 1962 Aidit gave it official PKI blessing.[18] A more precise formulation of the doctrine was given by Sukarno in a speech on Scholars' Day, September 29, 1962, in which he defined the new emerging forces as "the states, the people of Asia, Africa, Latin America, the socialist states."[19] Later, the "progressive" forces in the capitalist states—those supporting national

[16] See *Harian Rakjat,* May 15, Aug. 28, Sept. 1, 1961.
[17] *Ibid.,* Sept. 4, 7, 15, and 22, 1961.
[18] *Problems,* pp. 487–88.
[19] Quoted by Aidit in November 1962; *Problems,* p. 215.

liberation struggles—came to be included in the NEFO ranks. The OLDEFO forces were usually left to be determined by inference, but Aidit in November 1962 characterized them as "all imperialist states, all forms of colonialism and neocolonialism, and all the reactionary forces in the world."[20]

Ideologically, the NEFO-OLDEFO doctrine meant that Sukarno had identified the Western powers as a whole with Indonesia's enemies, imperialism and colonialism. Whereas once he had been attracted to some extent by Jeffersonian principles of democracy and progress, and had been prepared to see current American statecraft as having some sort of connection with these principles, he now implicitly rejected the entire Western tradition as a camouflage for predatory aims toward new nations striving to realize their place in the world. His world outlook was thus cast in the same mould as that of the PKI leaders and the Chinese Communist Party.

But few other Indonesian leaders were as yet prepared to go this far, and the president's concepts were not embodied substantially in Indonesian foreign policy until the logic of a new confrontation—that of Malaysia—had taken hold. A gap between the president's rhetoric and state policy continued to exist for some time, and PKI criticisms of dualism in foreign policy, which it said could only be overcome when the president took full charge of its conduct, were pertinent as well as being useful in underlining the party's own fidelity to the official ideology.[21]

THE LIBERATION OF WEST IRIAN

The West Irian campaign, which reached its height in 1961–62, took place, then, in the context of closely related concepts of international relations developed by Sukarno and the Communists. Constant reiteration and elaboration of the themes embodied in these concepts served to justify the emphasis placed on the campaign and to arouse the public enthusiasm necessary to gain acceptance for the sacrifices it entailed. Likewise, the president's masterly rhetoric and the PKI's mobilizing capacity, assured both parties of prominence in the determination of the goals and tactics associated with the confrontation with Dutch power.

[20] *Ibid.*, p. 213.
[21] For PKI attacks on dualism at the seventh party congress in April 1962, see *Problems*, pp. 492–94, 500; *Madju Terus*, pp. 268–69.

The issue began to pass from the realm of agitation to that of hostile action late in 1960. In August, diplomatic relations with the Dutch were broken off and the PKI, in response to the United States' refusal to supply Indonesia with the weaponry she sought, called for the takeover of American enterprises in Indonesia. But these were gestures, aimed at keeping the issue alive, rather than signals for immediate action. The close of the year, however, brought news of small parties of Indonesian infiltrators landing in West Irian. Although of little military effect, the landings marked a new stage in the conflict. In January 1961, amidst reports of further small landings, an arms purchasing mission to Moscow led by Defense Minister General A. H. Nasution concluded with what Nasution described without exaggeration as "highly satisfactory" results: the immediate grant to Indonesia of $400 million worth of modern military equipment for the West Irian campaign and the promise of further aid of a similar kind.[22]

The Nasution mission, and its outcome, marked a decisive switch in policy, which Sukarno had been urging, and the army resisting, for some time. Army leaders wanted to keep Indonesia within the Western orbit, in order to minimize Communist influence, and had striven hard to persuade the American government to meet Indonesia's requirements for modern weaponry and training. During the regional rebellion, however, when United States' policy had favored the regionalist cause, they had been obliged to take up Soviet offers of military aid. They had hoped this necessity would not recur, and throughout 1960 Nasution and other generals had repeatedly explored the possibility of obtaining through Washington the heavy equipment they needed. The attempt did not succeed; America was suspicious of Sukarno's motives and felt bound by its ties to Holland under the NATO treaty not to aid Indonesia's bid to force the Dutch out of West Irian.[23] Meanwhile, the Dutch in 1960 had been strengthening their military position in West Irian and hastening moves toward Papuan self-government. Consequently, by the close of the year Sukarno was able to override army opposition and force acceptance of the offer Khrushchev had made during a visit to Indonesia several months earlier.

Soviet intervention was not slow to have its effect on American

[22] Guy J. Pauker, "General Nasution's Mission to Moscow," *Asian Survey*, I, no. 1 (March 1961), 13–22.
[23] *Ibid.*

policy. A change had taken place at the White House, with John F. Kennedy assuming the presidency in January 1961. The new president immediately showed himself to be more concerned than his predecessor had been with the importance of Indonesia in America's policy calculations. Although a meeting with Sukarno at this time was not a success,

The President regarded Indonesia, this country of a hundred million people, so rich in oil, tin, and rubber, as one of the potentially significant nations of Asia. He was anxious to slow up its drift towards the Communist bloc; he knew that Sukarno was already turning to Moscow to get the military equipment necessary for invasion. And he was also anxious to strengthen the anti-Communist forces, especially the army, in order to make sure that, if anything happened to Sukarno, the powerful Indonesian Communist Party would not inherit the country.[24]

Kennedy acted with promptness and decision. In February 1961, he revoked a plan for a United States representative to attend the opening of the New Guinea Council, a new legislative body regarded by the Dutch as a landmark in their policy of preparing the people of West Irian for self-government. Shock and dismay in the Netherlands, and elation in Indonesia, marked the recognition by both parties that the U.S. was in the process of abandoning its "neutrality" on the issue and moving toward active intervention favorable to Indonesia's interests.

In April Sukarno ordered the armed forces to prepare a military plan for the liberation of West Irian. He was thus putting pressure on Nasution and other army leaders, who were opposed to a major military effort before late 1962 or 1963. Nasution, indeed, had not only urged caution so far as hostilities were concerned but had also taken a personal hand in several initiatives to settle the dispute peacefully.[25] The failure of these negotiations, however, strengthened the president's hand, and by September the landings of Indonesian infiltrators were being stepped up. At this point Holland forced another UN debate on the issue; on the eve of the departure for the UN of the Indonesian delegation, led by Subandrio, Sukarno in a speech in

[24] Arthur M. Schlesinger, Jr., *A Thousand Days: John F. Kennedy in the White House* (Boston, 1965), p. 464.

[25] Justus M. Van der Kroef, "The West New Guinea Settlement: Its Origins and Implications," *Orbis,* VII, no. 1 (Spring 1963), 129–30.

Jogjakarta (October 7) announced his lack of faith in an outside solution and stated that Indonesia could settle the issue through mobilization of its own forces.

Several factors appear to have contributed to Sukarno's tougher line. He was well aware of the change in opinion in Washington and calculated that the likelihood of a serious armed clash would speed American moves for a settlement acceptable to Indonesia. The Indonesian government was also becoming concerned at the signs of awakening Papuan nationalism under the stimulus of Dutch moves toward self-government and was anxious to reach a conclusion of the issue before this new factor gave rise to problems inside and outside West Irian.[26] Finally, a big increase in the price of rice in the last quarter of 1961 threatened the government with internal instability, which an upsurge of public sentiment on the nationalist issue would help it to contain.

Subandrio made it clear at the UN that Indonesia would accept United Nations assistance in resolving the West Irian dispute only if Indonesian sovereignty over the territory were recognized. On his return to Djakarta on October 24 during a recess in the UN debate, he said that Indonesia would liberate West Irian by force if Dutch preparations to grant independence to the territory were carried further under armed protection. A flurry of diplomatic activity marked Indonesia's efforts to lobby the uncommitted nations. At the same time preparations for military action were pushed forward; civil airline pilots were placed on active alert, and the formation of a West Irian task force was put in hand. On November 11 Sukarno stated that his final command for the liberation of West Irian only awaited the decision of the UN; if it accepted the Dutch proposal for internationalization, Indonesia would use force. In the event, the UN debate proved inconclusive, neither side being able to muster the required number of votes.[27]

On November 15, Nasution dropped a mild hint to army veterans of the "possibility of operations" in West Irian; ten days later he spoke of the desirability of military training for university students. On December 13, a National Defense Council was formed with Sukarno at its head, and the following week the president gave his long-

[26] *Ibid.*, pp. 136–38.
[27] For a fuller account of the UN debate, see *ibid.*, pp. 134–36.

awaited final command. Instead of the expected declaration of imminent invasion, however, Sukarno's slogans were rather anticlimactic: he called on the nation to thwart the formation of a "puppet" Papuan state, to prepare to raise the Indonesian flag in West Irian, and to ready itself for general mobilization.[28] Three days later he called for volunteers—a signal for political parties, functional groups, and unions to prepare lists and submit them to the National Front for registration.

The PKI reacted to the increase in the tempo of the West Irian campaign with declarations of support for the government stand and calls for mass mobilization. Prior to this, on September 30, the Politburo had issued a statement saying that the patience of the people was exhausted and that they would liberate West Irian "by whatever means are necessary."[29] On October 13, the Front Pemuda Pusat, the central leadership of the youth section of the National Front, in which PKI influence was already dominant, called for liberation along the "Djalan '45," that is, "confrontation in all fields."[30]

During this period, Aidit was absent in Europe, attending the twenty-second congress of the Communist Party of the Soviet Union and a series of congresses of other European Communist parties. It was at these congresses that the Sino-Soviet dispute at last erupted into open polemics when the CPSU attacked China-leaning Albania. Aidit used the congresses to obtain declarations of support for Indonesia's stand on West Irian, including a joint statement of the Indonesian and Dutch Communist parties declaring that "the CPN and the progressive Dutch people will side with the Indonesian people should a war break out over West Irian between Indonesia and the Netherlands."[31]

Late in 1961, President Kennedy succeeded in overcoming resistence in the State Department to his revised policy toward Indonesia. In December he wrote to Sukarno offering to find a solution to the West Irian dispute by direct negotiations; at the same time he asked British Prime Minister Macmillan to persuade the Dutch and Australians to be more flexible.[32] The Dutch premier, De Quay, re-

[28] *Ibid.,* p. 136.
[29] *Harian Rakjat,* Sept. 30, 1961.
[30] *Ibid.,* Oct. 13, 1961.
[31] See Aidit's speech on his return from Europe; *Problems,* pp. 187–95.
[32] Schlesinger, p. 465.

sponded by expressing willingness to open new discussions without prior acceptance of self-determination, but Indonesia rejected the offer on the grounds that it still contained a Dutch commitment to the self-determination principle.[33] Mobilization plans went ahead in Indonesia, and in January 1962 the most serious armed clash to date took place off the West Irian coast, producing a humiliating defeat for Indonesia and the loss of the deputy commander of her navy. Excitement in the country reached a new pitch, with the PKI well in the van of the agitation. In December, the Politburo had called on all Pemuda Rakjat members to volunteer and declared that if their numbers were insufficient the entire party was ready to join the ranks.[34] After the January 15 incident, the party called for all-out attack and the outright confiscation of Dutch business interests that had been nationalized in 1958.

The international aspects of the dispute were now thoroughly worked over. Yugoslavia was criticized for favoring a peaceful solution; Malaya was scolded for adopting a neutral attitude; and every item of evidence that could be interpreted as indicating support for or connivance with Holland on the part of the United States, Britain, Australia, and Japan was featured. NEFO solidarity with Indonesia was stressed again and again. In February, pressure was exerted for the establishment of training centers, and demonstrations were organized outside the United States Embassy.[35]

Meanwhile, President Kennedy initiated the steps that were finally to lead to fruitful negotiations. In February he sent his brother Robert to Indonesia bearing a letter urging the Indonesians to come to the conference table without preconditions.[36] Robert Kennedy made his partiality toward Indonesia sufficiently clear to set up resistance on the part of the Dutch, but on March 20 the parties finally came together in the presence of U.S. mediator Ellsworth Bunker.[37] Five months of difficult negotiations followed, with first the Dutch and then the Indonesians dragging their feet in an attempt to extract further advantages. At strategic points during the negotiations, Indonesia

[33] Van der Kroef, "The West New Guinea Settlement," pp. 138–39.
[34] *Harian Rakjat,* Dec. 26, 1961.
[35] *Ibid.,* Feb. 6, 8, and 19, 1962.
[36] Schlesinger, p. 465.
[37] For details, see Van der Kroef, "The West New Guinea Settlement," p. 139.

landed further troops on the West Irian mainland, at first with the aim of putting pressure on Holland but later, when the outline of the solution was clear, with the additional objective of frustrating any bid by Papuan nationalists to usurp her victory.[38] On August 15 agreement was finally announced on terms highly favorable to Indonesia. The United Nations would take over administration of the territory on October 1, 1962, and gradually effect a transfer to Indonesia by May 1, 1963; before the end of 1969, Indonesia would conduct an "act of free choice" to enable the Papuans "to decide their own future."

The PKI had followed the course of the negotiations closely and with a certain amount of caution. On August 7, Aidit had welcomed Sukarno's decision to enter into formal discussions with the Dutch but had accompanied this with reminders that the people would only be satisfied with the complete surrender of West Irian to Indonesian authority.[39] While the talks were going on, agitation against compromise was resumed and advance denials were offered against any view that an agreement, if arrived at, would be in any way due to American good offices.[40] The final agreement was hailed as a great success for "the road of the *Trikora*" (Sukarno's tripartite "final command" of December 1961)—in other words, for the line of "confrontation in all fields."

REAPING THE POLITICAL HARVEST

Once negotiations over West Irian had begun, and the Americans, Dutch, and Australians had all started to abandon their previous positions, a good deal of attention in Indonesia shifted to the question of who within the leadership would be able to claim credit for the anticipated victory. Three groups, each of which had had its own line of approach to the West Irian issue, were contenders: one, surrounding Foreign Minister Subandrio, had argued for a diplomatic course (in the latter months of the campaign Adam Malik became Subandrio's rival as the leading exponent of this line); another was led by Defense Minister Nasution, who in early 1962 had switched to

---

[38] The course of the negotiations, and the tactics of the parties, are described in *ibid.*, pp. 138–46.

[39] *Harian Rakjat,* Aug. 7, 1962.

[40] *Ibid.,* Aug. 10, 1962.

support of a major military effort; finally there was the camp of President Sukarno, backed by the PKI, which had all along favored an agitational campaign, with only a minor military component.

On the whole, the presidential party emerged from the settlement with the strongest claim to have steered the campaign to victory. No one could deny the extent of Indonesia's success. She had achieved virtually everything she had aimed for, while the Dutch had suffered deep humiliation, especially when it was demonstrated during the negotiation phases that they could be forced to talk even while Indonesia was flagrantly carrying on military action against West Irian. The United States came out of the affair reasonably well in Indonesia, as did Subandrio and Malik, since the issue had been settled at the bargaining table without major military action. Nasution and the army did less well; their forays into West Irian had been far from impressive, and they had been denied the opportunity to launch an all-out invasion attempt.[41] But Sukarno and his radical supporters could and did argue that their tactics of creating a national and international furore, pressuring the Americans to come down on their side and unsettling the Dutch by a combination of bluff and threat, had provided the winning formula. The radicals claimed that, while the good offices of the United States had opened the way for and defined the terms of the final agreement, American benevolence had been secured above all by the determination Indonesians themselves had shown to push their campaign to the limit. The PKI in particular went further and suggested that United States intervention had done no more than save Holland from an even more ignominious surrender at the point of the bayonet.

Sukarno's tactics had been well calculated to take advantage of the prevailing international situation. The bitter cold war postures of the two great powers in the fifties had moderated to the point where each recognized the necessity for and desirability of some easing of tensions. They had modified their tendency to regard all countries as either firm allies or actual or potential enemies and were devoting great attention to wooing the uncommitted nations of the third world. Taking advantage of their new flexibility in international relations, the new states for their part were organizing among themselves to obtain greater leverage in the world arena. It was a situation in which

[41] See Feith, "Dynamics," pp. 353–54.

even relatively weak powers might hope to be able to play one side off against the other, with profit to themselves. This in fact was what Sukarno had succeeded brilliantly in doing. He had traveled widely enough to be able to gauge international trends, and his political shrewdness is beyond doubt. There seems reason therefore to credit him with executing quite a masterly coup in his handling of the West Irian issue.

At the same time there were other factors inclining him toward the course he followed. Despite his apocalyptic speeches, the president had usually been cautious, even timid, when it came to action, and the confrontation tactics offered the maximum in political pressure with the minimum of risk of armed conflict on a scale threatening Indonesia's security and political stability. At the same time, a confrontation strategy, involving appeals within and without Indonesia to solidarity, anti-imperialism, and national independence, was one that best accorded with his gifts and emphasized his unique role. It is perhaps not too much to see in Sukarno's actions, too, the influence of that traditional Javanese idea of power which holds that it brings greater credit upon a ruler to force an enemy to bow to his superior demonstration of strength than to crush the enemy by physical force.[42]

Soviet military aid had been of great importance to Indonesia in waging the West Irian campaign, and especially in enabling the country to threaten much larger military offensives than were in fact undertaken. In its wake, economic and technical assistance was extended on a lavish scale, and commercial and cultural relations were expanded in a relatively short period. These developments were naturally welcomed by the PKI: they drew Indonesia closer to the Communist bloc and away from the United States; at the same time they promoted greater interest in and sympathy for Communism and gave the party an opportunity to act as a political broker between the two governments, as Aidit had done at the twenty-second congress of the CPSU with regard to West Irian.

Indonesia's ambition to become the militant center of the Afro-Asian bloc was also advanced during the course of the West Irian dispute. The Indonesian government gained considerable respect for

---

[42] For a discussion of this theme, see Benedict R. O'G. Anderson, "The Idea of Power in Javanese Culture," in Holt, ed., *Culture and Politics in Indonesia,* pp. 1–69.

the success with which it had pursued its national claim. Over the same period, despite the demands of the liberation campaign, it had devoted an enormous range of organizational and material resources to preparing the Asian Games that took place in Djakarta in August 1962. As it happened, however, Indonesia's handling of issues that arose regarding participation in the Games aroused mixed reactions. She had originally agreed to admit Israel and Taiwan to the Games, but then, under pressure from the Arab states and China, had reversed her position. This incident caused an international scandal; violent polemics were engaged in by Indonesia and India, whose representatives on the International Olympics Committee had strongly criticized the political character of the Games, and Indonesia was ultimately barred from participating in the 1964 Tokyo Olympics.

The impressive stadia complex built with Soviet help and the unexpectedly good organization of the Games helped somewhat to restore Indonesia's tarnished reputation, but even some of the militant African states must have been shocked by the tactics Indonesia had employed. The PKI, on the other hand, fully supported the government's handling of the entire affair, finding in international reactions to the exclusion of Taiwan and Israel an imperialist plot to sabotage the Games and undermine Indonesia's free and active foreign policy.[43]

The PKI leaders had consistently supported the president's line of attack on the West Irian issue, except for some reservations about the possible political implications of negotiations conducted under the aegis of the United States. They had no reason to welcome a military dimension to the struggle, since this would either rebound to the credit of the army or, in the event of defeats and setbacks, provide an excuse for the imposition of even tougher martial law powers. Similarly, a primary accent on negotiations, as advocated by Subandrio, would have left the party largely out in the cold and fearful of behind-doors deals inimical to its interests. The combination of low-profile military sorties, agitation, and negotiations advocated by Sukarno was admirably suited to the PKI's requirements; this approach not only put its presidential patron at the center of the stage, as it wished, but also gave full rein to those mass agitational capabilities that the party possessed in a measure unmatched by any other organization in the country.

[43] See, for example, *Harian Rakjat*, Feb. 10, 1962.

Steadfastly supporting the president's foreign policy approach, and stressing its own militancy by opposing all forms and appearances of compromise on the West Irian issue, the PKI enhanced its reputation for patriotism and national devotion in an atmosphere where these qualities were all-important in winning prestige and public acceptance. Although the army authorities continued to harry the party, they could do little to restrain the revived dynamism that it displayed on an issue central to the national interest.

Moreover, the loyalty of the PKI to the official ideology and Sukarno's policies was by this time causing a shift in alignments within the officer corps itself, with a greater number of officers inclining toward acceptance of Sukarno's leadership, with its implication that the Communists could be tolerated while they continued to abide by the policies and goals of the state. Sukarno took advantage of this trend to initiate a series of transfers and changes in army commands in June 1962, his object being to strengthen his influence over the military and weaken the position of Nasution and other rigidly anti-Nasakom generals.[44] As a result of the acquisition of Soviet hardware the army was by the end of 1962 a more formidable force in terms of physical power, but it had lost some of its political cohesion and drive, which had been built up in large part around anti-Communism. Its popularity had also waned as restiveness grew at the manner in which the army's martial law powers were exercised. A further downgrading of the army's political role was signaled by Sukarno's announcement at the end of the year that martial law powers would be repealed on the following May 1.

The PKI's strong position in the National Front by 1962 gave it a respectable official base from which to launch its mass demonstrations and displays of revolutionary fervor. The National Front became the agitational center of the West Irian campaign, and the tone-setting role of the PKI was unmistakable. The party had recovered the ground it had lost in 1959–60 and had reached a highwater mark comparable to its position at the height of the regional crisis in 1958. Throughout the West Irian campaign it had reiterated a number of themes, all carefully designed to highlight its concepts of struggle or to advance its domestic position. The major slogans were:

[44] Feith, "President Sukarno, the Army and the Communists."

Success will come through democracy, unity, and mobilization. This slogan expressed the tactical approach that the party shared with Sukarno and at the same time emphasized the wider interests of the Communists in the repeal of martial law, the holding of national and local elections, and the disavowal of anti-Communism, all three of which the PKI's notion of democracy demanded.

There must be confrontation in all fields. Again a particular tactical line was advanced, and this time it was linked with propaganda on the need to tackle economic and welfare problems in order to strengthen the nation's potential in the struggle against colonialism and imperialism. In this way, the PKI was able to some extent to raise issues of social welfare within a patriotic context without giving its enemies grounds for charging it with endangering national unity. As part of this approach, the party in February 1962 launched its "1001 Movement," a mass campaign stressing that there were "1001 ways" in which production might be increased by popular effort with governmental assistance. The central slogan of the production campaign urged the masses to keep "one hand on the gun and one hand on the plough." The drive was not notably successful, but it helped to maintain the party's reputation for attention to the people's needs and probably also reassured the cadres that the leadership was genuinely concerned about the decline in popular living standards.

The imperialists only understand strength. From this premise it followed that the government must take resolute action to pursue its objectives. In this context, constant evidence was presented of the imperialists' aggressiveness and perfidy and of the danger of flirting with them.

There should be no negotiations except on the basis of Dutch surrender. Secret discussions are bad, the PKI argued, because they are used by the imperialists to delay matters and sow confusion, and a compromise should be avoided. The party was apparently worried lest the government do a deal with the United States resulting in a new Western orientation and an influx of American aid, which would be disastrous for its political prospects.

The West Irian struggle is a classic illustration of NEFO-OLDEFO conflict. As already mentioned, the PKI was assiduous in canvassing support for Indonesia from the "progressive" forces in the world, and in citing examples of opposition among the "reactionary" forces. This activity was of paramount importance in establishing general acceptance of its international concepts.

Sukarno's call to free Irian in 1962 must be fully realized.

Remaining Dutch capital should be seized.   Enterprises previously nationalized should be confiscated outright.

The people should be armed.   This would enable the armed forces to be augmented with volunteers and would provide the country with a huge militia reserve in the case of enlarged hostilities. The PKI had previously proposed the arming of the masses in the mid-fifties, as an aid in suppressing the Darul Islam rebels in West Java, and again during the regional rebellion. On neither occasion had the proposal been taken up. Army leaders were naturally opposed, seeing in the idea a PKI ploy to get its hands on weapons and organize a force that could undermine the military's monopoly of arms. During the West Irian campaign, however, the president endorsed the proposal, which accorded with his vision of a united nation ready to storm the citadels of imperialism. However, Nasution was able to restrict the volunteer plan largely to university students and to keep strict army control over the issue of weapons and training of volunteers. The PKI at this time was weak among the students, and army screening methods kept out most of its legion of volunteers.[45]

NATIONALISM GAINS GROUND IN THE PKI

At the conclusion of the West Irian campaign the PKI judged the time appropriate to proclaim the United States both number one enemy and most dangerous enemy of the Indonesian people, thus arriving at a position toward which it had been working since 1954.[46] The PKI leaders understood very well that Indonesia was unlikely to stand alone in international affairs, if for no other reason than that, with mounting inflation and government deficits, it stood in great and urgent need of foreign aid to cover its deficits in international payments. The question was, would the government continue its course of the last year or two and lean closer to the Communist

[45] Note the speech of Pemuda Rakjat leader Sukatno to the PKI seventh congress in April 1962: "A quarter of a million Pemuda Rakjat members registered for military training, but the greater part of them were not given any training" (*Madju Tersus,* pp. 185–86).

[46] See Aidit, *Dare, Dare and Dare Again!* p. 36.

camp, or would it revert to dependence upon the United States? For the Communists, the answer was crucial to their future, and they were determined to leave no stone unturned to make the American way unacceptable.

The close of the West Irian campaign, however, left Indonesia's relations with the United States still unresolved. During its course the PKI had been able to stimulate considerable anti-U.S. feeling, both in relation to the dispute itself and on other issues such as the Congo and Cuba. Nevertheless, the United States had played a positive role in the ultimate settlement, and the argument that it had only done so to save Dutch face, while persuasive, did not alter the fact that its intervention had avoided for Indonesia the necessity for more severe and conceivably dangerous measures.

Thus, among elite circles in particular, opinion had by no means solidified in favor of a decisive break with the United States and total commitment to the Communist bloc. On the contrary, the PKI very soon began to suspect that the Irian settlement had been accompanied by an unpublicized agreement by Indonesia to accept an American-supported economic stabilization scheme.[47] This aim, in fact, had constituted the entire logic of U.S. policy, which was concerned to shore up the Indonesian political structure.[48]

Overall, then, the PKI had made significant gains during the West Irian campaign, both in having an official ideology adopted and consolidated that accorded with its views and in obtaining through its own activities and its alliance with the president at least a temporary enhancement of its place in the Guided Democracy order. But the party's position was still very insecure, and might rapidly deteriorate should there be a new governmental swing to the right in conjunction with a flow of American aid.

In these circumstances, it was clear enough that the PKI's policy would be to continue to rely as far as possible on radical nationalism to maintain the leftward momentum of Indonesian politics and to surround itself with powerful political allies. Three events occurring outside Indonesia late in 1962 served to keep the anti-imperialist spirit alive and maintain the momentum of PKI activities. In November the Cuba crisis erupted, with its threat of nuclear engagement between the

[47] See the editorial in *Harian Rakjat,* Aug. 22, 1962.
[48] Schlesinger, p. 466.

United States and the Soviet Union. The official Indonesian attitude was one of "no comment," but there was no doubt where the sympathies of most of the parties and political leaders lay. Former Premier Ali Sastroamidjojo spoke in support of Cuba; the National Front condoned a peaceful demonstration by twenty-eight of its member organizations, and the Partai Murba somewhat vaingloriously announced that it was prepared to send volunteers to Cuba. As was to be expected, the PKI took the most vigorous anti-U.S. action, calling for the seizure of American enterprises, sponsoring a boycott of U.S. ships by Surabaja dockworkers, and organizing a demonstration in the same city that did some damage to the U.S. consular office. Although the PKI did not voice any direct criticism of the Soviet Union's handling of the crisis, it made its attitude quite clear by endorsing Castro's five-point proposed solution, one that was much more radical than the agreement arrived at between Kennedy and Khrushchev.[49]

In the same month, major clashes on the Sino-Indian border broke out. Initially, Foreign Minister Subandrio stated that Indonesia did not intend to intervene; later, however, Sukarno claimed to be working as an intermediary, in association with the five-nation group of Colombo powers, and Subandrio subsequently held talks with the Chinese and Indian ambassadors in Ceylon. Indonesian mediation efforts went on for some time, but it was obvious that she would take no steps that would antagonize China. In view of Sukarno's rivalry with Nehru, and Indonesia's opposition to the Indian concept of neutralism, this was hardly surprising; China had shown herself during the Irian and Asian Games issues much more willing to back Indonesia's radical intransigence. The PKI press was predictably anti-Indian and pro-Chinese. The Indian Communist Party, which denounced Chinese aggression and adopted a patriotic progovernmental stance, was accused of succumbing to chauvinism. While the Soviet Union's scarcely disguised sympathy for India was passed over publicly, Aidit sent a cable to Khrushchev congratulating him on the decision to suspend the supply of MIG's to India.

Closer to home, and as it turned out of greater moment for the future course of Guided Democracy politics, a revolt began in De-

[49] See *Harian Rakjat,* Oct. 26, Nov. 8, 1962.

cember in the North Borneo Sultanate of Brunei. A British protec-
torate, Brunei was one of the territories scheduled for incorporation
in the proposed Federation of Malaysia. However, strong opposition
came from the Brunei People's Party, which held all but one seat in
the kingdom's elected but purely advisory assembly and was in conflict with the Sultan over demands for greater political power. Judging by subsequent events, the Brunei party also seems to have regarded itself as part of a broader alliance, within all North Borneo
territories, opposing the Malaysian Federation, an opposition that
Malaya was later to allege had been encouraged by Indonesia. The
actual revolt in early December followed the Sultan's dissolution of
the assembly.

Indonesian official and party opinion came out strongly on the side
of the Brunei rebels. Sukarno declared that the revolt would surely
win. The Front Marhaen, a PNI subsidiary, and the Front Pemuda,
the youth section of the National Front, called for volunteers to be
enrolled to help the rebel struggle. Seeing in these declarations hostility toward the proposed Malaysian Federation, the Malayan government reacted with sharp criticisms of Indonesian policy, which were
promptly returned by Subandrio and other spokesmen. While affirming that Indonesia did not aspire to enlarge its territory, Subandrio
threatened that if the Malayan premier, Tunku Abdul Rahman, used
the situation to aggravate tensions between Malaya and Indonesia,
then Indonesia would have no alternative but to accept the challenge.

The PKI had opposed the idea of the Malaysian Federation soon
after it was propounded in May 1961. It described the project as a
British neocolonial plan to suppress the national independence movements of the territories concerned and suggested that the continued
presence of British bases and influence in the area posed a potential
threat to Indonesia's security. Immediately on the outbreak of the revolt
Harian Rakjat declared that it showed that most people in Brunei did
not want Malaysia and that the colonialist system was shaky in that
country.[50] On December 13, the day following the issue of Sukarno's
first statement on the revolt, Aidit issued a declaration refuting
charges that the PKI was involved in the rebellion but hailing the revolt as a "just revolution [which] must be supported with all energies

---

[50] *Ibid.*, Dec. 10, 1962.

by progressives all over the world, and especially by the people of Indonesia," and accusing Malaya of "expansionism."[51] In succeeding weeks, *Harian Rakjat* bristled with adverse comment on Britain and Malaya.

All these developments intensified the nationalist orientation of the PKI and steered it in directions more and more at odds with Soviet policies and in line with Chinese Communist attitudes. One aspect of this tendency was the heavier emphasis that Aidit in particular began to place in the latter part of 1962 on the role of spirit, resolve, and enthusiasm in transforming political situations to advantage. This emphasis accorded both with Sukarno's longstanding political style and the similar emphasis apparent in Mao's writings for a considerable time. By contrast, the Soviet Union, as befitted a "have" power, adopted a much more economic determinist approach to international affairs, one clearly signified in the concept of peaceful coexistence and competition that stressed the inevitability of the victory of socialism through peaceful competition with the West. The difference in political style is characteristic of all controversies between the proponents of world stability and the radical advocates of revolutionary change. It will be met with again frequently in the course of the following chapter.

[51] *Ibid.*, Dec. 13, 1962.

5. Nationalism:
The Malaysia Phase

Indonesia's first major exercise in foreign confrontation played an important part in rescuing the PKI from the tight corner into which it had been driven in 1959–60 by army power and the restrictive controls of the Guided Democracy order. The second confrontation—against Malaysia and its British sponsors—proved signally less successful from the Indonesian government's point of view than the West Irian campaign, but still more efficacious for the PKI. It changed the direction of Indonesian foreign and domestic policies decisively in the party's favor and presented it with opportunities so promising that the leadership began to comprehend for the first time since the introduction of Guided Democracy how they might achieve power within the terms set by that system.

The PKI was the first political group in Indonesia to condemn the proposed Malaysian Federation, and this fact, together with the party's prominence in the subsequent official hostility to the Federation, has prompted the view that the Communists were largely instrumental in precipitating the conflict and that they did so as part of a wider Communist offensive against Western positions in Asia, principally directed by the Communist Party of China.

This view does not find support in the analysis put forward here. It will be argued that the PKI's major concern during the early stages of the dispute between Indonesia and Malaysia was to counter what it perceived as the threat of renewed American influence on Indonesia's domestic policies. The Communists were slow to recognize that the Malaysia issue might serve as a means of thwarting this development, and, even when they did so, they were not in a position to affect Indonesia's policies crucially in the period before the onset of full scale confrontation in September 1963.

More importantly, a radically different view will be taken of the PKI's motivations in supporting the confrontation of Malaysia. Far from aiming to change the balance of power in Asia by precipitating a major clash between Indonesia and foreign powers, the PKI was most anxious not to inflame the Malaysia dispute into a large scale military conflict. Such a course, in the leadership's view, would have been detrimental to the party's interests.

The uses of the Malaysia campaign for the PKI were at the same time symbolic and instrumental: symbolic in the sense that while the party's policy statements were couched in terms of the destruction of the Malaysian edifice their actual aim was the inculcation of a radical mood in Indonesia rather than the promotion of an external venture; instrumental in the sense that the development of the spirit and outlook sought by the PKI was calculated to strengthen its hand in internal politics at the expense of its rivals and enemies. Any separation of these two facets of PKI strategy produces misleading conclusions. Taking the party's symbolic utterances literally gives an entirely mistaken impression of its objectives. Alternatively, exclusive concentration on its instrumental aims and activities overlooks the key role that the symbolism of the anti-imperialist struggle played in enabling it to pursue its objectives successfully.

During the West Irian campaign the ideological setting had been provided by Sukarno, and the PKI, cognizant of its weakness, was largely content to follow his guidelines and improve its position by demonstrating its zeal as the president's most ardent and effective supporter. As confrontation against Malaysia reached a crescendo, however, the party escaped its subordinate ideological role and began to provide the theoretical concepts that underwrote the campaign. Sukarno's themes remained prominent, but they were progressively overshadowed by the innovations devised by the PKI leadership, and Sukarno himself came to borrow more and more extensively from the PKI's ideological armory.

This subtle change in the relationship between the president and the Communists was symptomatic of the new political balance that had been struck by the enhancement of the PKI's position. By late 1963, the party leaders felt more secure and capable of taking political initiatives, and they had built up the detachments of their followers to the point where their influence could be brought to bear upon events rapidly and decisively. Sukarno, for his part, seems to have exhausted most of his ideological imagination; he had come to regard the Communists as his staunch allies and close confidants and was more content to use their formulations, so long as his prestige was not undermined.

Inspiration for the Indonesian Communists' concepts came from the international line of the Communist Party of China, but the PKI used that inspiration for its own political purposes in a manner that differed in vital respects from the CPC's design. The differences stemmed from the fact that the PKI leaders were using Chinese international theses to give theoretical force to their radical symbolic activity, while their purposes were located in the domestic sphere and were directed toward an essentially peaceful road to power.

It was due to the political craft of Aidit above all that the PKI came to possess by December 1963 a comprehensive theory of political change adapting the united national front strategy to the circumstances of Guided Democracy. One aspect of that theory—Aidit's definition of the Indonesian state—has already been outlined. In this chapter another major element in the theory will be discussed—the manner in which anti-imperialist sentiment was to be used to radicalize politics and ensure the PKI of a commanding position in the life of the nation. In order to follow the process by which this understanding of PKI strategy was arrived at, the stage for confrontation must first be set.

CONFRONTATION: THE PRELUDE

In the aftermath of the successful West Irian campaign, it appeared that the Indonesian government might turn its attention to the tasks of economic stabilization and development, as it had long been urged to do by critics outside and within the country. The United States in particular had been intent for some time on encouraging such a course, which, it believed, would promote stability in Indonesia, combat Russian influence, and undercut the appeal of the PKI.[1]

In mid-1961, President Kennedy had appointed a survey team led by Professor D. D. Humphrey to look into Indonesia's needs, and after an on-the-spot investigation the team had issued a report in mid-

[1] F. P. Bunnell, "The Kennedy Initiatives in Indonesia, 1962–63" (Ph.D. Thesis, Cornell University, 1969), pp. 60–148.

1962 recommending United States' assistance of between $200 million and $235 million, together with multinational finance to the order of $125–155 million.[2] These offers of assistance were tied to a series of proposals for economic reform in Indonesia, in effect an austerity program to be tailored by the International Monetary Fund. By the latter months of 1962 discussion was rife in the Indonesian capital about impending measures to implement the proposed stabilization scheme.

There was as yet little sign, however, that the government was geared for the rigorous and politically unpopular steps that would have to be taken if stabilization was to be thoroughgoing, including retrenchment in the expensive prestige projects associated with Sukarno's grandiose conception of Indonesia's place in the world. A lot of people stood to be hurt by a belt-tightening policy, including such politically powerful groups as the armed forces' leaders, the chiefs of large government departments, and various private businessmen. In addition, strong opposition could be expected from the PKI, whose leaders would feel the pressure of discontent from their supporters as prices were adjusted upwards.

Little effort was made to prepare the country or the affected groups for the sacrifices that would lie in store; it was as if the government had been persuaded of the necessity of taking action but was hoping that it would not have to face up to the unpalatable consequences. Later events suggest, in fact, that important figures in the government, including the President, were less than enthusiastic about the proposed policy of restraints but were overborne in this period by the arguments of ministers and advisers, headed by Prime Minister Djuanda, who pointed to the desperate state of the country's foreign exchange reserves and the general rundown in production and exports. In retrospect, it is clear that the balance in favor of retrenchment was a delicate one and that if a way out of the tough political decisions involved should present itself key power-holders would be greatly tempted to grasp it.

The PKI had a great deal more to fear from the projected stabilization scheme than just the adverse effects austerity would have upon its

[2] *Indonesia: Perspectives and Proposals for United States' Economic Aid: A Report to the President of the United States* (Southeast Asian Studies, Yale University, 1963).

electorate; and it is not necessary to assume, as some commentators have, that the PKI leaders welcomed the prospect of economic collapse as an aid to their revolutionary objectives to appreciate why they should have been alarmed by signs that stabilization was being seriously contemplated.

Indonesia, in fact, stood at an important political crossroads, and the choice made of which road to follow was bound to have decisive consequences for the fate of the Communists. The West Irian campaign had moved politics somewhat to the left compared to the situation in 1960–61, the tone being set by the president's radical nationalism, which the PKI underwrote and made the vehicle of its resurgence. Army leaders had faltered in this political climate, and the improvement in the country's security situation had undermined the basis of their authority to some extent; in addition, the replacement of Nasution by Jani in 1962, and the antipathy between these two, had strengthened the president's hand in dealing with the officers. The military and economic aid furnished by the Soviet Union had helped to shift the orientation of Indonesia's foreign policy away from the West and toward the Communist countries, to the point where the USSR was reportedly using its influence in late 1962 to press for the inclusion of the PKI in the cabinet.

The new course was by no means securely established, however, and the renewed relationship with the United States implicit in the serious consideration being given by high officials to the stabilization scheme threatened to reverse it. Since a major interest of the United States in Indonesia was to counter domestic and overseas Communist influence, it was not to be expected that she would come to Indonesia's aid if the government opened its ranks to the Communists, and this was clearly understood in Djakarta; if the stabilization scheme went ahead, this must mean the end of talk about a Nasakom cabinet.

The PKI leaders were well aware of what was at stake. From the time that serious negotiations on the West Irian issue had been initiated, they had warned that United States mediation was linked with neocolonialist plans to dominate the Indonesian economy and promote the interests of reactionaries among the political elite. The vehemence with which they pushed the issue of a Nasakom cabinet late in 1962 and early in 1963 was closely related to the strengthening trend toward acceptance of the stabilization proposals. The

Communist leaders understood that once a right wing policy course had set in there was no telling where it would end, or what measures against the party would be considered necessary to reassure the Western powers and foreign investors. With powerful enemies anxious to block its future growth, and martial law powers still in force, the PKI's position would be bleak if President Sukarno decided to sacrifice the party on the altar of economic rehabilitation.

Indonesia's hostile reaction to the formation of a Malaysian Federation, sparked off by the revolt in Brunei, could be seen as one potential barrier to stabilization. If the dispute worsened, it could easily provoke a new burst of nationalist sentiment detrimental to economic concerns and at the same time make the American government and Western investors more cautious about putting money into Indonesia. As 1962 ended, however, this prospect did not seem strong. After the initial furore over the Brunei revolt in mid-December, a steady propaganda barrage against the Malayan and British governments was maintained in Indonesia, but President Sukarno seemed to be genuinely in two minds about how far to push the conflict and how to balance the competing priorities of stabilization and his NEFO crusade. Without doubt he would have preferred to confront Malaysia and attract American aid for the economy simultaneously, but he had not at that stage conceived a definite strategy to these ends.[3]

The ambivalence persisted into the first weeks of 1963. While Indonesia made a number of hostile gestures toward Malaya and the Federation proposal, there were also signs of official restraint on the issue, among them Sukarno's virtual silence on the subject of Brunei and Malaysia throughout much of January. At the same time, the government pursued its discussions on the implementation of the stabilization scheme.[4]

The relative calm was broken on January 20, however, by a speech by Foreign Minister Subandrio in which for the first time he officially labeled Indonesia's attitude toward Malaysia as one of "confrontation." Judging by the West Irian experience, this could only mean a calculated resort to diplomatic, propaganda, economic, and military pressures against the proposed Federation. Subandrio's speech was followed on January 28 by a bitter attack on the Malaysia project

[3] See Bunnell, pp. 273–82.
[4] *Ibid.,* pp. 282–83.

by Philippines leaders, who had laid claim to the North Borneo colony of Sabah.[5] The hardening of the Philippines' attitude was not overlooked in Djakarta, and could not fail to encourage its efforts to torpedo the proposed Federation.[6]

There were more portents of trouble in late January and February, with bellicose speeches by Jani and other army leaders; a statement by Subandrio of Indonesia's willingness to use guerrilla harassment against Malaysia; and, on February 13, a scathing anti-Malaysia speech by Sukarno in which he described the proposed Federation as a neocolonialist enterprise intended to encircle Indonesia, expressed his support for the "struggle of the people of North Kalimantan," and endorsed the policy of confrontation. At the same time Sukarno demonstrated that stabilization had no strong hold on his affections. In response to the action of the International Olympics Committee in suspending Indonesia for its exclusion of Israel and Taiwan from the Asian Games, he announced an ambitious and inevitably expensive plan to organize a Games of the New Emerging Forces later in the year as a rival sports festival to the Olympics.[7]

It would be surprising if PKI leaders had failed to note the developing contradiction between the demands of stabilization and those of confrontation and the opportunities it offered them to recapture the atmosphere of the West Irian campaign and so fend off the threatening rightward political trend. The party had, after all, led the attack on Malaysia as far back as July 1961, and in a Central Committee resolution of December that year had rehearsed both the themes that later became embodied in official Indonesian propaganda. The proposed Malaysian Federation, it had declared, was intended "to suppress the democratic and patriotic movements of the peoples of Malaya, Singapore and North Borneo which aim at the attainment of genuine national independence and freedom from imperialism," and it was "also aimed against Indonesia."[8] To isolate party statements on this issue from the general context of its political agitation at the time, however, is to risk overestimating the significance the

---

[5] *Ibid.,* pp. 291–92.

[6] An enthusiastic editorial comment appeared in the foreign ministry mouthpiece, *Indonesian Herald,* on Jan. 30, 1963.

[7] Bunnell, pp. 287–97.

[8] *Strengthen National Unity and Communist Unity,* pp. 58–61.

PKI attached to the Malaysia issue at this date. Generally speaking, PKI comments on Malaysia prior to the outbreak of the Brunei revolt in December 1962 did not occupy great prominence in the party's arsenal of propaganda and frequently occurred in the course of lengthy reviews of the international situation, in which a host of issues of greater or lesser concern were also taken up. Thus, in Aidit's report to the PKI seventh congress in April 1962, Malaysia was treated as subsidiary to such other crisis points of anti-imperialist struggle as the Congo, Algeria, Cuba, and Syria, and Aidit's advice to the party was merely to "pay close attention" to British plans and "be very vigilant" toward the plots of the imperialists in Southeast Asia.[9] It is most unlikely that the PKI leaders, at this point or even much later, anticipated the overriding place Malaysia would occupy in the politics of 1964–65, and still less likely that they had decided to elevate it into a central issue in their drive for power and influence. Apart from anything else, as we shall see, they did not yet consider themselves to be in a position where they could exercise a determining initiative in national politics; the general approach of Aidit, the party's leading strategist, was not to risk the party's safety or standing by attempting to dictate the course of national policies but rather to be on the alert to fend off and defeat policies harmful to the party or, where possible, to turn events to its advantage.

Even after the evident hardening of Indonesian attitudes toward Malaysia in late January 1963, the PKI did not immediately grasp the opportunity presented to it. In his report to the plenum of the Central Committee that met on February 10, 1963, Malaysia was still far from being uppermost in Aidit's concerns. Due tribute was of course paid to the struggle of the people of North Kalimantan, and a determination was expressed to do all possible to support them,[10] but Aidit left his listeners in no doubt about what constituted the primary threat to independence:

British imperialism has recently come to the fore with its Malaysia plan, in addition to West German imperialism and Japanese imperialism with their penetration. All this certainly arouses the vigilance of the Indonesian people. But of all these imperialisms that are playing their

[9] *Problems,* p. 492.
[10] *Dare, Dare and Dare Again!* pp. 58–59.

role in Indonesia, the enemy number one and the most dangerous enemy of the Indonesian people is American imperialism. This is the imperialism that must be made the main target in the struggle against neo-colonialism. . . .

The danger that comes from . . . Malaysian neo-colonialism must of course be opposed, but the people quickly get to know about it and it is easy to mobilize opposition to it. When it comes through the "economy," it is "unfelt" and there are some who even think things are very nice, but the independence of our country is being undermined and whittled away.[11]

Aidit appeared still to regard the Malaysia issue as a comparatively minor one, a ploy by a declining imperialist power that did not unduly threaten Indonesia's interests or impinge heavily on the PKI's strategy. His mind was concentrated on what he considered to be the far more serious and urgent threat posed by U.S. imperialism through the proposed stabilization scheme. His entire report hinged on this question and the grave neocolonialist threat it embodied. Either the idea that the Malaysia issue might serve as a means of combating and defeating the stabilization proposals, and driving a wedge between the Indonesian and United States governments, did not occur to Aidit at this time (if it had he would surely have sought to stimulate, rather than play down, feeling on the question), or he felt that the time was not propitious to hint at such a prospect.

The line advanced by Aidit at the February plenum was one focusing on the threat of U.S. neocolonialism via economic penetration. The door to the imperialists, he suggested, was being opened by reactionaries and right wing advisers in the government who were intent on undermining Sukarno's struggle against the old established forces. In contrast to those who argued that U.S. aid was vital in arresting economic decline, the report stressed that economic difficulties could be solved without surrendering Indonesia's independence. Aid should be sought from "friendly" countries (presumably mainly Communist countries), but the major effort should lie in mobilizing Indonesia's economic and political resources.

The appeal of the PKI to Sukarno's political susceptibilities was obvious enough, but either it lacked a sufficiently compelling perspective to persuade the president to break with his advisers or he had

[11] *Ibid.,* pp. 40, 44–45.

decided that he could have confrontation and stabilization at the same time. On his instructions, the PKI was compelled to call off its campaign for a Nasakom cabinet, thus leaving the door open for the adoption of the stabilization scheme. Confrontation pressures were maintained, however, and in March 1963 there began a prolonged struggle between these two competing priorities that was to end only with the launching of all–out struggle against Malaysia in mid-September. It was a dramatic and breathless period, during which the president kept everyone guessing about his intentions, appeared continually to veer from one tack to another, and maintained an atmosphere of tense excitement that served among other things to emphasize his determining role in the country's political system.

Despite the impression of bewildering confusion in the pattern of events between March and September, it is apparent in retrospect that Sukarno was attempting to carry through a shrewdly conceived operation to enhance Indonesia's standing in Southeast Asia and the world and gratify his own ambition to appear as his nation's savior and the architect of the struggle against imperialism. His strategy was modeled closely on the precedent of the West Irian struggle, incorporating a campaign on several interacting levels—diplomatic, military, agitational, and economic. The diplomatic aspect was directed toward gaining recognition of Indonesia's right to have a determining voice in political and military arrangements in the region of Southeast Asia, while at the same time demonstrating her willingness to enter into negotiations and make reasonable compromises with the legitimate interests of other states. The struggle aspect, involving limited guerrilla warfare across the border between Kalimantan and the North Borneo states (frequently timed to fortify Indonesia's bargaining position), and propaganda against imperialism and its designs on Indonesia's security, served to emphasize Indonesia's determination to fight for what she saw as her interests and wear down her opponents. Finally, the economic aspect—adoption of the stabilization scheme— had in addition to its own justification the function of reassuring the United States of the Indonesian government's intention to follow a constructive political course so long as her interests were respected.

For, as in the West Irian campaign, it was the aim of Sukarno's policy to enlist indirect American support for a settlement of the Malaysia dispute that would be favorable to Indonesia's interests, or, failing this, at least to ensure U.S. neutrality in the conflict. The alternation of brinkmanship and reasonableness in Sukarno's attitude was calculated to exploit American concern to keep Indonesia out of the hands of the Communists and stabilize the situation in Southeast Asia. Sukarno, it hardly needs to be added, also kept a close eye on conditions at home, and in particular on the competing factions that favored stabilization over confrontation and vice versa. His policy gave something to each, without settling his final options, and increased the dependence of all groups on his decisions.

Sukarno's ultimate objectives in the confrontation of Malaysia were never clearly defined and have been the subject of controversy. In the short term, he manifestly aimed at delaying the formation of Malaysia, in the hope that internal strains within the constituent elements of the proposed Federation would frustrate its foundation. Ironically, Brunei, where the revolt that triggered confrontation had taken place, did pull out of the Malaysia project when the Sultan failed to obtain a satisfactory arrangement for the disposition of his oil revenues; but the other entities—Malaya, Singapore, Sabah, and Sarawak—reacted to Indonesian hostility with an increased determination on the part of their political leaders to go ahead with the Federation scheme. Beyond delay, however, it would appear that,

While Sukarno ultimately envisioned Indonesia supplanting the British— and the Americans—as the dominant influence in the region, his short-term goal seems to have been to harass and humiliate the British in hopes of not only expediting their withdrawal but magnifying Indonesia's (Sukarno's) importance in the eyes of his own people. For, apart from the political benefits from twisting the lion's tail, Sukarno saw himself engaged in the most fundamental tasks of nation-building—sowing self-respect and national feeling.[12]

In the March–September 1963 period, Sukarno's maneuvering did

[12] Bunnell, p. 499. For other interpretations of Sukarno's and Indonesia's motives in confrontation, see Bernard K. Gordon, "The Potential for Indonesian Expansionism," *Pacific Affairs*, XXXVI, no. 4 (Winter 1963–64), 378–93; Gordon, *The Dimensions of Conflict in Southeast Asia* (New York, 1966), especially Chapter 3; Donald Hindley, "Indonesia's Confrontation of Malaysia: A Search for Motives," *Asian Survey*, IV, no. 6 (June 1964), 904–13; George McT. Kahin, "Malaysia and Indonesia," *Pacific Affairs*, XXXVII, no. 3 (Fall 1964), 253–70; and, especially stressing the centrality of the PKI's role, Van der Kroef, *The Communist Party of Indonesia*, Chapter 7.

bring about a measure of U.S. conciliation, to the great chagrin of the British, who were never disposed to make concessions to Sukarno and who became increasingly convinced in the course of the negotiations and conflicts that his aims were irreconcilable with the formation of Malaysia, to which they were dedicated. But in the end the attempt to tie confrontation and stabilization together failed, and the United States gave up the hopeless attempt to both support Malaysia and placate Indonesia. The West Irian precedent was not repeated, partly because Indonesia's objectives were at the same time larger and more ill-defined, partly because this was not a clear cut issue of colonialism versus national self-assertion on which she could count on considerable international sympathy, and partly again because the volatile pressures generated in Indonesia in the course of confrontation proved incapable of being countered by Western economic inducements and a sufficient show of deference to her self-esteem.

After some preliminaries, serious moves for a settlement of the dispute between Indonesia and Malaya got under way at the end of May. Simultaneously the long-awaited measures associated with the IMF-sponsored stabilization and aid scheme were promulgated, and became known as the May 26 regulations. If this conjuncture was coincidence, it was a convenient one. The economic measures were unmistakably liberal in intent and effect, providing for sharp increases in many prices and charges, a de facto devaluation of the currency, and heavily reduced government expenditures.[13] They were accompanied by other indications on Indonesia's part of a desire to propitiate the United States, notably a decision to admit the Peace Corps and the successful negotiation of new agreements with the foreign oil companies operating in Indonesia.[14]

The course of negotiations on the Malaysia issue was protracted, tortuous, and punctuated by frequent and dramatic changes of mood, bitter exchanges between the principal participants, blatant Indonesian border incursions, and mutual misunderstandings. An informal meeting between Sukarno, Malaysia's Tunku Abdul Rahman, and Philippines President Macapagal in Tokyo on May 31 and June 1 paved the way for a meeting of the foreign ministers of the three states in

[13] J. A. C. Mackie, *Problems of the Indonesian Inflation* (Monograph Series, Modern Indonesia Project, Cornell University, 1967), p. 37.

[14] On the oil agreement, see Bunnell, pp. 351–79.

Manila a week later.[15] There it was agreed that an independent ascertainment of the wishes of the people of the North Borneo states should be undertaken at the instance of the UN Secretary-General and that the signatories should explore the formation of a loose confederation among them, to be known as "Maphilindo." More precise details of these proposals were left to be worked out at a meeting of the three heads of state scheduled to be held on July 30, again in Manila.

Prospects for this summit meeting were clouded by the signing in London on July 9 of an agreement between Britain and the constituent states of the Malaysian plan whereby the Federation would come into existence on August 31 irrespective of the UN ascertainment. Although not contrary to the letter of the Manila accord, this agreement was taken as a slap in the face in Indonesia and aroused intense resentment against the Tunku. For a time it appeared that Sukarno would ignore the summit meeting, but eventually, only three days before it was due to begin, he announced that he would attend but would use the occasion to continue confrontation![16]

The summit took place in an atmosphere of tension generated by the recriminations of the previous month. In addition, Sukarno's options had been narrowed by mounting domestic unrest over the impact the austerity measures associated with the stabilization program were having on wide sections of the public, including business interests and the armed forces. The PKI, which from the outset had opposed the measures, found its case buttressed not only by popular discontent among its electorate but also by mounting adverse opinion within the political and military elite. Sukarno could not help but be aware that his "moderate" course was becoming increasingly unpopular at home. At first it appeared that the summit would collapse, but a last minute intervention by UN Secretary-General U Thant proposing a form of ascertainment in the North Borneo states that would require only a short postponement of the date that had been selected as Malaysia Day saved face for all sides and permitted an agreement to be initialed.[17]

Throughout the remainder of August, Indonesia's ultimate inten-

---

[15] *Ibid.,* pp. 442–43.
[16] For accounts of the July crises see *ibid.,* pp. 452–63.
[17] *Ibid.,* pp. 483–501.

tions toward Malaysia remained in doubt. On the one hand there were indications of a willingness to accept the UN findings and pursue stabilization. On the other hand, military efforts across the border slowly escalated, and increasing doubts were expressed in Indonesia that the UN mission would take a truly "fresh approach" in its ascertainment of opinion in the North Borneo states, as stipulated in the tripartite agreement. Two issues in particular added fuel to the fires of discontent in Indonesia that were fanned by the expectation that the mission findings would favor the Malaysian case. The first was a tendentious dispute regarding the number and rank of Indonesia's observers at the inquiry.[18] The other was a decision by the Malayan Cabinet, in accordance with constitutional requirements, to set September 15 as the new date for the formation of Malaysia.[19] Whatever the justification for the latter action, it was interpreted in Indonesia as a decision to anticipate the results of the UN findings and proceed as planned in disregard of Indonesia's interests.

By early September the indications were that Indonesia would repudiate the UN report. Objections to the manner in which the inquiry had been conducted were canvassed openly in the press by high-ranking officials, and on September 10 the government submitted to U Thant an appreciation of the ascertainment by its observers which stated unequivocally that "the 'fresh approach' was not apparent in the whole operation."[20] Two days later the UN Secretary-General released the report of his mission, with its predicted finding that a majority of the people of the North Borneo territories supported Malaysia. Indonesia immediately called for a new ascertainment, but signs of mounting tension and excitement in Djakarta gave warning that a more violent and drastic form of retaliation for the blow delivered to Indonesia's prestige might be in the offing.

The PKI leaders had followed the course of negotiations with evident trepidation and disapproval. Seen in conjunction with Sukarno's endorsement of the stabilization scheme, the diplomatic moves demonstrated that Indonesian policy between March and August was veering unmistakably, if erratically, to the right, and the Communists had every reason to fear the continuation and consolidation of this trend.

[18] *Ibid.*, pp. 543–67.
[19] *Ibid.*, pp. 557–73.
[20] *Ibid.*, pp. 595–622.

Early in the diplomatic phase of confrontation an editorial in *Harian Rakjat* queried the advisability of a summit meeting between Sukarno, the Tunku, and Macapagal, reminding Indonesians of the perfidy of the imperialists and their henchmen as exemplified by the Dutch during the West Irian dispute.[21] Once negotiations had actually begun, however, the party was constrained to avoid highlighting its disagreements with official policy so as not to risk isolating itself, alienating Sukarno, and hence strengthening the political influence of those who favored stabilization and a generally pro-Western policy. The PKI press organs, therefore, largely confined themselves to straight reporting of the discussions between the three countries, with a minimum of restrained comment. PKI pressure was exerted instead by utilizing incidents in the confrontation to gather support for its policy of resolute struggle against the neocolonialists and repeatedly emphasizing the political and economic dangers involved in the stabilization scheme. Clashes across the border between Kalimantan and the North Borneo territories in May were greeted with a demonstration at the British Embassy and demands by PKI organizations for a takeover of British capital in Indonesia.[22] On May 22, the Party newspaper reported another demonstration and a union ban on BOAC landings at Djakarta airport, but this had to be abandoned on government orders.[23]

The informal talks between Sukarno and the Tunku in Tokyo at the end of May, which opened the way for the subsequent foreign ministers' conference and summit meeting, were reported with careful neutrality and played down on the news pages of *Harian Rakjat*. It was clear from the guarded and suspicious tone of the newspaper's initial comment on the foreign ministers' meeting that it did not anticipate much good coming out of it from the party's standpoint,[24] and even after the announcement of the conference communiqué, Aidit declared that it was not yet clear what had been agreed upon and called on the Indonesian delegation to give a full explanation to the people. On one aspect of the conference decisions—the acceptance in principle of a Maphilindo confederation—the party was more out-

[21] *Harian Rakjat,* March 9, 1963.
[22] *Ibid.,* May 10, 1963.
[23] *Ibid.,* May 22 and 25, 1963.
[24] *Ibid.,* editorial of June 8, 1963.

spoken, however. Although studied and moderate in tone, its comment left no doubt of PKI opposition to the concept:

The Indonesian Republic is an independent state which freed itself by revolution. . . . The Federation of Malaya is not completely independent, its military affairs still being in the hands of the British imperialists. . . . The Philippines on the one hand is a member of the Bandung family, but on the other hand is still bound to SEATO. . . . What will be the basis for cooperation among the three states? On the one hand, it is not likely that Malaya will accept the independent principles of Indonesian policies, and on the other hand it is out of the question that Indonesia should revert to the semicolonial level of Malaya or the SEATO level of the Philippines.[25]

Gradually, over the ensuing months, this cautious criticism of Maphilindo was to give way to a vigorous attack on the proposal, on the grounds that it was an American-conceived supplement or alternative to Malaysia designed to draw the teeth from Indonesia's radical foreign policy and coax her into the U.S. fold. The PKI leaders gave no public indication that they were aware of the implications carried by some statements supporting the Maphilindo proposal that it was designed to combat Peking's potential use of the overseas Chinese in the area, but it is unlikely that they were either unaware of this aspect or unaffected by its anti-Communist undertones.

By June 20 the PKI's attitude toward the foreign ministers' agreement at Manila had hardened somewhat. The Politburo of the party, in a special statement entitled "The People of North Kalimantan will Decide their own Fate," declared emphatically that a plebiscite in the North Borneo territories was unnecessary in view of the opposition to Malaysia revealed by the Brunei uprising and added that if, despite this, a further gauging of opinion were to be held then it must be subject to the prior withdrawal of British troops, the release of political detainees, and a guarantee that the outlawed Brunei People's Party led by Sheik Azahari would be free to campaign. Moreover, the referendum should not be confined to Northern Borneo, but should be held also in Malaya and Singapore.[26]

---

[25] *Ibid.,* June 13, 1963. The previous year a *Harian Rakjat* editorial (Oct. 2, 1962) had attacked "right wingers" associated with the magazine *Gema Islam* for supporting Malaysia and the idea of a larger federation between Indonesia, the Philippines, and Malaya.

[26] *Harian Rakjat,* June 20, 1963.

The statement was shrewdly calculated to bring out the ambivalences in the Indonesian official approach to the Malaysia problem. It had been one of Indonesia's major contentions in her objections to the proposed Federation that it was being thrust upon the people, of North Borneo in particular, without proper ascertainment of their desires. Yet Subandrio had intimated at Manila that Indonesia was generally satisfied that the Federation was acceptable to the people concerned and merely wanted a gesture to satisfy its own people on this score. The PKI, however, was taking Indonesia's initial stand at its face value and insisting on a thorough polling of opinion under conditions that would not have appeared to many Indonesians at any rate to be unreasonable. If there was any feeling in Indonesian official circles that the Tunku and the British were being let off too lightly, the PKI statement was designed to probe it and bring it into the open.[27]

The troubled period between the foreign ministers' conference and the Manila summit gave the PKI many opportunities to commend a policy of unequivocal anti-Malaysia struggle and expand upon the deceits and machinations of the British and U.S. imperialists. In the aftermath of the London agreement the party energetically supported the antagonistic reaction this caused in Indonesia; Aidit attacked Maphilindo in more forthright terms and declared that a summit meeting was now out of the question.[28] On July 19, the expulsion of two Indonesian diplomats from Sabah on charges of subversion provided the opportunity for another outburst of anti-Malaysian propaganda and a further demonstration at the British Embassy. With opposition to the steep price rises and financial restrictions set in train by the regulations of May 26 becoming generalized and more outspoken, the Communist leaders had some grounds for hoping that Sukarno would turn the wheel away from negotiations and propitiation of the United States and embark on a new NEFO crusade.

---

[27] This was not the only ambivalance in the Indonesian approach. Its other major objection—that Malaysia represented a means of stabilizing British military power in the area, and was therefore a threat to Indonesian security—presumably applied irrespective of popular acceptance of the Federation by the people to be incorporated in it. The stress by the PKI and other nationalists on this aspect of Malaysia helped to give all the bickering over the ascertainment of the wishes of the people of North Borneo something of an unreal and hypocritical character.

[28] *Harian Rakjat*, July 11 and 15, 1963.

A great deal hinged on Sukarno's decision on whether or not to attend the summit, a decision that was delayed until the last minute. The announcement that he would go was obviously not to the party's liking. On the eve of the meeting of the heads of state, a *Harian Rakjat* editorial made an unusually strong and forthright call for the continuance of confrontation. Significantly, the central issue dealt with in the editorial was not the right of self-determination for the people of Northern Borneo but Indonesia's security and her dedication to the crusade against imperialism and neocolonialism. Declaring that the United States was using economic pressure to compel the president to go to Manila, and calling for the abandonment of conventional practices in diplomacy, the editorial demanded the immediate takeover of British enterprises and more concrete assistance to the "Azahari government" in North Borneo.[29]

Once the summit decisions had been taken, the PKI as usual outwardly if grudgingly accepted them. It warned that neither the Tunku nor the British could be trusted,[30] and Lukman indicated the party's dissatisfaction and continued determination to keep the issue alive by stating: "We Indonesian Communists do not find it necessary to be in a hurry to celebrate the results of the Manila summit, because what resulted is only a beginning"; the struggle must be intensified, he said, and the people must be prepared for any eventuality.[31]

Later, in December, when it was safe for the PKI to express its views on the Manila agreement more frankly, Aidit declared that the party had "never agreed to the holding" of the conference and that it took place "despite the wishes of the Communists," and, further, that the PKI opposed the fact that in the agreement Malaysia was accepted in principle subject to the fulfillment of certain conditions. He made it clear that in the PKI's view the outcome of the conference had been positive not due to any skill on the part of Indonesia's negotiators but owing to the stupidity and stubbornness of the British imperialists:

The Manila Agreement could have become negative; it could have been harmful to the struggle of the Indonesian people and the struggle of the people of Malaya, Singapore, Sarawak, Sabah and the Philippines,

[29] *Ibid.,* July 29, 1963.
[30] *Ibid.,* Aug. 7, 1963.
[31] *Ibid.,* Aug. 9, 1963. Aidit was out of the country during August and September on extended visits to the U.S.S.R., China, Cuba, and North Korea.

and to the struggle of the people of Southeast Asia in general, if the British had had full confidence in themselves and had followed the stipulations in the Manila Agreement. If this had happened, then "Malaysia" would have become "legal" and the initiative in this question would have shifted into the hands of the British and their Tunku.

The impatience and stupidity of the enemy has helped to make "Malaysia" a means of arousing the struggle of the peoples of Southeast Asia to direct powerful blows against imperialism in this region.[32]

Throughout August and early September, however, the PKI refrained from generalizations about the import of the summit meeting, preferring instead in its propaganda to take up and make the most of the conflicts developing around the conduct of the ascertainment. By September 12, when Indonesia transmitted her advance objections to the manner of assessing opinion in the North Borneo territories, the Communists had geared up their organization for a massive protest against the expected results of the UN inquiry.

THE SEPTEMBER UPHEAVAL

On September 13, the presidium of the National Front issued a call to "thwart Malaysia, help the struggle of the peoples of North Kalimantan, boycott the British and recognize the government of Prime Minister Azahari."[33] The following day, the date of the release of the UN report, anti-Malaysian posters were reported going up all over the capital and other major centers, demonstrations took place in Medan and Surabaja, and a huge demonstration in Djakarta was announced for the next day by the Youth Front. *Harian Rakjat* rejected in advance any unfavorable decision by the fact-finding mission and denounced the United States for having allegedly manipulated the ascertainment through the person of its chairman, Michelmore.[34]

The anti-Malaysia mass meeting on September 15 was the occasion for fiery denunciations of Malaysia and calls for "crushing" the Federation. The Pemuda Rakjat representative urged the takeover of British enterprises and the recall to duty of the West Irian volunteers. There began a week of escalating crisis, at the end of which the die had been cast and Indonesia launched into full-scale confrontation of

---

[32] *Set Afire the Banteng Spirit!*, p. 35.
[33] *Harian Rakjat*, Sept. 13, 1963.
[34] *Ibid.*, Sept. 14, 1963.

Malaysia. On September 16, a large and unruly demonstration in Djakarta marched on the British and Malayan Embassies and damaged them extensively. On the 17th, Malaysia broke off diplomatic relations with Indonesia, and a riotous counterdemonstration in Kuala Lumpur attacked the Indonesian Embassy and desecrated the Indonesian flag. On the 18th, another huge demonstration outside the British Embassy in Djakarta got completely out of control, and before the day was out the Embassy had been burned to the ground and 21 staff houses gutted. PNI-influenced unions initiated a wave of unofficial takeovers of British enterprises, and the PKI quickly joined in and enlarged the campaign. On September 21, Indonesia severed all commercial and financial relations with Malaysia, thus putting an end to her close trading relationship with Singapore and dooming the stabilization scheme. The following week, the International Monetary Fund suspended standby credits to Indonesia.[35]

In the early stages of the Malaysia dispute Indonesia was subject to conflicting pressures: on the one hand to accept a negotiated compromise and pursue its stabilization program, and on the other hand to embark on a new and uninhibited confrontation crusade. What part did PKI opposition to the Malaysia project, and its campaign against the Federation, play in determining Indonesia's course? An answer to this question must take into account not only PKI strategy over the period prior to September 1963 but also the party's weight in the political system at the time.

The view has already been expressed that, prior to the Brunei revolt, the Malaysia issue did not occupy a prominent place in PKI concerns or calculations and that, even after the outbreak of the revolt, it was still of decidedly secondary importance to the problem posed by the Indonesian government's acceptance of American aid in tackling its economic difficulties. Judging by Aidit's report to the Central Committee in February 1963, the Communist leaders were surprisingly slow in recognizing the opportunity offered by anti-Malaysian feeling in Indonesia to stem the rightward course of government politics and disrupt the trend toward closer relations with the United States. It is safe to assume that they had grasped the connection by March, however, and from that time onward their attempts to

[35] Bunnell, pp. 624–67.

link the United States with support for Malaysia, and later the Maphilindo scheme, demonstrated their awareness of the fact that the issues of confrontation and stabilization were closely bound together. Nevertheless, as was indicated earlier, the PKI leaders had to tread warily while the official tide flowed in favor of compromise and retrenchment. Sukarno appeared to be very much master of his house, as his skillful handling of the drama preceding his decision to attend the Manila summit showed. The party could not openly oppose the negotiations, although it feared greatly that out of them might come an agreement confirming the rightward political course and blighting their hopes of advance. They played adroitly on mounting nationalistic feeling in the country and the resentment generated by the effects of the stabilization measures on small traders, civil servants, and other vulnerable groups.

As evidence of United States interest in a settlement increased, so did the concern of the PKI grow. The emergence of the Maphilindo project, which it was convinced was an American substitute for Malaysia, or a supplement to it, put the party thoroughly on its guard.

It was imperative that the PKI leaders resist a sellout at their expense, but their room for maneuver was not great. They could not attack their own government's motivations openly without risking either punitive action or a rebuke from President Sukarno. Until May, militant challenge could still be dealt with by an invocation of martial law powers, and even after that it could be used as an excuse to reimpose them. More intimidating still was the prospect of bringing about the party's political isolation, the avoidance of which Aidit had made the pivot of his strategy for thirteen years.

Consequently, the Communists did what they had done so many times before; they avoided a direct clash with their governmental allies and plugged away at issues on which they knew a large element of shared feeling existed between themselves and sizable sectors of the elite. On the one hand they emphasized the adverse effects the economic stabilization measures were having. On the other hand they took up and reiterated continually the anti-imperialist, anti-Malaysian, anticompromise themes that Sukarno and other government leaders had themselves stressed. By taking these declarations at their face value and seeking to demonstrate their mass popularity and their fidelity to "revolutionary" principle, PKI leaders sought to stimulate nationalist consciousness and erect psychological barriers against a decision to accept the Malaysian state-to-be.

As late as August 17, however, in his Independence Day address, Sukarno appeared still to be tending toward moderation and pursuit of a restrictive economic policy. Only as it became apparent in late August that Indonesia's blocking tactics toward the formation of Malaysia were headed for failure, leaving her with the prospect of a diplomatic debacle and consequent loss of face, did the government show unmistakable signs of acceding to the view of those opposed to a climbdown.

Being in the agitational van, the PKI certainly contributed substantially to the furore in mid-September; but it is difficult to view its role as at any stage a determining one. From the defensive position it was forced into in the early stages of the Malaysia dispute, it had by September been able to move into the offensive, but only in circumstances that (its own contribution notwithstanding) had been created by the interaction of many forces, among which the president was clearly predominant.

The critical events of the week beginning September 14 have less the appearance of a carefully organized and calculated campaign than of a spillover of the passions and tensions that had built up in Indonesia over the preceding months. It was as if the genie of nationalism, exploited by many groups in the struggle for political survival and advantage, had suddenly escaped the bottle and gone on a rampage. The government had certainly encouraged a violent reaction to the UN ascertainment but appeared genuinely disconcerted and alarmed when the violence got out of control. The PKI, too, had set itself to profit to the utmost from the sudden turn in its fortunes, and undoubtedly played a leading part in the upheaval. But the party generally prided itself on the discipline of its massed detachments, a factor of no small importance to it in its delicate political maneuvering. On the morning of the demonstration that led to the gutting of the British Embassy, the party daily had specifically called for careful organization and the avoidance of provocations;[36] and afterwards PKI leaders disclaimed responsibility for the disorders. There is some basis for believing that non-Communists and anti-Communists may have

---

[36] *Harian Rakjat,* Sept. 18, 1963.

had some part in the proceedings of that day. Likewise, as noted earlier, it was not the PKI union apparatus but unions linked with the PNI that initiated the wave of takeovers of British enterprises.

Certainly the PKI had no cause to rue the fact that full–scale confrontation was now the order of the day, and still less that in its wake economic stabilization had gone by the board. The party had scored a major victory, but one which brought new dangers in its train. The party's leaders had no interest in inflaming things to the point where war might threaten or a new state of emergency be declared. Yet the trend of events in that tempestuous week must have raised this fear in their minds, to be succeeded by a sigh of relief when the tumult largely died down in the following weeks.

In the immediate aftermath of the euphoric events of mid-September, the Indonesian government moved to bring some semblance of order into its new policy course. Efforts were made to devise fresh avenues for the disposal of the country's exports now that the Singapore outlet was closed. At the same time measures were taken to limit the economic effects of the takeovers of British properties. Despite vigorous PKI calls for nationalization, these properties were placed under the "protective custody" of the appropriate ministers, and moves against oil installations, which represented Indonesia's steadiest source of foreign currency, were prohibited. Confrontation settled down into a fairly humdrum affair for the remainder of the year, more notable for its propaganda fireworks than for any drastic action on the military front. There were occasional border clashes, but the economic aspects at this stage were most evident on both sides.

Both Singapore and Indonesia suffered appreciably from the cessation of commercial dealings between them; but of the two Indonesia suffered the worst, her problems growing greater the longer confrontation continued. The inability of the Indonesian government to organize efficiently the services that Singapore middlemen had previously performed greatly hampered its efforts to find alternative export outlets, and the resumption of large scale smuggling to Singapore in 1964 both robbed Indonesia of much-needed income and eased the strain on Singapore. Inflation in Indonesia put on a new spurt in September and was to gather still more pace in 1964 and 1965.

Toward the end of September, a training movement for volunteers was inaugurated by the National Front, but it was not to achieve great mass proportions or major symbolic importance until the following year. Nonetheless, the PKI was quick to seize the opportunity for patriotic prestige, not to mention military training for its supporters, and the Pemuda Rakjat was soon reporting progress figures on the enrolment of its members.[37] On September 28 the Central Committee submitted proposals to the National Front for the conduct of confrontation, stressing the importance of strengthening the economy in the campaign to crush Malaysia. Statements of opposition to renewed negotiations appeared from time to time, and SOBSI continued to wage a rearguard action against the return of seized British enterprises.[38]

AIDIT PROPOUNDS A WORLD CONCEPT

A coherent and authoritative PKI policy on confrontation only emerged after Aidit's return, late in September, from an extended foreign tour with a party delegation that had spent more than three weeks in the Soviet Union, one week each in Cuba and the German Democratic Republic, three weeks in China, and one week in North Korea. The rapid turn of events at home during his absence must have come as something of a surprise to Aidit, since in none of his speeches abroad did he give any indication of anticipating the new upsurge of anti-imperialist militancy that engulfed Indonesia in the second half of September. Indeed, in Pyongyang on September 11, Aidit had still treated United States economic penetration as the main danger for the PKI,[39] and even on September 25, in a lecture in Canton, he did not venture to comment on the recent events at home.[40]

Nevertheless, the situation that greeted Aidit on his return fitted well with the concepts he had formed while abroad. His first speech on Indonesian soil, delivered at a welcome home meeting on September 29, indicated an important shift in his general approach to international and national politics. Whereas until this time the PKI had shown decided sympathy with the Chinese position on the issues being debated in the international Communist movement, it had not fully

[37] *Ibid.*, Sept. 24, 1963.
[38] *Ibid.*, Oct. 23, 1963.
[39] *Review of Indonesia*, VIII, no. 2-3-4 (Oct.–Nov.–Dec. 1963), 25.
[40] *The Indonesian Revolution*, pp. 102–32.

incorporated the views of the CPC into its strategic thinking and had formally adopted a neutral stance in the Sino-Soviet dispute. Now, however, Aidit came down strongly and unmistakably on the Chinese side. In particular he took up and elaborated the current Chinese analysis of imperialism, and the requirements of the struggle against it, and denounced those Communist parties that supported Soviet policies of coexistence as out-and-out revisionist.[41]

The circumstances leading the PKI to come out decisively on China's side in the Sino-Soviet dispute, and the significance of the new orientation for the PKI's relations with the Communist movement abroad, will be dealt with in a later chapter. At this point, interest lies in the fact that the theories of anti-imperialist struggle that Aidit outlined on his return from abroad, and elaborated in the following months, were to form the framework of the party's entire strategy over the succeeding two years; more, they were to be taken over in their essentials by President Sukarno and used by him as the ideological justification for his new radical course in foreign and home affairs.

Two weeks after arriving back in Indonesia, Aidit applied his theory of anti-imperialist struggle to the Malaysia question, distinguishing between "reformist," "adventurist," and "revolutionary" approaches to confrontation and defining the contribution that Indonesia's offensive against the neocolonialists was making and would make to the worldwide assault on the bastions of imperialism.[42]

In a report to the Central Committee plenum in December, Aidit presented a comprehensive outline of his new thinking and its practical implications for the work of the party in all major spheres. An examination of this report throws considerable light on the aims of the PKI leadership in the following months, and in particular on the motivations underlying its concept of confrontation.

Two connected propositions formed the core of Aidit's views on the character of the anti-imperialist struggle as a whole. The first was that "a revolutionary situation . . . is continually surging forward and becoming riper in Asia, Africa and Latin America," as a result of which "the contradiction between the oppressed nations and imperialism" had become the main contradiction in the world. It followed that:

[41] *Harian Rakjat,* Sept. 30, 1963. Aidit did not, however, attack the Soviet Union by name or attribute his new approach directly to the Chinese. The PKI was still careful to safeguard its reputation for independence.

[42] *Harian Rakjat,* Oct. 14, 1963.

In order to consolidate the Socialist system, the most important task of all Socialist countries is to support the struggle of the peoples on these three continents. . . . On a world scale, Asia, Africa and Latin America are the villages of the world, whilst Europe and North America are the towns of the world. If the world revolution is to be victorious there is no other way than for the world proletariat to give prominence to the revolutions in Asia, Africa and Latin America, that is to say, the revolutions in the villages of the world. In order to win the world revolution, the world proletariat must go to these three continents.[43]

The notion that the national independence movements of the third world represented the central focus of anti-imperialist struggle derived directly from the stated arguments of the CPC in its polemics with the CPSU.[44] The colorful imagery in which Aidit presented it, on the other hand, with its transposition to the international arena of Mao's strategy during the Chinese revolution of "surrounding the towns from the villages," appears to have been Aidit's own inspiration.[45]

The major implications of this thesis were twofold. First, it meant that Communists and Communist states had to be judged primarily by the importance they attached and the support they gave to revolutionary struggles by the people in the three continents against imperialist domination. By this yardstick, the Soviet Union failed to measure up to Communist standards, since it insisted on the primacy of the contradiction between Communism and imperialism and argued that this contradiction could be solved in favor of the Communist camp through peaceful competition; the struggle for peaceful coexis-

[43] *Set Afire the Banteng Spirit!* pp. 84–85, 87. It is interesting to compare this bold assertion with the more cautious analysis of a year before, which was moving in the same direction but still sought to find a middle way between Soviet and Chinese theories: "The struggles of the people against imperialism and for national independence form an unconditional and inseparable part of the struggle for a new world, a socialist world. The national independence movement no longer forms only a reserve of the world socialist revolution but a most important part of the world socialist revolution. The perspective of the revolutionary movement for national independence is socialism" (D. N. Aidit, *Anti-imperialisme dan Front Nasional,* Speech to a National Front cadre course, Oct. 19, 1962; [Djakarta, 1962]).

[44] See the CPC's letter to the CPSU dated April 14, 1963, in *A Proposal Concerning the General Line of the International Communist Movement* (Peking, 1963), pp. 12–18.

[45] See Schramm, *Mao Tse-tung,* p. 313.

tence therefore should take precedence in Communist concerns, and the revolutionary movements in the third world were required to subordinate their aims to the overriding one of preventing the outbreak of a third world war.[46] Secondly, the thesis clearly indicated that Communists in Asia, Africa, and Latin America ought to project their struggles within the framework of anti-imperialist policies and slogans rather than within the narrower context of a struggle between the proletarian and antiproletarian forces within each country. As both the CPC and Aidit made clear, revolutionary nationalists could take part in the anti-imperialist struggle, and hence the tactic of a united national front could be employed.[47]

There was ambivalence in the Chinese position, since it also stressed the importance of the Communists' striving for hegemony in the anti-imperialist struggle and provided no clear guidance for those parties that found themselves in a position where their governments (as in Cambodia, for example) were "opposing imperialism" but keeping a tight rein on domestic Communists. This dilemma did not exist for the PKI, however; its government could be considered both anti-imperialist and tolerant toward home-grown Communism. Therefore the PKI could continue to pursue its accommodating policies toward the Indonesian rulers, while at the same time justifying this by reference to their "revolutionary" character.

The second proposition concerning the character of the anti-imperialist struggle contained in Aidit's report to the Central Committee was peculiar to his own elaboration of the Chinese thesis. Southeast Asia, he said, formed a central focus of the world contradiction between imperialism and the oppressed nations and peoples; this region was a target of neocolonialist subversion, but on the other hand it was also a region where Communist states already existed and the national independence revolution and the socialist revolution had "continued to rage without stop" since the end of World War II. Patriotic forces of the national bourgeoisie were growing alongside

[46] See the CPSU letter to the CPC dated March 30, 1963, republished in *A Proposal Concerning the General Line*, pp. 63–98.

[47] According to the Chinese statement, even "certain kings, princes and aristocrats who are patriotic" could take part; *ibid.*, p. 15. Or, as Aidit put it in one of his lectures in China. "The nationalists who oppose imperialism are far better than those dogmatists and revisionists who embrace the imperialists so affectionately"; *The Indonesian Revolution*, p. 131.

Communist parties that had strong mass connections and were free of the revisionist taint. Consequently

Southeast Asia is one of the central points in the region of main contradiction in the world . . . [and] with the upsurge in the wave of revolution in Southeast Asia, it is no longer possible to prevent the total destruction of imperialism in Southeast Asia headed by the USA. . . . The collapse of the imperialist fortress in this region will constitute a mighty tidal wave overrunning imperialism, it will be a great help to the development of the world socialist revolution.

Indonesia was destined to play a decisive role in the ousting of imperialism from the area:

Indonesia's role is very important indeed in the struggle for independence in Southeast Asia. . . . In Indonesia today there is no armed struggle such as is taking place for instance in South Vietnam. But it is a mistake to think that because of this, Indonesia's role in Southeast Asia is not very important. In Indonesia, it is not only the people but also the Government that is waging a struggle against imperialism, if necessary with arms too. . . . The victory of the Indonesian revolution will signify a mighty breakthrough in the fortress of imperialism, it will signify a great stride forward in the anti-imperialist struggle and its rays will shine from afar, even beyond the borders of Southeast Asia. This is the reason why the imperialists, in particular the USA, devote such great attention to the developments in Indonesia and make it the main target of their intervention and subversion in Southeast Asia.[48]

There are two points of interest about these passages. First, while their nationalist bias is too evident to need emphasis, there is at the same time more than a suggestion in the boastful exaggeration of the role of Indonesia (and, indirectly, the PKI) in the Southeast Asian revolutionary upsurge that Aidit is seeking to compensate for the relative peacefulness of the party's strategy. It is as if he were saying to the Indonesian Communists, "Although our path is a peaceful one, we are still destined to play a role second to none in the transformation of this region. Do not be misled by our moderation; we are in the vanguard of the world revolution." Perhaps he was answering those in the party who were restive at the PKI's accommodating policies, or perhaps he was exhorting members to put greater fervor into their

[48] *Set Afire the Banteng Spirit!* pp. 95–98.

work in order to realize the potentialities that were present in the political situation.

Secondly, it is by no means clear that Aidit conceived Indonesia's role in the struggle against imperialism as consisting mainly of external ventures; rather, he appears to be thinking in terms of the impact that a successful coming to power by the PKI itself would have on the balance of power in the Pacific. This interpretation takes on still stronger credence when Aidit's approach to confrontation is analyzed.

The apocalyptic vision painted by Aidit of a Southeast Asia aflame with revolution, with Indonesia fueling the fire, would incline us to expect him to advance a bold and militant concept of confrontation involving the mobilization of all the resources of the country for a desperate and final onslaught on the imperialist power at Indonesia's doorstep. But this is very far from what he was urging, as his analysis of the "three lines on confrontation" makes clear.

According to this analysis, there existed first a "moderate or reformist" line on confrontation. The followers of this line, while paying lip service to the goal of crushing Malaysia,

still nurture the hope that the British imperialists and Tunku Abdul Rahman will be willing to settle the "Malaysia" question "peacefully," and for this purpose they are prepared to make certain concessions. They still dream of holding a second Manila Summit meeting in order to "settle" the "Malaysia" question. . . . In principle, they accept neo-colonialism; it is only the methods by which the neo-colonial structure is set up to which they take exception.[49]

Aidit may well have meant this characterization to apply to Subandrio, of whom the PKI at this time was still highly suspicious and whose attitude at the foreign ministers' conference at Manila in July had been a conciliatory one. However it was equally applicable to some of the attitudes expressed by Sukarno at various times. In all probability Aidit recognized that the views he was here apostrophizing represented a strain in the approach of the government as a whole and by labeling it as the outlook of "reformists and moderates" was seeking both to discredit it in the eyes of all "revolutionaries" and to make it repugnant even to those who had earlier been drawn to the

---

[49] *Ibid.,* p. 39.

idea of a negotiated settlement. His real concern was that the policy of concessions "can win popularity among the very large number of vacillating middle-of-the-roaders."[50] Again the PKI's fear of a deal being done behind its back comes out quite strongly in this appraisal.

The second erroneous and harmful confrontation line was that of the "counterrevolutionary adventurers," who were accused of having long aimed to bring about the downfall of the Sukarno regime by means of coup d'état, rebellion, assassination, etc. Behind their fiery opposition to Malaysia, these elements concealed the base motive of,

fishing for limited military action by the British so as to arouse panic at home which they hope will present them with a good opportunity to put an end to the "Sukarno regime" or at the very least to make Bung Karno their political captive, willing to sign whatever they present him with, and then finally establish good relations with "Malaysia" and the British, as well as presenting their victory to the USA.[51]

In this case, there is very little doubt that Aidit had specific targets in mind, namely the anti-Communist groupings, particularly within the leadership of the armed forces. Identifying these groups with past coup attempts, the regional rebellions, and the attempted assassinations of the president may have been unscrupulous, but no doubt in the minds of the Communists there was nothing to choose between the anti-Communist frontrunners of former years and their successors, particularly since the latter were known to maintain connections with prominent rebel leaders and influential figures in the banned parties. More relevant to the point at issue, Aidit was aware that the army high command was attempting to compete with the PKI in nationalism by adopting a tough military posture, as it had done in the last phases of the West Irian campaign. Whatever the general logic of Aidit's call for all–out anti-imperialist struggle might seem to imply, neither Sukarno nor the PKI wanted a strong military emphasis in the campaign. The situation was in fact very similar to the later stages of the Irian dispute, characterized by competition between the diplomatic, agitational, and military approaches, with the political right wanting either of the two extremes and Sukarno and the Communists the middle course.

[50] *Ibid.,* p. 40.
[51] *Ibid.,* pp. 40–41.

This point is made clearer still in Aidit's elaboration of the "revolutionary" line on confrontation. He held that the contradiction between the Indonesian people and other anti-imperialists on the one hand, and the forces of imperialism and colonialism on the other, was fundamental and one that "cannot be settled at the negotiating table but that must be settled through confrontation in all fields." Negotiations were useful only at the stage where the imperialists had been compelled to retreat, when they could be held in order to accept their surrender. The "revolutionaries" recognized that British imperialism was stronger than Dutch imperialism, but they did not exaggerate the strength of this "moribund imperialism"; confrontation must not be seen, therefore, as something that could be settled in great haste. Neither should it be forgotten that the British were only a secondary enemy, while the main enemy, which was propping up Malaysia for its own counterrevolutionary purposes, was United States imperialism.

It was basic to the revolutionary concept of confrontation that it must be waged in all fields—political, economic, and military—and must be combined with persevering work in "internal matters." Confrontation in the political field comprised exposure of Malaysia throughout the world and the enlistment of the new emerging forces on Indonesia's side, the improvement of the composition of the government, and the recognition of the Unitary State of North Kalimantan led by Azahari. In the economic field it involved sapping the economic interests of Britain and at the same time strengthening the functioning and independence of Indonesia's economy.

The most striking features of the revolutionary line on confrontation are paradoxical: it was a moderate line, and it had relatively little to do with the struggle against Malaysia as such. The only aspect touching directly and specifically on the conflict between Malaysia and Indonesia was a requirement that aid be rendered to the guerrillas in North Kalimantan, and even this was treated as secondary to the efforts of the insurgents themselves. Since the real strength of the guerrillas, as distinct from their role in Indonesian propaganda, was very slight, the military implications of Aidit's policy were minimal. Apart from vague references to economic warfare against the British and Malaysia, which Aidit can hardly have taken too seriously himself, this is the beginning and end of confrontation as an international conflict.

The kernel of the revolutionary line lies in its prescriptions for political activity *inside* Indonesia and Malaysia, where the insurrectionary Malayan Communist Party was still active along the border with Thailand. The Malaysia issue in fact was seen primarily as a symbolic struggle, providing a policy orientation that would strengthen left wing trends in domestic politics. The crucial goals of the PKI did not lie in leading a crusade against imperialist battlements in Southeast Asia but in bringing Indonesia itself closer to a socialist transformation. This was to be the party's contribution to the revolutionary struggle against imperialism. To recall Aidit's words again, "The victory of the Indonesian revolution [a formulation that Communists could read to mean consummation under Communist leadership but that Sukarnoists would find unexceptionable] will signify a mighty breakthrough in the fortress of imperialism . . . and its rays will shine from afar."

Under the slogans of confrontation, the immediate tasks of the PKI, as Aidit outlined them, were therefore to strengthen Indonesia's ties with the militant anti-imperialist countries, expel U.S. influence from the country, radicalize the government, and remove right wingers ("unpatriotic elements") from administrative posts. These were to be precisely the objectives preoccupying the party throughout 1964–65. The struggle against Malaysia, the importance of which consisted primarily in providing a patriotic and national revolutionary context for the pursuit of these aims, was to be waged at a low key but over a long term, in order to keep alive the anti-imperialist momentum on which the party's strategy depended without precipitating a major clash that would threaten its plans by promoting either strong arm government or a retreat. The West Irian precedent, which had consolidated the PKI-Sukarno alliance, was probably very much in Aidit's mind; in many ways, the Malaysia struggle was even better, as it was likely to drag on indefinitely with little or no prospect of an Indonesian victory.

It was still very much in the PKI's interest to turn the heat of confrontation as much as possible against the United States. Although events since September had greatly lessened the likelihood of an American-sponsored compromise designed to draw Indonesia into the U.S. sphere of influence, efforts were still being made in this direction, and it remained the goal of those in the Indonesian government and other influential circles who recognized that the post-September course of events was playing into the PKI's hands. The Communists had attempted throughout 1963 to discredit America's world role and intentions toward Indonesia, castigating U.S. aid schemes to Latin America to draw invidious comparisons with the economic stabilization scheme; attacking U.S. policies in the Congo, Guatemala, Cambodia, Vietnam, and toward the Negro; branding the Peace Corps as an instrument of the Central Intelligence Agency; and, from mid-1963, making a particular feature of U.S. "cultural penetration." But its strongest theme had been the allegation that the U.S. government was supporting Malaysia and in particular using economic pressure as a weapon to force Indonesia into a compromise. Nevertheless, the possibility of a resumption of friendly relations between the two countries was still not beyond the bounds of possibility.

In the post-September period, Aidit was no longer interested in advocating reliance on Soviet economic aid as an alternative to an American scheme. That argument had lost its plausibility early in the year, when it had become clear that the U.S.S.R. was unwilling to offer sums comparable to those Kennedy was foreshadowing, and this fact may well have been important in pushing Aidit toward the anti-Soviet position he had reached by September. The vehemence of his December attack on Soviet ideological positions, including Khrushchev's plan for the construction of Communism in the U.S.S.R., indicated how poorly Russia now stood in the eyes of the Indonesian Communist leaders. We do not know to what extent Aidit may have been influenced by his discussions with Soviet leaders during his overseas tour in August-September, or whether the reportedly chilly reception he was given in Moscow played some part in his violent repudiation of Soviet policies. If, as it appears, the Russians were pressing for interest payments on their loans to Indonesia, and proving cool to confrontation, this would help to explain the PKI attitude.

Aidit did not come out directly in support of an alliance with China as an alternative to American or Soviet aid, partly no doubt owing to a desire to maintain the PKI's reputation for independence. In any case, relations between the two countries at the governmental level had been steadily firming during the year, as a result of close collaboration at various Afro-Asian conferences, China's enthusiastic support for the Games of the New Emerging Forces, and Peking's strong endorsement of confrontation. Given the sensitivity of the "Chinese question" in Indonesia, it made best sense for the PKI to throw its weight behind official government policies toward China, extol Sukarno's role in the common anti-imperialist preoccupations of the two state leaderships, and make the party's distinctive contribution to the accord in the form of ideological pronouncements and slogans derived from or congenial to Chinese concepts.

The Games of the New Emerging Forces having concluded successfully in November,[52] the next major symbolic enterprise in the international sphere to engage Sukarno's attention was the staging of a second Afro-Asian conference in succession to the one held in Bandung in 1955. Both the Indonesian and Chinese governments saw in this project an opportunity for gathering support for a new anti-imperialist "International," which they envisaged as undermining great power dominance and providing them with a lever in the game of international power politics. The major obstacle to their aspirations lay in the rival plans of India, Yugoslavia, and the United Arab Republic for the holding of a further conference of nonaligned countries dedicated, not to anti-imperialist struggle, but to the quest for peace in cooperation with the Big Two.

Accordingly, in his report to the Central Committee plenum in December, Aidit urged the party to back the proposal for a "second Bandung Conference" and attacked the alternative of a nonaligned conference as a "criminal attempt to murder the Bandung Spirit" and "torpedo the concept of NEFO [New Emerging Forces] cooperation." The major abuse was heaped on India, which was branded as "the US watch-dog in Asia and a fifth column within the ranks of the Asian-African countries." As a further indication of how far relations between the PKI and the U.S.S.R. had deteriorated, the latter was accused, in veiled form, of supporting the nonaligned as opposed to the Afro-Asian concept, and it was hinted that Soviet economic and military aid to India was furthering U.S. plans.[53]

Aidit recognized that the state of the economy remained the weak point in his strategy. There was a pronounced disposition at this time for the political elite to take the inflation problem seriously. If inflation and the breakdown in production and exports became appreciably

[52] See Ewa T. Pauker, "Ganefo I: Sports and Politics in Djakarta," *Asian Survey*, V, no. 4 (April 1965), 171–85.
[53] *Set Afire the Banteng Spirit!* pp. 71–72, 76–77.

worse, then one of two dangers could arise: either pressure from the right would force acceptance of a retreat on confrontation and a new arrangement with the United States, or economic discontent would precipitate disorders that would upset the party's delicate and gradual consolidation of its position. Consequently Aidit devoted considerable attention in his report to the handling of the economic aspects of confrontation.

China was not in a position to offer Indonesia aid on anything like the scale of what was being forfeited with the lapsing of the U.S.-sponsored economic stabilization plan, and Aidit was therefore left to make a virtue of necessity by stressing the slogan of self-reliance or "standing on one's own feet."[54] Recognizing that economic deterioration had hurt the workers, he nevertheless argued that the main cause of the country's economic difficulties was not confrontation but the manipulations and corruption of administrators and "bureaucratic capitalists." A turn for the better would not be achieved until politics had taken a decisive swing to the left, and the anti-imperialist focus was essential for bringing this about. Campaigns against those who sabotaged the economy would be waged in the context of confrontation, but essentially Aidit appealed to the party and its followers to sacrifice their present needs for the sake of the ultimate but certain benefits that would accrue from a Communist victory in the political contest. In an attempt to use nationalist sentiment to make self-abnegation palatable, he coined new slogans to urge the masses to follow the path of austerity: "the heart is stronger than the stomach" and "freedom comes before material welfare."[55] Perhaps fearing more right-wing-organized disorders such as those that had occurred in West Java the previous May, Aidit advocated the (for a Communist) highly unorthodox policy of cooperating closely with the police to maintain public order.[56]

THE USES OF CONFRONTATION, 1964

The close parallels between the policies of Sukarno and the PKI after September were vividly illustrated by the virtual identity of their

---

[54] The weakening effect of relying on socialist aid, together with strong suggestions that it was being used for conservative purposes, were emphasized in the report; *ibid.*, pp. 90–94.

[55] *Ibid.*, pp. 13–31.

[56] *Ibid.*, pp. 7–8.

ideological slogans and appeals. Both were borrowing extensively from Peking's propaganda arsenal, and both were at the same time coining distinctively Indonesian variants and flourishes on anti-imperialist themes. It became increasingly difficult to distinguish the authorship of specific ideas and catchcries. The PKI quickly took up presidential themes that were congenial to it, but it also seemed on occasion to initiate ideological novelties which the president in his turn soon made his own. If ideologizing had been an Indonesian political disease, it now took on epidemic proportions, with politicians and officials scrambling over one another to win favor in the president's eye and justifying any conceivable attitude and decision by reference to the virtues of NEFO struggle, *berdikari* (self-reliance), living dangerously, etc.

The repudiation of the West opened the way for uninhibited indulgence in revolutionary and anti-imperialist heroics. By the same token, increased tensions within elite groups precipitated by the drastic leftward plunge taken by national policy created a need for the controlling mechanisms of symbols emphasizing national unity in the face of threatening enemies. To these factors was added that of mounting economic distress; and the inculcation of an atmosphere of "the enemy at the gates" operated, if not to solve economic problems, at least to divert attention from them and from shortfalls in government performance.

The PKI flourished in this heady atmosphere, following through on its policy formulations with a consistency and organizational vigor unmatched by any other political grouping. Enjoying more marked indications of Sukarno's favor, and utilizing its capacity for mass mobilization, the Communists took the political offensive over a wide range of issues.

In some policy areas—such as the developing Sino-Indonesian entente, the convening of a second Afro-Asian conference, and reform of the United Nations—the party could count on President Sukarno to make the running[57] and confine its own role largely to backing

[57] For more extensive discussion of these issues, see D. P. Mozingo, *Sino-Indonesian Relations: An Overview, 1955–1965* (The Rand Corporation, 1965), and the articles by Mozingo and McVey in Tang Tsou, ed., *China in Crisis,* vol. II; Franklin B. Weinstein, "The Second Asian-African Conference: Preliminary Bouts," *Asian Survey,* V, no. 7 (July 1965), 359–73; Frederick

him up and demonstrating mass enthusiasm for his initiatives.[58] But on issues having a more immediate impact on the internal political process the president tended to tread more cautiously and to compromise to a degree incompatible with the PKI's interests and its assessment of the possibilities. His desire to maintain his own authority over the warring political factions, and to keep them in some state of balance, inclined him to postpone crises and propitiate elements in all camps. In these areas, the decisive ones for the PKI's strategy, the party had to take more of the burden of initiative and struggle.

In relation to confrontation itself, the danger of a negotiated compromise persisted throughout the first half of 1964 and presented the PKI leaders with considerable problems. The first major test came in January 1964, when President Johnson sent Robert Kennedy to talk to the Indonesians and Malaysians regarding the Malaysia dispute. Kennedy met Sukarno for exploratory talks in Tokyo in mid-January, and then proceeded to Kuala Lumpur and Djakarta.

Kennedy succeeded in inducing Sukarno to issue on January 31 a ceasefire order to the "volunteers" in Northern Borneo, preparatory to the convening in Bangkok of a conference between the foreign ministers of Indonesia, Malaya, and the Philippines. But this promising beginning, which appeared to demonstrate a desire on Sukarno's part to find a way out of the confrontation impasse, failed to establish a viable basis for compromise. The Malaysian government was anxious not to undo any of the progress that had been made in consolidating the new Federation, and it was under strong pressure too from the British, who felt that they had shored up the new state's defenses adequately and resented American moves toward what they saw as appeasement of an expansionist Indonesia. Kuala Lumpur was thus disinclined to make the kind of concessions Sukarno was seeking as his price for abandoning opposition to the new state. The president was facing his own pressures at home, which made it difficult for him to make the ceasefire effective or to advance new concessions. The talks dragged on desultorily until June 1964, but ultimately fizzled out indecisively.

The PKI from the outset made little secret of its distaste for the

---

Bunnell, "Guided Democracy Foreign Policy, 1960–1965," *Indonesia*, no. 2 (Oct. 1966), 68–69.

[58] See, for example, *Harian Rakjat*, April 15, Sept. 29, Oct. 12, 1964.

renewal of negotiations, the party daily greeting the first meeting between Sukarno and Kennedy with the statement that, whereas the event had aroused hopes amongst "reactionaries," there was full confidence among the people that whatever pressure was applied Indonesia would not be diverted from its struggle.[59] On this occasion, the party's opposition was not confined to words. While the Tokyo talks between Kennedy and Sukarno were still in progress it initiated a second round of seizures of British enterprises. It was a measure of the PKI's new-found boldness that this was the first occasion on which it had taken the lead in a major takeover movement, and also the first occasion when it appeared to challenge the president directly over the conduct of foreign policy. Aidit in effect was indicating to Sukarno that he could not restrain his followers in the event of a deal being made with the imperialists, as well as striking at the president's sensitivity about being identified with right wing policies.

Confusion reigned within the government for several days on the issue of the takeovers, some ministers seeking to reverse or at least stop the workers' actions and others giving verbal support to them. Finally, in a typical compromise solution, the enterprises were placed under state control and the issue of their final disposal was shelved.[60]

Writing in the party's theoretical journal at this time, Aidit clearly indicated the PKI's concern at the possible implications of the new phase of negotiations:

The PKI is of the opinion that tactics can certainly change, so long as strategy, in this case the destruction of "Malaysia," does not change, so long as these tactics serve the strategic task. . . . But if not, then it means capitulation. . . . Our concern [at the hostility shown by the government towards the takeovers] was a little eased when President Sukarno instructed his assistants to hold discussions with the workers. In truth, this is wise. Discussion with workers certainly brings better results than discussions with Robert Kennedy, Tunku Abdul Rahman or his crowd.

The PKI's position is clear; the PKI fully supports the action of taking over British enterprises, and moreover believes that all British enterprises

[59] *Ibid.*, Jan. 18, 1964.

[60] Extensive coverage of the takeover movement and political reactions to it appeared in *Harian Rakjat* during the second half of January and the whole of February.

should be taken over. This is important for strengthening Indonesia's position in the event of discussions concerning "Malaysia" such as have occurred previously.

If the British are stubborn, and do not wish to order their lackey Tunku Abdul Rahman to dissolve "Malaysia," then the enterprises that have been taken over should be confiscated. But if they base themselves on a realistic judgment and dissolve "Malaysia," then the enterprises taken over can be nationalized, meaning that the owners will be compensated according to the financial capability of the Indonesian Republic.[61]

The opposition manifested by the takeovers did not prevent Sukarno making his gesture toward a settlement by issuing the ceasefire order from Tokyo, but it may well have contributed to his inability or unwillingness to make the order effective. This failure in turn proved a major stumbling block in the subsequent negotiation efforts. When the second round of ministerial talks at Bangkok failed to reach any agreement, the PKI called for the abandonment of further discussions, and it greeted the breakdown of the meeting between Sukarno and the Tunku in June with undisguised satisfaction.[62]

All along, the PKI was convinced that U.S. initiatives in these talks presaged an attempt to involve Indonesia in a Western-devised security pact built around Maphilindo, with consequent implications for the course of her domestic policies. Warnings to this effect were issued from time to time,[63] and in a speech in Surabaja on 23 May, on the occasion of the forty-fourth anniversary of the foundation of the PKI, Aidit claimed to discern a long-range scheme by the United States whereby it would ultimately agree to the dismantling of the Malaysian Federation and the grant of nominal independence to the North Borneo states, provided these, along with Malaya, Singapore, Indonesia, and the Philippines were drawn together into a "Greater Maphilindo."[64] If we accept these fears at their face value (and the "Greater Maphilindo" idea did conform rather closely to some suggestions made by Subandrio), then it is small wonder that the PKI winced and struck out at the very mention of negotiations.

---

[61] *Bintang Merah,* XI (Jan.–Feb. 1964), 18–20.

[62] *Harian Rakjat,* June 22, 1964.

[63] See, for example, the *Harian Rakjat* editorial of Jan. 22, 1964.

[64] "Djadilah Komunis jang Baik, dan Lebih Baik Lagi," *Harian Rakjat,* June 11–12, 1964.

The military side of confrontation proceeded in somewhat desultory fashion throughout the first half of 1964, punctuated by few genuine pauses and fewer still dramatic clashes. But in the furtive jungle skirmishes, the British and Malaysians gradually gained the ascendancy over the rebels and Indonesian "volunteers," bringing the border under fairly effective control by June. At this stage, in the aftermath of racial riots in Singapore and Malaya, the Indonesian high command decided on a series of forays on to the Malayan mainland, in an apparent attempt to capitalize on the communal tensions that had erupted there.

Between July and September these landings gradually escalated to the point where, despite their lack of conspicuous success, they aroused intense feeling in Malaysia itself and lost Indonesia any lingering sympathy among most Afro-Asian neutrals. The British, anxious to give a crushing rejoinder to Indonesian agression, toyed with the idea of naval and air attacks on Indonesian bases, thus bringing the conflict closer to the point where a major military engagement might be unavoidable. Tension rose sharply in Indonesia, but the British challenge had its effect—the scale of operations on the Malayan mainland dropped, and before long the pattern of conflict returned to the form it had taken most of the time previously and that it was to follow throughout the remainder of confrontation.

Publicly, Aidit greeted the escalation of the military struggle with bold defiance, declaring that the imperialists knew that they could not possibly occupy Indonesia and that their real aim was to "create fear and panic among cowards and weaklings and at the same time smooth the road for their hirelings in the country to seize political power." But, he countered, "If the British and U.S. imperialists dare to make an armed attack on Indonesia, then they will not only lose 'Malaysia,' but all their positions in Southeast Asia. The whole of Southeast Asia will go up in the flames of revolution, and it will certainly not be confined to Southeast Asia only."[65] But this was probably little more than ritual morale boosting. In his report the previous December, Aidit had shown his concern at the danger of a large scale military conflict precipitating a military takeover, or at least a marked expansion of army powers. His fears were not ungrounded,

[65] Address to BTI national conference, printed in *Harian Rakjat*, Sept. 11, 1964.

for the crisis over the mainland landings did lead to the imposition of a modified state of emergency, and a British retaliatory strike would almost certainly have been followed by full scale reversion to martial law rule. Privately, therefore, the PKI leaders expressed strong opposition to the landings, which they branded "adventurist" actions by military leaders with "Bonapartist" ambitions.[66]

The enrolment of volunteers had been stepped up in February, partly in response to the introduction of conscription in Malaya. In a wave of patriotic enthusiasm, the political parties, mass organizations, factories, and enterprises enrolled en masse in the volunteer movement, and before the month was out Sukarno announced that 21 million volunteers had registered. Like his claims to have abolished illiteracy, however, these grand figures were more symptomatic of the style of the times than the scale of the movement. Needless to say, the PKI was in the van of the volunteer movement, not only being conscious of the patriotic prestige associated with it but also hoping to get a good many of its members and supporters trained in the use of arms. Few of the volunteers received serious military training, however, and the army was careful to keep a close check on the rifles that were handed out at volunteer parades. It was a customary sight in Djakarta and the provinces late in the year to see units of volunteers from workplaces and offices drilling in waste lots, but most of them were armed with nothing more lethal than sticks. The volunteer training program was to acquire major significance in 1965, however, when it became the basis for the campaign to "arm the workers and peasants" and create a "fifth force" alongside the army, navy, air force, and police.[67]

PKI attempts to arouse national sentiment against the United States to the point where friendly dealings with it would be unthinkable received a boost in December 1963 with America's decision to extend the operations of its Seventh Fleet to the Indian Ocean.[68] This was

---

[66] Interviews with Aidit, Lukman, and Karel Supit (head of the Foreign Affairs Bureau of the PKI), November 1964, in Djakarta. The PKI leaders informed me that they could not make their views public without inviting punitive action by the authorities at the instigation of the generals.

[67] The link between the two campaigns was drawn explicitly by Aidit, when he claimed to have thanked the British ambassador at a reception for sending armed forces to Malaysia and so giving him "a good reason for proposing the arming of the workers and peasants"; *Harian Rakjat,* Feb. 1, 1965.

[68] Or, as Sukarno insisted, the "Indonesian Ocean."

taken by the government and the political parties as a move hostile to Indonesia, and the PKI's fulminations against it fell on fertile soil. Following up its advantage, SOBSI called for the nationalization of U.S. firms in Indonesia,[69] and the PKI, through its cultural organization LEKRA, announced at year's end a boycott of American newsreels and shortly afterwards the extension of the boycott to all American films. The film boycott became the high point of struggle in the campaign against U.S. "cultural penetration" that had been launched in vigorous style in the middle of 1963. In point of fact it was not a new issue but one on which Sukarno and the PKI had long seen eye to eye—the president had attacked youthful enthusiasm for Western music and dance in the fifties as an affront to "Indonesian identity." But, from being mainly a propaganda issue, the campaign against American culture was now transformed by the PKI into one of its major agitational platforms.[70]

Other U.S. agencies and institutions were brought into the line of fire; the Peace Corps was constantly harried by PKI groups until it was ordered to depart, and the United States Information Service suffered attacks on its premises and libraries. The escalation of American intervention in Vietnam following the Tonkin Gulf incident in August 1964 was used to rally public opinion against the United States, the "Asia for Asians" theme being particularly effective in the nationalist climate of Indonesia.

A measure of the change in climate that confrontation had wrought during 1964 is given by the fact that when the PKI initiated seizures of U.S. enterprises, in February 1965, it confronted only a mild repetition of the official resistance it had met in its actions against British enterprises in 1963 and 1964.[71]

Although there was continuous economic decline throughout 1964, for most of the year its effects were not as disastrous as some had feared at the time of the jettisoning of Western aid and the severing of trade relations with Malaysia. It appeared to many confrontation

[69] *Harian Rakjat,* Jan. 3, 1964.

[70] See *Harian Rakjat,* Aug. 31, 1964, for a PKI riposte to Trade Minister Malik's opposition to its campaign.

[71] For an account of the PKI's anti-U.S. campaign in 1964 and early 1965, see Van der Kroef, "Indonesian Communism's 'Revolutionary Gymnastics.' "

advocates that in a war of attrition Indonesia might hope to wear out the British, for whom the costs of supporting Malaysia were considerable. A measure of relief was expressed by nationalist ideologues that things were not so bad as they might have been. Ruslan Abdulgani, minister of information and a leading commentator on Sukarno's ideology, argued in March that economic collapse was impossible but Indonesia would collapse if its mental outlook collapsed. In other words, spirit and resolve could achieve miracles.

While similarly reassuring their followers, the PKI leaders constantly emphasized the need to stiffen the economy in the context of confrontation. They, after all, had a great deal to fear from either economic disorders or a reversion to foreign aid solutions. Nevertheless, for that very reason, they were compelled to join with Ruslan and other optimists in dismissing the argument that confrontation was undermining the economy and insisting that Indonesia could solve her own problems. *Berdikari* became the catchword on the economic front. Only in the last quarter of 1964, when economic conditions worsened markedly, did the PKI at length begin to show serious concern at the prospect of breakdown.

Under the cover of an external crusade against imperialism, then, the PKI was working assiduously to strengthen its domestic position and concentrate political attention on those areas where it could assert its strength within the protective coloring of patriotism. Since Sukarno by now had substantially abandoned his lingering attachment to a middle course and come to see things very much as the Communists did, they could count on his support in their initiatives so long as they elevated his role and inspiration in their activities and avoided steps he regarded as too premature or extreme. By the same token, once the army leaders saw the political drift being taken by confrontation, they began to lose their enthusiasm for the anti-Malaysia crusade and to contemplate with increasing concern the rise in PKI fortunes.

It is apparent that nationalism had worked signally to the advantage of the Communist Party. Between the beginning of 1961, when the West Irian campaign began to gather steam, and the end of 1964, when the political implications of the anti-Malaysia campaign were being fully exploited, the position of the PKI had been radically transformed from one of defensiveness and insecurity to one of boldness and assertiveness. Confrontation had provided the climate making this change possible. Though not of the party's making, the two anti-imperialist ventures had been made to order for its requirements.

The skill of the PKI leadership, and above all Aidit, lay in recognizing the ways in which nationalist crusades could be made to serve its united national front strategy and compensate for the political avenues closed to it by the dissolution of the parliamentary system. Initially approaching events in a somewhat pragmatic fashion, seizing hold of opportunities as they presented themselves and adapting quickly to the swings of the political pendulum, by the latter part of 1963 Aidit had grasped in a total theoretical framework the connection between the symbolism of the anti-imperialist crusade and the instrumentalist needs of the party in the prevailing political constellation. By persevering application of his strategy, the PKI had succeeded in altering the balance of power significantly to its advantage.

By the end of 1964, the PKI still stood a good distance from the halls of power, but it was at least in a position to contemplate the entrances to them. On the other hand, one of the crucial side effects of confrontation—a seriously declining economy—represented a destabilizing factor in the political situation that the PKI could not afford to ignore. As the next chapter will disclose, the party had in fact been paying close attention to this problem.

6. The Politics of Economic Mismanagement

From the outset of Guided Democracy, the PKI found itself on the horns of a dilemma so far as its economic policies were concerned. If it had wished to promote radical industrial actions in 1959–60 (and there is some reason to believe that this was its wish) in order to reassure its supporters of its continued independence and militancy and show the power-holders that its rights had to be respected, then it soon came to realize that such a path was closed to it. The army crackdown of July 1960 brought home the fact that these tactics involved risks; true, Sukarno rescued the party from the worst effects of army repression on this occasion, but by placing it on a good behavior bond he indicated that the party could not pursue this kind of approach with impunity.

By the latter part of 1960 the Communist leaders had decided to "subordinate class tasks to national tasks," as they put it. Consistent with this decision, agitation on issues affecting the material welfare of the masses was largely confined to propaganda and moderate forms of pressure. Accordingly, economic problems could not be used to forward PKI interests as against those of more powerful political groups.

At the same time, however, Sukarno's devotion to nationalist and prestige projects was not only costly in itself but also tended to divert attention from the tasks of economic stabilization, development, and welfare. A development program with state socialist characteristics was drawn up in 1959, and a number of measures designed to put the program into effect were inaugurated. For a time this seemed to offer the PKI an alternative vehicle to class agitation for advancing its claims to recognition and political advancement. Being in basic accord with its proposals, the party threw its weight behind the program and sought to demonstrate the PKI's dedication to the goals of progressive development. Initially, the Communist leaders apparently believed in the possibility of combining nationalist self-assertion with economic advancement. Their confidence was soon shattered, however, and economic decline, which had been relatively constant for a number of years, began to assume more serious proportions from late 1961, when the costs of the West Irian campaign and government failings worked together to undermine the currency and throw the economy into disarray.

The PKI leaders, as political realists, could not ignore the dangers this deterioration held for them. Their followers looked to them for remedial action on their behalf, as real wages and incomes began to fall drastically. There was a mounting risk that discontent would be fanned into disorders, either by grassroots radicals or by right wing forces intent on disrupting the alliance between the president and the party and thereby arresting the latter's political advance. Finally, economic decline provided a strong argument for influential political figures close to the President to use in urging the necessity of attracting Western aid to restore the economy—a recourse that would have been to the disadvantage of the Communists.

In coping with these problems, the range of options open to the PKI's leaders was narrow. They could not abandon their commitment to the nationalist crusade without removing the lynchpin of their political strategy and even calling into question Sukarno's primacy in the political system. As the crisis over the 1963 stabilization scheme demonstrated, nationalism remained their strongest weapon in the fight against closer economic relations with the West. So far as the state socialist development program was concerned, their attempts to persuade the government to carry it out, and to bring order into the economy, could go no further than exhortation and example—and these were clearly inadequate. Similarly, neither such respectful pressure as they could apply, nor negotiation, was very successful in either arresting the decline in the living standards of their followers or promoting the independent fighting character of their massed urban detachments.

Once again the onset of full-scale confrontation was a turning point, providing the PKI with a transformed political climate in which a new approach to the problem of the economy could be worked out. Even the concept of development underwent a decided change. In place of the Soviet-style model of development they had adopted formerly, the PKI leaders, drawing once again on Chinese views, proposed a strategy of self-reliance for Indonesia giving primary emphasis to the agricultural sector. In part this reformulation was a reaction to the country's economic troubles and international isolation, but it also reflected the party's need to concentrate attention on the internal political changes that were required if economic improvement was to be achieved.

In the early stages of confrontation the PKI tended to minimize economic deterioration, in order to discourage any thoughts of reverting to a U.S.-sponsored stabilization program. But by late 1964, when such a prospect had become remote and the drift toward economic anarchy could no longer be played down, it prepared a new offensive aimed at corrupt officials, "bureaucratic capitalists," and other "economic saboteurs." There was ample justification for an attack on the manner in which large segments of the politico-bureaucratic elite had amassed wealth; PKI forecasts of the emergence of a "new rich dynasty" were proving all too accurate. The party could point to peculation and mismanagement, and at the same time stress its own readiness to provide honest and capable state functionaries to replace those unfit to continue in office. Its leaders had devoted a great deal of attention to analyzing economic problems, devising credible development programs, and promoting programs to train personnel in managerial skills. The traditional Communist emphasis on industrialization and modernization had operated in this respect to provide the Communists with a unique combination in the Indonesian context of expressive and practical problem-solving skills.

The PKI could not afford to go after official profiteers indiscriminately, however. It was still obliged to rely on the goodwill of its "progressive" allies among the elite for opportunities to acquire greater power. Accordingly, it directed its anticorruption drive against those in high places who were also the party's enemies. Such an opportunistic strategy was essential in the party's view. It reassured allies that they need fear no indictment so long as they played the Nasakom game; at the same time it provided discontented party members and followers with clearly defined targets for their hostility, demonstrated the PKI's organizational power to friends and opponents alike, and worked toward the isolation of those who stood in the way of its aspirations.

THE SOCIALIST PHASE AND ITS DISSIPATION, 1959–1962

Sukarno's proclaimed goal under Guided Democracy was to lay the foundations for a socialist society in Indonesia, and in accordance with this objective one of his first actions after restoring the 1945 constitution was to specify the outlines of a "Guided Economy" and have his proposals ratified by the MPRS, the highest formal authority in the land.

In some respects, circumstances were propitious for the initiation of experiments in a state-managed economy. A considerable body of opinion in Indonesia followed Sukarno in attributing the mistakes and divisiveness of the parliamentary period to the vices of "liberalism" and the capitalist spirit. Reaction against the failures of this period created a political mood that was receptive both to socialist concepts of planning and control and to styles of leadership that broke away from the Western pattern to pursue an authentically Indonesian identity.

Materially, the takeover and nationalization of Dutch enterprises had for the first time placed the country's major industrial, commercial, and financial undertakings under government control. At the same time, the defeat of the regional rebels had greatly weakened the influence of private entrepreneurial groups in the community whose standing had already been undermined by their association with, and defense of, the discredited parliamentary system.

None of the major political parties supporting Guided Democracy had any very strong commitment to economic individualism, and the same was true of the leadership of the armed forces. To quote Lev:

Once ensconced in the economy, the army elite lined up with other groups that favored a thoroughgoing state economy. . . . Apart from a strong ideological predilection for socialism inherent in the nationalist movement since the 1920's, there was also a natural impulse for groups grounded in the government to favor state ownership. And this meant not only the bureaucracy itself and those parties, like the PNI, closely related to the bureaucracy, but also the officer corps, which possessed no legitimate basis for individual commercial activity and had no appreciation of the private economy.[1]

As against these positive indicators, however, there were others of a

[1] Lev, *Transition,* p. 70.

less encouraging kind. Any sustained attack on Indonesia's economic problems entailed decisions that would prove unpopular with large sections of the public and, more specifically, with influential groups among the elite. Structural defects in the economy had been accentuated in the period since 1954; financial instability had increased and economic development had been inhibited as a result of inflation, deficit financing, declining prices for exports, and the neglect of factors vital to the maintenance of productive capacity and the functioning of the infrastructure.[2] To these structural defects was added the dislocation caused by the regional rebellion and the takeover of Dutch enterprises.

Only a strong and highly motivated government leadership could have pushed through a plan of stabilization and development in the face of these formidable obstacles; and such a government was precisely what was lacking. The state leadership had a bill to meet: having attributed all the ills of the body politic to political and economic liberalism, with the implication that matters would take an immediate turn for the better once the revolution was "put back on the rails," it was in no good position to ask its supporters and the political public for sacrifices and austerity. It was, moreover, poorly legitimated, having pushed aside the parliamentary system which from the time of independence had constituted the only consensus basis for the state—and that in the face of opposition from the political parties. Sukarno and the army represented a combination that was formidable in terms of physical power and mass appeal, but not one that could easily embark on deprivational policies guaranteed to arouse the opposition and resistance of the political parties and other powerful groups such as the bureaucracy.

It is conceivable that these difficulties could have been overcome had there existed among the elements gathered together in the Guided Democracy complex a substantial identity of views concerning the goals of the society and the methods by which these were to be attained. This was far from being the case, however. None of the groups associated with the regime, with the partial exception of the PKI, had any very definite ideas on priorities in economic decision-making.

---

[2] For an examination of economic policies in the fifties, see Feith, *Decline*, pp. 303–9, 373–78, 445–49, 570–72; Mackie, *Problems of the Indonesian Inflation*, pp. 2–24.

Moreover, in the years since independence, the government and its apparatus had come to be viewed as vehicles for the realization of clique and personal advantage rather than for the advancement of broad social interests. The groups brought together under the banner of Guided Democracy expected and demanded tangible rewards in the form of patronage and access to spoils in return for their concurrence in the new dispensation.

Finally, Sukarno, the dominant ideologue of the regime, saw national unity and national greatness not as a painful labor of material construction but as an imaginative leap into the future, a "mental revolution" which, by envisioning and willing the fulfillment of the nation's destiny, would bring the target within reach. Prestigious symbols, both ancient and modern, together with the ritual and titles that went with them, appealed more to him, both intrinsically and as instruments for binding the populace to him, than the prosaic evidences of material progress. Given his own disposition, and the pressures upon him to shore up the cracks in the society, it was unlikely that he would provide the inspiration or the authoritative direction for a concerted attack on economic problems.

The Political Manifesto, as the authoritative statement of Sukarno's teaching, laid down the general guidelines for Indonesia's development in the economic as well as other spheres. It proclaimed as its goal the establishment of a socialist society founded on principles of social justice. Before this objective could be attained, however, the country had to complete its national revolution by laying the foundations of an economy that was both integrated and democratic. The main tasks to be undertaken in this field were: government supervision and control of the key productive and distributive sectors, retooling of the economic apparatus to bring it into accord with social objectives, planning, popular participation in economic administration, and the indigenization of land ownership. While the state would control the heights of the economy, some limited scope would be left for private enterprise, including established nonindigenous capital.[3]

The generality of this program, and the vagueness of provisions relating to such contentious issues as the roles of foreign capital and private enterprise, ensured that it was acceptable to the varied groups

[3] *Political Manifesto, Republic of Indonesia of 17th August 1959* (Djakarta, 1959); *Manipol-Usdek in Question and Answer* (Djakarta, 1961), especially pp. 13–14, 16–18, 27–30.

associated with the regime. The rejection of liberalism in favor of an interventionist role by the state was clear; but there was still ample room for interpretations to fit the interests of all the parties and factions that, in characteristic Sukarno fashion, had been involved in the formulation of the program and were therefore committed to whatever it should prove to mean in official terms.

A trend in government policy toward greater intervention in the economy had actually begun earlier, in 1958. As Mackie says:

It was a time of intense reaction against "liberalism" and capitalism, the high tide of *Socialism à la Indonesia* and trust in the Guided Economy as a panacea. Private importers were excluded from a wide range of imports and left a mere 25% of the market. State enterprise and an ambitious new Development Plan were to create an entirely new society. Government-supplied *sandang-pangan* [food and clothing] shops and *kampung* cooperatives were to serve as a channel for essential commodities, to be sold at fixed prices on a ration-card system.[4]

The Eight Year Plan of National Development formed the most ambitious element in the Guided Economy program. It also illustrated vividly the basic flaws in the regime's approach to national economic development. The formulation of the Plan was entrusted, not to a committee of economic experts, but to a large and unwieldy political body representative of the major streams in the Guided Democracy complex and headed, significantly, by the radical nationalist ideologue Mohammad Yamin. The ritualistic and symbolic aspects of the exercise are graphically revealed in the Plan's division into 8 volumes, 17 parts, and 1945 clauses, an organization designed to celebrate the date of the proclamation of independence. It was bound in *batik,* the handmade cloth that customarily bears traditional motifs of royal and magical significance. Described by President Sukarno as being "rich in fantasy," the Plan has been evaluated more critically as "in no sense a rational allocation of priorities for the utilization of available resources, but a mere heterogeneous ragbag of projects and financial estimates which in many cases bore little relation to reality." No clear line of responsibility for the execution of the Plan was ever devised, and its vague financial provisions, which appeared to depend primarily on foreign capital and profits from state enterprises, proved largely illusory. As Mackie comments, "With the virulent inflation and

[4] Mackie, *Problems of the Indonesian Inflation,* p. 24.

acute foreign exchange crisis of 1961–62, little more was heard of the Plan or its executive body. Other organizations set up in the crisis period of 1962 soon superseded it in importance."[5] The Plan was finally abandoned in March 1965, long after it had ceased to exist except on paper.

None of the more specific proposals for implementing the Guided Economy program of state socialism fared well. The state enterprises, laboring under a shortage of managerial and technical expertise, were stymied by inadequate and often contradictory government controls, a political climate inimical to nonrisk operations, and the corruption which these circumstances encouraged.[6] The Chinese traders and manufacturers, who dominated small and medium scale enterprise and the distributive sector, were discouraged from performing their functions by active persecution and bureaucratic hostility. The weaker indigenous entrepreneur either went to the wall or came to depend on protective connections with state officials.[7]

The cooperatives and *sandang-pangan* shops, initially regarded as a socialist solution to the distribution problem, steadily lost ground; undercapitalized, lacking in competent staff, and inadequately supervised, they could not cope with the general financial insecurity and sporadic supply deliveries and frequently fell victim to the peculations of their officials.[8] Land reform laws that had been passed in 1959 and 1960, while going further on paper than the Manipol program, were rendered ineffective by bureaucratic inertia and the resistance of rural landed interests.[9]

Controls against inflation began to break down seriously in late

[5] *Ibid.,* pp. 27–28. For more detailed discussions of the Eight Year Plan, see Guy J. Pauker, "The Indonesian Eight-Year Overall Development Plan," *Pacific Affairs,* XXXIV, no. 2 (Summer 1961), 115–20, an early and charitable summary; D. D. Humphrey, "Indonesia's National Plan for Economic Development," *Asian Survey,* II, no. 10 (Dec. 1962), 12–21; Paauw, pp. 220–231.

[6] See J. A. C. Mackie, "The Government Estates," in T. K. Tan, ed., *Sukarno's Guided Indonesia* (Brisbane, 1967), pp. 58–72; J. Panglaykim, *An Indonesian Experience: Its State Trading Corporation* (Monograph, Fakultas Ekonomi Universitas Indonesia, 1965).

[7] Feith, "Dynamics," pp. 348–50; Lance Castles, "Socialism and Private Business: The Latest Phase," *Bulletin of Indonesian Economic Studies,* I, no. 1 (June 1965), 29–32 and *passim.*

[8] Castles, "Socialism and Private Business," pp. 32–33.

[9] Land reform will be discussed in more detail in the following chapter.

1961, and thereafter the cost of the West Irian campaign was a major factor in creating a virulent inflationary spiral.[10] "Social control" and retooling made little headway and came to be operated, if at all, more as weapons to ensure official loyalty to the regime than as checks on economic mismanagement.

PKI POLICY IN THE SOCIALIST PHASE

So far as can be ascertained from the PKI's statements and actions, the economic policies and program outlined in the Political Manifesto substantially accorded with the party's own understanding of how the foundations of a national economy ought to be laid, although it would no doubt have wished for a more emphatic rejection of dependence on foreign capital and a more radical agrarian program. The PKI saw the economic provisions in Manipol both as committing the government to building up the state sector of the economy and as giving the party a suitable framework in which to advocate many of the *political* changes it wanted. Accordingly, there was agreement between the Communists and the government on the goals toward which economic policy ought to be directed, and also a considerable measure of support by the PKI for specific governmental measures. This was especially true of those steps taken to strengthen the role of the state sector. The party had naturally supported the idea that the Dutch enterprises seized in December 1957 should be nationalized, and even after a law to this effect had been enacted the Communists continued to press for provisions to strengthen the law and extend nationalization to all Dutch firms, including mixed enterprises. It further advocated that a final decision on compensation to former owners be withheld as a means of putting pressure on Holland to cede West Irian.[11]

In February 1959, the PKI held a national economic seminar at which it advanced general proposals regarding development and industrialization. The conclusions of the seminar were that the state sector should be given the prime role in transforming the country from a backward, agricultural, export-oriented economy into an advanced, industrialized, balanced economy.[12] They called for an ex-

[10] Mackie, *Problems of the Indonesian Inflation,* pp. 28–37.
[11] See, for example, the SOBSI statement of August 19, 1959, in *Review of Indonesia,* VI (Sept–Oct. 1959), 28.
[12] "C.P.I. National Economic Seminar: Documents," Djakarta, February 2–4, 1959, *Review of Indonesia,* VI (April–May 1959, Supplement), 5.

pansion of the state sector, with priority being given to heavy industry.
State enterprises, the seminar declared, should be regulated by a law,

laying down the principles of management, business and responsibility,
and defining such matters as the link between such enterprises and the
state which must be organized in such a way as to give the state full
control over these enterprises while at the same time ensuring that they
have the freedom to regulate their own business affairs.

The government should draw up a national plan emphasizing development of the mining industry, construction of an iron and steel industry,
provision of replacement plant and essential agricultural supplies and
consumer goods, and electricity production.[13] More than two years
later, at a lecture to the Aliarcham Academy on August 25, 1961, in
which he outlined the PKI's economic proposals at considerable
length, Aidit advanced very much the same view of the place of the
state sector in development.[14]

With regard to the preparation of a national development plan, the
PKI approved Sukarno's declaration that the formulators must be
politically reliable as well as technically qualified, arguing that patriotism was the first qualification for participation in a project of such
fundamental importance.[15] Both the president and the Communist
leaders had good political reasons for mistrusting Indonesia's professional economists, since the most highly regarded of them were in
the PSI camp and were likely to advocate greater financial prudence,
liberal market policies, and favorable opportunities for the participation of Western capital. Having participated in the drafting of the
Eight Year Plan, the PKI leaders enthusiastically supported its provisions, claiming that for the first time "the ideas of the people regarding economic development have significantly influenced" official concepts of development.[16]

At the PKI's seventh congress in April 1962, a time of rising rice
prices and general economic panic, Aidit conceded that the implementation of the Plan was not going well. This was due, he main-

[13] *Ibid.,* pp. 6–7.
[14] *Socialisme Indonesia dan Sjarat-sjarat Pelaksanaannja* (Indonesian Socialism and Ways of Implementing it) (Djakarta, 1962), pp. 76–77, 90–91.
[15] See Aidit's report to the Central Committee of the PKI in November 1958;
Review of Indonesia, V (Dec. 1958, Supplement), 11–12.
[16] *Harian Rakjat,* Apr. 14, 1961.

tained, to the presence of reactionaries in the state apparatus and the government's failure to fill out the general contours of the Plan with "a detailed annual plan based on definite priorities and the organisation of implementation"; other factors hindering its execution were the absence of effective coordination between government bodies, the lack of popular control, and the diminution of mass enthusiasm as a result of the difficulties the people were experiencing in their daily life.[17] In other words, Aidit was arguing for a more consistent and determined application of socialist principles and suggesting that the PKI possessed the conviction and know-how to do a national job that those in power were failing to do.

The state enterprises presented the PKI with a ticklish problem. Since the party's leaders had consistently argued that foreign economic domination was the major barrier to Indonesian development, and that the state sector was the essential basis of a program for a national economy, they had a stake in the progress of the enterprises, since their successful operation would enhance the popularity of socialist solutions and make resort to foreign capital less necessary. On the other hand, from the outset they could find little to approve in the conduct of the enterprise operations. They objected to the degree of military influence, the dismissal of workers, the rejection of workers' claims to participation in management, and declines in output.[18]

In September 1959, in his report to the sixth congress of the party, Aidit was still relatively mild in his criticism of the state enterprises, though he did demand the inclusion of trade union representatives on democratically-organized executive bodies of the enterprises.[19] In 1960 the PKI's hostility to the managements hardened considerably. At this time the party and SOBSI were displaying an uncharacteristic militancy on industrial issues, and conflict was particularly acute in the state enterprises, owing to the abolition of bonuses at Lebaran and other benefits that workers in Dutch-owned enterprises had traditionally enjoyed. The army, using its martial law powers, kept the Communists' industrial agitation under control, much to the latter's

[17] *Problems*, pp. 479–80. See also the congress speech by M. Zaelani, printed in *Madju Terus*, pp. 281–84.

[18] See the PKI's press statement on the occasion of the nationalization of the Dutch enterprises; *Review of Indonesia*, V (Dec. 1958), 5–6.

[19] *Problems*, pp. 295–96.

indignation, and the PKI leaders drew the conclusion that army administrators and their colleagues on the boards of the state enterprises
were making common cause against the party. They also suspected
the enterprise managers of aiding the labour minister's plans to create
an all-embracing labor front, a move that was generally seen as aimed
at curbing the power of SOBSI.[20] The PKI struck back with accusations of mismanagement by those in charge, and it was in these circumstances that the label of "bureaucratic capitalists" first came to
be attached to the enterprise managers.

From this time forward, the Communists were to wage an unre-
mitting campaign against those whom they regarded as constituting an
emerging new class that was enriching itself from peculations in state
property, sabotaging the program for a national economy, and allying
itself with the militantly anti-Communist forces in the country. At the
seventh party congress in April 1962, Aidit went so far as to say that
the state enterprises could be a liability instead of an asset to national
development. The remedy, however, lay in retooling the personnel
and democratizing the management; the PKI remained adamantly
opposed to the transfer of the enterprises to private control.[21]

The utilization of foreign capital and aid remained a source of controversy between the PKI and the government between 1959 and
1962, although the dispute was not as sharp as it was to become in
1963, for the simple reason that the amount of Western aid (government or private) received by Indonesia between 1959 and 1962 was
very modest. The PKI's attitude, which subsequently found substantial support in the Political Manifesto, was that Indonesian development should be financed as far as possible out of domestic resources,
but that if recourse to foreign aid were necessary then this should
take the form of government-to-government loans from Communist
and other "friendly" countries.[22] There is little doubt that the party's
intransigence on this issue was prompted in large part by the political
threat the leadership saw in closer relations between the Indonesian
and United States governments. In 1961, when there was discussion

---

[20] See, for example, Njono's report to the third national congress of
SOBSI, in *Review of Indonesia,* VII (Sept.–Oct. 1960), 23.

[21] *Problems,* pp. 473–76.

[22] "C.P.I. National Economic Seminar: Documents," *Review of Indonesia,*
VI (April–May 1959, Supplement), 11.

of various forms of joint ventures with foreign capital to solve the problem of lagging development, Aidit rejected them all as devious forms of "penetration."[23]

The PKI found little to criticise in the government's restrictions on the role of private enterprise in general. The party had consistently supported a limited role for the individual businessman, though it was not very explicit about the scope to be allowed him. In a theoretical disquisition on the struggle between socialist and capitalist factors in Indonesian development in his 1957 training manual, Aidit had taken a rather liberal view:

The growth within certain bounds of national capitalism is only one aspect of the victory of the Indonesian revolution. Another aspect is that the victory of the democratic revolution will mean the development of *socialist factors,* such as the growing political influence of the proletariat, the growing recognition by the peasants, the intellectuals and other petty bourgeois elements of the leadership of the proletariat, the growth of state enterprises as well as co-operatives among the peasants, the handicrafts men, the fishermen and other sections of the people. All these are socialist factors which will provide the guarantee that the future of the Indonesian revolution is socialism and not capitalism.[24]

The PKI fought hard against discriminatory measures aimed at Chinese businessmen, running considerable risk of army displeasure by campaigning vigorously against attempts in the latter half of 1959 to oust alien Chinese traders from rural areas.[25] These anti-Chinese policies were inspired in part by economic competition and reflected the resentment of indigenous business groups at Chinese domination of retail trade; but there was also an important political dimension. The 1959–60 measures, like the racial riots of 1963, have been seen as "largely army instigated and aimed as much at the embarrassment of the PKI and the exacerbation of relations with China as at the harassment of the local Chinese."[26] The reason for the PKI's strenuous defense of the Chinese minority, in the face of the political dangers such action involved, has been seen by some commentators as

---

[23] *Socialisme Indonesia dan Sjarat-sjarat Pelaksanaannja,* pp. 52–53.

[24] *Problems,* pp. 60–61.

[25] See *Review of Indonesia,* VI (Nov.–Dec. 1959), 3–4, 5, 19–20.

[26] Ruth T. McVey, "Indonesian Communism and China," in Tang Tsou, ed., *China in Crisis,* II, 361–62.

lying in either the financial dependence of the party on donations from Chinese businesses or pressure from the CPC. McVey has argued convincingly, however, that neither of these influences was of decisive importance and that the main explanation is to be found in "the internationalist, anti-racialist character of Marxist ideology" and the fact that anti-Chinese actions were initiated by right wing political forces.[27]

The PKI's attitude toward cooperatives underwent a marked change in the late fifties. Earlier on, the party had opposed government moves to promote cooperatives, branding them "demagogic" and describing those already in existence as organizations of middle class people with no prospect of making a successful entry into spheres of production.[28] This attitude was prompted by Hatta's espousal of cooperatives as the basic form of Indonesian socialism, a policy that the PKI excoriated as a diversionary attempt to bypass the problem of the domination of Indonesia's economy by foreign capital.[29]

By early 1959, however, the PKI was favoring the encouragement of cooperatives, provided that Communists took care to avoid suggesting that these organizations could solve economic problems if there were no struggle against foreign monopoly capital and the landlords.[30] The party turned its attention to training cadres to work in cooperatives and began to emphasize the importance of setting up credit cooperatives and cooperatives for the joint marketing of agricultural products in the villages.[31] Further elaboration of the party's policy on cooperatives was undertaken at the PKI national peasants' conference in April;[32] and in September, in his report to the sixth congress, Aidit called on the government to provide greater protection and facilities for cooperatives.[33] During the following year the BTI undertook an investigation of existing cooperatives, exposing deficiencies in their operations and urging a new start in accordance with

[27] *Ibid.*

[28] Aidit, Report to the Fifth Congress of the PKI, *Problems*, p. 247.

[29] *Ibid.*, pp. 247–48.

[30] Speech by Lukman at the PKI national economic seminar; *Review of Indonesia*, VI (Apr.–May 1959, Supplement), 4.

[31] Conclusions of the PKI national economic seminar; *Ibid.*, pp. 12–13.

[32] *Review of Indonesia*, VI (June–July 1959, Supplement) 7–9, 13–14.

[33] *Problems*, pp. 294–95.

the principles of "voluntary membership, open dealings, democracy and beneficial undertakings."[34]

The change in PKI policy can be attributed partly to the eclipse of Hatta and his identification with cooperative projects, and more substantially to the fact that the PKI, having decided to direct its main mass work to the villages in future, saw in the cooperative movement a means of building up popular support. The party seems also to have hoped that cooperatives would provide the poorer peasants with a cushion against economic distress, and that this would increase their sense of identity with the party.

Reflecting the party's view that survivals of feudalism constituted, after imperialist economic domination, the major factor holding back the national development of Indonesia, land reform was a key element in the PKI's program.[35] Accordingly, the party welcomed the laws on maximum and minimum landholdings and on sharecropping that were passed in 1959 and 1960. It criticized them as not going far enough but was obviously prepared at that stage to settle for their implementation. A more detailed examination of the operation of these laws, and PKI policy in relation to them, will be reserved for the next chapter. As an earnest of its practical support for the socialist orientation of the government's economic program, the PKI began in 1958 to campaign for increased national production. At first, apparently, a patriotic contribution to the struggle against the regional rebels,[36] the effort on the production front in time became a routine element in the party's propaganda, being intended as a symbol of its responsible national outlook and its concern to get things done. At the same time, production campaigns were a suitably loyal context in which to raise demands for greater democratic rights and social participation for the masses.

Proposals directed to increasing food production were first drawn up at the national economic seminar in February 1959, and these were followed by regular exhortations to the cadres and by reports of activities undertaken and results achieved.[37] Borrowing from Chinese

[34] *Review of Indonesia*, VII (Aug. 1960), 34.

[35] The PKI's slogan since 1953 had been "land to those who till it"; *Program PKI*.

[36] See Aidit's speech on May 1, 1958, in *Review of Indonesia*, V (June 1958), 6.

[37] See, for example, Aidit's speech to the national peasants conference,

slogans and policies, the PKI called on its members and the peasantry to "plough deeply, plant closely, use more fertilizer, improve seeds and irrigation," and emulate the pioneering work of such farming innovators as Dr. Tjokronegoro and Pak Jagus.[38] Early in 1962, the production efforts of the PKI blossomed into the "1,001 Movement," whose title summed up its aim of suggesting that there were countless small ways by which production of food and clothing could be increased.[39] The movement was featured in the party's newspaper, where a column was devoted each day to proposals for planting new vegetables, raising chickens and goats, improving irrigation, etc. Judging from press reports, however, little in the way of a mass response developed, and the campaign faded away toward the end of the year. SOBSI and the BTI adopted their own production plans in 1962 also, and from this time onward PKI leaders made a point of developing detailed plans for the renovation and expansion of various branches of industry and transportation.

Steady pressure was maintained for retooling and worker participation in management. In 1961 Aidit expressed these demands in essentially populist terms:

There are some people who have no faith in the people's ability to develop a national economy and place the blame for our economic failures on the fact that the people are not sufficiently educated, many are still illiterate, they do not have the managerial know–how, they work badly, they are superstitious, etc. . . . More serious still, some of these people are in important positions in the state power. . . . The trouble is due to the fact that the people have not been given an active role in economic development but have been exploited."[40]

Criticism of government economic policy varied greatly in tone and extent during the 1959–1962 period. Throughout 1959 and 1960, as noted previously, relations between the PKI and the government were noticeably strained. The strongly critical tone of PKI statements

---

Review of Indonesia, VI (June–July 1959, Supplement), 14; Aidit's report to the eighth plenum of the Central Committee (*Bintang Merah* XV [July–Aug. 1959], 303–4); and an interview with Aidit reported in *Bintang Timur,* Nov. 20, 1959.

[38] *Bintang Timur,* Nov. 20, 1959.

[39] *Harian Rakjat,* Feb. 9, 1962.

[40] *Socialisme Indonesia dan Sjarat-sjarat Pelaksanaannja,* pp. 70–74.

on economic policy was in part a reflection of this general estrange-ment, but specific actions of the cabinet in the economic sphere also added to the strain, as we have seen. Liberal policies, as they mani-fested themselves in price increases, came under particularly heavy fire. After the storm over the July 1960 evaluation, however, the PKI was more subdued, and its opposition was reduced in 1961–62 in the improved political climate of the West Irian campaign. Criticism did not cease, and Aidit stressed—for example in his report to the seventh congress in April 1962—the seriousness of the economic decline that had taken place in the previous few years; but the tenor of the attack at this time was different from that of 1960. Though the government was taken to task for its weaknesses and deficiencies, there was no question of withdrawing Communist support or seeking drastic changes in the government's composition; rather, the major blame was placed on the imperialists and those elements in the state ap-paratus that were pursuing reactionary and antipopular policies. The government might be misguided in certain respects, but its intentions were regarded as honorable.

It is clear, then, that the PKI's basic attitudes toward the govern-ment were not decisively influenced by economic policies or economic conditions in themselves; the party's constant and earnest concern was whether its political standing and influence were being enhanced or diminished. So long as these interests were being catered for, it was prepared to excuse manifest failings in the sphere of the economy and to direct its main attack at those who, because they were the party's political enemies, could be made to bear the blame.

THE STABILIZATION CRISIS, 1963

Relations between the cabinet and the PKI deteriorated rapidly at the end of 1962, as the likelihood of an American-sponsored stabiliza-tion scheme increased. The background and political implications of the stabilization plan have already been discussed, but the far-reach-ing effects of the new course in economic policy require further con-sideration. The general lines of action that were being urged on the Indonesian government by the IMF mission were well known in political circles in Djakarta by the last two months of 1962. In February of 1963, when the issue of whether the government would steer to the left, by relying on Russian aid and installing a Nasakom cabinet, or would take a rightward course, was still in the balance, Aidit tried to persuade Sukarno and his followers of the advantages of a radical economic approach. In his report to the Central Committee, Aidit offered a wide-ranging analysis of the economic situation and the remedies proposed by the party. Aidit's argument was summed up in the following passage:

The real way out of Indonesia's economic difficulties is not by begging for loans from abroad or making the Indonesian people the servants of foreign capital invested in Indonesia, but by the development of a national economy that can stand on its own two feet. This means that there must be the daring to change the system of society at home by sacrificing the interests of the minority of big exploiters in the towns and the villages, that is, the bureaucrat capitalists, the compradores and the landlords, and defending the interests of the masses of the people. For this, there must be the appropriate political power, Gotong Rojong power with Nasakom as its fulcrum.[41]

This solution was patently a nationalist one; Aidit was frankly appealing to national sentiment and pride by suggesting that resort to foreign aid represented subservience and dependence. And to support this argument he painted a dismal picture of the economic and political consequences that the countries of Latin America and elsewhere had experienced as a result of their subjection to United States aid schemes. Indonesia, he urged, could and should "stand on its own two feet" and mobilize its own resources for independent development. In this endeavor, efforts should be concentrated on raising production. The implication here was that there were no objective barriers to increasing production; the obstacles lay in governmental weakness, mismanagement, and the presence of reactionaries and saboteurs in the state apparatus. The way out, therefore, was fundamentally a political one, lying in the formation of a Nasakom cabinet, the retooling of public functionaries, and the mobilization of popular energies.[42]

This appeal to the susceptibilities of Sukarno and a wider circle of radical nationalists was unsuccessful at the time. In the conflict between pro-Western and pro-Communist policies, the likelihood that the Americans would be prepared to lay out greater sums than the

[41] *Dare, Dare and Dare Again!* pp. 34–35.
[42] *Ibid.,* pp. 12, 24, 32–37.

Russians, who were now very cautious about further aid for Indonesia, and the opposition of influential groups in both the government and the army to greater dependence on the Communists, decided the day.

In his economic declaration (known as Dekon) at the end of March (drawn up on the basis of a multiparty committee's recommendations), Sukarno still tried to follow a middle course between interventionism and liberalism, and so to give comfort to all. In all probability, he was genuinely in two minds about which course to take, as his radical inclinations vied for supremacy with the advice of his ministers; presumably he also wanted to leave himself in a position where he could disassociate himself from any course which later proved to be an economic or political failure. As Mackie describes the Dekon,

It contained references to certain phrases and principles which had often been decried in the period of enthusiasm for a Guided Economy. The role of small producers was extolled, as well as the large state enterprises; the need for incentive to private producers and for deconcentration of management in the State sector was mentioned; the price mechanism was (in rather gingerly fashion) unveiled from behind the screen of disdain which had surrounded it. Altogether, it contained a number of pointers towards a slightly more "liberal" or market-oriented approach to economic policy, although to describe it baldly as "liberal in tone" is an exaggeration.[43]

On the antiliberal side, it included a condemnation of drastic devaluation measures.

Whatever the PKI leaders privately thought of the Dekon, their tactic had to be to support it against the more forbidding measures anticipated under the stabilization scheme and seek to influence its implementation after their own aspirations. Especially was this the course they must follow since the declaration had the personal authority of the president behind it and contained sufficient concessions to PKI views to enable the party to interpret it as being opposed to liberalism and dependence on foreign aid. This line of reasoning was advanced in an editorial in the party daily on March 30, and the party organization was immediately mobilized to marshall resolutions of support for the Dekon.[44]

[43] *Problems of the Indonesian Inflation*, p. 38.
[44] See the statement of the Politburo of the PKI in *Harian Rakjat*, April 1,

In comparison with the mildness of the Dekon, the governmental regulations issued on May 26 as the first instalment of the IMF-endorsed stabilization program provided a stiff dose of liberalism. Price controls were largely dismantled; big increases were made in rail, bus, and plane fares; the salaries of civil servants were roughly doubled; a new set of foreign exchange regulations was introduced to stimulate exports; foreign exchange (swelled by an injection of U.S. aid) was released for a crash program of imports; and an austerity campaign was inaugurated to achieve a balanced government budget.[45]

The immediate effect of the regulations was to stimulate exports and stabilize prices; at the same time, the increases in prices and utility charges hit many, urban dwellers in particular, quite severely, and the tight money policy provoked a liquidity crisis that hurt importers and industrialists, and particularly the smaller firms among them.[46] A political storm whipped up by the parties and businessmen burst about the heads of the unfortunate ministers, whom Sukarno, by departing on another world tour, shrewdly left to take the odium of the belt-tightening policy.

The PKI entered the lists eagerly. On June 4, the Politburo issued a special statement attacking the May 26 measures, which it attributed to "false Manipolists" who had the audacity to put their program forward in the name of the Dekon. The PKI's aim was to protect Sukarno from blame and leave him room to reverse governmental policies without loss of face; indeed, Aidit argued that, since Sukarno frankly admitted his ignorance of economics, he could not be blamed for the mistakes of his advisers![47] The party's attack was concentrated on First Minister Djuanda, the most prestigious supporter of the stabilization scheme, whom Aidit accused of the heinous "liberal" sins of conventionalism, disregard of the people's welfare, and reliance on foreign

---

1963, and the subsequent reports in the paper throughout April and May. Aidit gave three lectures in May and June acclaiming the Dekon as proof that Sukarno and the people together could solve the country's economic problems (*Dekon Dalam Udjian*).

[45] See Mackie, *Problems of the Indonesian Inflation*, p. 39; K. D. Thomas, "Recent Developments in Indonesia," *Australia's Neighbours*, 4th series, nos. 11–12 (Jan.–Feb. 1964).

[46] Mackie, *Problems of the Indonesian Inflation*, p. 40.

[47] Thomas, p. 8.

capital.[48] By the latter part of June the PKI chairman was speaking of the "price terror" that had been unleashed to accompany the "racial terror" (directed against Chinese citizens) that had broken out in May in a number of Javanese provincial centers.[49] Sukarno's return at the end of the month prompted an appeal to him to take note of the mess things had got into in his absence and to set the nation's house in order.[50]

A NEW ORIENTATION, 1963–1965

The campaign against the May regulations continued throughout July and August, and was rewarded on September 7 by a statement from Sukarno agreeing that they should be corrected.[51] A week later, the stabilization scheme and its rationale were wrecked in the storm of confrontation against Malaysia. From then on, the atmosphere was one of militant nationalism. As such it was conducive to the adoption by Sukarno and the dominant wing in the government (headed, after Djuanda's death in November 1963, by Subandrio) of the economic slogans of the PKI: self-reliance (*berdikari*), radical retooling of personnel, all-out efforts to raise production, and social control. Economic policy-making, however, drifted aimlessly between various ad hoc devices for obtaining the finances necessary to keep the government functioning. Supplies of foreign aid were virtually exhausted, and there was a huge bill outstanding for repayment of principal and interest; exports were declining under the impact of confrontation and smuggling, and heavy demands were being made on government revenue by both the military and the political aspects of confrontation. In such circumstances the government was forced to live a hand-to-mouth existence. The May 26 regulations were formally superseded in April 1964, but the government had nothing very definite to put in their place. Mackie's comment is apt: "By 1964 there was little that the government could do to re-establish control over the economy and there are few signs that it ever had any positive economic strategy to do so. It was fully occupied with coping with the most immediate crises as they occurred."[52] The government deficit soared, reaching

---

[48] *Harian Rakjat,* June 7, 1963.
[49] *Ibid.,* June 18, 1963.
[50] *Ibid.,* June 27, 1963.
[51] *Ibid.,* Sept. 7, 1963.
[52] *Problems of the Indonesian Inflation,* p. 41.

about 50 per cent of total expenditure in both 1963 and 1964 and generating a steady increase in the volume of money, which in turn precipitated uncontrollable inflationary pressures.[53]

Making a virtue of necessity, Sukarno and Subandrio lauded the virtues of placing political before economic considerations, made *berdikari* the principal ideological foundation of economic policy, exhorted the population to make sacrifices in the cause of national goals, inaugurated production drives, and in 1965 told the already thoroughly disenchanted Americans to "go to hell with your aid."[54] While the dynamic of the Malaysia struggle dominated political concerns, the accelerated economic decline produced remarkably little in the way of overt protest; but by late 1964, with stalemate in confrontation and PKI pressures undermining the security of the elite, dissension and intrigue began to dominate the life of the capital.

Argument that retooling would cure all assumed new force in the nationalist atmosphere of confrontation, and between 1963 and 1965 campaigns urging that officials and managerial personnel be purged reached their height. In some cases, the PKI was able to place trained economists and administrators sympathetic to it in middle-level posts in government departments and other bureaucratic positions; but these men, though often able and usually highly motivated to resist the temptations of personal enrichment, were able to make little if any impact on the general decline in standards of probity and efficiency. In general, political rather than professional qualifications remained essential for entry into the victorious bureaucratic cliques.[55]

Paradoxically, private businessmen fared reasonably well in this period, especially if they had good political or bureaucratic connections, were able to do things for the state enterprises that they themselves could not do, or contributed heavily to such pet projects of Sukarno as the huge statue and complex to celebrate the Indonesian identity and the world's biggest mosque. The contribution of the private entrepreneur to national development was even recognized officially in the establishment in February 1964 of Bamunas, a consultative body of businessmen, including alien Chinese, whose aim was to mobilize capital for development; in practice, the main role played

[53] *Ibid.*, pp. 41–42.
[54] Tan, pp. 39–40.
[55] See Castles, "Socialism and Private Business," p. 29.

by Bamunas was in raising special contributions for Sukarno's monuments and similar priority projects.[56]

With the onset of confrontation and the abandonment of the stabilization program, the sting was taken out of the conflict between the PKI and the government over economic policy. The adoption, by Sukarno and Subandrio in particular, of the party's economic slogans contributed to the improvement in relations. The economic decline of 1964–65 and the inconsistencies of government policy were matters of concern to the PKI, but the fact that opportunities were now being opened for the party to expand its political influence outweighed any other consideration. The Communists continued to make "constructive" criticisms of government policy, but they were much more concerned to load the blame for the deteriorating economy on to their political enemies, the "reactionaries and bureaucratic capitalists," and to demonstrate, by suggesting practical ways to increase production and improve this or that aspect of industry, their strong qualifications for cabinet portfolios.

In his report to the PKI Central Committee in December 1963 Aidit set out an economic program consistent with the aims of confrontation. He declared that anti-imperialist struggle could not harm Indonesia, pointing to various adverse economic consequences that had flowed from the May 26 regulations to buttress his argument that the alternative to confrontation was even worse. The masses of the people, who had been hurt by the stabilization program, must see their salvation in "shifting politics further to the left"—in other words, in bringing the PKI into the government.[57] Implicitly conceding that economic conditions would get worse before they improved, he urged the workers to make sacrifices and commended to them the slogan, "our hearts are harder than hunger."[58] Nevertheless, he said, Communists must not just accept economic deterioration but must make every effort to raise production even while they were waging confrontation

[56] *Ibid.,* pp. 29–39.

[57] *Set Afire the Banteng Spirit!* pp. 16–20, 36–39. For later variants on the theme that anti-imperialist struggle was fundamentally beneficial to popular interests, see Aidit, "Djadilah Komunis jang Baik, dan lebih Baik Lagi," *Harian Rakjat,* June 11–12, 1964; and Aidit's address to a national conference of economists reported in *Harian Rakjat,* July 8, 1964.

[58] *Set Afire the Banteng Spirit!* pp. 18–19.

in all fields.[59] The main effort should be directed toward arousing the peasants to carry out radical land reform.[60]

Aidit put forward a number of proposals to the government in his report, most of them aimed at restoring the interventionist character of the economy.[61] But he also outlined a new basic economic strategy. It will be recalled that at the PKI economic seminar in early 1959 the party had advocated that priority should be given in development to the construction of heavy industry. In 1961, Aidit had changed this emphasis, giving pride of place to "light industries producing food and clothing and lessening dependence on imports."[62] Now he further modified the PKI's position, urging that primary efforts in development be directed toward agriculture and the estates.[63]

This shift in economic strategy paralleled developments in the economic thinking of the CPC, which was at this time moving decisively away from the traditional Soviet emphasis on heavy industry. Just as Chinese Communist policy was strongly influenced by the investment difficulties China faced after the breach with Russia, so did the changes in Aidit's approach find their rationale in domestic economic and political circumstances. The change in emphasis from heavy to light industry could well have reflected a more realistic assessment by the party of the economy's capabilities and the weaknesses in government programing. The more substantial shift to a focus on agriculture, however, probably related less to economic considerations than to the PKI's imminent political offensive in the villages; if general acceptance could be won for the party's economic viewpoint, then there would be added justification for insistence on the urgency of land reform.

Another innovation introduced in Aidit's report was the extension of PKI strictures against foreign capital to embrace economic assistance from the Communist countries.[64] From the context, it is clear that this change was prompted by the party leaders' deep suspicion of Soviet policy. Rejection of foreign aid on principle and advocacy

[59] In early 1964 there followed a new spurt of Communist production activities; see, for example, Asmu's article in *Review of Indonesia*, XI (March–April 1964), 7–10.

[60] *Set Afire the Banteng Spirit!* pp. 22–30.

[61] *Ibid.,* pp. 57–60.

[62] *Socialisme Indonesia dan Sjarat-sjarat Pelaksanaannja,* pp. 95–96.

[63] *Set Afire the Banteng Spirit!* p. 30.

[64] *Ibid.,* pp. 92–94.

of self-reliance were again items to be found in the economic thinking of the CPC, which thus made a virtue of the withdrawal of Soviet aid from China and attempted to insulate the movements China sought to influence from "revisionist" temptations.

The PKI's attitude toward private enterprise remained relatively liberal. In 1963, the party's position had been that the foreign trade sector ought not to be open to the operations of private capitalists,[65] possibly because this field offered profitable avenues for association between individual businessmen and state enterprise managers and so laid the former open to "contamination" by the "bureaucratic capitalists" among the latter.[66] But in his lectures on the Dekon, in the same year, Aidit had actually proposed that more national capitalists be encouraged to establish businesses, especially in the industrial sphere;[67] and this proposal was repeated in a series of lectures in the latter half of 1964 arranged by the National Front.[68] In part, this concern for the interests of private business was probably designed to aid and protect Chinese entrepreneurs, who had been threatened during the racial disturbances of May 1963; but it was also consistent with an important strand in PKI thought (evident as far back as 1952), which followed Chinese Communist doctrine in regarding the national capitalist as a positive force in economic development so long as he was production-oriented and not linked to the politically reactionary bureaucratic capitalist complex. By 1963 Aidit may well have considered that an injection of private initiative could help overcome some of the crisis features in the economy.

The PKI continued to promote the cooperative movement among the peasantry, though results were far from satisfactory. Sakirman claimed that by late 1963 a majority of village, neighborhood, and public servant cooperatives had gone bankrupt ("rolled up their mats") because of price increases and transport difficulties;[69] and in his December 1963 report to the Central Committee Aidit said that the "progressive" cooperatives were not proceeding well and that

[65] *Harian Rakjat,* Feb. 15, 1963.
[66] See Castles, "Socialism and Private Business," p. 28.
[67] *Dekon Dalam Udjian,* pp. 26–29.
[68] *Revolusi Indonesia, Latarbelakang, Sedjarah dan Haridepannja,* pp. 57–8.
[69] Sakirman, *Laksanakan Konsekwen Patriotisme Ekonomi* (Put Economic Patriotism into Effect Resolutely) (Djakarta, 1964), p. 11.

the majority of cooperatives remained under the control of exploitive elements.[70]

On several occasions during 1964 Aidit stressed the necessity and possibility of combining the struggle against imperialism with an attack on economic difficulties. In a speech to a student delegation in May he described as "fantasy" the notion that Indonesia would collapse under the weight of its problems and added: "While the Indonesian people are united and strongly determined to crush imperialism, Indonesia will not collapse because of economic difficulties."[71] He returned to this theme in a PKI anniversary speech in Surabaja later the same month:

> It is indeed true that the economic situation in Indonesia is not good, but this is not caused by the policy of confrontation; on the contrary, it is caused by the fact that not enough is yet being done to crush imperialism. . . . As the political situation becomes more and more revolutionary, so the possibility opens up ever wider for improving the economic situation.[72]

The positive demands made by the PKI in the economic sphere mainly took the form of *political* agitation for the replacement of corrupt and "liberal" officials, the introduction of enterprise councils with worker participation in the state enterprises, the enlistment of the masses in "social control," and the formation of a Nasakom cabinet.[73]

The party claimed that land reform, for which it was campaigning by means of militant peasant action, was the basic way to solve the food and clothing problem, since this would "liberate the productive forces" in the countryside and raise the peasant's capacity to purchase the products of national industry.[74] This argument notwithstanding, it seems likely that in fact the political, rather than the eco-

[70] *Set Afire the Banteng Spirit!* p. 30. See also the report on research into peasant life in West Java led by Aidit, *Harian Rakjat,* May 11–16, 1964.

[71] *Harian Rakjat,* May 14, 1964.

[72] *Ibid.,* June 11–12, 1964. See also Aidit's speech to the national conference of Indonesian economists on July 8, 1964; *ibid.,* July 10, 1964.

[73] See the Politburo's theses on the occasion of the PKI's anniversary; *Review of Indonesia,* XI (May–July 1964), 15ff.

[74] Aidit, *Revolusi Indonesia, Latarbelakang, Sedjarah dan Haridepannja,* p. 56.

nomic, implications of the land reform campaign were uppermost in the party leaders' minds.

In the last quarter of 1964, as the effects of inflation and the run-down in production became more serious, the tone of PKI statements on the economy underwent some change. The party still argued that confrontation was not a significant cause of the troubles, but, in place of previous assurances that the workers faced their difficulties with firm resolve and enthusiasm, it was now admitted that spirits were being affected and that the stability of the country was being gravely undermined.[75]

This admission formed the prelude to an offensive against the "bureaucratic capitalists" unleashed at the beginning of 1965.[76] Again, however, it is a moot point whether the PKI really saw the assault on the bureaucratic capitalists as a means of arresting the economic decline, or whether the party was reacting to symptoms of economic unrest and aggravated material deprivation among its supporters by directing the resentment toward those whom it regarded as its primary political opponents. In view of Aidit's often repeated assertion that political change would have to precede economic change, the latter interpretation is probably closer to the mark.

Economically, the greatest beneficiaries of the Guided Democracy order were those who stood at the pinnacle of the politico-bureaucratic edifice: the court circle around the president, ministers and heads of government departments, the state enterprise managers, favored businessmen, and armed forces heads. But beyond this group, corrupt practices and the operation of the patronage system spread the benefits down through the bureaucracy, even to its lower reaches.[77] The economic effects on the population at large are more difficult to gauge. Undoubtedly the contrast between rich and poor sharpened, but the impact of hardship was uneven. Workers suffered a severe decline in real wages and in standards of consumption; on the other hand, they were cushioned to some extent against the effects of inflation by the state's distribution of certain goods at fixed prices, and their working conditions were considerably better than before the

[75] See for example *Harian Rakjat,* Sept. 18, 1964; *Review of Indonesia,* XII (Jan. 1965), 4.

[76] *Review of Indonesia,* XII (Jan., 1965), 4.

[77] See Feith, "Dynamics," pp. 398–99.

revolution.[78] Thousands of lower civil servants who either had no access to spoils or resisted the general trend toward corruption suffered acutely as a result of their diminished real incomes; nevertheless, in many cases they too had some means of relieving their distress—in particular, many were able to engage profitably in small trading.[79] The situation of the peasantry is much harder to assess since conditions varied greatly according to place, size of harvest, time of the year, and other factors; that there was a general trend toward impoverishment, at least in Java, is certain, but the incidence and precise effects have never been computed.

It is even more difficult to deduce from the socio-economic forces at work under Guided Democracy any general definition of the system's evolution in class terms. The paradox lies in the fact that, while on the one hand the *economic process* was gradually crystallizing in the emergence of an identifiable stratum of wealthy, politically powerful, and conservative politician-bureaucrats, the *political process* was undermining the security of this incipient new ruling class and increasing the possibility of a radical, Communist-led attack on their privileges. President Sukarno not only presided over each of these contradictory processes; he also gave sustenance to both. Thus, analyses of Guided Democracy that stress the social conservatism of the elite as well as those that emphasize the radical Jacobinism of its leader have to be taken into account. The regime embodied a contradiction, one that was mirrored in the personality structure of its leader; the conflicts inherent in this contradiction were, as we shall see, crucial to the crisis that developed in the system in 1965.

The Indonesian Communists were unable to assail the basic causes of the economic drift under Guided Democracy because their future prospects depended on their preserving close relations with the Sukarno wing of the elite and supporting those nationalist policies that, while detrimental to stability and development, furthered the consolidation of their political alliance. They had to pin their faith on a political transformation that would bring them out on top of the governmental pyramid, and for this reason their attacks on economic failure and elite self-enrichment had to be angled mainly against those

[78] Castles, "Socialism and Private Business," pp. 75–80; Paauw, pp. 189, 200–203, 211.
[79] Feith, "Dynamics," pp. 389–90.

who obstructed their path to power. Their practical economic proposals, which stood in such strong contrast to the sterile emotionalism of most other support for Guided Democracy, were chiefly designed to demonstrate their expertise in the field and to indicate the kind of economic policy they would follow if they gained power.

As has been argued previously, the PKI did not stand to gain from economic decline; outbursts of discontent, whether stimulated by the political right or left, could easily upset the process of political advance the Communist leaders were so carefully nurturing. The party was engaged in a game of controlled political pressure; if the game was to be won, the unpredictabilities of social unrest had to be kept to a minimum. As a result both of the hold the PKI had on the allegiance of large parts of the organized mass movements and of the control mechanisms employed by the regime,[80] overt expressions of disaffection were in fact kept in check until the outbreak of clashes over land reform in the latter part of 1964. Just how this new factor influenced political developments we shall now consider.

[80] For a study of the operation of these mechanisms, see Feith, "Dynamics," pp. 400–409.

7. Class Struggle in the Countryside

The PKI program drawn up at the 1954 congress stated that "the Indonesian revolution is above all an agrarian revolution," a formulation that allowed for the possibility that at some stage the party might elevate the struggle for basic peasant reforms into a major arm of its strategy. Ten years later this possibility was transformed into fact when a full-scale offensive was launched in the villages under the slogan, "land to the tillers."

Until 1959 the Communists had merely concentrated on strengthening those weak links with the peasantry to which Aidit had referred in his fifth congress report. Village support was won largely by demonstrating, by vigorous welfare activities, that the PKI was the party most concerned with the villagers' overall interests. Membership was greatly increased by these means, especially in Central and East Java, but the depth of peasant commitment earned by such moderate methods was shallow and, outside the more militant squatter and estate areas, based to a considerable degree on the leadership of well-to-do villagers.

In 1959, the PKI leaders launched a campaign to improve the quality of their support in the rural areas through a more systematic mobilization of the peasantry, though still around rather moderate demands. Considerable effort was devoted to training cadres for work in the villages, educating the peasants in the party's policies, and trying to promote activists from among the ranks of the poor. In large measure, it will be argued below, this turn to the peasantry was dictated by the atmosphere in which the party had to operate in the cities, where its opportunities for grassroots agitation were severely circumscribed. Once the turn was made, however, it was followed in the succeeding years by a gradual ideological shift in emphasis away from the proletariat and toward the peasantry, which came to be seen as the decisive revolutionary force for Indonesian conditions.

In late 1963, in the context of the thorough overhaul of party strategy that was prompted by confrontation, the PKI determined to capitalize on its patient work among the peasants by encouraging and leading a campaign of unilateral actions (*aksi sepihak*) to enforce the land reform laws that had been promulgated by the government in 1959 and 1960.

The campaign had a definite and precise political objective within the scope of the party's overall strategic plan. As we have seen, Aidit had by this time reinterpreted the united national front strategy to conform with what he perceived to be the necessities and potential of the political situation that obtained following the onset of full-scale confrontation. His aim was to gain access to power through an alliance with progressive elite groups; for impetus to carry the party forward he relied principally on the wave of nationalism and the Communists' ability to ride it further than any other group. But he recognized that appeals and demonstrations of patriotism and capacity would not be sufficient by themselves to overcome either the reluctance of his allies to share power or the opposition of the party's enemies to power being shared with the Communists. Action in the villages, therefore, was to supply an additional lever for use in the political contest.

The *aksi sepihak* campaign represented a unique facet of the PKI's drive to power, in that it was the only major struggle the party precipitated outside the confines of the united front alliance. It was from the outset an independent PKI initiative and, although appeals were made to other parties and groups for support, there is little room for doubt that the Communists were bidding in their own name for command of the villages. At the same time, however, the campaign was not intended to mark a break with the overarching strategic guidelines drawn up by Aidit; rather, it was to serve as a demonstration of the PKI's mass power and the legitimacy of its claims to full participation in government. A successful display of massive support for the party among the peasantry would, Aidit reasoned, make it impossible for the elite to go on denying the force of PKI claims, cast as they were in nonexclusive terms. At the same time, there was apparently a minimum as well as a maximum objective; in the event of untoward developments at the political center, the party would by its radicalization of the villages provide itself with a firm base for continuing the struggle outside the bounds of the system.

This was a bold move for a party that had for so long followed the cautious and moderate path and suggests that the Communists felt, in the latter part of 1963, that the time was approaching when their political fate would be decided one way or the other. In an important sense, too, the decision to follow this course constituted a partial reversal of the ideological trend that downgraded class in favor of other factors in the interests of strengthening the PKI's political position.

THE TURN TOWARD THE VILLAGES

By the late 1950's the PKI had a firm organized base among city workers, estate laborers, and squatters on forestry lands. As the cast of national politics grew more authoritarian, however, this base became more vulnerable. Accordingly, the party's leaders decided to enlarge and intensify their work among the peasant population. In 1958 they began preparations for a national peasants' conference, to be held early in 1959, at which they intended to launch a concerted drive to organize the peasantry. The main feature of the preparatory activities was what was called a "Go Down" movement, a campaign to encourage party cadres in the cities and towns to go to the villages, familiarize themselves with conditions there, and educate the peasants in the policies and programs of the party. Based on considerations similar to those that inspired a movement of the same kind in China prior to the land reform movement there of the early fifties, the PKI's "Go Down" movement was directed toward overcoming the acute shortage of activists in the villages who understood the party's aims and were willing to work for their realization in the face of opposition from village authorities, the well-to-do, and the traditionalist advocates of harmony at all costs.

At this date, the limits of PKI penetration of the villages were largely determined by the strength of the peasants' prior loyalties to the Islamic and PNI parties. In Central and East Java, many whole villages of the *abangan* persuasion had gone over to the party; others, however, were divided into hostile factions of followers of the PKI, the NU (or Masjumi), and the PNI. In multiparty villages, PKI sup-

port tended to come from unaccommodated youth and other radicalized elements; in single party villages, by contrast, the leading Communists were often those who had the most prestige and could
command the greatest patronage in traditional terms—men of substance, either in land or in political authority, and frequently in both.
Such leaders were quite capable of promoting the welfare programs
(e.g., mutual help schemes to improve irrigation or repair houses)
that characterized PKI peasant policy in the early and middle fifties,
especially where these were designed to benefit all villagers irrespective of social standing and economic need. But they were clearly not
suitable for mobilizing the peasants around more militant policies,
such as campaigns for rent reductions, since many of them were
moneylenders and landlords themselves.

There was no easy solution to this problem within the villages,
since most of the peasants were illiterate, accustomed to show deference toward those better off or of higher status than themselves, and
only minimally versed in the ways of modern organizations. It was
necessary to introduce education and organizational training from
outside the village, but party cadres in the towns were generally reluctant to leave urban life for prolonged periods of work in the villages and were daunted by the formidable tasks that awaited them
there. The "Go Down" movement was an attempt to place the authority and prestige of the leaders behind such an enterprise.

The national peasants' conference took place in April 1959. Both
Aidit and Njoto gave keynote speeches emphasizing the inadequacies
of party work in this area and the need to devote major attention to
its improvement. In Njoto's report, and again in the published conclusions of the conference, particular stress was laid on the fact that
too few cadres were prepared to work in the villages; they were said
to be "evading" decisions of the party in this regard.[1] The conference
conclusions also referred to the need to enhance the "class stand" of
village cadres, a stand holding that "in all forms of activity, the Party
based itself upon the landless labourers and the poor peasants, united
with the middle peasants and neutralised the rich peasants so as to
isolate the landlords and gradually inflict blows upon them." This
class stand of the party obliged all peasant cadres to abjure landlord

[1] *Review of Indonesia,* VI (April 1959, Supplement), 3, 7.

and moneylending practices and to break off relations with the exploiting classes in the villages.[2]

The major means proposed for overcoming the lack of contact between the party apparatus and the villages was rural research. Aidit emphasized that much of the research done to date had been poorly conceived and hastily carried out; nevertheless, he argued, sufficient had already been done to show that there was extensive landlordism and village exploitation through low wages, high rents and interest rates on loans, and such forms of "feudal servitude" as compulsory labour.[3] The conference resolved that research should constitute the most important aspect of party work in the villages. Such an emphasis would ensure that cadres would become acquainted at first hand with the conditions of exploitation operating in the villages and thus avoid making "subjective" errors in assessing the tactics of struggle and methods of work that should be applied in mobilizing the peasants, either by overestimating the peasants' willingness to fight for their interests or by underestimating the extent of class conflict in the villages. Research should be conducted through the method of the "three togethers," according to which the cadres were exhorted to live together with the peasants, eat together with them, and work together with them.

There was a good deal of sound common sense in this approach. The party's leaders wanted to get the cadres from the cities involved in village work, but there were obvious dangers in directing them into immediate activity in unfamiliar surroundings. They could make serious mistakes, particularly by running ahead of peasant preparedness to embark on militant struggles, and they could arouse a good deal of pointless discord if they acted as officious leaders sent to stir things up in rural backwaters. Research, on the other hand, would give them something useful to do without precipitating premature actions; at the same time, if instructions about the "three togethers" were carried out, the cadres would become familiar with prevailing conditions and the villagers would be persuaded of the genuine and devoted concern of the PKI for their interests.

The Communist leaders were clearly not anticipating a sudden

[2] *Ibid.,* p. 4.
[3] *Ibid.,* pp. 11–12.

upsurge in rural class activity at this stage. Their references to the tasks of isolating the landlords and purifying the class stand of the village cadres stressed gradualness. These admonitions were supported by a strongly stated warning about the protracted nature of the task of winning peasant confidence:

The task of cultivating the confidence of the peasants is a difficult one: the more so if we bear in mind the backwardness of the peasants. Over a long period of time, after having gone through many trials and difficulties, after having worked consistently and thoroughly, the Communists will eventually succeed in winning the confidence of the peasantry so as, together with them, to enter upon the threshold of liberation.[4]

Peasant activists were instructed that no movements should be initiated without thorough preparation, during which the proposed campaign must first be discussed and approved by the village party organization and then submitted to the peasant organization (BTI) for its agreement. It was of the utmost importance, if confidence among the peasants was to be created, that actions be successful; for that reason the accent should be on small projects that would have every prospect of success and that would "draw in and arouse 90 per cent of the inhabitants of the village."[5]

These cautious pronouncements involved little change in the PKI's approach from that obtaining in earlier years, and indeed, with one major qualification, the significance of the national peasants' conference lay mainly in the effort of the party leaders to encourage harder work on the village front. In one respect, however, the conference did venture a further step forward in the cultivation of a class-based approach to peasant activity. Aidit's report raised the issue of land reform and defined the party's immediate policy with regard to it, stating that the PKI's program of demands did not include the confiscation of all landlords' holdings but only land owned by foreign imperialists and landlords who had sided with the Darul Islam and regional rebels. The reason, declared Aidit, was that for the time being the anti-imperialist struggle had to be given tactical precedence over the antifeudal struggle.

Translating this proposition into practical terms, it is apparent that

---

[4] *Ibid.,* p. 6.
[5] *Ibid.,* pp. 6–7.

Aidit was saying that the party leadership was intent on consolidating and developing the party's alliance with Sukarno and the state leadership, by promoting the nationalist causes its allies held dear, and was not ready to put at risk the close cooperation that was developing between the party and Sukarno by stirring up a major conflict in the countryside, for which in any case it considered the peasants ill-prepared. Nevertheless, Aidit did authorize a moderate attack on landlord interests. The demand for land redistribution was to be confined to the holdings of foreigners and "traitor" landlords, but the party would take up the demand for the reduction of land rents by all landlords:

Whereas today the division of the harvest is generally 50:50 [i.e., 50 per cent to the tiller and 50 per cent to the landlord] the PKI now demands that the division should be 60:40, that is, the cultivators should get a minimum share of 60 per cent as against a maximum of 40 per cent for the landlords. It is necessary to stress that it is a minimum of 60 and a maximum of 40, because in some parts of the country there are cultivators who, thanks to their resolute struggle, are getting a share of more than 60, with the landlords getting less than 40.[6]

The demand for rent reductions had been made before, at least as early as July 1956.[7] At the fifth conference of the BTI in September 1957, it was suggested that at least in some areas the peasants were prepared to act on the issue. Now, however, this demand was elevated, in Aidit's words, to the status of "the most important practical policy of the PKI" toward the peasants.[8]

Although the PKI leaders' decision to concentrate seriously on the peasantry was a logical next step, given the bases of support it had already consolidated, the timing of the drive seems to have been influenced also by prevailing political circumstances. The heavy hand of the army rested uncomfortably on the Communists in 1958–59, severely cramping their activities in the major urban centers. The insecure place the party occupied in the emerging Guided Democracy complex gave its leaders grounds for hesitation and fear, and they may well have viewed the villages as safer areas in which to work and expand their support. Since the size and discipline of their or-

[6] *Ibid.,* p. 12.
[7] *Harian Rakjat,* July 10, 1956.
[8] *Review of Indonesia,* VI (April 1959, Supplement), 13.

ganization was an important factor in their appeal to Sukarno, on the success of which their future to a great degree depended, it made sense to enlarge and tighten up the party in that sector where the room for expansion was greatest and the circumscriptions of army power least operative. There is just a suggestion of this line of thought in Njoto's report to the peasants' conference, when he stated that the conference, "can and must discuss what concrete steps have to be taken and what program has to be fought for so as to give content to Guided Democracy and ensure that its benefits are not confined to a small group but are felt by the vast majority of the Indonesian people, in particular the peasants and fishermen."[9]

Bearing in mind that the party leadership at this time was coming under attack from radicals in its own ranks for its accommodating posture toward the more authoritarian structure of Guided Democracy, it is also possible that a more energetic peasant policy was intended to pacify critics by indicating a resolve to keep options open for an armed agrarian struggle after the Chinese or Cuban models. Van der Kroef has suggested that the decisive turn toward the peasant was dictated by the PKI leaders' realization of the possibilities for class agitation opened up by the deterioration in the village economy. He may be right, but in view of the extreme caution with which the Communists pushed class issues, it seems more likely that political considerations of the kind mentioned were uppermost in their minds.[10]

In December 1958, PKI and affiliated members had introduced a bill into parliament which, if passed, would have limited land rent to between 10 per cent and 30 per cent of the value of the crop (depending on the type of crop grown) and providing other forms of security for tenants and sharecroppers.[11] In all likelihood, the parliamentary initiative was designed in large part as a propaganda exercise (it went beyond the PKI's policy of a 60:40 division of the harvest, presumably to allow leeway for bargaining), but it may have played some part in inducing the government to put forward its own crop-sharing law, which provided for a minimum 50:50 division and

---

[9] *Ibid.,* p. 3.

[10] Justus M. Van der Kroef, "Peasant and Land Reform in Indonesian Communism," *Journal of Southeast Asian History,* IV, no. 1 (March 1963), 31. The article reviews earlier PKI policies toward the peasantry.

[11] *Review of Indonesia,* VI (Jan. 1959), 27.

specifically upheld those agreements already in force that were more favorable to the tenants. This bill became law on November 20, 1959, but it was left to the heads of level-two autonomous districts (*kabupaten* and some municipalities) to issue regulations on its implementation. Steady pressure from the PKI and BTI was instrumental in having such regulations issued throughout most of Java by October 1961.

The crop-sharing law was a mixed blessing for the PKI. As Aidit had mentioned in his report to the national peasants' conference, the 50:50 division was already the norm in rental arrangements; consequently the law did not provide anything like the same scope for peasant agitation as did the PKI's own 60:40 demand. It was still open to the party to go beyond the minimum standard laid down in the law, but such a course would lead it into something like the difficulty faced by trade unions in industrial countries that lay down minimum wage rates for employees: the minimum rate, having legal sanction, tends to be regarded as the lawful arrangement, and those seeking to go beyond it are easily represented as being against the law or its spirit.

The solution adopted by the PKI's leaders was to urge the peasants to fight for the implementation of the legal minimum, but, where the landlord resisted this demand (which the law required to be agreed to in writing), to go further and insist on a 60:40 division. The problem remained hypothetical for some years after the passage of the law, however, since most peasants remained ignorant of their rights. Thus in January 1960, the BTI journal reported that "the 60:40 action and other actions against the landlords' exploitation are entirely new for the peasants and even for most BTI cadres. Examples of successful action will facilitate our work to convince the peasants of the justice of the 60:40 demand and of the power of the peasants' unity."[12] Again, in March 1961, the BTI chairman, Asmu, stressed that "the work of arousing, organizing, and leading 60:40 actions is hard, difficult, and many-faceted."[13]

THE LAND REFORM LAW OF 1960

Meanwhile, in January 1960, Sukarno's Supreme Advisory Council held a special session devoted to the subject of land reform, and the

[12] *Suara Tani,* Jan. 1960, p. 3.
[13] *Ibid.,* March 1960.

government moved speedily to introduce a new law. Discussion in the Supreme Advisory Council, and later in parliament, revealed three general views on land reform. A radical group, consisting mainly of men of PKI, Murba, and PNI outlook who had been appointed as functional representatives of the peasantry, supported by PKI and PNI spokesmen, proposed a far-reaching redistribution of land based on the single principle that those who worked the land should own it. Such action would have had extensive social effects, since many besides large landowners would have been affected. All absentee owners would have forfeited their land, as would those small peasants who were obliged to let out their land to more well-to-do peasants in return for loans. A conservative group, made up largely of representatives of the Moslem bodies and parties, was opposed to any ceiling being placed on land ownership on the grounds that any law to this effect would be contrary to the precepts of Islam. The compromise faction, including Sukarno and Agriculture Minister Sardjarwo, accepted the radical position in principle but argued that reform should proceed by stages, with the first step concentrating on laying down maximum and minimum limitations on landholdings. The compromise was eventually embodied in the draft law submitted to parliament, to which the PKI gave its substantial support.[14]

When the matter came before parliament, PNI spokesmen were initially the strongest advocates of further radicalization of the law, proposing that the right of foreigners to own land be canceled and that *gadai* (a form of land mortgage) be marked down for ultimate abolition. This PNI move may have been an attempt to prevent the PKI obtaining the credit for land reform. In any event, when the government intimated that it wanted the original provisions retained, PNI members of parliament tried to back down on their amendments, only to find that the PKI had now swung in behind them and it was too late. The amendments were carried into law in a hurried debate pushed through at the president's insistence before he left to attend the September 1960 session of the United Nations General Assembly.[15]

[14] E. Utrecht, "Land Reform," *Bulletin of Indonesian Economic Studies,* V, no. 3 (Nov. 1969), 71–73.

[15] I am indebted to Daniel S. Lev for the information on which this paragraph is based.

In its final form the agrarian law contained the following major provisions:

> A maximum was placed on the amount of land any one family might own, the amount varying according to the region and type of land use. Thus, for example, the amount of *sawah* (irrigated rice land) that a family might own varied from five hectares (approximately 12.3 acres) in very densely populated regions to fifteen hectares in sparsely populated areas. To determine the maximum, land held under several kinds of lease or mortgage was treated as if it were owned by the family to whom it had been leased. The law did not interfere with the use of land below these maxima; crop-sharing arrangements were therefore not affected, except as they were regulated by the previous year's crop-sharing law.
>
> Every family holding land in excess of the maximum laid down by law was required to register the excess within three months, and any transfer of the surplus other than as provided for by law was prohibited.
>
> Excess land deriving from surpluses in private hands would be distributed by the government to landless peasants, as would property taken over from foreigners and princely estates. The government would compensate the owners over a period of years, and the recipients of the land would in turn be obliged to repay the government for the sums expended on compensation.
>
> Absentee owners of land were obliged to give up their holdings, except in the case of those in active state service and certain other defined circumstances.
>
> The government laid down a minimum holding of two hectares (approximately five acres) for every nuclear family engaged in agricultural production.[16]

The dearth of statistics on landholdings and the complexity of village arrangements regarding land use, embodied in custom and informal practice, make it extremely difficult to gauge the import of the law. As Utrecht says,

[16] For general outlines of the provisions of the agrarian law, see Utrecht, pp. 71–76, and Selosoemardjan, "Land Reform in Indonesia," *Asian Survey,* I, no. 2 (Feb. 1962), 23–30.

It had been found that while in Java, Madura, South Sulawesi, Bali and Lombok there were only 5,400 persons who owned *sawah* of more than 10 hectares a much larger number of rich people held more than 10 ha. of irrigated land owned by others, mostly by poor peasants who did not have the means to till the soil themselves or whose land was so small that it did not pay to work it, so that of necessity they had surrendered it in *gadai* and *sewa* [rental] to richer fellow-villagers or town inhabitants. For dry fields the respective numbers were 11,000 persons owning more than 10 ha. each and a much larger number of people having at their disposal on conditions of *gadai* or *sewa* more than 10 ha. of land belonging to others.[17]

Unfortunately, we have no way of knowing how great the "much larger" numbers of lessees were.

The Agrarian Department originally estimated that about one million hectares of land would come up for redistribution, and in 1963 the surplus deriving from the first stage of the law's implementation (covering Java, Madura, Bali, Lombok, and Sumbawa) was quoted at 337,445 hectares.[18] One thing was abundantly clear from the outset: it was an arithmetical impossibility to provide a minimum of two hectares of land per peasant family on crowded Java. With the average existing plot size being 0.65 hectares, there was simply not enough arable land available to go round.[19] To meet this problem, the government spoke of providing the guaranteed plots in the Outer Islands to migrants from Java, but since transmigration schemes had never absorbed more than a tiny fraction of Java's annual population increase it was inconceivable that they could now be accelerated sufficiently for the two hectares minimum to be realized by even a major proportion of Indonesia's peasants, let alone all. The minimum land stipulation was clearly included as a symbolic display of goodwill rather than as something to be given practical effect.

The PKI had objected to a number of features of the law during debates in the Supreme Advisory Council and the parliament. It had wanted provisions protecting the rights of squatters on government and estate lands; a lower maximum on holdings; confiscation of the

[17] Utrecht, p. 75.

[18] *Ibid.*

[19] See Karl J. Peltzer, "The Agricultural Foundation," in McVey, ed., *Indonesia*, p. 130.

land of "traitor" landlords (Darul Islam and regional rebellion supporters); nationalization of foreign-owned estates; elimination of the minimum limit on holdings (a provision the party regarded both as impracticable and as liable to arouse fears among peasants with small holdings that they were destined to be pushed off their land); abolition of land grants to village officials and local government authorities; redistribution on an individual rather than a family basis; and either no charge or ("where circumstances compel") at most a modest charge to the peasants to whom land was distributed.[20]

It is significant, however, that the Communists did not press at any stage for radical land reform as an immediate government program; they proclaimed their support for the ultimate goal of "land only for those who work it" but lowered their sights for the moment to measures aimed at reducing the intensity of village exploitation. They specifically stated during parliamentary debates that their criticisms were not ones of principle, and they joined in the unanimous vote in favor of the amended bill that was finally adopted. Once again, the Communists were playing consensus politics, guarding their alliance with the president and demonstrating to the elite groups that they were men of moderation and responsibility. This did not prevent them from stressing afterwards, however, that the agrarian law embodied only moderate reforms and fell far short of the PKI's objective of abolishing landlordism and all elements of exploitation in the countryside.

In the same spirit of moderation, the Communists did not raise the issue of eventual collectivization of land, although some other participants in the debates did refer to this as an ultimate objective.[21] If the PKI leaders shared the Leninist view that land reform was no more than a necessary concession to the proprietary instincts of the peasantry along the way to collectivization, they did not show it. One of the few official party references to collectivization was made by Njoto in a series of lectures at the University of Indonesia in December 1962; Njoto named collectivization as an ultimate goal, but stressed

[20] See Asmu's speech to the Supreme Advisory Council, January 1960 (notes of which have kindly been made available to me by Daniel S. Lev); Asmu, "Masalah Land Reform," *Suara Tani*, March–April 1960; *Review of Indonesia*, VII (Sept.–Oct. 1960), 20–21.

[21] For example, Bambang Murtioso, representative of the peasant organizations in the Supreme Advisory Council, in January 1960.

that it must come about voluntarily as a result of the peasants' own experiences and only when the government was in a position to provide adequate technical assistance.[22] On the other hand, PKI leaders did make the point from time to time that land reform could only succeed in permanently benefiting the peasants if it were accompanied by cheap government loans and the provision of fertilizer, seeds, irrigation, etc.; otherwise, inexorable economic pressures would lead to land becoming concentrated once again in the hands of the rich.[23]

Considerable difficulties were experienced in putting the provisions of the land reform law into effect and progress was very slow. In part the difficulties were administrative. Given the chaotic state of Indonesia's statistical and recording apparatus, the task of registering land was a formidable one, especially since the responsibility was entrusted to untrained or poorly trained officials at low governmental levels. Frequent bottlenecks in the bureaucratic process did nothing to ease matters. But probably of greatest moment was the obstruction offered by landlords and their protectors in official positions. Evasion of the law, particularly by illegal transfers of land to relatives and dummies, was widespread, difficult to detect, and frequently acquiesced in by those charged with the implementation of the reform.[24]

In a report issued on January 14, 1965, the agrarian minister itemized the major difficulties experienced in putting the law into effect: deficiencies in registration of land surpluses, hampering redistribution and opening the way for abuses and falsifications; obstruction by some groups, particularly the landowners; problems on the land reform committees created by the limited time many members had to devote to their responsibilities and the presence on the committees of people with a vested interest in the failure of the reform; difficulties placed in the way of peasant organizations' playing their full role on the committees, as provided for in the law; strong psychological and economic pressure on the peasants by landowners to prevent them asserting their rights; and confusion about the application of the law in many instances, leading to prolonged disputes

[22] Njoto, *Marxisme Ilmu dan Amalnja* (Scientific Marxism and its Practice) (Djakarta, 1962).

[23] See, for example, Aidit, *Socialisme Indonesia dan Sjarat-sjarat Pelaksanaanja.*

[24] Utrecht, pp. 78–80.

involving the political organizations. A factor not mentioned by the minister, but raised by Professor Utrecht, is that landlord resistance was fortified by the failure of the government to honor its promises regarding compensation.[25]

Sukarno had ordered that the first stage of land reform be completed by the end of 1963 or, at the latest, the beginning of 1964. In a report to the PKI's Central Committee in February 1963 Ismail Bakri claimed that only 1,500 hectares of land had been shared out by then.[26] According to official figures, 35,978 hectares had been distributed in Java by the end of the year. Even if the figures were correct, they indicated that implementation was far behind schedule;[27] but the PKI challenged their accuracy, claiming that the true figure was only 19,000 hectares.[28] In interviews with the author in November 1964, officials of the BTI stated that no more than 57 per cent of the land scheduled for distribution during the first stage had by then been parceled out and that, if allowances were made for frauds (principally distribution by landlords to relatives, friends, and others not entitled under the law), the real figure would be closer to 9 or 10 per cent. Early in 1965 the agrarian minister reported that the first stage of redistribution had been completed.[29] Once again the PKI demurred; a report in the party's daily, for example, claimed that in East Java only 18,000 hectares had been redistributed, leaving 30,000 hectares still to be shared out in that province.[30]

The only figures the writer has on the progress of crop-sharing agreements are some supplied by BTI leaders in November 1964 indicating that the government had recorded 25,345 written agreements. In this case, BTI leaders claimed, the real figure was much larger, though only a small minority of sharecroppers had yet succeeded in obtaining the legally guaranteed minimum share of the harvest. They

[25] *Ibid.* It is pertinent to point out that the minister's report was issued after the full force of the PKI's unilateral peasant actions to implement land reform had been spent. The reference to disputes involving political organizations will become clear in the course of our discussion of this campaign.

[26] *Harian Rakjat,* Feb. 19, 1963.

[27] *Suluh Indonesia,* Jan. 5, 1964.

[28] Ismail Bakri's report to the PKI Central Committee meeting in December 1963, *Harian Rakjat,* Jan. 13, 1964.

[29] Utrecht, pp. 85–86.

[30] *Harian Rakjat,* Feb. 10, 1965.

also stated that, under their leadership, a number of peasants had won a 60:40 division. They attributed the progress made in implementing the crop-sharing law entirely to PKI and BTI pressure tactics against landlords.

PKI PEASANT POLICY, 1960–1963

The PKI began to apply pressure for the implementation of the land reform and crop-sharing laws as soon as they were promulgated. An energetic campaign was waged throughout 1961 in the columns of the party's daily. Major attention was paid to:

> Publication of laws and regulations dealing with land reform, and extensive commentaries on them. The Chairman of BTI, Asmu, began a regular question and answer column in the party's newspaper during the course of the year that explained the provisions of the laws and their application and detailed how the peasants should go about having them implemented.[31]

> Descriptions of the character of landholdings in various regions and how they would be affected by the laws. These descriptions drew on an earlier article by Asmu, published in the party's theoretical journal in January 1960, which reported the results of research carried out by the BTI in Java and purported to show that landlord monopoly of the land was extensive and that the rent levels and other burdens on the peasantry were onerous and hampered production efforts.[32]

The regions outside Java were less well covered.

> Reports outlining the progress made in implementing land reform. Apart from information about the establishment of land reform committees and other official activities, these reports contained mostly accounts of pressure from mass organizations on the central government and local authorities for greater speed in carrying out the provisions of the law. Organized action seems to have been confined to the crop-sharing law, and to have been on a minor scale and relatively peaceful in character. On May

[31] Asmu's columns were later republished in booklet form: *Masalah-masalah Landreform* (Djakarta, 1964).

[32] Asmu, "Masalah Landreform," *Bintang Merah*, XVI (January 1960).

9, 1961, *Harian Rakjat* reported that peasants in the Garut district, under BTI leadership, had succeeded in thwarting the attempt of a landlord to cancel the land leases (*tanahgarapan*) of eleven peasants and compelled him to sign crop-sharing agreements as the law laid down. Three days later BTI issued figures on the number of peasants who had obtained written agreements: 3,773 in Central Java, 3,500 in West Java, and 2,872 in East Java. Even at this early stage, the PKI and BTI were emphasizing that peasants should not rely on the authorities to give them their rights but should take their emancipation into their own hands.[33] Quite apart from the *fact* of official dilatoriness, the PKI stood to gain no political leverage unless the land reform resulted in greater peasant social awareness and identification with the party.

Demands for the inclusion of peasant representatives on the land reform committees.

General attacks on the sabotage of the laws by landlords and officials. The most specific of these was a broad hint in an editorial that land marked for distribution was finding its way into the hands of landlords' *kakitangan* (stooges).

Articles analyzing the commitment of government leaders, political parties, and mass organizations to land reform. There was little, if any, overt suggestion at this stage that any political groupings were opposing the laws, although it was well known that NU leaders were generally far less than enthusiastic about it.

Tactical guidance to party cadres. Apart from the emphasis placed on encouraging the peasants to become active on behalf of their rights, party activists were told to concentrate on the crop-sharing law, to popularize the slogan of the "Six Goods," to adhere to a firm class line in the peasant movement, and to be selective in attacking landlords by acting indulgently toward those willing to make concessions.[34] (The "Six Goods" movement was aimed at popularizing six demands among the peas-

[33] See the BTI New Year Message: "Experience teaches the peasants that the implementation [of the land reform laws] depends on the unity and actions of the peasants themselves" (*Suara Tani,* Jan. 1961, p. 1).

[34] See especially Aidit's speech to the second national peasants' conference, *Harian Rakjat,* July 17, 1961.

ants: lower land rents; lower interest rates; raise the wages of agricultural workers; increase agricultural production; raise the peasants' cultural level; and raise the political consciousness of the peasants.)

The PKI and BTI leaders continued to complain of the "impure" class composition and low ideological level of their village activists. Ismail Bakri told the PKI Central Committee meeting at the end of December 1960 that, "Because many of the cadres in the revolutionary peasant movement consist of middle peasants, the principle of placing the interests of the farm laborers and poor peasants first is still limited to words, while in practice the problems of these strata are given least attention."[35] He claimed that the cadre situation was changing and that the initiation of peasant action for land reform could be expected to bring forward natural leaders from among the poorer strata, who could then be trained to become cadres. But similar criticisms (together with the expression of similar hopes) persisted throughout the succeeding years.

In March 1961, a writer in the BTI journal spoke of "idealistic ways of thinking among cadres," examples of which were views that "there are no landlords and usurers in this district" and that "peasant laborers and poor peasants are hesitant and do not want to be asked to oppose the landlords."[36] (The second view, as has already been noted, applied to at least some BTI leaders themselves.) Shortly afterwards, in a report to the National Council of the BTI, Asmu indicated some of the difficulties the organization was having in taking politics to its peasant members: "The majority of the mass membership of the BTI and the peasants are still illiterate and their cultural level is in general still backward, so they are not very aware of the necessity of reading the organizational publications and listening to the lectures of the BTI."[37]

[35] *Harian Rakjat,* Jan. 16, 1961.
[36] *Suara Tani,* March 1961, p. 2.
[37] *Ibid.,* May–June 1961. No figures on the circulation of *Suara Tani* are available, but its readership was probably very small. According to party officials, the circulation of *Harian Rakjat* in November 1964 was only 49,000, partly due to newsprint restrictions. There were also a number of PKI-influenced papers in the provinces. But the newspaper reading public in Indonesia has been confined largely to the politically aware in the cities and towns.

At the PKI's seventh congress in April 1962, both Aidit and Asmu discussed the problem again. Aidit declared that "cleansing the revolutionary peasant organisations and the Party in the countryside from the influence of landlords and rich peasants [not merely 'middle peasants,' as Ismail Bakri had tactfully put it in December 1960] is an absolute condition for making the movement for rent reduction a success, for the consistent implementation of the Crop-Sharing Law."[38] Asmu admitted that even the leading bodies of the BTI had not yet been freed of landlords and rich peasants but claimed that some progress had been made.[39] At year's end, Asmu spoke once more of the efforts of the BTI "to place peasant laborers and poor peasants, both men and women, in the leading bodies of the BTI, as well as purging the exploiting class from the BTI organization."[40]

Ismail Bakri returned to the subject again at the February 1963 meeting of the Central Committee of the PKI: "The enforcement of the crop-sharing law is also not going as well as it ought, because of hesitations on the part of BTI cadres and leaders in the face of violent opposition by the landlords, sabotage by reactionary officials, and the fact that prior attention was concentrated on land reform."[41] The problem was still being described in much the same terms in 1964, after the peasant unilateral actions had been initiated. The membership of the BTI was increasing rapidly at this time, no doubt adding to the problems of disciplining the organization and inculcating the desired outlook among its members.[42]

Overall, 1962 saw the PKI devoting less attention publicly to the crop-sharing and land reform issues than in the previous year; rather, in 1962, priority was given to the agricultural production campaign, the "1,001 Movement." Undoubtedly the major influence in this

[38] *Problems,* p. 525.

[39] *Madju Terus,* pp. 194–96.

[40] *Suara Tani,* Nov.–Dec. 1962, p. 22.

[41] *Harian Rakjat,* Feb. 19, 1963. The last phrase is puzzling. All the indications are that, both in speeches and actions, primary attention up to this point had been given to the crop-sharing law.

[42] At the PKI's seventh congress Asmu stated that between 1957 and 1959 BTI growth had been small, but between the latter year and the end of 1961 it had risen from 3.5 million to 4.5 million (*Madju Terus,* pp. 194–96). Later membership claims were 5.6 million in July 1962 and 7.1 million in August 1963 (*Harian Rakjat,* Nov. 27, 1963). See also Aidit, *Set Afire the Banteng Spirit!* pp. 122–23.

change of emphasis was the West Irian campaign, which was absorbing the greater part of PKI energies and prompting a more national approach to social questions. In his report to the seventh congress, Aidit stressed the 1,001 campaign and the peasant reforms that were being negotiated with the government, such as the lowering of official interest rates on loans and the repeal of regulations compelling sugar cane growers to sell their product to state sugar enterprises. The 60:40 movement was said to be expanding, but no directions were given for its future development.[43] Little more was heard of land reform for the remainder of the year.

No discernible change had taken place by the time of the important Central Committee meeting of February 1963, when Aidit gave a lengthy report on the party's current policy imperatives. The report addressed itself primarily to the threat which the projected adoption of the U.S.-supported stabilization plan held of a move to the right by the Indonesian government; land reform was dismissed in one short paragraph devoted solely to the role such reforms could play in raising agricultural production.[44] On the occasion of a statement in March by the agrarian minister calling for the completion of the first stage of land reform that year, the BTI contented itself with a comment urging peasants to give the minister active cooperation in fulfilling his plans and stressing the necessity for strengthening the land reform committees.[45] Asmu, writing in the BTI journal, called on sharecroppers not to make any payments to the landlords outside the terms of the crop-sharing law, but his proposal was not a signal for militant action; where landlords failed to respect the law, Asmu enjoined the peasants to go to the police or the offices of the public prosecutor.[46]

AIDIT CALLS FOR A RURAL OFFENSIVE

Only after the onset of full-scale confrontation against Malaysia in mid-September 1963 did the PKI begin to resuscitate the theme of

[43] *Problems,* p. 523.

[44] *Dare, Dare and Dare Again!* p. 26.

[45] *Harian Rakjat,* March 23, 1963.

[46] *Suara Tani,* March–April 1963. See also the lectures given by Aidit in May–June 1963 and collected in *Dekon Dalam Udjian.* Aidit complained of the poor implementation of land reform, but his general remarks were moderate (pp. 22–24).

class struggle in the countryside. An editorial in the PKI daily suddenly called attention to the importance of the crop-sharing law and commented that, while official opposition to it had declined, most officials were passive toward it and ought to be replaced by people with a more positive outlook.[47] This was mild enough, but on November 1 Aidit fired a more significant shot in a speech to peasant cadres, in which he explicitly linked the land reform campaign with the Malaysia struggle and, by enlarging on what he claimed had been the vital role played by the peasants in the national revolution, impliedly equated the importance of the current crusade against the imperialist enemy with that epochal struggle.[48] This was the prelude to Aidit's report to the December 1963 meeting of the Central Committee, in which he placed radical land reform in the center of the "revolutionary offensive" that he called for. This report marked the beginning of the campaign which produced the *aksi sepihak* movement of 1964.

It will be recalled that the December Central Committee report analyzed at length the changes brought about in the political situation by the dramatic events of September 1963, which had toughened Indonesia's anti-Malaysia posture. Aidit appreciated that the government had embarked decisively on an anti-Western course and that, so far had it committed itself to this new course, it would be extremely difficult for it to disengage itself. He set before the PKI the task of keeping the fires of confrontation burning vigorously in order to consolidate the new course and derive every possible advantage from it in strengthening the party's political position. He estimated that the Communists could now pass over to the political offensive against all those in positions of authority who were resisting the growth of PKI influence. For the first time in many years, he gave strong emphasis to those aspects of the party's policy that distinguished it from the government and other political groupings and made it clear that the PKI aimed to press its program on the government by means of mass mobilization and intense campaigning.

Aidit's views on the land reform question need to be assessed in the light of this general appraisal and perspective. In the first place, he made the most vigorous attack to date on the ambivalence of the

[47] *Harian Rakjat,* Sept. 25, 1963.
[48] *Ibid.,* Nov. 1, 1963.

national bourgeoisie toward land reform, the inadequacy of the land laws, and the lack of progress in carrying out redistribution:

Indonesia's national bourgeoisie is still young and has many family ties with the landlords. One of its legs is capitalist while the other is feudal. In particular, the position of Indonesia's industrial bourgeoisie is very weak indeed. As a result of all this, they have no stake in an increase in the purchasing power of the masses of the peasants in order that the peasants are able to purchase their industrial products. Thus, although the Indonesian bourgeoisie is objectively anti-feudal, it cannot possibly have a radical agrarian program. . . . The only class that has the necessary conditions for possessing a radical agrarian program is the proletariat. It is the proletariat that is objectively capable of drawing the peasants over to its side, to the side of the revolution.[49]

In a tendentious account of the political negotiations preceding the passage of the basic agrarian law, Aidit claimed that the national bourgeoisie had rejected the PKI's program of radical land reform and teamed up with the landlords. Unable to resist completely the mass pressure for reform, these classes had put forward the unsatisfactory compromise embodied in the law. Since then they had done everything possible to sabotage the execution of the law. At the current rate of implementation, land reform would take decades to complete.[50]

Radical land reform, Aidit argued, was essential to raising production of food and clothing, the foundation of the *berdikari* program, and to making it possible for Indonesia to industrialize and modernize. By *radical* land reform, he meant *confiscation* of all landlord holdings and their distribution *free* to landless and poor peasants. The party did not reject the existing reforms but valued them, not for their intrinsic value, but only as a basis for stimulating peasant actions and raising their political consciousness.[51]

---

[49] *Set Afire the Banteng Spirit!* p. 22. It is interesting to compare Aidit's analysis here with that of Lenin in *Two Tactics of Social Democracy in the Russian Revolution.* Lenin, in arguing that the Russian bourgeoisie feared to arouse the peasants to take part in the bourgeois democratic revolution, stressed that the main inhibition on the bourgeoisie was its fear that the peasants would go beyond their aspirations and prove impossible to keep within the bounds of bourgeois right (*Selected Works* [Moscow, 1950], I, no. 2, especially 49).

[50] *Set Afire the Banteng Spirit!* pp. 23–25.

[51] *Ibid.,* pp. 22–25.

Aidit demanded the Nasakomization of the land reform committees, the retooling of functionaries of the Agrarian Department (whom he accused of dragging their feet), and the establishment of land reform courts, with peasant participation, to try landlords and officials who failed to carry out the reforms.[52] But his main concentration was on the encouragement of peasant actions and the thorough integration of the party with the villagers.

Unilateral peasant actions had already taken place in some regions, Aidit stated, but they were not as widespread as they ought to be. Given the obstructions that land reform had met, the peasants could not be blamed for taking the law into their own hands. On the contrary, all revolutionaries must welcome, encourage, and lead such action by the peasants. This should be done in a disciplined and measured way, however:

The unilateral actions will be successful if at least three conditions are met: one, compact organisation, especially in the standpoint and resolve of the leadership of the actions at the *kabupaten* [regency], *ketjamatan* [subdistrict] and village level; . . . two, education should proceed apace, namely, emergency courses for village cadres which deal specifically with the practical side of actions; and, three, actions to proceed under leadership, avoiding "leadership action" without the masses, or "mass actions" without leadership, as well as actions being consistently based upon the farm labourers and the poor peasants. . . . These actions must therefore be capable of winning the sympathy and support of more than 90 per cent of the village inhabitants and the non-reactionary state officials.[53]

The report stated that the PKI had basically succeeded in integrating itself with the peasants; the revolutionary peasants' organization, BTI, had achieved a membership of more than seven million and had extended its organization to nearly fifty per cent of the villages, more than eighty-four per cent of the subdistricts and almost ninety-seven per cent of the second-level government regions in the country. As a result, "The united national front in our country has a sound and militant base and is therefore becoming more and more invincible, [and] there is an ever greater guarantee of the defeat of every attempt at splitting by the rightwing socialists, rightwing religious persons,

[52] *Ibid.,* p. 26.
[53] *Ibid.,* pp. 27, 134–36.

rightwing nationalists and the other reactionaries."[54] Nevertheless, there was much still to be done in improving the party's position among the peasants, particularly in overcoming the continuing tendency of some city cadres to remain aloof from the peasantry, in bringing forward poor peasants to leading positions at the village level, and in raising the cultural level of the villagers.[55]

There can be little doubt that, in deciding to stimulate unilateral peasant actions in support of the land reform provisions, the PKI leaders were consciously stepping outside the bounds of the united front strategy they had been pursuing for many years. Aidit's analysis of the attitudes toward the reforms held by officials, "rightwing nationalists and rightwing religious groups," and his general remarks to the effect that the "radical way" on land reform could be taken only by the proletariat, show clearly that he understood that this was a go-it-alone enterprise. He appealed for the support of progressive elements and may even by then have had an assurance of presidential sympathy—sympathy that, as we shall see, was openly expressed in August 1964. But essentially he conceived of the peasant struggle as one in which the alliance strategy that had governed all major Communist activities since 1952 would be subordinated to the need to mobilize the villages behind PKI goals. This is not to suggest that the PKI was abandoning its alliance strategy overall; indeed, as has been pointed out, the fundamental tendency of Aidit's report was not to forsake the alliance with the political elite but to secure for the party a more prominent position in it. Apparently, then, the objective was to build up the PKI's following among the peasantry and to demonstrate the intensity of peasant support, in order to compel the party's allies to grant it a greater role in the central governing apparatus of the country, and, conversely, to deter the party's powerful opponents from organizing a successful resistance.

In a sense, Aidit had arrived at a peaceful version of Mao Tse-tung's strategy in the Chinese revolution. Mao too advocated an alliance with the national bourgeoisie and was prepared to cooperate with the Chiang Kai-shek government at different times, but never at the price of surrendering exclusive control over his peasant bases and peasant armies. Apart from the question of armed struggle, how-

[54] *Ibid.*, pp. 122–23.
[55] *Ibid.*, pp. 124–28.

ever, there was another crucial difference between the Chinese and Indonesian cases: Mao had the immense advantage that the consolidation of his control over extensive peasant areas *preceded* his overtures to the Kuomintang and did not, as was the case with the PKI, have to be built up within the confines of a top-level alliance.

Aidit, it is safe to say on the basis of his report, must have known that the party's espousal of unilateral peasant action would arouse intense opposition and place heavy strains on the alliance. What, then, made him and his colleagues willing to take the risks involved in violating the unwritten political compact against class-type struggles? One possible explanation is that the growth of rural distress and unrest obliged the PKI leaders to direct it lest it erupt outside their control, and that lower level cadres in the party organization and in the BTI were giving expression to this unrest in ways that threatened the discipline of the movement.[56] There is evidence that conditions in the countryside had deteriorated markedly in the preceding months. The late 1963 harvest in Java had been heavily depleted by the worst drought and rat plague in living memory, and accounts of privation were common. Aidit himself in his report of December 1963 mentioned that "the people are now eating virtually anything edible,"[57] and in the following months various sources drew attention to misery on a huge scale. Reuters Newsagency reported on February 16, 1964, that in Central Java, where the crop failure had been particularly severe, one million people were starving; in the district of Wonosari between two and six people starved to death daily; and the deputy governor of Central Java said that 12,000 people were being treated for malnutrition and 15,000 families had deserted their barren rice fields. The crisis was not confined to Java: Antara detailed that 18,000 people were starving in Bali and that there were serious rice shortages in South Sumatra. *Harian Rakjat* reported on February 18 that people were selling everything including their children.[58]

[56] W. F. Wertheim has advanced the view that PKI leaders acted under the impact of pressure from below. See his "Indonesia Before and After the Untung Coup," *Pacific Affairs,* XXXIX, nos. 1 and 2 (Spring and Summer 1966), 115–27, and "From Aliran towards Class Struggle in the Countryside of Java" (paper delivered at the International Conference on Asian History, Kuala Lumpur, August 1968).

[57] *Set Afire the Banteng Spirit!* p. 22.

[58] I am indebted to J. A. C. Mackie for the data on economic conditions cited in this paragraph.

Despite such evidence of widespread rural distress, the Djakarta press contained no references during this period to food riots or other forms of overt social unrest in the villages or small towns that were unusual in their size or extent. Aidit's report extolled the spirit of the workers, and the people generally, as being prepared to face even greater difficulties in the interests of the patriotic struggle against imperialism.[59] While this can largely be dismissed as flummery, it does suggest that at that stage the Communist leaders felt able to control mass unrest and were not impelled to give it its head.

There is a similar lack of evidence to sustain the suggestion that restiveness in the lower ranks of the PKI and the BTI pushed the party leaders into taking a stand they would not otherwise have ventured upon. The unilateral actions Aidit referred to as having occurred in some regions before December could conceivably be interpreted as the work of grassroots radicals, but the absence of further information makes it impossible to form a useful opinion. So far as can be discovered, no reports of militant peasant actions outside the normal range of PKI activity appeared in the national press in 1963, and the disposition of the PKI leaders to use the unilateral label for any organized peasant initiative in support of their rights (including the presentation of a petition, the holding of a peaceful procession, or squatter actions), makes it impossible to isolate the substance of Aidit's reference. Nor was 1963 distinguished by criticism by PKI leaders of "adventurism," the usual label attached to views and actions going beyond leadership policy directives.

Finally, it seems doubtful that, if they had been under pressure to undertake actions about which they were reluctant, the PKI leaders would have urged peasants to go beyond the land laws in their action, as they did for example in urging peasants to press the 60:40 demand on crop-sharing. They would have been more likely to have endorsed unilateral actions while seeking to confine them to the limits laid down by law. Such a course would have made some concessions to their radical followers but at the same time maintained the general conditions of the party's alliance with the political elite. Instead, as we shall see, the PKI leaders urged their own radical agrarian program as a basis for action. This is not to argue that indications of grassroots militancy, combined with deteriorating rural conditions, had no effect

[59] *Set Afire the Banteng Spirit!* pp. 18–19.

on their calculations. On the contrary, such manifestations may well have been very important in persuading them that the time was ripe for taking a step that, on other grounds, they were already keen to take.

The view to be advanced here is that the Communist leaders soberly and judiciously embraced the *aksi* in their plans for a political offensive set within the framework of confrontation and aimed at decisively strengthening their hand with their governmental allies. That they were now thinking seriously about the problem of obtaining substantially greater political power in the not-too-distant future is indicated by, among other things, the following significant passage from Aidit's report to the Central Committee:

Our cadres are aware of the fact that all national democratic revolutions in Asia that have won victory and have been able to follow up victory by speedy Socialist construction have been able to do this first and foremost because of the integration of the Marxist-Leninist parties and the peasants of the countries in question. The Cuban Revolution also won because of this. Yes, our own experiences too indicate the same thing about the importance of the role of the peasants.

Aidit then spoke of the peasants having been decisive in helping the armed forces to crush the rebellions in Sumatra and West Java (Darul Islam), and in ensuring the victory of the armed national revolution. During the national revolution, he said, the villages were the source of foodstuffs and soldiers, the line of retreat for the revolution at times of setback, and the bases for launching counterattacks against the enemy. "In brief, the question of the peasants or the villages is the question of life or death for the revolution, and even the question of life or death for revolutionary cadres."[60]

Taken alone, this section of the report could be interpreted as referring to a foreshadowed switch to an armed peasant struggle for power. The general tenor, however, is otherwise: there is no reference to the armed aspect of the peasant struggle in China or Vietnam, even though this may well be considered the decisive element in the strategies of the Communists in those countries; and stress is laid on the *survival* value of the village sanctuary. In the context of the overall line laid down by Aidit at the meeting, the program of action

[60] *Ibid.*, pp. 129–30.

among the peasants appears to be intended to act as a battering ram to force open the doors of power, still locked against the party, and at the same time as a means of creating safe places of retreat in case the army should succeed in turning the tables on the party in a showdown.

PREPARATIONS FOR ACTION

The PKI was not slow to follow up the lead given in Aidit's report. Throughout January 1964, the party's daily made a feature of increased agitation over land reform and carried reports on the obstructions being encountered in the Outer Islands as well as Java.[61] On January 12, the paper published Ismail Bakri's contribution to the Central Committee's discussions, in which he argued that "It has now become clear to the peasants that their only way out of their poverty is to take their fate into their own hands." For the first time, Bakri gave some hard evidence of the extent of rural struggle in Java:

The enthusiasm of PKI cadres working in peasant circles is soaring in proportion as the numbers and breadth of the peasant masses taking part in actions grow. For example, in the Central Java regional BTI conference, of the 160 participants, 48, or 30 per cent, had been arrested or sentenced for leading peasant actions. In the West Java regional BTI conference, of the 44 participants, 38, or 85 per cent, had been arrested or sentenced to from 10 days to 4 years. Despite this, not one among them regretted having taken the side of the peasants in the actions.[62]

The impact of this statement is diminished, however, if one bears in mind that, if there were delegates who had served four years in prison, their activities would have had nothing to do with the current land reform agitation. In all probability their sentences would have related to earlier conflicts over squatter-occupied estate or forest lands.

On February 3, in a speech to party cadres, Aidit returned to the question of land reform. Declaring that the implementation of the agrarian law had been very disappointing, he urged peasants to withhold rent payments from landlords altogether as a means of inducing them to carry out their obligations. At the same time he called on

---

[61] See, for example, the articles dealing with Atjeh (*Harian Rakjat*, Jan. 9, 1964) and Minahasa, in Sulawesi (*ibid.*, Jan. 18, 1964).

[62] *Ibid.*, Jan. 12, 1964.

peasant sharecroppers to take sixty per cent of the produce of the land they worked by unilateral action.[63]

Again on March 17, in a lecture to air force officers, he attacked the sabotage of the reform law and described the unilateral action movement as just and "a revolutionary action that benefits the government, not only by enabling the speeding up of the implementation of the laws, which ought to have been completed in 1963, but also by giving the government a basis for making a success of its food and clothing program."[64]

On March 6 it was announced in the party press that since February Aidit had been leading research into agrarian conditions and the peasants' movement in West Java; forty-six teams had been assisting him, two in each of twenty-three of the largest subdistricts in all regencies of the province. The report stated that the research teams were using the "three togethers" method of ascertainment and criticized the "superficial question-and-answer method" that, it claimed, was used in "bourgeois" studies.[65] An article in the March issue of *Ilmu Marxis,* a party publication directed toward intellectuals, quoted the chairman in greater detail on the aims of the research. According to his own account, Aidit had decided to undertake the study for five reasons: because the better a Marxist understands the objective situation, the better he is able to propound correct policies and apply Marxism to Indonesian conditions; in order to understand better why the land laws were not being implemented satisfactorily; to aid the integration of the PKI with the peasantry; to train cadres in social research; and to make the conditions of the peasantry better known to all revolutionaries.[66]

Publication of the results of the research in West Java began in the PKI daily on May 11 and extended over six issues. Shorter summaries of similar studies in East and Central Java were published early in June.[67] Aidit kept up a full round of public activity during this period, so it is probably fair to say that his participation was confined to taking part in briefing meetings for the researchers and possibly visit-

[63] *Ibid.,* Feb. 3, 1964.

[64] *Revolusi, Angkatan Bersendjata dan Partai Komunis,* p. 33.

[65] *Harian Rakjat,* March 6, 1964.

[66] *Ilmu Marxis,* no. 3 (1964).

[67] The East Java account appeared in *Harian Rakjat* on June 3 and the Central Java account on June 5, 1964.

ing a few villages to set an example. Most of the work was carried out by party cadres under the supervision of university-trained people.

The West Java report began by listing the villages which had been visited and then explained why they had been chosen, stressing their typicality for the province. After the methods of the researchers had been described, a long section analyzed the class structure of the village and the characteristics of each class, beginning with the landlord.[68] The report tacitly admitted that most landlords owned relatively small holdings. Special reference was made to landlords who owned only 3–4 hectares of land, who of course were not covered by the provisions of the agrarian law. The authors added, however, that it had proved impossible to obtain full details of land ownership, since holdings were commonly spread over several subdistricts and often registered in the names of dummies, and also emphasized the many other forms of income accruing to landlords from money-lending, pawnbroking, etc. This led to the general assessment that "landlords who own a relatively small area of land carry out exploitation which is as cruel as that of those who own a large amount of land, and indeed there are cases where the small owner is even more cruel."

Most landlords in West Java were "evil landlords"—that is, rigid opponents of land reform or former members of the banned Masjumi party. Many landlord *hadjis* (men who had made the pilgrimage to Mecca) used religion to extend their land ownership and intensify their exploitation of the peasants, and an organization called the Madjelis Ulama (Council of Religious Scholars) had taken on many of the reactionary aspects of the Masjumi. In addition, the landlords sheltered behind civil and military officials, including village heads.

The report found evidence that landlords were shifting part of their funds into capitalistic (retail trading) enterprises and changing over from renting land to peasant sharecroppers to employing wage labor on their holdings. Other exploitive elements singled out for attention were moneylenders, *tukang-idjon* (dealers who bought up crops cheap in the preharvest season), the middlemen who acted as transmission belts between towns and villages, and bureaucratic capitalists, agents of state enterprises who signed up peasants in advance to sell their crops to the enterprises.

[68] The report was a general appraisal of the entire study, no village-by-village data being given.

The characterization of the other farming groups—rich peasants, middle peasants, poor peasants, and landless laborers—added nothing to previous PKI analyses, and forms of village exploitation or survivals of feudalism were described in exactly the same way they had been since 1953.

Concerning village government, the report declared that no fundamental changes had taken place since Dutch colonial times, because the pattern of class domination had remained substantially unaltered, despite the introduction of full adult suffrage for village elections. Village government was still feudal in essence because government officials there had the same economic interests as the landlords. Some changes had followed the entry of the revolutionary movement into the villages: before that event, "the peasants looked upon the feudal power as something sacred, eternal, and unshakable, and their misery and backwardness as predestined and unchangeable"; now they were beginning to understand their rights, with the strength of their understanding varying according to the strength of the PKI and BTI in particular places.

On the subject of peasant actions, it was noted that unilateral actions relating to the crop-sharing law had taken place in several districts, including Bandung, Tjirebon, Indramaju, and Krawang, as a result of which about 52,000 agreements had been entered into, 21,750 of them in writing. BTI figures for the entire province gave the number of crop-sharing agreements as 51,750, generally achieved as a result of unilateral actions.[69] With regard to land reform, official figures were quoted as showing that 21,000 hectares had been distributed to 33,573 tillers; the report did not consider these estimates at all reliable, however, and stated that all of the unspecified number of distributions that had benefited the poor and landless peasants had been the result of unilateral actions. Agitation to raise laborers' wages was said to have increased, and there had also been attempts to cancel pawnbroking pledges, to retool bad officials, and to safeguard peasant squatters.

Guidance was laid down for the promotion of future unilateral actions. They should be "just, beneficial, and within prescribed

[69] Compare this estimate with the official figure of 25,000 *written* agreements for the whole of Java released some months later, a figure which, as noted above, BTI leaders claimed was a considerable understatement.

bounds"; they should aim at small results, be combined with agitational work, and be waged perseveringly. "Social-economic actions must always be connected with political actions, such as democratizing the villages, retooling bad officials, Manipolizing village government, crushing Malaysia, opposing the presence of the U.S. Seventh Fleet in the Indonesian Ocean, etc."

Once more, reference was made to deficiencies in the local leaderships of the revolutionary organizations:

Too many of the leadership groups of the party at the district and village levels are composed of people of rich peasant social origin . . . [who] originally took shelter from the fire of the revolutionary peasant movement but who, because of their higher cultural level, were able in a short time to occupy leading positions in the PKI and BTI and to gain the peasants' trust for a time.

This situation had to be changed by intensifying Marxist-Leninist education and promoting activists from among the poor peasants.

The East Java and Central Java reports contained basically similar findings with regard to village social structure, the character of village government, and the growth of peasant actions. A point was made in the Central Java report of refuting the widespread belief that in the Surakarta and Jogjakarta regions, seats of Java's most deeply entrenched princely traditions, communal land ownership remained largely undisturbed:

Even though in these regions a peasant was officially allowed one *patok* [approximately one-ninth of a hectare], the landlords have nevertheless succeeded in gaining control of the land and using it as a means of feudal exploitation through such methods as land mortgage, unrestricted sales, or season sales lasting for decades (some of them for 72 seasons or 36 years). Thus those people who are of the opinion that there are no landlords in these regions are very much mistaken.

Furthermore, the agrarian law had actually aggravated landlordism in the communal ownership areas, "because it legalizes the emergence of landlords by officially permitting a person to own land up to the maximum set, which is far greater than one *patok*."

An indication of the difficulties posed for the party in promoting village militancy within an overall strategy that stressed accommodation with the regime and the building of a mass Communist party was provided in the section on village government, where it was noted that "it not infrequently happens that good persons who obtain power by democratic means turn into feudal officials."

Considering the scope of this research effort, organization for it must have been going on for some time before February 1964. The question therefore arises: what were the leadership's motives in undertaking such a survey, under the leadership of the chairman, at a time of mounting political activity? As has been noted, PKI leaders had frequently drawn attention in the past to the importance of village research and the deficiencies of such studies as had been undertaken. But it is hard to accept that the project was inspired by no more than a desire to obtain firsthand data on rural conditions and show the cadres how the job ought to be done. Major PKI campaigns almost always had definite political aims in view, and the involvement of Aidit in the village research points strongly in this direction.

A notable precedent forces itself on our attention. In 1955, when differences of opinion arose on the Central Committee of the Communist Party of China as to whether or not the peasants were ready to embrace collectivization on a mass scale, Mao Tse-tung himself went off to the villages and returned with an authoritative direction to proceed at once with the campaign. It seems possible that Aidit was taking a leaf from Mao's book and that his research program was intended to enhance his personal authority and so enable him to overcome doubts and hesitations within leading circles of the party about the wisdom of embarking on a class struggle in the countryside. If definite evidence of such a dispute existed it would of course go a long way toward settling the question of the party leadership's role in promoting the *aksi*. As is so often the case, however, we are left to deduce the preceding course of events from the results and from such few obscure general references as are to be found in PKI materials.

The case for viewing the *aksi* as primarily the outcome of PKI high policy has already been argued. That the decision is likely to have provoked disagreement and trepidation, in view of the radical reinterpretation of the national front strategy it involved, stands to reason. But the only hints to be found in the PKI press of the time of the existence of disagreements and ideological problems in the party are annoyingly vague. Consider, for example, this item from mid-1964:

Internal contradictions in the party cannot be avoided but must be faced, taken care of, and terminated. In resolving the party's contradictions in a correct manner, the leadership improves its skill and quality. Bringing to an end the internal contradictions in the Party is an indispensable condition for enhancing the ability of the party to resolve external contradictions.[70]

Another possibility is that the BTI leadership wavered. An examination of the BTI monthly journal and the speeches of BTI leaders other than Ismail Bakri, who was the party's *aparatchik* within the peasant organization, reveals a softer line on peasant actions than that advanced by the party. Particularly was this so in the case of Asmu, the chairman of BTI. It seems extraordinary, for example, that, in a speech to a BTI seminar on food production and the 1,001 movement in January 1964 (that is, immediately after Aidit's Central Committee report), he should have made only routine mention of the land reform issue and none at all of unilateral actions.[71] The decision that Aidit himself would oversee a program of village research may well have reflected dissatisfaction with the BTI's work in this direction. This dissatisfaction in turn may have arisen from broader disagreements as to what was to be done among the peasants.

UNILATERAL ACTIONS: THE FIRST ROUND

During the period between the announcement of the PKI's rural research program and the publication of its results, the first serious conflicts over peasant actions were reported in the national press. On April 14 the PKI daily reported a mass meeting in Klaten (Central Java), attended by Njoto, at which slogans were displayed proclaiming "Land for the peasants who till it" and "Crush the seven village devils."[72] Njoto "warmly greeted the peasant actions now developing in Wedi, Trutjuk, Djogonalan, Prambanan, Wonosari, and other

[70] *Harian Rakjat,* July 6, 1964. The context suggests a concern for the effect of "bourgeois" pressures on the PKI, a subject to which Aidit gave some attention at this time.

[71] See the report in *Review of Indonesia,* XI (March–April 1964), 7–10.

[72] Both were PKI slogans and embodied demands going beyond the terms of the land reform laws. The "seven village devils" were exploitive elements; landlords, usurers, *idjon* dealers, etc.

places," and declared that "the land reform laws can only be carried out by peasant actions in close cooperation with patriotic and democratic state instruments."[73] On April 27 further actions were reported in the Jogjakarta area.[74] Klaten appears to have been the center of particularly serious conflicts, and it is also one of the very few cases in which anything like a coherent account of events appeared.[75] On April 30 *Harian Rakjat* carried a story by an Antara newsagency reporter in Solo on the origins and development of the *aksi* there, which said:

> The peasants, especially small peasants who have lost their land in pawn or have had to rent it out, are now acting in a body to fight for its return; at the same time, landless laborers are taking action to obtain shares of the crop under the crop-sharing law.
>
> Before taking unilateral action, the peasants first go to the landlord's house to hold discussions and consultations, in which they make clear that their demands are genuine and not excessive. Because these discussions fail or are refused by the landlord, the problem is then reported to the village head's office. In most cases the discussions fail. From here on, the procedure is for the head to submit the problem to the land reform committee of the subdistrict. Then, when this path is blocked by the landlord's obduracy, the peasants concerned take unilateral action. The intention of these actions is in part to bring about a return of the land by *gotong rojong*.
>
> Generally the actions are successful, but they are not carried out without sacrifice. Not all the landlords give in in the face of the actions. Some of them use the local state power to have the peasants arrested. But in the last month or so, in one village (Lumbungkerep) alone, twenty-six families have succeeded in obtaining the return of their land or have implemented a sharing of the crop and freed themselves from the *idjon* system.
>
> Some of the land which is the subject of actions for its return has been rented by the landlord for as many as twelve, twenty-four, or thirty-six

[73] *Harian Rakjat,* April 14, 1964.

[74] *Ibid.,* April 27, 1964.

[75] Most newspapers lacked the resources for extensive coverage of events in the provinces; more importantly, being for the most part the vehicles of political parties or cliques, they both concentrated on capital city affairs and reported contentious episodes with a minimum of factual material and a maximum of bias. *Harian Rakjat* was no exception with regard to the *aksi*.

years. The basic agrarian law lays down that land that has been rented out for seven years must be returned.[76]

Beyond suggesting (in the first paragraph) that not all actions were strictly in support of rights conceded by the land laws, this account sounds more like an idealized version of how an *aksi* ought to be conducted than a description of how any specific action developed. Utrecht has provided us with the kind of information about the *aksis* that cannot be obtained from the Indonesian press, and from his account it seems clear that both the PKI and its opponents were defying the letter of the law.[77] Thus, he instances occasions when neither side waited for a land reform committee to rule on a claim to disputed land before taking direct action. In addition, the PKI sometimes encouraged a landless peasant to stick to a claim for land that was not surplus within the meaning of the law. On the PKI's side, justification could be found in the "corrupt decisions" of local land reform committees and delays in implementing the laws; on the landlord's side, the strength of property attachments and determination to defend the status that ownership of land conferred was intensified by the failure of the government to provide compensation. Poor peasants who had caught on to the notion that the government was obliged to give them land were often not concerned with the details of legal categories, especially if their neighbors had suddenly come into possession of land and the PKI was agitating among them with its own more radical slogans.

The PKI quickly became aware that the *aksi* were arousing serious political dissension in Klaten and elsewhere in Central Java. On April 29, Aidit followed up Njoto's visit to Klaten and handled the explosive situation there with a combination of firmness and conciliation:

The intensification of peasant unilateral action means that the political parties, people's organizations, and officials cannot adopt a neutral attitude any longer. A process of selection and crystallization is appearing in all political parties and among all officials, determining who is a true revolutionary because he is on the side of the peasants, and who is a dilettante revolutionary because he is hostile to the peasants. This selec-

---

[76] *Harian Rakjat,* April 30, 1964.
[77] Utrecht, pp. 81–84.

tion and crystallization is also taking place in the PKI; those members of the PKI who are not on the side of the peasant actions have been left behind by the peasants, and their role as revolutionaries is over. . . . And don't blame the PKI if other parties get into a mess and many important people take a fall because they procrastinate or don't adopt a correct attitude toward the peasant actions.

After referring to the commencement of a "poisonous whispering campaign against the PKI" that alleged it was "enemy number one," Aidit went on to stress the party's continued concern for National Front considerations: "I wish to make clear that the PKI's enemy is not the other parties but the imperialists, especially the U.S. imperialists, the landlords, and their hangers-on. I call on all Indonesian Communists to implement the policy of national unity more strenuously."[78]

Back in Djakarta a few days later, Aidit addressed a PKI May Day reception and delivered a warning to the "right wing of the middle forces" in terms that suggested he was relying on national political pressures to keep these forces from going too far in opposing the PKI:

Anti-Communist policies will not profit the middle elements, will not elevate them to greater power. The weak economic and political position of the middle forces in Indonesia makes it impossible for them to rise on the political stage without uniting with the left forces. . . . Supposing they [the pro-American reactionaries] succeed in wiping out the Communists (a very dubious possibility), then the reactionaries will take the stage and the middle elements will very quickly become no more than their errand boys. . . . The best thing for the middle forces is to follow the advice given by President Sukarno ever since 1926, that is to support Nasakom cooperation.[79]

The fact that the earliest major reported *aksi* clashes took place in Central Java may have been the result of considered party policy or may have merely reflected the fact that PKI cadres in that province, faced with conditions of extreme privation and backed by a long established and well organized party machine, were the first to move into action. The Klaten area was one where clashes might have been expected to become quite widespread and to arouse intense feelings.

[78] *Harian Rakjat,* May 4, 1964.
[79] *Ibid.,* May 6, 1964.

It is a densely populated district and at that time probably had a PKI majority among its voters, even though Masjumi was strongly supported among the *santri*. It is also a district with many rich peasants (among whom those who did not work their land would have been classified by the PKI as landlords) growing the rather "capitalist" (i.e., commercial) crop of tobacco.[80] Political rivalry between the PKI and Masjumi groups for the control of the village leadership had been endemic since the fifties, with threats of violence from both sides.[81]

The wider tension aroused by the *aksi* in Central Java, however, involved the PKI in conflict with its Nasakom partners, as Aidit's remarks about the middle forces make clear.[82] In particular, the party encountered intense opposition and resentment from leaders and branches of the PNI. This antagonism too had a long history, going back at least as far as the 1955 elections, after which the realization by PNI officials that the PKI was advancing at its expense prompted bitter attacks on the Communists and calls for the renunciation of the party's political alliance with them. Since then the Central Java PNI had been a stronghold of the right wing of the party. The unilateral actions were bound to exacerbate the antagonism, both because they were promoted by the "upstart" Communists in defiance of the (predominantly PNI-attached) officials and because, as Utrecht points out, "the influence of the landowners and rich farmers was very strong" among PNI leaders in the province.[83]

The provincial PNI could still command considerable peasant support:

Most of the richer farmers, who still exerted traditional and economic influence on their labourers, were naturally anti-Communist. But so were many of the landless peasants who, however desperate their position might become, would never join the BTI. They remained "loyal to the landowner," or rather, "loyal to the party," the party they shared with their landlord, and "loyal to the Pantjasila," which meant "loyal to

[80] Lance Castles, "Notes on the Islamic School at Gontor," *Indonesia*, no. 1 (April 1966), 38.

[81] Based on notes made by Daniel S. Lev during a field study in 1964 and kindly made available to the writer.

[82] The term "middle forces" was never applied to Masjumi or ex-Masjumi elements, but only to the legal parties.

[83] Utrecht, pp. 81–83.

God"! PNI indoctrination, which appealed to traditional and religious feelings, had been effective, and party discipline stood strong.[84]

It followed that the class-based appeals of the PKI would come up against entrenched loyalties founded on patron-client relationships between richer and poorer villagers.

NATIONAL CONTROVERSY AND GOVERNMENT POLICY

By June the *aksi* controversy had become a major national issue and the actions themselves had spread from Central to East Java, where they were to produce still greater violence and political dissension. A bitter press polemic commenced in the Djakarta press in mid-June, with the anti-PKI forces being led by *Merdeka,* an independent Djakarta daily put out by the PNI-leaning publicist B. M. Diah. *Harian Rakjat* replied blow for blow, at the same time publishing extracts from the articles of its opponents, apparently in the belief that their antipopular character was self-indicting.[85] The lines of the argument were familiar; the PKI stressed the reactionary nature of feudalism and the role of the peasants as one of the principal pillars (*sokoguru*) of the revolution (with liberal quotations from Bung Karno), and its opponents charged the Communists with destroying national unity and acting in a counterrevolutionary manner (with liberal quotations from Bung Karno).[86]

On June 13, Agrarian Minister Sardjawo and the Central Java board of the PNI were reported as having condemned the Klaten *aksi* as counterrevolutionary, with the latter demanding punishment of the offenders.[87] The PKI countered with a list of supporters of the peasant actions that included the leaders of five peasant organizations.[88] On

[84] *Ibid.,* p. 83. In an interview with the writer in November 1964, BTI leaders put the membership of Petani (the PNI peasant organization) at three million, compared with the BTI's seven million; cf. Utrecht's rather dubious statement that "by far the greater part of the peasants not belonging to religious organizations were Petani members" (p. 81).

[85] The Chinese Communists adopted the same tactic in their polemics with the CPSU, out of a similar confidence in the self-apparent rightness of their own viewpoint.

[86] The press controversy was collected and published by the PKI in a booklet entitled *Polemik Merdeka-Harian Rakjat* (Djakarta, 1964).

[87] *Trompet Masjarakat,* June 13, 1964.

[88] *Harian Rakjat,* June 20, 1964.

June 15, Acting President Leimena, in Sukarno's absence, issued an instruction stating that "unilateral actions by any group cannot be approved." But the PKI was by now too far committed to its campaign to withdraw, and probably still confident that the gains that would follow would outweigh the opposition aroused. After waiting a short time to test reactions to the instruction, Aidit commented on it in such a way as to encourage the continuation of the *aksi*. Declaring that the instruction had been widely misinterpreted as aimed at the peasants, he went on, "I am of the opinion that if the instruction is implemented correctly, then what is condemned in the first place are the unilateral actions of the landlords who are resisting the basic agrarian law and the crop-sharing law. On the other hand, the peasant unilateral actions are only the rejoinder to this landlord resistance." If the government took resolute actions against sabotage of the laws by landlords and officials, Aidit argued, then the peasant actions would not be necessary.[89]

Lukman struck a tougher note at the policy level in a speech to the first national conference of the PKI on July 4:

The meaning of our party's theory concerning the national united front is clear. It is that the peasants are the principal and most reliable allies of the working class, and because of that the alliance between the workers and peasants forms the basis of the united national front. This being so, it becomes clear that the national bourgeoisie, although very important as an ally of the working class in the struggle against imperialism, forms an additional ally, meaning one not so important as the peasantry. For this reason, although our party must with all its strength tug at and cultivate the national bourgeoisie so that it remains in the united front with the working class, nevertheless at no time can it sacrifice the unity of the worker and peasant. This means that, whatever the reaction, and however great the violence attending the work of the party among the peasants, we cannot be in the least vacillating in our vanguard role of protecting and leading the peasants.[90]

In point of fact, if Lukman's interpretation of the party's strategy was the correct one, it had been well and truly obscured during the previous ten years. Overall, the PKI had avoided as far as possible making this kind of evaluation of the respective weight of the national

[89] *Ibid.*, July 2, 1964.
[90] *Untuk Perbaikan Perkedjaan dalam Front Persatuan Nasional.*

bourgeoisie and the peasantry in the united national front. In 1957, and again in 1959, Aidit had stressed the tactical necessity of subordinating the agrarian revolution to the prior demands of the national revolution against imperialism. The practical effect of this approach by Aidit could only be to afford priority to relations with the national elite, and this was how Njoto expressly interpreted it at the time.[91] Aidit was careful never to express a preference between the two classes, and the general tenor of his analyses was to give equal weight to both alliances. If Lukman's statement presaged a revolt against Aidit's line, it appears to have come to nothing; all later PKI statements during the *aksi* period attempted the difficult task of reconciling the stimulation of peasant militancy with the preservation of Nasakom unity. In a series of lectures sponsored by the National Front between September and November 1964, Aidit again strongly emphasized the *aliran* aspect of national unity and the importance of good relations between the political parties. In what may have been a reference to continued disagreement in the party, he criticized cynical views that suggested the National Front was only "a meeting between workers and nobles" and specifically referred to the role of the Front "in combating unnecessary contradictions among the people."[92] Whatever restiveness there may have been in the party as a result of the political disputes brought on by the *aksi,* it did not get out of hand, and Aidit's line prevailed.

On July 12 Sukarno called a special session of the Supreme Advisory Council to discuss the vexed issue of land reform. The Council resolved to speed up implementation of the reform;[93] at the same time, it imposed a ban on further polemics over the issue, a move which *Harian Rakjat* purported to welcome, declaring that there were urgent national tasks to concentrate on and that it had not started the controversy.[94] One result of the latter decision was that reports of *aksi* in the national press became sparser and more circumscribed,

[91] *Review of Indonesia,* V (Oct. 1958), 33. B. O. Hutapea contradicted Njoto a few months later, though without reference to Njoto's statement (see *Review of Indonesia,* VI [Aug. 1959], 34). According to PKI expatriates interviewed by the writer in 1968, these two were bitter personal and political enemies by 1964.

[92] *Revolusi Indonesia, Latarbelakang, Sedjarah dan Haridepannja,* pp. 67–70.
[93] Utrecht, p. 85.
[94] *Harian Rakjat,* July 14, 1964.

making it difficult to gauge the extent of the troubles and the reactions of various parties to them. Generally, the provincial press retained considerably greater latitude on the question, particularly in East Java.

VIOLENCE IN EAST JAVA

Meanwhile, a conflict of major proportions had begun in East Java. By June 1964 the Surabaja newspapers, each of them strongly identified with one or other of the basic viewpoints on land reform, were reporting almost daily incidents in the villages, some of them entailing disputes between PKI and PNI supporters but most involving clashes between PKI-led peasants on the one hand and supporters of the NU and ex-Masjumi followers on the other. The areas of Banjuwangi, Djember, Djombang, Kediri, Sidoardjo, and Bangil experienced the most serious conflicts, but many others were affected to one degree or another. The clashes were marked from the outset by acts of violence such as stabbing and kidnaping, and before long large scale confrontations between opposed forces armed with *kris* and other weapons were taking place. Factions took to burning down the houses of hostile elements and destroying their crops in the fields. In a number of places, police intervention led to serious loss of life and injury.

Almost from the outset, religious passions were injected into the conflict over land. NU groups accused the PKI and the BTI of attacking religious schools and insulting Islam, while the Moslems in turn were alleged to be inciting their followers to crush "the atheists" and defend their property in the name of Allah.[95] The NU youth group, Ansor, organized flying squads from the towns to go to villages where peasant militancy was being expressed in order to support landholders and local officials against their challengers.[96]

The intensity of the social and political conflict in East Java is explained partly by the pattern of allegiance: PKI support came prin-

[95] See Jacob Walkin, "The Moslem-Communist Confrontation in East Java," *Orbis*, XIII, no. 3 (Fall, 1969), 829. This account by a U.S. Foreign Service officer stationed in Surabaja in 1964–65, though partisan and overreliant on Moslem press services, gives a valuable description of the East Java clashes.

[96] For details of these clashes during the *aksi* period, see the items culled from the Surabaja press cited in Rex Mortimer, *The Indonesian Communist Party and Land Reform, 1959–1965* (Monograph Series, Southeast Asian Studies Centre, Monash University, 1972), pp. 48–50.

cipally from the poorer peasants, especially those of the *abangan* persuasion, while most of the holders of sizeable plots were *santri*. An element adding heat to the religious aspect of the conflict was the fact that Moslem religious institutions often owned quite large tracts of land, and in addition frequently became the recipients of land from landlords seeking to escape the application of the reform law. This device of transferring land to Islamic schools and other religious institutions was apparently a legal loophole in the law, but not unnaturally it aroused the ire of PKI cadres and active peasants.[97] Faced with the PKI challenge, committed Moslems turned to the *kjai* and *hadji* for leadership, and these men, imbued with religious zeal and dedicated to turning back the Communist tide, which they saw as engulfing the country and threatening the true faith, made the most of religious appeals in countering Communist land tactics.[98]

To a large extent, also, the attack on the land rights of Moslem landowners represented the last straw for a large religio-cultural group that was feeling increasingly threatened under Guided Democracy. In the late fifties, Moslem hopes for an Islamic state system had been defeated by the combination of secularists and Communists. The outlawing of Masjumi, while not altogether unwelcome to many of the conservative leaders and supporters of NU, had nevertheless robbed Islam of its most capable and dynamic leaders, and by so doing had weakened the whole Moslem cause. Under Sukarno's leadership, government policies had hurt the economic interests of many *santri* businessmen and allowed the "atheistic" Communist Party to grow unchecked and flaunt its rising influence in high places. In recent times the PKI had used its enhanced power in an attempt to have the Moslem student organization, HMI (which it alleged, with some justice, to be under the control of ex-Masjumi elements), outlawed and to snipe at other "reactionary" Moslem organizations.

After a period of disorientation, younger Moslem activists in particular had become restive at the paralysis and ineptness of their elders in suffering this decline in the position of the *santri* community

[97] Lance Castles, in "Notes on the Islamic School at Gontor," pp. 36–37, notes that the Gontor *pondok* had received 240 hectares in this way and that the PKI was trying to prevent the transfer. See also Utrecht, p. 84.

[98] Castles, "Notes on the Islamic School at Gontor," indicates in the case of the Gontor school the manner in which anti-PKI sentiment was nurtured among the pupils; see p. 44.

and the influence of its social precepts. Something of a religious revival had begun among sections of the Islamic youth;[99] and Castles detected signs in 1964 of a reassertion of unity among the conflicting currents of Moslem opinion.[100]

The land disputes, with their direct attack on the vested interests of staunch Moslems and often on the authority of local NU officials, sparked deep frustration among the *santri* and focused this on the Communists. Under the banner of religion the devout poor could be mobilized against the PKI and the BTI, in a manner that cut across the class basis on which the BTI had intended to wage its campaign and undermined the efforts of the party's leaders to avoid Nasakom conflict by stressing unity against the imperialist enemy.[101]

Although in many places the authorities did their best to moderate the conflict and reconcile the warring factions, on the whole official attitudes at the regency and provincial levels appear to have favored the propertied as against the landless and the anti-Communists against the Communists.[102] Moslem and PNI newspapers generally praised the firmness of the authorities, while the pro-PKI newspapers were unmistakably critical toward them and frequently reported cases where local officials either sided with the landlords or failed to take action to prevent intimidation of the peasants. The East Java leadership of the NU noted its "high appreciation of the firm action taken by the provincial authorities"[103] quite early in the *aksi* campaign and maintained a benevolent attitude toward them throughout. On the other hand, demands by the PKI and its affiliates for the retooling of officials who had failed to support land reform became increasingly frequent and outspoken in the course of the campaign.

A third major area of conflict over land was Bali, where tension began to appear as early as mid-1963, against a background of land shortage and overpopulation. Conflict developed around both the land distribution law and the crop-sharing law, with the PNI in each case supporting the interests of the landlords and more well-to-do

---

[99] Castles, *The Kudus Cigarette Industry,* pp. 67–68.

[100] "Notes on the Islamic School at Gontor," pp. 42–44. See also Walkin, pp. 822–23.

[101] See, for example, a speech by Aidit in Banjuwangi; *Djalan Rakjat,* Sept. 27, 1964.

[102] See Walkin, p. 826.

[103] *Manifesto,* Aug. 24, 1964.

peasants and the PKI agitating among the landless and the share-croppers. Early in July 1964 there was a report of a hand grenade explosion in Denpasar; the incident was apparently related to party political tensions, since the police chief and the public prosecutor called the parties together and issued guidelines for the holding of meetings and avoidance of inflammatory speeches.[104] In the following month several small but significant incidents involving conflict between PNI and PKI members took place, and at Tabanan all peasant organizations except the BTI declared their disapproval of the unilateral actions.[105] Still, by late November, no major clashes had occurred, although direct confrontations between rival groups on disputed plots of land were becoming more common and PNI representatives were quoted as expressing stronger determination to meet illegal actions with force.[106]

The policy of the central government on the land conflict was the subject of intense political infighting in mid-1964. Acting President Leimena's instruction of June 15 expressing strong disapproval of unilateral actions was the most authoritative expression of the government's viewpoint to date, but throughout the next two months there was tense speculation on the position President Sukarno would take. In fact it appears that, although this was not generally known at the time, he had already been disposed more toward the attitude of the PKI than to that of its opponents at the Supreme Advisory Council Meeting on July 12.[107] He declared his position, however, in his Independence Day address on August 17, giving indirect support to the PKI by confining his comments on land reform to expressions of sympathy with the peasants and criticism of the pace at which the land laws were being executed. Reminding his audience that he had previously proclaimed the peasants, together with the workers, to be the pillars of the revolution, Sukarno declared that the liberation of the productive powers of the villages was the essential condition for industrialization. He stated his dissatisfaction with the progress of the land law, demanding its immediate and complete implementation in

[104] *Suara Indonesia,* July 13, 1964.
[105] *Ibid.,* Aug. 12, 1964.
[106] Much of the information in this paragraph is based on field notes made by Daniel S. Lev in Bali in November–December 1964 and kindly made available to me.
[107] Utrecht, p. 85.

the areas covered by the first stage of the reform program. Early the following month, he addressed a BTI conference in similar vein, extolling the peasants as pillars of the revolution, the nation, and the people's livelihood, calling for vigorous implementation of the land reform and crop-sharing laws, and denouncing "BTI-phobia."[108] But while this intervention may have helped to keep Nasakom relations at the political center from breaking down, it seems to have had little effect in the regions where land conflict was in open and fierce display.

By September 1964, there were indications that the PKI was being bested in the rural conflict and was seeking to bring the situation under stricter control.[109] The resolutions of the September BTI conference repeated the guidelines previously laid down for initiating *aksi* and criticized the tendency of cadres in some places to launch actions at the leadership level, on the basis of "subjective" estimates of the situation, without consultation with the masses and government bodies.[110]

In November, PKI concern grew and became more open. On November 8, the East Java BTI frankly admitted that counterrevolutionaries were causing chaos in the villages.[111] Then, on December 3, a speech by Aidit was reported in the party newspaper in which he tacitly acknowledged the success of the opponents of the *aksi* in dividing the peasants. Subversives and counterrevolutionaries did not oppose the land reform law openly, he said. Instead, they concentrated on splitting the people's unity by inciting peasant against peasant and members of different peasant organizations against each other, hoping through this conflict to disturb conditions in the country, gain political advantage for themselves, and stimulate anti-Communism. "I appeal to the peasants not to allow themselves to be set against each other, but instead to forge a closer unity and crush the instigators of division." At the same time Aidit appealed to all groups and state forces not to confront the peasants but to take their side in all circumstances.

Lukman, too, was in anything but the ebullient mood of the previous July. In a message to the BTI on its anniversary, he appealed for

[108] *Harian Rakjat,* Sept. 8, 1964.
[109] See Walkin: "The impression I got from reading the Surabaja press . . . was that the Communists had taken much more punishment than the opposition" (p. 826).
[110] *Harian Rakjat,* Oct. 3, 1964.
[111] *Djalan Rakjat,* Nov. 8, 1964.

efforts to avoid interpeasant conflicts.[112] And Asmu, speaking in East Java, warned that "terror must not be opposed with terror [but] with mass actions uniting the people together with the army and other patriotic forces."[113] Unmistakably, the party had decided to pull back from the go-it-alone spirit that had developed during the *aksi,* with the encouragement of the leadership, and to try to confine actions to situations where the concurrence, or at least the neutrality, of civil and military officials could be obtained and conflicts with Nasakom partners minimized.

At this stage the government intervened to curb the mounting violence in the villages and moderate political party passions. On December 12, Sukarno called all ten political parties together at the Bogor Palace to discuss a number of issues of national dissension, the *aksi* among them. Only a few weeks before the Bogor conference there had been a particularly serious armed clash in the village of Ketaon, in the Bojolali district of Central Java, in which three peasants were shot and killed by the police.[114] This incident had further inflamed feelings among the political parties, and the conference met in an atmosphere of tension. After a session lasting thirteen hours, a unanimous declaration was exacted from all present that reaffirmed the common adherence of the parties to revolutionary national unity based on Nasakom and committed the parties to doing their utmost to act in accordance with the spirit of Nasakom. On the land reform dissension, the Bogor declaration had this to say:

> To carry out the above matters and solve national problems, for example the agrarian law and the crop-sharing law, the system of consultation and consensus . . . will be given priority. . . . Particularly with regard to land questions, officials and peasants are obliged to consult without using insinuations, intimidation, and arms.[115]

AFTERMATH OF THE VILLAGE OFFENSIVE

Both sides in the land reform dispute claimed the Bogor declaration as a substantiation of their attitude. Anti-PKI forces interpreted it as

[112] *Ibid.,* Dec. 4, 1964.
[113] *Ibid.*
[114] For PKI accounts of the Bojolali incident, see *Harian Rakjat,* Dec. 1 and 3, 1964, and Jan. 5–9, 1965.
[115] *Ibid.,* Dec. 14, 1964.

a rebuff to the PKI's unilateral tactics. The PKI, on the other hand, affected to regard it as a remonstrance directed at those who had answered the peasants' just demands with force. In a New Year message, the BTI hailed the declaration as crowning the peasant actions "by stating explicitly that in settling problems with the peasants, consultation and consensus must be followed."[116] The party continued to speak of the necessity to support the peasants' just struggle, which, it asserted, was expressing itself in more than 2,000 mass actions every day.

Nevertheless, it is more than probable that the PKI leaders were happy with the compromise reached at Bogor and the opportunity it gave them to reduce the intensity of the *aksi* and (hopefully) the reaction that had been aroused. It is unlikely that they could have put a sudden stop to the unilateral actions, and they would presumably have preferred a gradual retreat, in any case, for the sake of the morale of their rural cadres. Consequently, *aksi* continued during the next two or three months, but on a decelerating scale.[117] The party leaders began to place greater emphasis in their speeches and reports on work of a welfare and cultural nature in the villages.

But there was no cooling the passion of the East Java Moslems. It seems that they had scented success in their struggle to turn the tide against the PKI and, imbued with religious zeal, were determined to press ahead with anti-Communist actions. Incidents multiplied in the following months, as the Moslems became increasingly willing to act in defiance of local authorities. Willingly or not, PKI activists were obliged to meet the Moslem crusade as best they could.[118]

In early February, a *Harian Rakjat* report gave the following figures of BTI losses in the "terror" in East Java (without, however, indicating the period over which they occurred): four BTI cadres killed, forty-three peasants injured, fifty hectares of peasant crops destroyed, thirteen houses of BTI cadres and peasants damaged, and twelve BTI nameplates destroyed. It added that, "These figures do not include a considerable number of casualties suffered by the PKI and other revolutionary mass organizations in East Java."[119]

[116] *Ibid.*, Jan. 1, 1965.

[117] See *Obor Revolusi*, Feb. 17, 1965; Walkin, p. 824.

[118] See Walkin, p. 832; Mortimer, *The Indonesian Communist Party and Land Reform*, pp. 56–59.

[119] *Harian Rakjat*, Feb. 10, 1965.

February and March 1965 appear to have been the high point of the post-*aksi* conflicts, but tension remained high thereafter throughout East and Central Java, with frequent incidents of violence and bitter recriminations between the PKI-led groups and their Moslem opponents. PNI leaders in East Java, who in many cases had allied themselves with the NU against the PKI, and whose press in Surabaja was hostile to the *aksi,* seem to have felt some concern as the specifically religious element in the Moslem protest became more extreme in the early months of 1965; from this time they tended to detach themselves from the NU and preach reconciliation.

At the national level, the PKI was now sounding a note of moderation and unity and endeavoring to make light of the disturbances wracking East Java and, to a lesser extent, Central Java. Thus, in a speech at Solo, Lukman referred to recent troubles in the city that had affected unity and pointed out that disunity only profited the imperialists and subversives.

For this reason the Communists in Solo, who are strong here, must find the tactics and wisdom to restore national unity based on Nasakom, must more wholeheartedly find the way to open consultations and reach agreement. I think the small problems that led to these conflicts can be solved by musjawarah.[120]

Oddly, in view of the apparently conflicting attitudes of Lukman and Aidit at one point in the previous year, the latter was reported the same day in a somewhat more aggressive vein. The peasants were not to blame for the disturbances in Solo, he stated, because of the slowness in carrying out land reform. Subversives and landlords liked to appeal to the Bogor declaration and the necessity for consultation, but this applied only to consultation among revolutionaries.[121] Later in the month, Aidit attributed the clashes between "nationalists and Communists, religious groups and nationalists, minority groups and minority groups, indigenous and nonindigenous," to incitements financed and organized by the United States Central Intelligence Agency.[122] The same day, the BTI leadership, after reporting the wave of violence sweeping East Java, called on BTI members and allies to resist provocations and improve Nasakom cooperation with

[120] *Ibid.,* Feb. 1, 1965.
[121] *Ibid.*
[122] *Ibid.,* March 1, 1965.

all patriotic elements including the armed forces.[123] Yet another speech by Aidit, later in March, denied that such incidents as had occurred in East Java and elsewhere had weakened national unity. "Of course these incidents are not good and we must work hard to overcome them," he said. But essentially they were the result of "leaps in the dark" by discarded forces that would be crushed, and, while they had caused contradictions among the Manipolists, these could and would be overcome, not by confrontation, but by consultation.[124]

A meeting of the Central Committee of the PKI in May 1965 was the occasion for Aidit to review the political situation as a whole, including the significance and effects of the *aksi sepihak* campaign. Within a general perspective of "revolutionary offensives," he placed great emphasis on the need to preserve and strengthen national unity. He defended the correctness of the decisions made by the party in launching the *aksi* and claimed that the peasant mass movement had been the cause of some improvement in the implementation of the land laws. Admitting that in some places the landlords had succeeded in mobilizing "counterrevolutionary mass actions" to suppress the peasant actions, he offered this explanation:

The efforts of these reactionary landlords succeeded because of the mistakes of some party cadres, including those who work among the peasants. In a number of places, BTI cadres are not implementing the directive concerning "small scale actions" that are just, beneficial, and within defined limits. To achieve success, actions must be prepared with an understanding of the position of the landlord who is the target of the action, by organizing and consolidating those who are to take part in the action, and by undertaking extensive, profound, and convincing propaganda, so that they will succeed in establishing the broadest front involving more than ninety per cent of the village inhabitants. In several places, BTI cadres, carried away by their desire to spread the peasant actions immediately, became impatient, indulged in individual heroism, were insufficiently concerned with developing the consciousness of the peasants, and, wanting a "definite event," were not careful enough in differentiating and choosing their targets.

Peasant actions should be intensified, Aidit stated, but in consultation

[123] *Ibid.*
[124] *Ibid,* March 23, 1965.

with the land reform committees and the National Front. If this was done, the landlords' terror could be defeated and the peasant actions would flare up and spread.[125]

This was as close as the PKI leadership was to come to admitting that its tactics had led the party into a precarious and isolated position in a number of regions of East and Central Java and Bali. In blaming the unfortunate cadres on the spot, the leadership left unstated the fact that its own directions had placed a wellnigh impossible task on the cadres' shoulders by requiring them at one and the same time to secure the utmost mass, political, and official support for the *aksi* and to go beyond what the law authorized.

To account for the setbacks suffered by the PKI in the campaign, one must look first at what appears to have been a considerable over-estimation of the party's own strength in the villages and an under-estimation of its opponents' ability to organize in opposition to the offensive. In all probability, as has been suggested, the Party's leaders had counted too heavily on the effect of high level political support in restraining opposition forces in the provinces. A campaign waged strictly within the terms of the land laws, if it could have been under-taken in a tightly organized fashion, might have placed the local authorities in much more of a dilemma and inhibited the landlord and Moslem reaction. On the other hand, of course, it would not have achieved anything like the mass mobilization at which the PKI aimed.

Ideological predispositions may also have played some part in Communist miscalculations. The PKI had come to view the peasantry as the revolutionary force par excellence, partly, it would seem, be-cause of the regard its leaders had for the Chinese Communist Party's experiences and doctrines. For once, doctrinaire influences may have overruled the party's traditional caution and launched it on a path which sober calculation would have counseled against. Yet there is a danger in making this assumption. In every other area, the PKI had shown itself to be highly selective in its borrowing from Chinese theories, the touchstone in all cases being the concordance of such doctrines with the Indonesian Communists' careful reading of their own conditions. On the whole, it would be safer to estimate that the crucial source of the mistake lay in the fact that, while Communist

[125] *Ibid.,* May 12–14, 1965.

village support was overt and demonstrable, the strength of Moslem allegiance was latent and unverifiable until the die was cast. On this interpretation, ideological factors would enter into calculations in support of a judgment reached in the first place by relatively pragmatic but, in the circumstances, fallacious reasoning.

The conflict certainly confirmed the strength of vertical attachments to party- and religious-based organizations among the rural population. The Communists had tried to fight on class lines for once, and to an extent they had succeeded; but in the end *aliran* loyalties tended to swamp them. The traditional socio-cultural cleavages among the population, which had been an important factor in dictating the PKI's strategic avoidance of class agitation in past years, could not be overcome in the short period in which they cultivated a class approach in the villages.

As other observers have pointed out,[126] the PKI itself probably departed to some extent from the class lines of its campaign by protecting sympathetic landlords in certain areas. The switch to a class strategy was less complete in practice than party writings might lead one to expect, and this fact was no doubt seized upon in some localities to brand the party as hypocritical and concerned above all with its own interests. But the significant fact is that the PKI did carry through a class campaign—and on a large scale.

It is difficult to estimate the extent to which PKI interests were harmed by the demonstration that, in the village sphere at least, the party's offensives could be blunted. It is not clear how widely the PKI's partial defeat was understood. It is important to bear in mind that this was a period when the national press was under great pressure to report only what accorded with Sukarno's view of events. But it is clear that all anti-Communists who became aware of what was happening were greatly encouraged. That PKI strength was preponderant in the villages of East and Central Java was no longer accepted as an axiom of Djakarta politics. On the other hand, the period of the *aksi* was one of considerable success for the PKI at the national level. Drawing a balance sheet of profit and loss, the PKI leaders may not have been too concerned by the partial failure of their peasant offensive. They had no doubt learned valuable lessons from it; they had

---

[126] Utrecht, for example, p. 83.

acquired a new set of arguments to use against militant critics of their basic strategy; they could hope for a gradual subsidence of rural tensions; and the left-leaning national alliance was still basically intact under the president's protection.

One important result of the campaign, however, was that its partial failure left the PKI once again dependent on maneuvering and applying pressure at the political center. The party could not count on a boost from the countryside, and the tactics employed at the elite level therefore acquired added significance. In the final analysis, this meant that an effective counter to army power short of direct confrontation had become more important than ever. This consideration, as we shall see, was to play a decisive role in political conflict in 1965.

8. Inter-Communist Relations and the Great Schism

The inauguration of Guided Democracy in Indonesia coincided with the emergence of another formidable problem for Indonesian Communists: the outbreak of open conflict between the Soviet and Chinese Communist parties. In the course of the next few years, the antagonism between these two Communist giants was to rend the international Communist movement, drastically weaken the capacities of the Communist states to undertake international initiatives, split and demoralize individual parties all over the world, and create a lasting atmosphere of dissension and bitterness among adherents to the Communist creed.

The PKI, almost alone among Communist parties, not only weathered the storm unscathed, with its unity unimpaired and its confidence unshaken, but actually grew substantially in numbers and political influence. Just as the party leadership successfully adapted to the novel conditions of Guided Democracy, so did it steer a skillful path between the rocks of discord upon which so many of its brother parties foundered. The major factor in this achievement was the long tradition of independence from outside control established by the PKI, which Aidit and his colleagues fostered and made a cornerstone of their policy.

Formally, the leaders of Indonesian Communism viewed their party in orthodox fashion as both an integral part of the Indonesian national movement and a detachment of the international Communist movement dedicated to the goals of overthrowing capitalism and imperialism and establishing socialism on a world scale. They recognized no contradiction between these two roles and continually stressed that, to be a good Communist, a PKI member had to be both patriotic and internationalist—to uphold Indonesian national interests while furthering the cause of world Communism. But in their application of this concept, PKI leaders acknowledged no other authority than themselves as entitled to determine how the national and international tasks of the party were to be reconciled. Consequently, their interpretation of their obligations was strongly colored by what they took to be the interests of their movement, and above all by the requirements of the party's domestic strategy for achieving power.

Several factors, which will be briefly canvassed, had combined to dispose the Indonesian Communist leaders toward this assertive independence and to create the conditions in which they could go their own way with only a minimum of interference from the established centers of Communist authority. So far as interparty relations were concerned, Aidit and his colleagues wanted only two things from the international movement: respect for the fact and reputation of their own independence, and an outward aspect of unity on the part of the world movement. They were able to obtain the first, and to protect it against all attempts to undermine it. With the intensification of the Sino-Soviet dispute in the early sixties, however, they had reluctantly to recognize that the unity of the world movement was disintegrating and to contrive means of compensating for this untoward development.

Gradually, after attempting for some time to adopt a middle course between the two disputants, the PKI shifted away from the generalized endorsement of Soviet world analyses that had marked its policy in the fifties and toward a close identification with the international standpoint of the Communist Party of China. The major influence leading the party to adopt this course was the encouragement that China's policies gave to the nationalist struggle so vital to the PKI's internal strategy. The Indonesian Communists had no desire to forfeit their treasured independence to Peking, however; it was neither politic to do so nor in conformity with their temperament and self-image. Accordingly, they incorporated only so much of China's theses as matched their own program, carefully played down the source of those appraisals they did owe to Peking, and followed a considerably more flexible policy in dealing with other Communist parties than that followed by the CPC. In this way, they were able to hold their party together, protect it from the imputation of foreign domination, and prevent developments beyond their own domain from impinging on the guidelines for obtaining power that they had painstakingly drawn up and were determined to carry through autonomously. Since identification with a foreign movement did not at any stage determine the course taken by the party, it was able to insulate itself against the effects of international Communist disarray and to enhance its standing as a genuinely Indonesian political body that could be trusted to represent national interests faithfully and fully.

INDEPENDENCE: A VITAL PKI REQUIREMENT

From 1920 to the emergence of the Aidit leadership in 1951, the PKI had been largely shielded from the domination exercised over most Communist parties by Russia's international apparatus. In its first heyday, between 1920 and 1926, the PKI had been too isolated geographically, too peripheral to Soviet concerns, and too closely circumscribed in its overseas communication by Dutch official harassment, to come under the tight control of the Comintern. As a consequence, it did not experience much of the kind of conditioning known as "Bolshevization," which involved the adoption by sections of the Communist International of strict Leninist norms of organization and the subordination of policies and leadership to the will of Moscow.[1] Then, throughout almost the entire period when Stalin exercised untrammeled authority over the world Communist movement and manipulated it for the advancement of Soviet state policies, the PKI was either nonexistent or consisted of a tiny collection of underground groups isolated from outside contact.

Musso's two brief appearances on the Indonesian scene, in 1935 and 1948, appear to have been the only occasions, prior to the establishment of Indonesia's independence from the Dutch, when attempts were made to transmit Soviet instructions directly to the Indonesian Communists. The death of Musso and many other PKI veterans during and after the Madiun affair of September 1948 once more severed the slender threads that bound the Indonesian party to the seat of Communist authority. During the revolution, more information on international Communist policies and techniques reached the PKI, first from members returning from Holland and Australia, later from Soviet broadcasts and publications; but while this strengthened

---

[1] See McVey, *The Rise of Indonesian Communism, passim.*

the party's sense of identity with the world movement, it did not appreciably alter its condition of de facto autonomy. The U.S.S.R. was still too far away, too preoccupied, and too ignorant of Indonesian conditions to exercise any appreciable influence on the behavior of the local Communists.[2]

Aidit and his colleagues, as we have seen, found their way to Communism by way of the Indonesian nationalist movement, and they owed their rise to leadership of the PKI in 1951 not to Moscow's fiat (or that of Peking, for that matter) but to their own qualities and the lack of effective alternative. They had no firsthand acquaintance with the Russian international political apparatus and its methods— Aidit, for example, made his first visit to the U.S.S.R. in 1953, after the death of Stalin—and hence had not acquired any habit of dependence on it for instructions or advice. They viewed the Soviet Union primarily as a state that they held in high esteem as the pioneer of socialism and the staunch ally of Indonesian independence.

The success with which the Aidit leadership rebuilt the shattered PKI and elaborated a strategy appropriate to their understanding of Indonesian conditions fortified their nationalism and their disposition to regard their problems as peculiarly their own province; they saw their policies as consistent with general Communist practice but in no way subordinate to any outside instructions or guidance.

As it happened, from 1953 Russian and Chinese policies began to favor the kind of strategy being pursued by the PKI and to allow individual Communist parties greater latitude in devising their own solutions to domestic power questions. Recognizing belatedly that a "relative stabilization" of capitalism in the economically advanced countries was evident, the new orientation presaged a period of peaceful coexistence and peaceful competition for influence and supremacy between the capitalist and Communist systems. So far as the new states were concerned, a moderate analysis and a patient strategy were adopted. Having previously been regarded as "appendages of imperialism," these countries were now recognized as having obtained varying degrees of political independence; and some of their leaders were accepted being genuinely concerned to defend and advance national interests. The threat of neocolonialist domination by the

[2] McVey, *The Soviet View of the Indonesian Revolution.*

United States and its lesser imperialist partners and rivals remained, but the presence of the Communist state system opened up the possibility that, with "disinterested socialist aid," the ex-colonial countries could, at least in some instances, avoid foreign subjugation and dependence, build up national economies based on state enterprise, and proceed by way of a stage of "national democracy" to socialism.[3]

The new doctrine advocated that indigenous Communist parties should seek a "united front from above" that embraced the bourgeois nationalists. The problem of hegemony in the united front was sidestepped, but implicit in the Soviet version at any rate was the notion that Communist leadership was not always necessary for the transition to socialism—economic and military assistance from the Communist powers could act as the vital lever in the transitional process.[4]

The new international line was elaborated at the CPSU twentieth congress and the 1957 meeting of the world's Communist parties. Although by the latter date significant differences in policy had begun to develop between the Soviet and Chinese Communist parties, there was no real challenge to the appraisal of strategies in and toward the new states until 1959. In the meantime the Communist nations assiduously wooed the governments of the new states and encouraged indigenous Communist parties in them to abandon tactics of root and branch opposition (including, in some cases, armed struggle) against existing regimes and to cooperate with the more militantly nationalist parties and governments.

For the PKI, the change was merely an ex post facto endorsement and confirmation of the political strategy its leaders had devised and begun to implement in 1952. The party had anticipated the new orthodoxy, and was to implement it more successfully than any other Communist party in Asia.

As these changes in Communist strategy were taking place, so was the long period of exclusive Soviet domination of the world movement drawing to a close; China was emerging as a major Communist power. At first, owing to the basic identity of interests and strategies between the two Communist giants, this development did not bring about any

---

[3] See McLane, pp. 353–64, 367–69.

[4] The evolution of the new strategy is well described in d'Encausse and Schramm, *Marxism and Asia*, pp. 66–72, where it is noted that Soviet and Chinese views were not entirely consistent at any stage.

clear bifurcation of loyalties, though it did introduce a new element of flexibility and variability into the authority structure of the movement. Nevertheless, the inspirational quality and down-to-earth character of Chinese theories and practices made a considerable appeal to those who made the pilgrimage to Peking, and China's concern with Asian problems enhanced the bonds that grew up between her and other Asian Communist groups.

Aidit and Lukman, it will be remembered, spent part of the period 1949–50 in China, though according to Aidit their political obscurity at the time meant that they learned relatively little from their visit.[5] Indonesian party cadres began traveling to Peking for prolonged political training in 1951,[6] and by 1954 Chinese texts occupied a major place in the educational and publishing activities of the PKI.[7] Although they adopted many Chinese political slogans and styles, however, the Communist leaders in Indonesia were at pains to distinguish their own political situation from that which had confronted the Chinese party leaders on their road to power and to prevent anything like an uncritical devotion to Chinese Communism growing up in their ranks.[8] Aidit's analysis of the international situation in his 1954 report appears, on the basis of the terminology and emphases adopted, to have followed Soviet rather than Chinese sources;[9] and despite the greater nationalist bias of his report to the sixth congress in 1959, he was still deferring to Soviet views, even to the point of treating Europe as the center of the most decisive struggle between capitalism and socialism.[10]

None of the PKI Politburo members, so far as is known, took part in the Chinese training programs, and for a long time they retained a primary attachment to the Soviet Union as the pioneer of socialism, the unswerving champion of Indonesian independence, and the source of greatest material support for young states seeking to carve out their own independent paths of development. Moreover, the image of the Soviet Union as the major center of Communism remained substantially intact until late 1961, despite the fact that by then disagree-

[5] McVey, "Indonesian Communism and China," pp. 367–68.
[6] McEwan, pp. 32–33.
[7] See Aidit's report to the 1954 Congress, *Problems*, p. 279.
[8] McVey, "Indonesian Communism and China," pp. 368–70.
[9] *Problems*, pp. 229–41.
[10] *Ibid.*, pp. 340–84, especially p. 366.

ments had arisen between the CPSU and the PKI.[11] In part this support for the Soviet Union can be explained by the important role Russian aid played in 1959–61 in preparing Indonesia for the campaign to liberate West Irian, aid which, to the Indonesian Communists, emphasized the strength of the U.S.S.R., its support of national liberation struggles, and its value in cementing the nationalist alliance between the PKI and Sukarno. By contrast, not only was China at this stage still weak and beset by economic difficulties, but its image in Indonesian eyes was at best ambivalent; as an example of a dynamic Asian socialist state China had an appeal for many Indonesian radicals, but as the aspiring guardian and protector of the Chinese minority in Indonesia, against whom there was a marked racial prejudice that was felt especially strongly in 1959–60, its standing was more questionable.[12] The PKI leaders' preference for Moscow over Peking may also have been related to the fact that, although the two ruling parties were in substantial agreement on international strategy between 1954 and 1959, the Soviet version gave more encouragement to Communist alliances with national bourgeoisies and the pursuit of peaceful policies than did the Chinese.[13]

The question of the PKI's independence from foreign control was vital to the party's position in the internal life of Indonesia. The party's enemies, knowing how sensitive this issue was, left no stone unturned in their attempt to brand the Communists as subservient to foreign domination. The PKI leaders themselves acknowledged no outside direction of their policies; indeed, the very success they had enjoyed in making those policies the vehicle for a dramatic resurgence of the party's fortunes convinced them that they had no need to turn elsewhere for guidance. They had no wish to sacrifice either their security or their prestige by bowing to outside authority. As Aidit expressed it in 1960:

[11] The only significant difference between the PKI and the CPSU in the fifties had been occasioned by Khrushchev's denunciation of Stalin in 1956. The PKI resented the CPSU's action in delivering a blow to a prestigious international Communist figure without prior consultation with other parties; see Aidit, "Tentang Perlawatan Ke-empat Negeri," *Bintang Merah*, XII (June 1956), 216–18.

[12] For a subtle exposition of the conflicting elements in Indonesian attitudes toward China, and the PKI's reactions, see McVey, "Indonesian Communism and China," especially pp. 357–70.

[13] See d'Encausse and Schramm, pp. 66–72.

The national character of the CPI . . . is an important matter, not only because the imperialists and their agents here in our country are spreading slanders about the CPI not being national, but also because it is important for the Communists themselves who have for long been making genuine efforts to discover the Indonesian way of applying Marxism-Leninism and to imbue all their work with a combination of the spirit of patriotism and proletarian internationalism.[14]

The party leaders frequently reminded their members and the public that the PKI had always been an integral part of the national movement against colonialism:

The CPI is the party of the working class, the Party of the Indonesian Marxists. But it is a mistake for people to think that the CPI is something that is separated from the general national movement, the movement for independence and democracy. Neither in theory nor in practice is this so. The CPI is the red thread in the Indonesian national movement.[15]

On another occasion, replying to those who sought to stress the foreign origins of Communist ideology, Aidit pointed out that the other major ideologies in Indonesia were no more native than Marxism:

In my opinion, Indonesian nationalism is much more influenced by Ernest Renan, Karl Kautsky, Karl Radek, Otto Bauer, Sun Yat Sen, Tilak, Kemal Ataturk and others than by the thoughts of our ancestors. . . . I think I need not say much about religion, since of all religions existing and having a great influence in Indonesia, there is not one that is "native."[16]

"The Indonesianization of Marxism-Leninism" became the phrase by which the Indonesian Communist leaders underlined their independence in determining their policies. They found considerable difficulty, however, in explaining precisely what characterized the Indonesian features of their theory and strategy. The difficulty lay not in the absence of such features but in the fact that their distinctiveness flowed basically from the adaptation of the Communist movement in Indonesia to the conditions established and imposed by a non-Com-

---

[14] *Problems,* pp. 137–138.
[15] *Ibid.,* p. 138.
[16] *Ibid.,* pp. 207–8.

munist elite. To have acknowledged this, however, would have lowered the PKI leaders' accomplishments, both in their own eyes and in those of their followers and other Communist parties, by drawing a contrast between their image as bold revolutionaries and their "revisionist" strategy toward the question of power.

They were never able to face up to and assimilate this contradiction, and the concept of the "Indonesianization of Marxism-Leninism" therefore did not offer a summation of their distinctive experience. Aidit's major statement on the question, made early in 1964, consisted substantially of the mere assertion that "Indonesianizing Marxism-Leninism means nothing more nor less than integrating the party with the peasantry."[17] This definition seemed to owe more to the immediate program of the party, which was then preparing its offensive on land reform, than to any distinctive theoretical approach. Aidit came a shade closer to alluding to the real state of affairs in a party anniversary speech in May that year, when he described four distinctive features of Indonesian Communism. Three of these (the united national front, the combination of patriotism and proletarian internationalism, and the tactical concept of progressive, middle-of-the-road, and die-hard forces) were in no way unique to the Indonesian party, but the fourth contained a kernal of truth: "That . . . we must combine three forms of struggle if we are to win the Indonesian revolution, namely, the struggle among the peasants, the struggle among the workers in the towns, and the struggle to *integrate the apparatus of the state with the revolutionary struggle* of the people."[18]

SINO-SOVIET DISCORD: EARLY REACTIONS

The theoretical poverty of the concept of an Indonesianized Marxism-Leninism in no way lessened its significance for the PKI, since its main function was to express the independence and self-esteem of the party's leadership. The interest of the PKI in maintaining the appearance of unity in the international Communist movement had a similar function in enhancing the party's popular appeal and promoting internal solidarity within its ranks.

[17] Marxisme-Leninisme dan Pengindonesiannja" (Marxism-Leninism and its Indonesianization), *Harian Rakjat,* Feb. 25, 1964. The article was subsequently issued as a pamphlet.
[18] "Djadilah Komunis jang Baik dan Lebih Baik Lagi," *Harian Rakjat,* June 11–12, 1964 (emphasis added).

One of the strongest bases of Communist attraction everywhere had always been the claim that Communism abolished strife within and between nations that had abolished class exploitation and oppression. This claim made a particularly strong impact on Indonesian nationalist sentiment, which possessed its own mystique of national oneness and aspired to create a socialist society. The PKI was endeavoring to persuade the radical nationalists to break decisively from the Western powers and throw in their lot with the Communist camp as the surest way of realizing their aspirations; consequently any open breach among the Communist states would undermine the strength of the PKI case. The Yugoslav heresy already posed a problem in this regard, one that was met by denying its Communist character. But the outbreak of the Sino-Soviet dispute, and the measures resorted to by the disputants, presented PKI leaders with a much more alarming and disconcerting problem.

It is not clear at what point the Indonesian Communists became aware of serious differences between the two major Communist powers, but by early 1959 the dispute was a matter of common knowledge within the Communist movement as a whole and the subject of public report by the world's press.[19] Nevertheless, Aidit branded the reports as "pure fabrication."[20] This reaction, a common one among Communist party leaders at the time, was no doubt due in large measure to a desire to fend off the problems that the fissure threatened. No Communist leader, Aidit or any other, wanted to believe that a split was in the offing, and all of them no doubt hoped and believed that the dispute would be resolved without an open breach.

By the time of the sixth congress in September 1959, however, the PKI leadership felt bound to make some acknowledgement of the indirect polemics that were in progress between the Soviet Union and China, in which Yugoslavia served as the Chinese stalking-horse and unnamed "dogmatists" as the Soviet target. Aidit's report referred to "efforts to create chaos and split the world communist movement," and in attributing responsibility for the evil he sided with the CPC: "It is clear that the Tito clique is carrying out a policy . . . of split-

---

[19] For a review of Sino-Soviet differences and their public expression up to this time, see Donald S. Zagoria, *The Sino-Soviet Conflict, 1956–1961* (Princeton, 1962), pp. 39–221.

[20] *Review of Indonesia*, VI (March 1959), 5.

ting the unity of the Communists of the world." At the same time he denied that the efforts were succeeding; on the contrary, he declared, the ranks of the Communists were being consolidated.[21]

The singling out of the Yugoslavs as the scapegoats did not mean that the PKI had swung behind the CPC position in the dispute. As we have seen, for reasons of their own the Indonesians had been anathematizing Yugoslavia for some time, and this may have appeared the most advantageous way of presenting the problem of the differences. Despite the nationalist bias already noted in the 1959 report, there was no sign that the PKI leaders had departed from their general endorsement of Soviet foreign policies. On the contrary, on issues that were by then already matters of dispute between the Russians and Chinese, the PKI adopted a position squarely in line with Soviet policy. Thus Aidit's report enthusiastically supported proposals for a summit meeting between the Soviet and United States leaders, presented the maintenance of world peace as the foremost task of Communists, and, as has previously been observed, placed Europe in the forefront of international Communist priorities.[22]

Throughout 1960 the PKI, facing a difficult year on its home ground, largely ignored the growing evidences of Sino-Soviet discord; its statements on issues involved in the conflict still largely accorded with Soviet positions. In May, Aidit again expressed support for the imminent summit meeting and for the Soviets' proposals for general and complete disarmament, another bone of contention between the CPSU and the CPC.[23] Nevertheless, the party was by this time deviating from complete conformity with Soviet attitudes. In January it sent a delegation to Albania, with whom (as it later transpired) the U.S.S.R. was already in dispute. A joint statement issued by the two parties stated their "complete identity of views" on subjects including "the world Communist and workers' movement" but also made suitable mention of the role played by "the glorious Soviet Union" in liberating and aiding Albania, defending world peace, etc.[24]

It would appear that the Albanian party deliberately sought the contact with the Indonesians (the delegation's visit was expressly

---

[21] *Problems*, pp. 358–60.

[22] The Chinese Communists by this time were attacking all of these Soviet approaches; see Zagoria, pp. 236–318.

[23] *Review of Indonesia*, VII (May 1960), 9–10.

[24] *Ibid.*, VII (Feb. 1960), 3–5.

stated to have taken place at Albanian invitation) because of the PKI's reputation for independence, and that this was a ploy to strengthen international support for the Albanians in anticipation of a Soviet crackdown. Whatever the PKI's state of knowledge concerning Soviet-Albanian relations, its leaders would have regarded a repudiation of Albania's overtures as a concession of dependence toward the CPSU of a kind that they were determined at all costs to avoid.

The PKI is also reputed to have given some support to minority views of the CPC at a meeting of the General Council of the World Federation of Trade Unions in Peking in June 1960, as it was again to do at the forthcoming world meeting of Communist parties five months later.[25]

The eighty-one parties' meeting, as it came to be known, was a landmark in the Sino-Soviet schism. Convened in Moscow in November 1960, in an attempt to shore up the divisions in the movement that were threatening to do what Aidit had feared—create chaos in the ranks—the meeting lasted many weeks and ranged over a vast array of ideological issues in contention. Stated in the broadest terms, these issues related to the three basic innovations introduced by Khrushchev at the twentieth CPSU congress: the doctrine of peaceful coexistence, the theory of the noninevitability of war, and the possibility of peaceful roads to power in non-Communist countries.

On all three general propositions, the PKI, as we have seen, had consistently supported the Soviet position, in public at least. But in 1959 the Chinese had introduced into the debate a question of great moment for the PKI. The CPC charged the Soviet Union with giving insufficient aid to colonial liberation movements because it feared harming its detente policies; the Chinese also challenged the notion that political hegemony in the new states could be left to the bourgeois nationalists right through the "national democratic" stage of development, suggesting rather that in most, if not all, cases the struggle between the Communists and the national bourgeoisie would eventually have to be settled by force of arms.[26]

The issue could not but closely concern the PKI and other Communist parties in the third world. An increased emphasis on nationalist issues and anti-imperialist struggle had already become apparent

[25] Zagoria, pp. 320–23.
[26] *Ibid.,* pp. 245–76.

at the PKI's sixth congress in September 1959, and by the time of the world Communist meeting the Indonesian party leaders were even more strongly convinced that their strongest hopes of averting isolation and making political ground lay in this direction. On the other hand, the issues of hegemony and armed struggle were not ones that the PKI wished or could afford to raise in a domestic context, especially since the army held the Damocles sword of repression over all the Indonesian political parties in the wake of the banning in August 1960 of Masjumi and the PSI.

The PKI representatives at the world meeting, led by Aidit, were not disposed, then, to come down firmly on one side or the other in the Sino-Soviet conflict. Their position was an intermediate one, and this was reflected in the fact that they endorsed most Soviet formulations, backed the Chinese on a number of points (particularly those calling for more militant anti-imperialist struggle), but above all associated themselves with a number of other (predominantly Asian) parties in independent initiatives to bring the two disputants together on an agreed statement.[27] Eventually a compromise declaration was hammered out that favored the general Soviet assessment but made concessions to Chinese views in a number of areas.[28]

This outcome was greeted with evident relief and approval by the Indonesian Communist leaders. On the three matters of greatest moment for them, they had fared reasonably well. First, the references to anti-imperialist struggle and the role of national liberation movements were strengthened somewhat, in comparison with the Soviet draft. Secondly, the Communist movement had emerged from the ordeal united, even if only on paper. Finally, the conference statement had affirmed the equality of Communist parties, and their independence in formulating national strategies, and had laid down procedures for resolving differences between them.[29]

The fragility of the compromise soon became apparent, however; the U.S.S.R. and China persisted in advancing conflicting interpreta-

[27] In interpreting PKI attitudes at the meeting I have relied, in addition to the cited texts, on discussions with participants from Australia, Ceylon, India, Italy, and Czechoslovakia.

[28] See Zagoria, pp. 343–69.

[29] This section of the document, like so much else in it, was nevertheless open to varying interpretations; see Zagoria, pp. 346–48.

tions of the statement and resumed their indirect polemics. The PKI largely ignored this evidence of continued strain and treated the conference declaration as the binding consensus of the international movement that had put an end to the quarrels of the previous years. Misgivings about trends in Soviet policy were allayed throughout most of 1961 by the size of Russia's military aid for the West Irian struggle, which also consumed most of the energies of the Indonesian Communists. No marked change in the party's attitude in fact took place until the twenty-second congress of the CPSU in October 1961.

Khrushchev chose the twenty-second congress platform to launch a violent attack on the Albanian Communist leaders, and created added dissension by further denunciations of Stalin and the antiparty group in the CPSU, headed by Molotov and Kaganovich, which was accused of seeking to restore the former dictator's views and methods. The excommunication of Albania (for such it proved to be, from the Soviet point of view), which was generally viewed as an attempt to force the CPC to come to heel, or at least to cease carrying its struggle against the CPSU into Russia's Eastern European empire, appears to have come as a complete surprise to the Chinese and other party representatives. Most of the delegates from foreign parties dutifully fell into line with the U.S.S.R., but the Chinese signified their outrage and intransigence by placing a wreath on Stalin's grave and then quitting the congress.[30]

The PKI delegation, along with a number of other parties, refrained from joining in the denunciations of Albania. Aidit and other members returned to Indonesia via China, where they held discussions with Mao Tse-tung and other CPC leaders; once home they initiated top level discussions to define their attitude toward this new and ominous development in the world movement. An initial statement was made by Aidit on November 23, the day following the delegation's return. Outlining the reasons why the PKI's representatives had not joined in the attacks on Albania, Aidit said that in the first place they had been unaware that the issue would arise and did not consider they had a mandate from the party's leading committees to take any stand on the matter; more fundamentally, he declared that differences between Communist parties ought to be settled on the

[30] See Zagoria, pp. 370–73.

principle of consultation and common assent and in accordance with the principles laid down at the 1957 and 1960 international meetings.

He made it crystal clear that the PKI would not bow to Soviet pressure to excommunicate Albania:

As long as a country genuinely conducts a socialist political, economic, and social system, although it is not bound by a treaty and even though matters arise which create conflict between that country and another socialist country, the country remains a part of the socialist camp. . . . Albania is a country which is building this type of society, a socialist society. Comrade Khrushchov himself does not deny this.

Aidit defended the right of the Soviet party to do whatever it liked about Stalin and its own antiparty group, but insofar as Stalin was an international figure in the Communist movement other parties had the right to evaluate his contribution after their own judgment. "The Communists of Indonesia continue to respect Stalin," he declared, and would treat his writings according to their value for their own struggles. At the same time, he was unstinting in his praise for the CPSU program for building Communism, describing its goals as "swords which pierce the hearts of the imperialists" and declaring that its implementation would benefit all people who opposed imperialism.

Once again, Aidit made a spirited and emphatic statement affirming the PKI's independence:

As I have said time and again, and this is in accordance with the spirit and content of the 1960 statement of the Communist parties, the PKI is an independent Marxist-Leninist party. It has the same rights as all other Communist parties; it does not accept the leadership of any other party, and it certainly does not claim leadership over other parties. Guided by Marxism-Leninism, the PKI determines its policies itself. The PKI is responsible to the working class and the working people of Indonesia. However, the PKI also has responsibilities toward the international working class movement at the same time. Therefore, Indonesian Communists cannot remain passive in facing the fact that antagonism exists among the Communist and workers' parties of the world.

Finally, on international Communist unity and the future of the world movement, Aidit expressed the PKI's abiding concern that differences should not "result in a weakening of the struggle against the common enemy, namely, world imperialism headed by the United States." Stating his confidence that the existing differences, like all previous differences in the movement, would be overcome without lasting damage to it, he twice declared, "the Communist movement will not collapse, just as the heavens will not collapse."[31]

Three weeks later, the PKI Politburo passed a resolution endorsing Aidit's statement and the delegation's stand at the twenty-second congress. The resolution indicated that the PKI still stood somewhere between the Soviet and Chinese positions on the major strategic questions in debate:

As regards international policy, it is very necessary that the policy of peaceful coexistence be continued, that general and complete disarmament be striven for, and, at the same time, that the struggle against imperialism, colonialism, and neocolonialism be given priority, since actually the struggle for peace and the struggle for freedom are truly one and indivisible.[32]

At the Central Committee meeting of the party that followed the release of the Politburo's resolution, Aidit once more emphasized the importance of the PKI's independence, but distinguished the Indonesian party's position from the Italian party's call for greater autonomy and a polycentric approach to interparty Communist relations. According to Aidit, the appeal for greater autonomy implied that a "kingdom" existed in the movement, which was not the case; polycentrism would create conflicting centers of authority and implied hesitancy about the leading role of the CPSU.[33] Circumlocutions notwithstanding, Aidit's argument recapitulated the PKI's two prime tenets: the party was independent and always had been so, and it desired the restoration of international unity as much as ever.[34]

---

[31] *Harian Rakjat,* Dec. 15, 1961. There is an interesting sidelight on the use of this final phrase. The Communist Party of Australia, which had sided with the Chinese party initially, switched after the twenty-second congress of the CPSU and endorsed Soviet positions in the dispute. In explaining the switch, L. L. Sharkey, the Australian party leader, frequently told members of his party (including the writer) of his horror at the opinions expressed to him on his return through China after the congress by Teng Hsiao-ping, general secretary of the CPC. The statement that Sharkey said appalled him most was the following: "Even if the international Communist movement should split completely asunder, it is no calamity—the heavens will not fall."

[32] *Ibid.,* Dec. 16, 1961.

[33] *Strengthen National Unity and Communist Unity.*

[34] See Donald Hindley, "The Indonesian Communists and the CPSU Twenty-Second Congress," *Asian Survey,* II, no. 1 (March 1962), 20–39.

NATIONALISM AND GROWING CONFLICT WITH THE CPSU

In weighing the impact of the twenty-second congress on the PKI's relations with other Communist parties, it is necessary to consider the implications of the measures taken by Khrushchev against Albania for the PKI's treasured image of its own independence. The Indonesian party leaders reasoned that by arrogating to itself the right unilaterally to determine which parties were and which were not acceptable as members of the Communist fraternity, the Soviet party was destroying the pretensions of all to independence and a national identity. For reasons already explored at some length, such an assumption of domination was not only deeply repugnant to the PKI leaders, but also dangerous to their party's domestic status.

Repudiation of the Soviet action was in the first place common prudence, since it demonstrated to the PKI's friends and enemies alike that the party was subservient to no outside body. But it was at the same time much more than a sign of the party's determination to pursue its own course in policy-making. The open defiance of the excommunication of Albania that the PKI demonstrated by sending warm greetings to Enver Hoxha both on the anniversary of the foundation of the Albanian party and at the New Year,[35] indicated the party's strong feeling of resentment toward the CPSU for its actions and loss of that respect and admiration which the Indonesian Communist leaders had previously evinced for "the vanguard of the world movement." Since this traditional devotion to the Soviet had impelled respect for Russian pronouncements on international Communist strategy, its loss removed an important factor inhibiting the PKI from following the bent of its own radical nationalist orientation.

A somewhat self-conscious article written during this period by Lukman is indicative of the unease the party felt at its divergence from the line adopted by the recognized center of the Communist movement. At the same time, it reiterated the Indonesian Communists' determination to stand by their position. Entitled "The PKI and the Eighty-one Parties' Statement," the article said in part:

The correctness of the PKI's stand concerning the nationalists and nationalism—that is, that the Communists are completely necessary in

[35] *Harian Rakjat,* Jan. 11 and 12, 1962.

the struggle for national independence and can in fact cooperate with the nationalists—can be supported by several statements by Lenin on nationalism. Lenin also reminds us to regard differently the nationalism of a nation under colonial domination. Lenin explains that nationalism in a colonialized nation "has the approval of history" and that "bourgeois nationalism in every oppressed (colonized) nation has a general democratic content that is directed against oppression, and it is this content that we support unconditionally." The PKI is of the opinion that nationalism in the countries of Asia and Africa generally is at this time nationalism of the type described by Lenin.[36]

It would seem that the PKI leaders were somewhat unsure of the orthodoxy of their policies and anxious to ground them in the sacred texts. Lukman's exercise in reconciliation was more than a little contrived, but with the self-confidence that came with success and association with boldly advanced Chinese theories later statements were to carry stronger conviction.

In the meantime, of course, Sukarno had moved decisively away from the Soviet world view, adopting the NEFO-OLDEFO frame that laid great stress on the primacy of anti-imperialist struggle. It was incumbent upon the PKI leaders to keep up with the president's nationalist radicalism and to try to exploit it for their own domestic advantage. It is not surprising, then, that from this time onward differences between Soviet and PKI attitudes began to be expressed more openly, while at the same time those elements that were common to both the Chinese and the Indonesian Communist world views were drawing these two parties closer together. As Ruth McVey has admirably put it:

In the charged atmosphere of guided democracy, aims and not institutions are real. Stability is tantamount to stagnation, motion to progress. If the economic situation worsens, if foreign relations grow more tense, the response must be more radical than before, for such things only indicate how many and how determined Indonesia's enemies are. The nation's aims cannot be achieved by compromise and calculation, but only by enthusiasm and faith; the goals themselves expand, become millenial: the revolution will not be completed until imperialism has been crushed and the just and prosperous society established over the entire world.

---

[36] *Ibid.*, May 26, 1961. The reference to a nation under colonial domination would hardly have applied to Indonesia any longer.

The pragmatic flexibility of Khrushchev's goulash communism was hardly compatible with this spirit; it appeared self-seeking, complacent, concerned with the petty problems of adjusting to the present rather than the monumental task of creating the future. Far more sympathetic was the Chinese stand, with its crusade against imperialism, its assertion that the underdeveloped countries are the world's revolutionary centres, and its assurance that even the poorest countries need not depend on foreign aid—all themes recurrent in the rhetoric of guided democracy.[37]

That the PKI should still have been trying, late in 1961, to adopt an intermediate position between the Soviet and Chinese strategies can probably be attributed to several factors. The advantages of party independence still weighed as heavily as ever with PKI leaders, enhancing their self-respect, consolidating their domestic political position, and aiding their efforts to restore the unity of the world Communist movement. In addition, they were not wholly attracted to Chinese doctrine, which contained propositions about Communist hegemony in the national struggle and the necessity for armed struggle that could not easily be reconciled with PKI practice, and it was probably not clear to them at that point how insistent the CPC would be in requiring adherence to these postulates.

A definite stand one way or the other may, too, have held the prospect of creating fissures within the PKI itself, a situation that the leaders had skillfully avoided up to that time and unquestionably wished to avoid in the future. Just how great this problem might have been is hard to assess. There were differences in the party about domestic strategy, as is attested to by the party's own materials, and taking sides in a major Communist schism could easily have transformed these differences into divisive factional struggles. The extent to which the leading stratum was divided on the Sino-Soviet issue is difficult to gauge. A number of academic analysts have claimed to discern evidence of opposed allegiances at this level, but the evidence is slight and in some cases mutually contradictory.[38] It would be

[37] "The Strategic Triangle: Indonesia," *Survey*, no. 54 (Jan. 1965), 115.

[38] Zagoria, p. 268, sees a marked difference of emphasis between Aidit and Sudisman in 1960; Hindley, *The Communist Party of Indonesia*, p. 298, quotes unverifiable rumors that Aidit was pro-Moscow and Lukman pro-Peking; Van der Kroef, *The Communist Party of Indonesia*, p. 158, writes that Lukman was "believed to be pro-Soviet."

surprising if the leaders' responses had not varied to some extent, and the adoption of an intermediate position in the earlier stages of the dispute probably served to unify them and to maintain the cohesion that flowed from their common interest in preserving the party.

Finally, the PKI in 1961 almost certainly understated its reservations about the Soviet policy of peaceful coexistence, probably because of concern over the risk that Russia would slow down military supplies, whose availability had greatly strengthened the PKI's domestic standing. Within a few months, however, once the West Irian struggle had been settled, the party's preference for the more radical anti-imperialist theses of the CPC was evident.

Th first major indication of the PKI's gravitation toward the general ideological position of the CPC came at the party's seventh congress, in April 1962. On this occasion, unlike 1954 and 1959, Aidit's review of the international situation owed little to Soviet analyses, although ritual tribute was still paid to Russian achievements. On the contrary, the primacy allotted to anti-imperialist struggle overshadowed the questions of peaceful coexistence and disarmament to which the Soviet government gave precedence; the first and longest place in the discussion of the international situation went to "the struggle against neo-colonialism in Asia, Africa and Latin America," the places where, according to Chinese theories, the decisive battles against imperialism were being waged and where the fate of the two opposed world systems would be determined.[39] No explicit reference to Chinese theories was made in the report, however; instead, credit for recognizing the potentialities of the colonial liberation struggle was given to President Sukarno, for his speech at the Belgrade conference of nonaligned nations the previous September stressing the division of the world into two conflicting camps—the new emerging forces and the old established forces. In other words, the PKI was stressing the national origins and character of its anti-imperialist policies and the identity that existed between its analysis and that of its presidential ally.

The seventh congress report still treated the differences in the international Communist movement as a passing phenomenon and one that reflected, not basic and irreconcilable conflicts, but merely vary-

[39] *Problems,* pp. 488–96.

ing estimates of how best to defeat imperialism. Consequently, the PKI resolved to expand its relations with all other parties and work for the restoration of unity.[40]

A gradual but consistent hardening of PKI positions was apparent throughout 1962 and 1963. Between April and June 1962, the party came into conflict with the Soviet-dominated World Peace Council over the agenda for the World Peace congress that was to take place in June, with the Indonesians criticizing the emphasis on peaceful coexistence and disarmament and the consequent neglect of national liberation struggles.[41] Toward the end of the year, the Sino-Indian border dispute and the Cuba missile crisis further stimulated the PKI's militant anti-imperialist outlook and brought the party into sharper conflict with the policies being pursued by the U.S.S.R. On the Cuba issue, Aidit was quoted by the Chinese official newsagency as saying: "It is a regrettable sacrifice that strategic defensive weapons are being dismounted in Cuba. It is regrettable because a sovereign state, Cuba, was forced to do things against its will."[42] In PKI eyes, the CPSU was once again violating the two principles the party regarded as being of supreme importance in the international movement. On the Sino-Indian border issue, it was creating disunity by failing to support a Communist state against an imperialist client state; on the Cuba issue, it was trampling on the independence of another Communist party by forcing Cuba to accept an arrangement reached with the imperialists behind her back. Compounding these offenses, the Soviet also used a number of European Communist party congresses in the latter half of 1962 to make violent polemical attacks upon the CPC, thereby, in the PKI's view, "exposing the crack and dispute within the communist family."[43]

Early in 1963, as the polemics between the Russians and the Chinese grew fiercer, the PKI began to publish various statements and documents relating to the international dispute; outwardly this enterprise affected neutrality and objectivity toward the disputants and their arguments, but in fact strong preference was given the pro-

[40] *Ibid.,* pp. 501–2.
[41] *Harian Rakjat,* April 7, July 5, 1962.
[42] New China News Agency, Djakarta, Nov. 7, 1962.
[43] Report to the Central Committee, Feb. 1963; *Problems,* pp. 594–96.

Chinese viewpoint. At the same time, contacts between the Indonesian party and other CPC-leaning parties were stepped up:

In April, M. H. Lukman attended the congress of the New Zealand Communist Party in the company of two Albanian delegates. In May, June and September, Australian Communist Party leaders visited Jakarta, as did New Zealand Communists in June and September. Japanese Communist Party leaders visited Indonesia in May and November, Albanian leaders in April and November.[44]

The PKI may still have been seeking to create a bloc of Communist parties that would be sympathetic to Chinese international theories but concerned to restore unity within the Communist movement; if so, its efforts were unsuccessful in the polarizing climate of the period.

The PKI's stronger alignment with Chinese policies owed a good deal to the internal dynamics of the party's political situation. After the close of the West Irian campaign in August 1962, the national unity sustained by this crusade showed signs of cracking, to the grave disadvantage of the party. Economic problems were thrown into high relief, and Sukarno appeared to be willing to countenance adoption of an American-backed stabilization scheme, which would inevitably have promoted a rightward political trend inimical to PKI prospects. To counter this threat, it was incumbent upon the PKI leaders to arouse anti-American sentiment in Indonesia by stressing the incompatibility of imperialist and Indonesian nationalist goals. A heightened anti-imperialist campaign was called for, and the Communists had an official ideological platform for one in Sukarno's NEFO doctrine. But if they were to be successful in encouraging Sukarno, and through him a majority of the government, to take the road of agitational nationalism rather than that of Western-financed retrenchment, they needed all the international support they could get. The Soviet, however, was not only preaching international restraint and opposing what the PKI regarded as legitimate anti-imperialist militancy but also indi-

---

[44] Donald Hindley, "The Indonesian Communist Party and the Conflict in the International Communist Movement," *The China Quarterly*, no. 19 (July–Sept. 1964), 105–6. Note, however, that Hindley does not distinguish between the pro-Soviet and pro-Peking Communist parties in Australia; leaders of both parties visited Djakarta several times in this period, but the pro-Peking group was shown much greater affection (see below).

cating that it had no intention of competing with the United States in granting further large scale economic credits to Indonesia.[45] That left China, whose propaganda matched the PKI's need and also harmonized with Sukarno's NEFO doctrine; it was, therefore, very much in the PKI's interest to strengthen its relations with China and support her defiance of the U.S.S.R. At the same time, given political feeling in Indonesia, as well as Sukarno's and the party's own pride, it was important that no suggestion of dependence on China should arise, and thus that the inspiration for PKI policies should be clearly located within the homeland.

A more wholehearted association with Chinese policies on the part of the PKI was facilitated by the fact that the CPC was making it abundantly clear in practice that it did not require its allies to adhere strictly to its theses about Communist hegemony and armed struggle. Far from being hostile toward all non-Communist states, China was busy seeking closer relations with independent states in Asia and Africa, including America's SEATO ally, Pakistan. After the resolution in 1961 of conflicts with Indonesia over citizens of Chinese descent, China had gone out of her way to demonstrate goodwill toward the Republic and to praise Sukarno's international policies. The identity of interests between the two countries demonstrated in various international organizations was growing stronger, and by early 1963 it was probably dawning on the Chinese leadership that if Sukarno could be induced to pursue the anti-imperialist logic of his NEFO doctrine actively, Indonesian and Chinese interests could be dovetailed over a considerable range of issues.[46]

The CPC continued to insist on the inevitability of armed struggle in its polemics with the CPSU, but the theory did admit of exceptions; and in any case the Chinese were disposed to judge other Communist parties primarily by their general orientation in the Sino-Soviet dispute and to leave the problem of power to them to work out for themselves. For its part, for all practical purposes the PKI came to endorse the road of armed struggle as applicable to everyone but

---

[45] D'Encausse and Schramm suggest (p. 87) that the Soviet at this time was restricting its foreign aid in order to concentrate on internal development.

[46] For a more thorough discussion of the converging trends in Chinese and Indonesian policies over this period, see Mozingo, *Sino-Indonesian Relations*.

itself.[47] By a curious twist of reasoning, Njoto even treated the PKI's experiences in the armed national revolution of 1945–48 as equivalent to the violent struggle for power demanded by the Chinese theses he was notionally endorsing.[48]

During 1963 and 1964, Chinese and Indonesian delegates (the latter including representatives of both the government and the PKI) collaborated closely in developing a congeries of international organizations of trade unions, youth, women, journalists, etc., based on Afro-Asian constituents and competing with Russian-dominated bodies in the same spheres. The first of these new bodies, the Afro-Asian Journalists Conference, was established at a meeting in Djakarta in April 1963, and at both the preparatory gathering in February and the inaugural meeting Indonesian representatives teamed up with the Chinese to exclude the Russians from membership.[49] Similar anti-Soviet collaboration became a standard feature of organizational maneuvers thereafter.

Until September 1963, nevertheless, the PKI continued to maintain a show of friendly relations with the CPSU and its supporting parties and to refrain from open polemics. Quite apart from its deeply felt urge to preserve its independence, the party still wished to restore the movement's unity, and to this end it was necessary to avoid ruptures. Thus throughout 1962 and 1963 it participated in or supported several moves to tone down the dispute and bring about a reconciliation between the CPSU and the CPC. In January 1962 it was one of several parties that appealed for a halt to the damaging public exchanges between the two parties.[50] The following year, it endorsed Khrushchev's proposals in January for a halt to the polemics and in May welcomed the prospect of a meeting between the principals.[51] Despite the failure of this meeting, held in July, the PKI continued its efforts at mediation, while making it increasingly clear that it would counte-

[47] In talks with PKI leaders in November 1964, I was struck by their ability in the same breath to insist on the necessity of armed struggle and to justify their own peaceful strategy.

[48] *Harian Rakjat,* Dec. 18, 1964.

[49] William E. Griffith, *The Sino-Soviet Rift* (Cambridge, Mass., 1964), pp. 125–26.

[50] Griffith, pp. 35–36.

[51] *Harian Rakjat,* Jan. 21, May 27, 1963.

nance neither condemnation of China nor a reimposition of Soviet control over the international movement.[52]

AIDIT'S THEORY OF THE WORLD COMMUNIST MOVEMENT

Aidit's world tour in July-September 1963, which took him to both the Soviet Union and China, among other places, put an end to this stage in the PKI's attitude to the international conflict and propelled it toward a much closer identification with Chinese positions. According to his own later account, Aidit was treated with rude condescension in Russia, while the Chinese showered honors upon him, among them the first foreign membership of the Academica Sinica.[53] Although his speeches while the tour was still in progress combined advocacy of a militant anti-imperialist line with studied moderation toward the international dispute itself,[54] he wasted no time after returning to Indonesia in demonstrating his much stronger commitment to the Chinese camp.

The change cannot be ascribed wholly to Aidit's personal experiences while abroad, however. During his absence, full scale confrontation between Indonesia and Malaysia had broken out, and relations with the United States had begun to deteriorate drastically. Russia showed no inclination to give substantial material backing to Indonesia's new international sally; and the implicit identity of Indonesian and Chinese views of the world began to take on more concrete shape. In these circumstances, the PKI could drop most of the inhibitions that had kept it sitting on the fence and give clear expression to the common features between its doctrine and the CPC's.

The PKI's new theses on the international situation, which achieved their most developed expression at the Central Committee meeting in December 1963, have already been described in Chapter 5. They were accompanied by a new appraisal of the state of the international Communist movement and the trends in it. A feature of Aidit's analysis here was that he no longer regarded the divisions in the movement as an unqualified evil. While the PKI was still concerned to work for the restoration of unity, it had nevertheless formed the opinion that if a party "hold[s] firmly to the standpoint of indepen-

---

[52] Griffith, pp. 103, 209–10.
[53] McVey, "Indonesian Communism and China," p. 376 and n. 29.
[54] See, for example, *The Indonesian Revolution,* pp. 44–47.

dence and equality [of parties, then] the difference of opinion in the international Communist movement cannot have a bad effect upon [it]." Speaking specifically of the Indonesian party, he added,

Because of the correctness of its attitude toward the differences . . . Indonesian Communists have not been harmed by their existence. On the contrary, a correct attitude, the attitude of independence and equal rights, the attitude of using one's own mind, has led to Indonesian Communists becoming more steeled by these differences of opinion.

Members of the party had been able to read all viewpoints in the dispute and thus to learn a great deal more about such problems as revisionism. Knowledge of Marxism-Leninism had grown, because the great debate in the international movement had constituted "a Marxist-Leninist University on a world scale."[55]

What was occurring in the ranks of world Communism, Aidit stated, was a process of "selection, crystallisation and consolidation."[56] This process was accompanied by a good deal of confusion and uncertainty, but the outlook was promising: genuine Marxism-Leninism would emerge victorious, and the reactionaries and revisionists would meet with defeat. He had concluded that there were four types of Communist Parties in the world at that time:

Communist parties that were Marxist-Leninist from the top-most leadership to the cadres and members and constituted the only Communist parties in their countries;

Communist parties whose leaderships were controlled by revisionists or which inclined toward revisionism, which constituted the only Communist parties in their countries, but in which there was a strong opposition or a rather strong opposition from genuine Marxist-Leninists;

Communist parties which were fully controlled by revisionists and constituted the only Communist parties in their countries; genuine Marxist-Leninists had been expelled and either in concert with others or on their own established Marxist-Leninist circles and in some cases reached the stage of publishing a magazine;

Communist parties that had already had alongside them for

[55] *Harian Rakjat,* Oct. 4, 1963. Cf. *Set Afire the Banteng Spirit!* p. 113.
[56] *Set Afire the Banteng Spirit!* p. 114.

some time new Communist parties, so that in these countries there were two Communist parties: the new one had been set up as a corrective to the old one which was regarded as having deviated from Marxism-Leninism or having taken the path of revisionism.[57]

Aidit advised the genuine Marxist-Leninists to stay inside the established parties and, where possible, fight out the differences there. Where new groups and parties had been formed, however, the PKI would in each case investigate to make sure that those involved were genuine Marxist-Leninists; if they were, then it was incumbent upon the Indonesian Communists to "give them a good reception." Where there existed two Communist parties in one country, the attitude of the PKI would be as follows:

The PKI will not break off its relations with the old Communist parties as long as they do, within limits, still oppose the imperialists and the domestic reactionaries, not only in words but also in deeds. The PKI at the same time would like to have relations with the new Communist party if . . . it genuinely upholds the banner of Marxism-Leninism [but] will have nothing to do with it if it is established by Trotskyists and other adventurers. Thus, the PKI will be as objective as possible, as patient as possible, in solving the difference of opinion within the international Communist movement.

Where the differences between the two parties were not too great, the PKI would do what it could to reunite them.[58]

Aidit indicated that there were two so-called Communist parties that, by their proimperialist actions, had placed themselves beyond the pale so far as the PKI was concerned: the Yugoslav League of Communists and the "Dange clique," the pro-Soviet leadership of the Communist Party of India, which had supported its own government in the border conflict with China.

The conflict between the Soviet and Chinese parties, which the PKI had previously minimized, was acknowledged to be deep and serious and unlikely to be easily resolved. The July meeting between the two parties in Moscow had been a good thing, nevertheless, despite the lack of any progress toward reconciliation. At least they

[57] *Ibid.*
[58] *Harian Rakjat,* Oct. 4, 1963.

had talked, and had undertaken to resume negotiations at some time in the future. The PKI hoped that the meeting would be reconvened, this time in Peking. At the same time, Aidit cautioned his listeners not to expect too much in this direction and to refrain from looking to the parties in power for guidance or comfort. Each party must stand on its own feet and solve for itself the problems of winning its own revolution.[59]

Finally, Aidit announced his discovery of a new model for the construction of socialism.

After visiting Korea this time, I am absolutely convinced that it is Korea that must be the example of how socialism ought to be built. In Korea the problem of economic construction is unified with political and ideological Marxist-Leninist education. In Korea they pursue the policy of giving priority to politics. The problem of agriculture and foodstuffs has been solved in the best way of all in Korea by comparison with the other socialist countries. . . . This has been made possible first and foremost because [the Korean party leaders] are pursuing a correct policy, namely an economic policy of standing fully on their own feet, relying on their own strength.[60]

Viewed in conjunction with the policy theses that Aidit developed contemporaneously, the PKI's standpoint on inter-Communist relations in the latter part of 1963 may be summed up in these terms:

The party would adopt those aspects of Chinese international strategies which advanced the radical nationalist course that was being followed by the Sukarno-PKI alliance and that found its most militant expression in the confrontation against Malaysia. In this area, the Indonesian Communists would cooperate closely with their Chinese comrades, in the interests of mutual advantage, but would present the common strategy of the two parties in their own idiom and without overt recognition of Chinese authorship. In the domestic sphere, the PKI would pursue its own strategy of peaceful penetration and pressure without regard for Chinese denunciations of the peaceful road to power.

In the conflict between the CPSU and the CPC, the PKI

[59] *Ibid.*
[60] *Ibid.*

would henceforth align itself fully with the latter against the Soviet's "collaborationist" relationship with the United States and its attempts to intimidate parties that declined to follow its ideological lead. At the same time, the PKI would make no formal break with the CPSU. Unlike the CPC, the Indonesian party was not aspiring to hegemony over the world Communist movement, and hence it had no interest in enlarging the fissures in it; although the split had not affected the PKI adversely to any appreciable extent, the party still had reason to fear that further exacerbation of the Sino-Soviet conflict might rebound to the advantage of those in the Indonesian governmental elite who were opposed to the current trend in the country's foreign policy and sought a return to a more independent stance or a pro-Western alignment.

Similar considerations, as well as a desire to demonstrate its independence, led the PKI to adopt a far more flexible policy toward Communist parties of differing views. Its sympathies with the pro-Chinese parties and groups were plainly revealed, but at the same time it proposed to continue tolerating contacts with "revisionist" parties other than those of Yugoslavia and India. In this way, it might hope still to exert some influence toward healing the international rift.

The sudden elevation of North Korea to the position of a socialist model, linked as it was to praise for that country's success in "standing on its own feet," was probably a product of the PKI's fear lest its affinity with the CPC should lead to its being taken as an appendage of Peking.[61] The fact that several other pro-Chinese parties also found great inspiration in North Korea at this time suggests that the ploy may have had China's blessing and that it may have served the additional purpose of flattering the Korean communists and binding them more closely to Peking.

THE BLENDING OF INDEPENDENCE AND INTRANSIGENCE

The air of self-confidence noticeable in Aidit's speeches during this period was not assumed. The split in the ranks of world Communism had in truth done the PKI little if any harm: the party remained free

[61] See McVey, "Indonesian Communism and China," pp. 376–77.

of serious factional conflict, and the decisive shift in Indonesian governmental policy signified by the initiation of full-scale confrontation had greatly strengthened its political position and presented it with opportunities for launching a vigorous offensive against officials and party cliques opposing its claims to stronger representation in the governmental apparatus. The party leaders could regard these gains as the results of their own political skill, achieved not only without aid or comfort from the international movement but despite its convulsions and internecine conflict.

This greater self-confidence found expression during the following year not only in the party's vigorous activities on the home front but also in its handling of relations with other sections of the international Communist movement. In the first place, the closer alignment with Chinese international policies was accompanied by a stronger and more elaborated insistence on the PKI's independence and its success in Indonesianizing Marxism-Leninism. One suspects that the tactical element in this emphasis was by now overshadowed by considerations of the prestige to which Aidit and his partners considered themselves entitled by reason of their capabilities. With Aidit in particular it became a matter of considerable pride that the Indonesian Communists should express their individual identity in their political work:

> We must always try to create forms which accord with the interests and tastes of our own people. This cannot be otherwise, since our party is the Communist Party of *Indonesia,* and is made up of *Indonesians.* Because of that, we must always make our point of departure the welfare and the thoughts and feelings of our own people, and what we say must be understandable and felt by our own people.
>
> Take for example the matter of opposing imperialism. The Chinese comrades crush imperialism, as also do the comrades of Albania, Vietnam, Korea, Japan, New Zealand, etc. Each of these parties has its own manner of crushing revisionism, and we have our own manner. . . . Marxist-Leninist parties have powerful creative capacities, each has its identity, and because of that all are healthy. . . . We have our own people, our own history of struggle, our own nature and national composition, our own traditions and customs and usages, and because of that we must discover and use our own style.[62]

[62] *Tentang Sastra dan Seni jang Berkepribadian Nasional Mengabdi Buruh, Tani dan Pradjurit,* pp. 73–74.

Party contacts with China were greatly expanded, in line with the trend evident in state relations between the two countries. At the same time, however, references to Chinese sources and authorities were kept to a minimum in party speeches and writings; if there was to be any personal cult in the Indonesian party, it was to be that of Aidit, and not of Mao Tse-tung, whose name was rarely mentioned except in his capacity as China's president.[63]

Relations with the U.S.S.R. deteriorated rapidly, but it is difficult to determine how much this was due to the logic of the PKI's orientation and how much to the party's bitter resentment of what it regarded as Soviet intrigues against it. There is no doubt that an increasingly strident tone in the PKI's nationalism became evident in this period, manifested for example in the tone of its propaganda against Western films and other forms of culture. In the latter part of 1964, Soviet art and literary forms shared in this odium, and PKI leaders made no secret of their contempt for the bourgeois themes and style of Soviet behavior in many spheres.

Whereas in the past admiration for the Soviet Union had led the PKI leaders to respect European values, insofar as they were identified with revolutionary promptings, now the dissipation of Soviet prestige lowered the barriers to revolt against all Western values (capitalist or Communist). The PKI leaders, like their Chinese allies, came to view the differences between the "cities" of the world and the "villages" of the world, or between the materially advantaged peoples and the dispossessed peoples, as more basic than those between proletariat and bourgeoisie, capitalist and Communist. A new revolutionary culture was to be founded on indigenous traditions combined with the anti-imperialist spirit of all the countries of Asia, Africa, and Latin America.[64] The cultural dimension assumed by the inter-Communist conflict, founded on the desire of formerly subject peoples to modernize while still remaining themselves, could only serve to make the resolution of that conflict immeasurably more difficult, if not impossible.[65]

At least some part of the anti-Soviet reaction, however, may be

---

[63] See McVey, "Indonesian Communism and China," pp. 368–69.

[64] See in particular Aidit's development of these themes in *Tentang Sastra dan Seni.*

[65] See D'Encausse and Schramm, especially p. 6.

attributable to the Russians' propensity to resort to tactics of intimidation and intrigue against their opponents. Mention has already been made of the rude reception given to Aidit in Moscow in August 1963; and in his statement on the results of his trip abroad Aidit also accused the Russians, indirectly, of branding the PKI leaders as "bourgeois nationalists or chauvinists."[66] In his report to the PKI Central Committee meeting in December, in which he made his first full-scale assault on Soviet policies (including the partial test-ban treaty and the program for building Communism in the U.S.S.R., which he had previously endorsed) Aidit replied at greater length to charges that the policies of the PKI were "national-chauvinist, separationist, racialist and goodness knows what else" and explicitly repudiated the idea that the new states must depend on Soviet aid.[67]

An indication of the growing bitterness between the two parties was given by an incident in April 1964. At a meeting sponsored by the Indonesian-Soviet Friendship Institute in Djakarta, Aidit spoke in terms strikingly similar to those of current Chinese polemics, and the Soviet ambassador, who was present, demanded the right to reply to the PKI chairman. At this point he was jostled by members of the audience and, when granted the right to reply, was assailed with jeers and calls for his "retooling."[68]

One month later, at a PKI anniversary meeting in Surabaja, Aidit made a serious attack on the Soviet. "The modern revisionists have recently been actively engaged in intrigues to split the Indonesian workers' movement," he said, "busily making preparations to attack the party by making use of degenerate elements who are easily susceptible to bribes, in particular the Trotskyites."[69] This allegation, which was repeated in May of the following year,[70] implied that there had been contact between Soviet representatives and leaders of the Murba Party with a view to harming the PKI. Some confirmation of the charge was obtained by Ruth McVey who, in interviews with Murba leaders in November and December 1964, learned that during

---

[66] *Harian Rakjat,* Oct. 2, 1963. The actual terms used to refer to the Russians were "dogmatists and revisionists."

[67] *Set Afire the Banteng Spirit!* pp. 78–94.

[68] McVey, "The Strategic Triangle: Indonesia," p. 118.

[69] *Harian Rakjat,* June 11–12, 1964.

[70] *Ibid.,* May 7, 1965.

that year "negotiations were taking place between Murba and the Soviets for the replacement of PKI mass organizations with their own in the eventuality of a split in such international groups as the WFTU; in return for this consideration, Murba supported Soviet inclusion in the Asian-African fraternity."[71] McVey goes further to interpret this intrigue as part of a wider Soviet policy of relying on the army rather than the PKI to advance its interests in Indonesia—a view made more plausible by the fact that about this time some Soviet theorists began to see in the armies of the new states what two Western scholars have described as,

a tendency to assume the role of a "vanguard," and to feel itself invested with an historic mission, both as regards the conquest of national independence and as regards economic development. In certain cases, this leads the army to transcend particular interests, including those of the class from which it is issued, and sometimes those of the government, so as to represent the nation as a whole.[72]

Whether or not the Soviets were actually seeking an alliance with the PKI's archenemy, their maneuvers seem to go a long way toward explaining the virulence of the party's disparagement, from about mid-1964, of all things Russian. The party hailed Khrushchev's fall in October 1964 as "a victory for the constantly expanding Marxist-Leninist forces throughout the world . . . [which] testifies to the bankruptcy of the modern revisionists' domestic and foreign policy, of capitulation to imperialism, of the policy of splitting the international Communist movement."[73] Initially, the PKI appeared to entertain cautious hopes that the new Soviet leadership would move to heal the breach in the Communist movement, but Russian attempts to convene a world Communist meeting in 1965 with the object of isolating China and possibly excommunicating her dispelled these illusions. The party, which had repeatedly stated its view that a world meeting must be thoroughly prepared and fully representative, announced that "the PKI will not take part in the international meeting of Communist and Workers' parties in Moscow on March 1, 1965,

71 "Indonesian Communism and China," pp. 23–24 and n. 28.

72 D'Encausse and Schramm, p. 91. Note also the comments of the authors on pp. 90–91 and 111 and the Soviet article of 1966 reproduced on pp. 345–48.

73 Joint statement of the PKI and the Communist Party of Australia (Marxist-Leninist); *Review of Indonesia,* XII (Jan. 1965).

as it has not been adequately prepared and will not be attended by all Communist and Workers' parties of socialist states."[74]

By this time, the CPSU had to some extent mended its fences with North Korea, North Vietnam, and Cuba, but Soviet plans for an anti-Chinese conference still met with resistance. A number of parties, including those of Rumania, Italy, and Great Britain, which held no brief for Peking but equally had no wish to see an unwanted ortho-doxy re-established within the movement, combined to water down the Soviet proposals. The world conference was downgraded to a "consultative meeting," emptied of all effective anti-China content, and attended by only nineteen parties.[75] PKI comment on the some-what futile exercise could afford to be patronizingly critical.[76]

True to the promise contained in Aidit's homecoming speech of September 1963, the Indonesian party lavished special affection and attention on pro-Chinese parties, welcoming them to Djakarta with high honors, signing joint statements with them, and singling them out for fulsome praise in its press. At the same time, its deteriorating relations with the Soviet did not lead the party to sunder all contacts with the "revisionist" parties. Thus, the Indonesians' partiality toward the Communist Party of Australia (Marxist-Leninist) did not mean that the doors were completely closed to representatives of the larger Moscow-leaning Communist Party of Australia, although in its case there could be no question of honors or joint statements.

Oddly, in view of Aidit's vehement dissociation from the Italian party's notions of polycentrism and "structural reform," several visits between representatives of the Italian and Indonesian parties took place in these years, the last high-ranking CPI delegation visiting Djakarta in May 1965.[77] Both jealous of their independence and both pursuing a peaceful path to power, perhaps they felt drawn to one another across the great ideological divide that separated them. These —the two largest Communist parties in the non-Communist world— had both largely succeeded in going their own way, despite the pres-sure to which they were subjected by the Communist giants. Both

[74] Letter of the PKI to the CPSU, *Review of Indonesia,* XII (Jan. 1965), 24.
[75] See William E. Griffith, *Sino-Soviet Relations, 1964–1965* (Cambridge, Mass., 1967), pp. 79–90.
[76] See *Harian Rakjat,* March 5 and 13, 1965.
[77] *Ibid.,* May 15, 1965.

evaluated international events primarily in terms of effects on their domestic strategies. In strikingly different conditions, both were pioneering novel approaches to the all-important question of succeeding to power. The specific circumstances of the environment in which each operated had dictated that each should combine an assertive independence with an identification with opposing forces in the Sino-Soviet conflict. In neither case had the choice of options created major problems of internal party unity. Italian Communism's situation and objectives made its espousal of the cause of world peace, and its identification of Communism with material plenty and pluralistic democracy, attractive to its followers. Vastly different circumstances had unified the PKI behind the policies of militant anti-imperialist struggle. If the PKI had the advantage that its orientation was also that of its government, it also suffered, as the next chapter will indicate, from the serious disadvantage that economic and political conditions in Indonesia were producing a crisis at a time when the Communists were unready for it.

9. The Final Year:
Climax and Catastrophe

The reconstruction of the PKI's strategic concepts undertaken in the previous pages has carried the account of the party's doctrine and action programs up to the end of 1964. It will be profitable at this stage to pause, before venturing into the final phase of the Aidit enterprise, in order to draw together the threads of the argument and try to assess how the PKI leaders at that time perceived their achievements, problems, and immediate tasks.

On the whole, Aidit and his colleagues could look back over the immediately preceding years with considerable pride and satisfaction. The party had come closer than ever before to establishing the legitimacy of its political aspirations within the ambit of the official state ideology as enunciated by President Sukarno. In terms of declared policy, the gap between the immediate program of the PKI and that of the government had closed appreciably. In the sphere of foreign policy, the United States had been humiliated and scorned, and its practical influence in Indonesian affairs had sunk to an all-time low; on the other hand, Indonesia's relations with China had been consolidated and made the cornerstone of the country's international diplomacy. So far as Malaysia was concerned, a bold show of pressure on the president by the PKI, at the time of Robert Kennedy's efforts to achieve a settlement, had met with success, and by the end of 1964 an end to confrontation seemed further away than ever. Yet at the same time, confrontation was being waged at a level consistent with the PKI's concern to avoid a national crisis that might imperil its interests.

On the domestic front, the party's stock had also risen. Its most important campaigns—against U.S. influence, for land reform, and to isolate and cast out anti-Communist politicians and officials—had all made significant progress. The party's ability to deploy its mass detachments effectively, and the support given to it by Sukarno, had led important politicians and officials to view the PKI as a valuable instrument for making government policies effective. Many others had concluded that it was now a force that it would be unwise to cross. The president's closer identification with the Communists, and his more frequent and emphatic condemnation of "Communist-phobia," strongly suggested that he was intent on harnessing the PKI's vigor and dynamism to achieve his Jacobin goals. Consequently, to work against the party meant seeking to reverse policy trends dating from September 1963, and so working against the president himself. To those who did not wish to take the painful road back, or who regarded such a course as impractical, the idea of admitting the PKI to a greater share of power began to appear more reasonable and logical.

But things had not gone all the PKI's way. As its boldness and assertiveness increased, so did the intensity of the resistance of at least some anti-Communist groups. The overt center of this opposition was the Murba Party leadership, but support came too from important figures in the army command, some prominent nonparty intellectuals and publicists, influential officials, and, on a mass scale, the organized Moslem reaction to the land reform campaign. The PKI had by no means overcome elite reluctance to recognize it as a part of the structure of government power and authority, and a crucial factor stiffening resistance to the party's ambitions was the political establishment's knowledge that the great majority of army leaders were determined to deny Communist claims.

The tensions caused by the Communists' political offensive were exacerbated by growing instability and doubts about the continued viability of the political system. Inflation had grown significantly worse in the last months of 1964, sharpening the economic crisis manifested in falling secondary production, declining government income, a run-down infrastructure, and mounting unemployment.[1] Confrontation appeared to have reached a state of deadlock, intensifying the unease and alarm felt by important political groups at the country's international isolation and its alliance with China. Equally disturbing was the report current in official circles that Viennese doctors had pronounced seriously on Sukarno's longstanding kidney

[1] Mackie, *Problems of the Indonesian Inflation*, p. 42.

disease during his absence abroad in October and November 1964.[2]

In the atmosphere of uncertainty and malaise induced by these developments, speculation about the country's future became rife and constituted, in the hothouse environment of the capital, a consuming preoccupation fed by rumor, intrigue, and palace gossip. It was vitally important to those who valued their positions and status within the governmental complex to anticipate political trends, but the number of imponderables was agonizingly large.

The president seemed determined to try to force the issue of the PKI's entry into the government in a substantial way, but could he succeed in the face of entrenched opposition from the army and civilian elites, and would he live long enough to accomplish his grand political design? Only time could answer these questions, but a related one—the current strength of the PKI and the extent of its infiltration of other power groupings—was debated feverishly.

There was no doubt that the Communists had built up a vast organization with formidable energies and a high degree of internal coherence. The exact size of the PKI and its affiliated bodies could not be established independently, but the party's new figures found sufficient support in the range of its mass activities to enjoy considerable credence. The last figures ever issued by the Aidit leadership, in August 1965, made these claims for membership of the PKI and related organizations:[3]

PKI	3.5 million
Pemuda Rakjat (youth)	3 million
SOBSI (unions)	3.5 million
BTI (peasants)	9 million
Gerwani (women)	3 million
Lekra (writers and artists)	5 million
HSI (scholars)	70 thousand
TOTAL	27,070,000

[2] Eric Schmeits, "The '30th September Affair' in Indonesia," *France-Asie,* XX, no. 2 (184, Winter 1965–66), 208–9, citing a Djakarta radio broadcast dated Dec. 13, 1964.

[3] *Harian Rakjat,* Aug. 20, 1965. The membership of Lekra seems inordinately large for an art and literary organization, but all Communists and supporters were urged to belong to the body and to encourage the popularization of traditional Indonesian art forms.

Allowing for considerable duplication of membership, this would have given the Communists a following approaching 20 million.

The level of organizational commitment and efficiency was generally high, by the prevailing standards of operation of Indonesian organizations, both official and voluntary. One demonstration of this strength lay in the ability of the party leadership to secure conformity with its guidelines and to mobilize large bodies of activists, in widely dispersed locales, for its campaigns. The long period during which the party had enjoyed stable and unified leadership must have contributed to an atmosphere in which members could feel confident of the authority and expertise behind instructions. No less important, the admiration and encouragement for the PKI expressed by the president invested the organization with a national legitimacy that could not but encourage members' devotion to its policies. The spirit of offense evinced by the Communists in 1964, though somewhat dimmed by the ambiguous results of the land reform campaign, indicated that the party could be expected to put up a determined and skillful struggle to assert what it considered its rights to a more prominent and assured place in the government.

On the other hand, there were evident weaknesses in the PKI's organization. Despite some gains in the Outer Islands, particularly in Bali and parts of Nusa Tenggara in 1963–64,[4] the party was still overwhelmingly Java-centered; strong backing at the political center would therefore be required to support any claim to a more pronounced national position. Again, despite some indications that the party had become more attractive to intellectuals and members of the bureaucracy in the preceding years, it still remained weak in both these spheres.[5] Ruth McVey may be right in doubting that the PKI's lack of appeal to Western-style intellectuals was a serious disability,[6]

[4] Interviews with PKI leaders, Djakarta, November 1964. At these interviews, PKI leaders informed me that Bali was at that time the fastest-growing center of PKI organization.

[5] Herbert Feith, "Some Political Dilemmas of Indonesian Intellectuals" (paper presented to the Australasian Political Studies Association, August 1964); Ruth T. McVey, "Indonesian Communism and the Transition to Guided Democracy," in A. Doak Barnett, ed., *Communist Strategies in Asia* (New York, 1963), pp. 160–61.

[6] McVey, "Indonesian Communism and the Transition to Guided Democracy."

but the relative immunity of officialdom to its appeals would obviously have had a bearing on the success of any strategy founded on a continuing alliance with the elite formations.

The big question mark that hung over the PKI, however, was how useful its vast following would be to the party leadership in the event of its being obliged to confront the government and/or the army in its bid for power. In 1962 Donald Hindley had argued that all roads to power for the PKI had been effectively blocked under Guided Democracy and that Sukarno had succeeded in "domesticating" the party in the sense that it was unable to move outside the bounds he set for its activities.[7] Although developments in the meantime had undoubtedly raised the PKI's capacity for independent action, as well as moving Sukarno toward more decided backing for the party's claims, some students of Indonesian Communism were still stressing in the mid-sixties the considerable obstacles that lay between it and effective power. These critics, among whom Hindley was particularly influential, argued that "the numerically large following of the PKI may be shown to be of dubious political usefulness," and that,

the peasantry . . . are "basically passive and conservative in their political outlook, not militant and revolutionary." Workers' membership in trade unions is "largely passive" and "the workers do not have the militancy, the training in direct action, or even the belief in their own strength to follow SOBSI and PKI against the 'authorities' if the 'authorities' were to demonstrate their determined opposition."[8]

Others, however, were inclined to rate the PKI's chances more highly and to stress the weakening resolve of the army and the political elite to resist Communist pressures:

Optimistic assessments point to the impressive numerical strength of the Party and its network of affiliated organisations. This mass following may be offered as evidence of the PKI's claim to legitimacy in Indonesia, and also as representing a source of great strength in the event of an ultimate showdown with the anti-communist elements, particularly the

---

[7] Donald Hindley, "President Sukarno and the Communists: The Politics of Domestication," *American Political Science Review,* LVI, no. 4 (Dec. 1962), 915–26.

[8] Stuart Graham, "Assessments of the PKI," *Australia's Neighbours,* 4th series, nos. 31–32 (Jan.–Feb. 1966), 5. Graham's quotes are from Hindley.

military. It may be argued that the Party, with its mass base and centralised hierarchical structure, is "filling a political vacuum," that it will come to be seen as "the last hope," the "saviour of the people" and "the genuine bearer of the sufferings of the people," because there are no competitors for this role. This notion is expressed by Pauker as PKI victory by "acclamation," and by Van der Kroef as the process of being "lifted to power on the crest of a popular wave." It is associated with the assumption that there must be some point on the downward graph of economic deterioration at which widespread disaffection will manifest itself in violence against the regime. Such disaffection would presumably be utilised by the PKI because it is the only party with the organisational structure and ability needed to aggregate widespread discontent.[9]

The PKI membership's readiness or otherwise to go all the way with its leaders, should the need arise, was only one element in the differing interpretations of the party's prospects, but in so far as it was one factor in the equation, the cautious view appeared to be more soundly based. Communist activists had been trained in militant activity over a considerable period, but the ideological climate in which this activity had been undertaken was largely that formed by the official policies of the regime. The leaders had taken great pains to convince everyone, including their own members, that Communists were national patriots, faithful followers of Pantja Sila and the Political Manifesto, ardent advocates of the National Front, and complete adherents to the Nasakom concept. A critical attitude toward the authorities and many official policies had been inculcated, but always with the proviso that reformation was possible within the terms set by Sukarno, to whom the party proclaimed its unswerving loyalty. It was uncertain, therefore, how far the PKI leadership could count on the rank-and-file following them, if a crunch developed between them and the authorities. The experience of the land reform campaign tended to show (to those who were sufficiently well informed of the circumstances) that, faced with strong resistance that was backed up

---

[9] *Ibid.*, p. 4. As Graham notes, the "pessimists" countered the argument based on economic discontent "by questioning the assumption that there will be any danger point in the graph of economic decline and by indicating the army as a viable alternative" (p. 5). See also Guy J. Pauker, "Indonesia: The PKI's Road to Power," in Robert Scalapino, ed., *The Communist Revolution in Asia* (Englewood Cliffs, 1965), and Van der Kroef, *The Communist Party of Indonesia*, pp. 295–304.

by the army and local officials, the Communist followers tended to wilt.

AIDIT'S STRATEGIC CALCULATIONS

There is no doubt, however, that the PKI leaders were aware of this limitation and that they intended to do all in their power to avoid any head-on collision. From all appearances, they themselves had little taste for a violent enterprise of this character. The abiding fear of political isolation they had repeatedly manifested had been reinforced by their considerable investment in the ongoing system, represented by a huge party apparatus and prestigious and influential official posts for their leading members. Aidit's awareness of the state of the party is indicated by the fact that, although he spoke at times of the thoroughly revolutionary character of the PKI, this morale-building praise was balanced by references to the pervasive effects of "petty-bourgeois" ideology in a country of small scale production and to the temptations by which Communists in official positions were beset. Both these themes found expression in a speech Aidit made in Surabaja on the party's anniversary in May 1964, though the major emphasis was on the dangers of embourgeoisement. He made particular mention of the fact that some Communist village heads had reverted to "feudal" ways, and warned against the degenerative influences threatening cadres who supplemented their incomes from the business activities of their wives.[10] Not surprisingly, he did not refer to the considerably greater embourgeoisement pressures on higher party leaders in their capacities as government ministers, presidential advisers, joint leaders of official bodies such as the National Front, mayors, deputy governors, etc.

The strategy that began to take shape in 1963 and that was reflected particularly in the major speeches and reports of Aidit, showed not the slightest disposition (if we except the strictly limited objectives of the land reform campaign) to abandon the alliance tactic in favor of go-it-alone policies. On the contrary, Aidit proceeded from the standpoint that the long established national front approach of the

[10] "Djadilah Komunis jang Baik dan Lebih Baik Lagi," *Harian Rakjat,* June 12, 1964.

PKI had proved highly successful, in a variety of political conditions, in gaining the party protection and promoting the expansion of its influence. True, the party had not obtained the entry to key positions in government and bureaucracy promised it under the Nasakom formula; nor had the problem of the virtual monopolization of arms by anti-Communist army commanders been solved. But Aidit envisaged the possibility that the strategy could still yield these crucial results in the more radical political climate created by confrontation.

The essential requirements for transforming influence into power, as Aidit saw it, were a more militant deployment of the PKI's enlarged organizational resources and the exploitation of Sukarno's left wing inclinations, benevolence toward the PKI, and commitment to a radical course whose reversal would have presented enormous prestige difficulties. At the Central Committee meeting in December 1963, describing, with considerable overstatement, the new political conditions created by confrontation as a "revolutionary situation," Aidit urged the party to "wage a revolutionary offensive in all fields." This offensive, he emphasized, was to be carried out "from above and below," that is, by the mobilization of the party's mass forces and the utilization of its influence in high places. The objective was to develop a momentum to the left that would isolate the party's enemies and exert irresistible pressure on the government to give the PKI leadership a larger place.[11]

The delicate subject of the army, which the PKI leaders well understood to be the most formidable obstacle to their aspirations, had to be approached with great circumspection; but it would appear, from the slant of Aidit's speeches in 1963 and 1964 on the role of the armed forces, that he hoped they could be neutralized. The stress he laid on the subordination of all forces in the state to the political line laid down by the president was designed to strengthen "loyal" sentiment among the officers against the anti-Communist radicals. The tactic of wooing the air force, navy, and police was calculated to supplement this process of neutralization. At the same time, of course, the Communists were busy cultivating as many potential supporters as possible within all the armed forces. The main drift of Aidit's reasoning seems to have been: If the PKI could project its goals within

[11] *Set Afire the Banteng Spirit!* p. 144.

the bounds of legitimacy conferred by the president, then the army would be faced with an agonizing choice between passively accepting the admission of the PKI to key posts and challenging the entire political order sanctified by Sukarno; and in view of the failure of previous military attempts to dictate to Sukarno, there were grounds for believing that many senior officers would hesitate before making another such attempt and for hoping that this hesitation would paralyze the high command.

In sum, then, there were four crucial strands in Aidit's strategy: militant mass mobilization, the extraction of every ounce of benefit from Sukarno's benevolence and his confrontation predicament, the "softening up" of the political elite, and the neutralization of the armed forces. By the end of 1964, the first two elements of the strategy had been put into effect, on the whole with considerable success. With regard to the latter two, however, results were more doubtful.

As already indicated, it had certainly become more difficult for officials and politician-bureaucrats to oppose, or even hold aloof from, the left wing trend that the president and the PKI were fostering in a wide variety of fields. Those who were incautious enough to attempt it were overwhelmed by demands for their retooling, and many felt the effects of the president's displeasure. The defeat of all efforts to establish organizational bulwarks against Communist advance was persuasive argument in favor of going along with the tide.

One indication that elite resistance was moderating was the change in the political stance of the astute foreign minister, Subandrio. Previously he had been the target of considerable PKI disapproval because he opposed a too prominent role for the Communists; by early 1964, however, he had begun to collaborate with the party and to echo its radical themes. Capital insiders hyopthesized that Subandrio, angling for the presidential succession, had concluded that, with the army strongly opposed to his claim, it made sense to go along with Sukarno in accepting the PKI as the wave of the future.

Subandrio was not alone in drawing the conclusion that, given Sukarno's partiality, the political odds were on the side of the Communists in their contest for supremacy with the army. But at the same time it is doubtful that the PKI had succeeded in winning wholehearted endorsement from any sizeable segment of the elite. The barriers of status and social outlook that divided the Communist leaders from the power-holders were formidable. Daniel Lev has admirably described some of the elements involved:

Unlike the PNI, the PKI was truly an ideological party; and, unlike Masjumi and the NU, its ideology was unquestionably modern. In this, and its obvious concern for popular social and economic interests, the PKI was able to extend its appeal beyond a simple *aliran* context. The PKI therefore threatened not only the other parties but the entire traditional elite. It has been mentioned that this elite is an ascriptive one, a main threat to whose position would appear to be the growth of a forceful egalitarianism. In fact, however, the elite escaped this threat partly by adopting egalitarian ideological symbols. Thus there developed the contradiction that while Indonesian ideology often appears to be radical, the social reality of Indonesia—the very elite which articulates the radical ideology—is decidedly conservative.[12]

Throughout the Aidit period, the PKI leaders had been obliged, in the interests of their own protection, to refrain from puncturing the radical pretensions of the elite (or at least the part of it that participated in the Guided Democracy dispensation). Thus they avoided the disparagement of whole parties or politically significant groups as distinct from the openly anti-Communist elements within them. But the party's propaganda and activity amply demonstrated its own more genuine social radicalism. The PKI's national front policies and repeated assurances that all genuine revolutionaries and patriots would share power under the Communists' formula for a people's democracy were designed in part to still elite fears about the party's intentions and secure the cooperation of as many important groups and individuals as possible.

The escalation of PKI pressure on office-holders in 1964, however, made it more difficult for the latter to escape their dilemmas. Nasakom began to appear less a device and symbol for domesticating the PKI than a drastic political rearrangement. Communist reassurances paled beside the vehemence of their political campaigning and the mass pressure techniques they used to implement them. Sharpness was thus added to the impression PKI statements had long given that

---

[12] *The Transition to Guided Democracy*, p. 10. See also the same author's "Political Parties in Indonesia," *Journal of Southeast Asian History*, VIII, no. 1 (March 1967), 52–67.

the political incumbents had performed less than adequately and that only the PKI itself possessed the fully correct policies for the nation and the expertise, integrity, and disinterested national and social concern to carry them out.

Few among the political elite could deceive themselves that the PKI, once it had its foot in the door, would forever be content with a modest or equal partnership in power. Just as those established in office had sought to treat the PKI leaders very much as junior and inferior allies, so could the latter be expected, should they get the opportunity, to try and reduce alternative centers of power; and the PKI was harder, less permeable, and more self-sufficient than those holding office. The experience of established Communist states amply confirmed this prospect. It followed also from the markedly different social and political perceptions of the two forces. The elite, despite the many conflicts within it, possessed its common code, derived from similar backgrounds and cultural traits and the shared experience of ruling; similarly the Communists had an exclusive ideological credo, a sense of mission, and a set of experiences that bound them together and defined their identity as against outsiders.

While Sukarno pressed on in pursuit of his goal of integrating the PKI into the system over which he presided, it appeared to many elite members that, intentionally or not, he was going dangerously close to handing the party the keys to power. Their difficulty was to find any effective way of opposing the accelerating trend in political life without risking their immediate futures. Caught between the pressures from two outsider groups, the army and the Communists, both possessing distinct organizational identities and ambitions, the civil authorities were largely incapable of influencing the course of events and dependent upon the president's directions.

Despite their more concentrated resources and relative autonomy vis-a-vis the president, the army leaders also faced awkward problems in making their opposition to Sukarno's policies politically effective. By the end of 1964, Nasution, Jani, and most other senior generals were cured of whatever enthusiasm for confrontation they had earlier felt by its military ineffectiveness and the political benefits it had brought the PKI. Most of them were deeply disillusioned by the drift of Sukarno's international policies and alarmed by the extent of his collaboration with the PKI. They had lent encouragement and support to anti-Communist movements and actions, but they were unable to prevent the president's proscription of the Body for Promoting Sukarnoism (BPS) or his imposition of sanctions upon those who publicly defied his Nasakom prescriptions.

The army leaders did their best to protect those who fell foul of the president on the Communist issue and assured anti-Communists that in a showdown the army could be counted on to prevent a PKI assumption of power. The problem for them, however, was whether they could count on a showdown at all. Sukarno and the PKI were taking care to move in ways that were outside recognized army prerogatives, and the president's charismatic hold on some senior officers (especially those of ethnic Javanese origin) was strong enough to make any concerted army defiance of his will unlikely. So long as he lived, therefore, the army faced enormous difficulties in passing from obstruction of his policies to decisive counteraction. If there was a line beyond which the generals would not permit the Communists to advance, at this time it was by no means clear either where it lay or how it would be drawn.

THE RADICAL OFFENSIVE, JANUARY-SEPTEMBER

Whatever the ultimate effects of growing political polarization might be, the president and the PKI held the political initiative at the beginning of 1965, and they were not slow to use it to speed up their radicalizing efforts and to discomfort their opponents. In international affairs, the first months of the new year brought Sukarno's shock decision to quit the United Nations and a series of meetings between Indonesian and Chinese government leaders which cemented their alliance, opened prospects of military cooperation, and laid down plans for advancing the cause of the new emerging forces.

On the domestic front, the PKI opened the year with a propaganda offensive against capitalist bureaucrats, corruptors, reactionaries in official posts, and the residues of United States economic, political, and cultural influence. While turning the heat on its enemies in this manner, the party also made more demonstrable efforts to create the impression of an irresistible tide in its favor. The highlight of this endeavor was the ambitious program of celebrations for the party's anniversary in April and May. Surpassing in scope and conspicuous display all previous occasions of the kind, the celebrations were described in retrospect by a PKI functionary as "giving the impression that Indonesia was already a people's democracy."[13]

Indicative of the leaders' bolder stance was their public acknowledgment of previously undisclosed sympathizers. To some extent, the party overreached itself. Its much vaunted "Long March" of supporters through Java was reported to have been something of a failure, possibly owing to the caution induced among its followers by Moslem reactions to the land reform campaign;[14] on the other hand, the celebrations in the capital appear to have been rather too successful, in that they aroused so much resentment from the PNI that the Communist leaders were obliged, for the sake of unity, to help that party make its anniversary junkets an equal success.[15]

From early in 1965, two specific groups emerged as the major targets of Sukarno-PKI campaigns: right wing elements in the political parties, and the army leadership. The offensive on the party front opened with the president's unexpected decision, announced on January 6, to suspend the operations of the Murba Party.[16]

Leaders and associates of Murba had been under severe attack from the PKI for some time. Their prominent role in several anti-Communist sorties during the previous year, including the BPS, their links with anti-Sukarnoist officers, their defense of American film imports, and their alleged machinations with Soviet officials had all drawn the party's fire. The PKI's response had been to single out Malik and Saleh,[17] ministers, respectively, of trade and basic industries, for special attention in its campaigns against rising price levels.

Murba leaders had laid themselves open to more specific attack on at least two occasions. Sukarni, chairman of the party, in a speech in Surabaja early in December, had made some tactless remarks about Sukarno's role that were eagerly seized upon by the PKI and other opponents of Murba.[18] And at the Bogor conference in mid-December

[13] Interview with "N," Nov. 1968.

[14] See the articles by Australian journalist Frank Palmos in *The Sydney Morning Herald*, Sept. 24, Oct. 5, 7, 8, and 12, 1965.

[15] Interview with "N."

[16] *Harian Rakjat*, Jan. 7, 1965; see also the favorable comment in the editorial of Jan. 8.

[17] Saleh was not in fact a member of Murba, but he had been generally identified with its personnel and policies.

[18] See *Harian Rakjat*, Dec. 7, 1964; *Suluh Indonesia*, Dec. 8, 1964.

Saleh had quoted from a document purporting to outline PKI plans to gain power by 1970 and, according to a public statement by Aidit after the ban on Murba, had been obliged to apologize later for disseminating a forgery.[19]

Why Sukarno chose this time to suspend Murba, when he might just as easily have done so at the time he banned the BPS, is not clear. Subandrio's influence may have lain behind the anti-Murba move, as he is reported to have supplied Sukarno with information purporting to show U.S. Central Intelligence Agency influence behind the BPS.[20] In any case, the vigor of PKI campaigning notwithstanding, the action against Murba represented for Sukarno a significant break with past ties; it was, accordingly, a suggestive pointer to the strength of his determination to put down opposition to his plans to bring the PKI into the central state power apparatus.

Malik and Saleh had been close to the president during the crisis of constitutional democracy in the late fifties, when they had been the most fervent and radical supporters of his antiparty concepts and had acted as his lieutenants in gathering support for the *konsepsi*. Under Guided Democracy they had formed part of the president's inner entourage and had occupied a succession of influential posts in the government and diplomatic corps. Even now, Sukarno declined to put them down utterly; Malik and Saleh were retained in the cabinet, though demoted in the reshuffle of March.[21] But he had signaled their decline and let loose upon them the full force of the PKI's wrath.

The weeks and months following the suspension of Murba resounded with demands for the dismissal of the Murba ministers, the expulsion of members of the party from the Journalists Association and other official and semiofficial bodies, the closure of newspapers sympathetic to it, and the expunging of every vestige of the party from public life. PKI language seemed inordinately violent in view of the fact that PKI-Murba relations had been very fluid in earlier years, with particular individuals being known as sympathizers of both. The "Trotskyites," the party charged, were imperialist agents, lackeys of

[19] *Harian Rakjat,* Jan. 22, 1965.

[20] Sukarno made this charge publicly in February; see *Harian Rakjat,* Feb. 24, 1965.

[21] The PKI welcomed the cabinet changes while noting that they were not radical; *Harian Rakjat,* April 1, 1965.

the bureaucratic capitalists, provocateurs and slanderers of the worst kind, with a long record of treachery behind them.[22] The PKI's belief that Murba, the Soviet Union, and army officers were collaborating against it may go far to explain the intensity of the vituperation. Ultimately, in September, Sukarno gave the seal of approval to the anti-Murba campaign by banning the party altogether.

The operation against Murba proved preliminary to an attack on a more deeply entrenched reservoir of anti-PKI sentiment in the party system. Although the National Governing Board of the PNI, led by Ali Sastroamidjojo and Surachman, had played the Nasakom game faithfully, despite private reservations on the part of Ali and other central leaders of the party, it had faced strong opposition from the dominant faction in the Central Java party apparatus, led by Hadisubeno Sosrowerdojo. The longstanding grievances against the PKI felt by Central Java PNI leaders as a result of the Communist erosion of PNI grassroots support in the province had been intensified by the land reform struggle, and the provincial leaders made little secret of their antagonism toward the central officers for their participation in Sukarno's efforts to curb anti-Communist sentiment. Moreover, they had active support in Djakarta from a determinedly anti-Communist group around former Deputy Prime Minister Hardi.

The president had more than once expressed his impatience with the PNI leaders for their lack of radicalism and loss of mass backing. In mid-1965, in tune with his more insistent demands for ideological conformity and the extirpation of Communist-phobia, he put pressure on the PNI Central Governing Board to purge Hadisubeno, Hardi, and their supporters, and they were expelled early in August, to loud PKI applause.[23] If it is true, as PKI Politburo member Sudisman alleged at his trial in 1967, that army leaders met in June 1965 with PNI leaders in a vain attempt to secure the latter's cooperation in blocking the growth of PKI influence, this may well have triggered Sukarno's counteraction.[24] The expelled group attempted to establish

[22] See for example Aidit's report to the PKI Central Committee, *Harian Rakjat,* May 12–14, 1965.

[23] See the *Harian Rakjat* editorial of Aug. 7, 1965.

[24] Sudisman claimed that the meeting took place on June 8, 1965, at the home of Chairul Saleh.

a rival right wing PNI, based in Central Java,[25] and reportedly gained the sympathy of some army leaders, including General Nasution, and civilian politicians concerned about the direction of Sukarno's policies.[26] Hardi himself told a Western correspondent at the time that he had been assured that the army would act in time to crush the PKI.[27]

The action taken against Murba and the right wing faction of the PNI broke up the last major legitimate bases of opposition to the PKI within the secular parties, and the president indicated that he also desired the purification of the NU leadership. But Sukarno was either unable or unwilling to aid the PKI in its campaign against the most activist anti-Communist force within the organized Islamic grouping, the student body HMI. In all probability the strength of Moslem antipathy to the Communists, as revealed during and after the land reform campaign, led Sukarno to hesitate to stir up a religious hornets' nest. In any case, both he and the PKI were more concerned about weakening the lynchpin that supported all anti-Communist blocks—the army leadership.

The PKI Politburo in its 1965 New Year message had designated as the first and primary task of the party, "the crushing of the capitalist bureaucrats."[28] The slogan was a highly flexible one. It was often used to attack economic deficiencies and malpractices and all officials allegedly responsible for them. But its main utility, especially in this period, was as a euphemism with which to indict army leaders for their *political* activities in opposition to Sukarno and the PKI. Thus the New Year message referred to the new alliance between "the imperialists, capitalist bureaucrats, and the Trotskyists" that had been formed in 1964 and that aimed "to convert the contradictions between the Indonesian people and the imperialists into a contradiction

[25] Daniel S. Lev, "Indonesia: The Year of the Coup," *Asian Survey*, VI, no. 2 (Feb. 1966), 104.

[26] Michael Van Langenberg, "The September 30 Movement: The Contradictions" (unpublished B.A. Honours Thesis, Sydney University, 1967), citing the researches of an unnamed scholar.

[27] I am indebted for this information to Mr. Huib Hendrikse, correspondent of *Trouw* (Amsterdam), who interviewed Hardi during an assignment in Indonesia in August-September 1965 and kindly read me his field notes.

[28] *Harian Rakjat*, Jan. 1, 1965.

among the Indonesian people themselves" by pursuing a policy of anti-Communism "disguised as 'Pantjasilaism' and 'Sukarnoism,' intriguing for the dissolution of parties, spreading slanders that the PKI intended to seize power, stressing the 'dangers of Communism' in view of President Sukarno's failing health, etc."[29] To anyone familiar with the political controversies of the previous year, it was obvious that the PKI was here striking at the collaboration between generals of the high command and right wing politicians, principally the Murba Party leaders.

The PKI stuck to this theme with vigorous persistence and mounting pitch in the months that followed, accompanying it with accusations that army-supported newspapers had spread slanders against the PKI, were undermining the National Front, were expressing peasant-phobia, etc. In the Politburo statement on the occasion of the PKI's forty-fifth anniversary in May, the "bureaucratic capitalists" were directly charged with preparing a coup, and this charge was repeated early in September.[30] Whatever the basis for this allegation (a subject to which we will return), the PKI appeared to be alarmed by persistent rumors that the army was preparing to use force against it and to be attempting to inhibit such action by public exposure.

The party was relying on official measures, backed up with mass pressure, to erode the army's strength as it had eroded that of other anti-Communist bodies. As the Politburo's anniversary statement, echoing Aidit's analytical formulations of 1963, put it,

The strength of the pro-people's aspect [of the state power] is already becoming steadily greater and holds the initiative and the offensive, while the anti-people's aspect, although moderately strong, is being relentlessly pressed into a tight corner. The PKI is struggling so that the pro-people's aspect will become still more powerful and finally dominate, and the anti-people's aspect will be driven out of the state power. . . . The struggle of the revolutionary Indonesian people is carried out by combining people's revolutionary mass actions from below with revolutionary actions by the bodies of the state power from above.[31]

What this meant in practice, so far as the army was concerned,

29 *Ibid.*
30 *Ibid.*, May 7, Sept. 4, 1965.
31 *Ibid.*, May 7, 1965.

was by that time clear. In a radio speech on January 14, Aidit had mentioned that during a meeting with Sukarno and other Nasakom leaders that afternoon he had proposed that, in response to the threat of British attack over the Malaysia issue, the Indonesian government should arm the workers and peasants. "President Sukarno laughed," Aidit told his listeners, "and nodded his head." He added, with what must surely have been intended irony so far as the army was concerned, "I am absolutely certain that our Armed Forces will be only too happy to train workers and peasants in the use of weapons."[32]

The PKI had, as has been mentioned, made this proposal many times before, but the army had been able to restrict intensive military training outside its ranks to relatively small numbers of civilians, generally considered by it to be politically reliable. But whereas on previous occasions the party had kept its agitation in a low key, knowing that there was no immediate prospect of its proposal being adopted, Aidit's broadcast on this occasion was to prove the beginning of a major drive against the army's bastion; this time associated demands were to be made for the establishment of a "fifth force" and the Nasakomization of the armed forces by the attachment to territorial commands of political advisers from the three ideological streams.

The crucial reason why the issue of arming PKI supporters was now being taken seriously was, of course, that this time it had the president's tacit blessing. Aidit would hardly have revealed the content of palace discussions on such a delicate matter without Sukarno's approval. As a matter of fact, Sukarno was later to state that the proposal for a fifth force had first been suggested to him by Chinese Premier Chou En-lai.[33] China's close interest in the scheme is confirmed by the fact that a long series of Chinese delegations to Djakarta in 1965 made repeated reference to the importance of an armed militia for all nations engaged in anti-imperialist struggle.[34]

Judging from the pattern of previous political ploys initiated by the president and the Communist leaders, Sukarno had given the PKI the task of mobilizing public support behind the fifth force demand so that he could later enter the lists in response to mass opinion. Ac-

[32] *Review of Indonesia,* XII (Feb. 1965), 1–2.

[33] *Suluh Indonesia,* June 2, 1965.

[34] See, for example, the reports of speeches by members of a delegation from the Chinese People's Congress; *Harian Rakjat,* Aug. 7–10, 1965.

cordingly, the president contented himself at first with guarded pronouncements to the effect that "the workers and peasants will be
armed if necessary."[35] The PKI for its part went to its task with a
will, and within a short time resolutions and declarations supporting
the idea of a fifth force were flooding in to the president. At first they
came from the PKI's own mass organizations, but the snowball effect,
combined with the PKI's increased leverage within such official organizations as the National Front and the Journalists Association,
gave them a more representative flavor.

On June 1, at a meeting with members of the National Defense
Institute, Sukarno urged the territorial commanders to give serious
consideration to the fifth force proposal.[36] If this was the president's
way of provoking dissension within the armed forces, it was not without results. In the context of a full-blown press controversy over the
issue, waged mainly between PKI-leaning newspapers and the army-
controlled publications, pressure was exerted on political and military
figures to declare their positions. Most of them took a cautious attitude, though none was prepared openly to oppose a project which
the president seemed to be favoring.[37] At the same time, a cleavage
opened up between the army and the other services. On behalf of the
army, General Jani declared that the matter of a fifth force was entirely up to the president to decide.[38] Air Force Commander Omar
Dhani, on the other hand, gave the proposal immediate and unequivocal endorsement, declaring that he agreed with the presidential inspiration.[39] Omar Dhani accompanied his endorsement with other
actions profoundly distasteful to the army: Marxism would be taught
in the air force staff and command school, he announced, and AURI
(Air Force) units in the provinces could on their own initiative com-
mence receiving instruction in Marxism from non-AURI people.[40]
A short time later he gave an assurance that the air force had no
objections whatever to Nasakom advisers being placed in its ranks.[41]

---

[35] *Harian Rakjat,* Feb. 12, 1965.

[36] *Suluh Indonesia,* June 2, 1965.

[37] See, for example, the guarded statements of Ali Sastroamidjojo and
other political party leaders; *Harian Rakjat,* June 26, 1965.

[38] *Harian Rakjat,* June 14, 1965.

[39] *Warta Bhakti,* June 5, 1965.

[40] *Ibid.*

[41] *Antara,* June 23, 1965.

His commitment was more than verbal; in the following month groups of volunteers, many of them from PKI organizations, began to receive weapons training at Halim air force base near Djakarta.

Admiral Eddy Martadinata, the naval chief, also declared for the fifth force in mid-June, however ambiguously. He described it as "a positive question in revolutionary development."[42] Later the same month, he became the first service head to pay a formal visit to Aidit at PKI headquarters, where he repeated his endorsemnt of the proposal.[43]

It seemed in fact that the patient efforts of Sukarno and the PKI to capitalize on the rivalry between the army and the other services were beginning to pay handsome political dividends. Despite Jani's officially noncommittal stance, it was known that army leaders were vehemently opposed to the idea of a fifth force, but their opposition was being undercut by support from the other forces. It is doubtful that the army feared any immediate military danger from the proposal, since the building up of an effective challenger to the army would have taken a considerable time; but if, as seemed likely, the PKI were to obtain significant influence in the new force, then a leftist influence would be admitted into joint services representation on official bodies, which would aid Sukarno's efforts to erode army domination of the other services.[44]

With the army leaders on the defensive, Sukarno proceeded to apply more pressure on them in his Independence Day address on August 17. In the course of a scathing attack on "corruptors and swindlers of the state wealth," he went out of his way to denigrate high-ranking army leaders by accusing them of luxurious living and reactionary attitudes:

Those who were progressive yesterday are possibly retrogressive, anti-progressive today; those who were revolutionary yesterday are possibly

---

[42] *Harian Rakjat,* June 18, 1965.

[43] *Warta Bhakti,* June 25, 1965. It was said at the time that Martadinata's stand on the fifth force was the price he had to pay for Sukarno's help in extricating him from a difficult position occasioned by a "rebellion" of junior navy officers in Surabaja earlier in the year. For a brief comment on the Surabaja episode, see McVey, "Indonesian Communism and China," p. 282 and n. 35.

[44] I am indebted to Ruth T. McVey for drawing my attention to this significant aspect of the proposal.

counter-revolutionary today; those who were radical yesterday are possibly soft and resistless today. Therefore, sisters and brothers, let none of us pride ourselves only on our past services. I am disgusted with that old rubbish! It makes me sick! Even if you were formerly a bald-headed general in 1945, but if you split revolutionary national unity today, if you create disorder in the Nasakom front now, if you are an enemy of the main pillars of the revolution today, then you have become a force of reaction!

Having thus provided more grist for the PKI's mill and catered for popular resentment against high-living officers, Sukarno then fore-shadowed an early decision on the fifth force:

People have lately been heatedly discussing the idea I launched [sic] about a Fifth Armed Force. . . . I feel grateful for all the support that has been given to my idea. We always have to begin with the facts. The facts are that the Nekolim are levelling their sword points and their gun barrels at us. The facts are that the defence of the State demands a maximum of effort from us all while, according to Article 30 of our 1945 Constitution, "Every citizen shall have the right and the duty to participate in the defence of the State." After an even more thorough consideration of this question, I will take a decision on this matter in my capacity as Supreme Commander of the Armed Forces. . . . The Armed Forces of the Republic of Indonesia will form an invincible power if they unite with the people like fish in water. Remember—water can exist without fish, but fish cannot exist without water. Integrate with the people because the armed services of the Republic of Indonesia are revolutionary armed services. The defence of the Revolution is the de-fence of the People. The armed services of the Republic of Indonesia must become the core of this noble defence, but with islands as numerous as ours, a coastline as long as ours, air space as vast as ours, we cannot maintain the sovereignty of our State without a people who, if necessary, are also armed—the people, workers and farmers and other groups, who continue to work in the productive sector but who, if necessary, also bear arms.[45]

The implication of Sukarno's speech was that his decision on the the fifth force would be a favorable one. The noose appeared to be tightening around the army's neck, and on September 27 General Jani broke a long public silence on the issue by stating the military's

[45] Sukarno, *Reach to the Stars!* (Djakarta, 1965).

firm opposition both to the fifth force and to the Nasakomization of the armed forces.[46] There the matter rested, the abortive coup and successful countercoup a few days later rendering all further consideration of the issue superfluous.

The months of August and September, during which the battle between the PKI and the army was being fiercely waged, had been ushered in by an event that caused uncertainty and alarm. On August 6 Sukarno suffered an attack of some kind, and official circles buzzed with rumors of his possible demise. Aidit was summoned home urgently from China, where he had arrived in the course of several weeks' overseas touring, ostensibly to help in the preparation of the president's Independence Day address. Despite his quick recovery, the president's attack set the capital ablaze with premonitions. The contending political forces were brought face to face with the fragile nature of the prevailing balance of power and the imminence with which they might have to meet a sudden crisis situation.

It is reasonable to assume that from this time onward, the PKI and army leaders hastened their separate preparations for such an eventuality. PKI leaders are reported to have been in a state of high tension in the succeeding weeks, sleeping at different addresses from night to night and taking other precautions for their safety.[47] Aidit dropped some hints that he anticipated some kind of a showdown. In a speech to party cadres in Djakarta on the occasion of the twentieth anniversary of national independence, he made what appears in retrospect a significant comment on the need for readiness on the part of the Communists in the capital:

> Reflect on the fact that twenty years ago the Communists and other revolutionaries in Greater Djakarta took a passive attitude toward the matter of the defeat of the Japanese fascists in World War II. . . . The vanguard position of the Djakarta Communists must be firmly adhered to by taking a more active and serious part in implementing Central Committee instructions.[48]

Ten days later he was reported as saying:

[46] *Mertju Suar,* Oct. 24, 1965.

[47] Arthur Dommen, "The Attempted Coup in Indonesia," *The China Quarterly,* no. 25 (Jan.–March 1966), 156.

[48] *Harian Rakjat,* Aug. 21, 1965.

The blows that have recently been delivered on an increasing scale to the counterrevolutionary forces are only one warning to the adventurers that if they try to oppose the current of the popular masses they will not destroy the Indonesian people but instead will themselves be cast into oblivion.[49]

The army leaders, for their part, are said to have been meeting regularly at General Jani's house to discuss developments.[50] As far back as March, General Ibrahim Adjie, commander of the Siliwangi Division, had been quoted by two American journalists as saying of the Communists: "We knocked them out before [at Madiun]. We check them and check them again." The same journalists claimed to have information that "in still another move to protect its political rear, the Army has quietly established an advisory commission of five general officers to report to General Jani, the Chief of Staff and General Nasution, the most prestigious military officer in the country, on PKI activities."[51] During the year the army had also moved to fill the vacuum created by the outlawing of anti-Communist newspapers associated with the BPS by establishing new press organs under its own patronage. These provided a steady counter to PKI propaganda and, according to the PKI, had revived the bogey of Madiun in late August.[52] Rumors were rife that a "generals' council" had been formed to foil the PKI, if necessary by staging a coup.[53]

The tension infected a political atmosphere already highly charged with insecurity, bitterness, and hyperexcitement. The economy had taken another turn for the worse, owing partly to expectations of a poor harvest but more especially to hoarding and speculative pressures reflecting political anxieties. The price of rice quadrupled between June 30 and October 1,[54] and the blackmarket price of the

---

[49] *Ibid.*, Aug. 31, 1965.

[50] Dommen, p. 157.

[51] *Bangkok World,* March 28 and 31, 1965. Quoted in Schmeits, pp. 210–11.

[52] *Harian Rakjat,* Sept. 1, 1965.

[53] The "advisory commission" mentioned above may have been one inspiration for these rumors. It is possibly significant that the number of generals involved (seven) corresponds with the number made the target of the October 1 plotters. On the other hand, so many varied accounts of the "generals' council" have appeared that it is unsafe to push this speculation too far.

[54] Frederick Bunnell, "Indonesia's Quasi-Military Regime," *Current History,* LII, no. 305 (Jan. 1967), 23.

dollar skyrocketed, particularly in September. Against this background, the PKI brought its campaign against corruptors and bureaucratic capitalists to a crescendo, mounting frequent and aggressive demonstrations and demands for retooling across the country and placarding the cities, towns, and villages with violent slogans and caricatures calling for the crushing of the people's enemies and death to corruptors. By late September the party was naming economic "criminals" (including one army captain) and demanding public executions.

Anti-Communist organs responded with equal vehemence; in the provinces frequent clashes broke out along a line of shifting alliances between PKI, PNI, and Moslem youth groups and some army groups.[55] Coup rumors came thicker and faster.

Foreign observers in Indonesia at this time were struck by the atmosphere of crisis, bordering on hysteria, that prevailed.[56] The hypocrisy with which many officials and politicians had formerly espoused the idea of Nasakom unity was wearing thin, and little coaxing was required to reveal the violently polarized attitudes of the politicized segments of the population. Javanese soothsayers, traditional harbingers of crisis and dynastic change, were announcing imminent cataclysm.

THE DESTRUCTION OF THE PKI

The denouement, when it came, lacked the clearcut lines of a PKI-army clash on which speculation had been concentrated. In the early hours of the morning of October 1, a small force of rebel armed forces officers, operating out of Halim air force base on the outskirts of Djakarta, organized the kidnap and murder of six generals of the high command and the seizure of a number of key points in the capital. They broadcast their intention of establishing a Revolution Council to take charge of the country on an interim basis in order to safeguard President Sukarno's policies from the machinations of a treacherous secret generals' council. Before the day was out, however,

[55] References to these disturbances, and efforts to avoid or control them, may be found in *Suluh Indonesia*, June 3, 1965, and *Warta Bhakti*, June 5, 13, 15, 20, 22, and 27, 1965.

[56] See, for example, Palmos' reports in *The Sydney Morning Herald* and the series of articles by Huib Hendrikse in *Trouw*.

the head of the army's strategic command, General Suharto, had put the rebel forces to flight and brought the capital under control. With the failure of the Djakarta initiative, similar ventures in several cities of Central Java also collapsed.[57]

In the immediate aftermath of the coup attempt, the capital was in a state of shock. Rumors and lurid reports relating to the affair swept the city, and those who had in any way expressed sympathy for the September 30 Movement, as the group responsible for the coup attempt had styled itself, sought to extricate themselves from identification with it. At the same time, there developed a sharp conflict between Sukarno and the army leaders, headed by Suharto, as to how the affair should be interpreted and the problems created by it resolved. Sukarno, who had been at Halim on the day of the coup, sought to limit the army's victory and protect the groups and individuals closest to him in outlook by minimizing what he termed a mere incident in the revolution and seeking to restore the status quo ante.[58]

In all probability, Sukarno had admonished those remaining at Halim while Suharto's net was closing on them to leave it to him to sort out the mess left by the abortive action and to aid his attempts by maintaining an atmosphere of calm in the country. At any rate, Aidit, who was also present in the vicinity of the coup group headquarters until late on the night of October 1, appears to have devoted the following weeks to a frantic effort to reassure the party following in Central Java and urge them to refrain from provoking the army and anti-Communist groups. Njoto and Lukman, who had both been out of Djakarta on the day of the coup bid, appeared as usual at the cabinet meeting on October 6 and, taking their cue from Sukarno, disowned the affair and denied any party involvement.[59]

On the day previous to the cabinet meeting, the PKI Politburo issued a statement giving direction to the party in the new situation. The statement opened by declaring the PKI's support for the guidelines laid down by Sukarno for solving the problem and called on all members and followers to help carry out the terms of the president's

[57] A brief outline of the main incidents connected with the October 1 affair is contained in Appendix A below.

[58] See, for example, his remarks to the October 6 cabinet meeting, reported in John Hughes, *The End of Sukarno* (London, 1968), pp. 122–29.

[59] *Ibid.,* pp. 128–29.

message. Ignoring a *Harian Rakjat* editorial of October 2 that had supported the September 30 Movement and reports of participation by PKI youth and women's auxiliaries in the coup, the statement said that the affair was "an internal problem of the army and the PKI does not involve itself in it." Like all others named to the Revolution Council, the PKI representatives were said to have been included without their knowledge or endorsement.[60]

But the generals, incensed by the murder of their colleagues, and in all probability seriously alarmed by the ramifications of the coup attempt, were determined to thwart the president's efforts to pass lightly over the matter and to punish their enemies dearly for their actions. This was their opportunity to destroy once and for all the forces lying behind the current dangerous tendencies in political life. According to a Western reporter on the spot, word was passed to Moslem anti-Communist groups during the funeral of General Nasution's small daughter on October 7 that a sweep of the Communists should begin; thereupon mobs in Djakarta began to destroy and burn PKI buildings and houses. In the following days, amidst reports that the Chinese Embassy had refused to lower its flag for the funeral of the six generals and rumors that China had played a part in the coup plot, the razzia extended to the shops, homes, and persons of Indonesians of Chinese descent.[61]

The campaign against the PKI and the Chinese was inflamed by frequent television broadcasts of gruesome pictures of the murdered generals, highly colored press accounts of the events of October 1, and a rising stream of anti-Communist propaganda. Most damaging to the PKI were reports that Pemuda Rakjat and Gerwani members who were receiving military training at Halim had participated in the coup and taken part in the brutal and reportedly orgiastic killings at Luang Buaja.

Although Sukarno insisted on devising a political solution to the crisis, and forbade punitive action, the army moved on its own initiative to ban PKI activities, arrest Communists and suspects, and suspend members of the party holding official positions.[62] On October 17, the army's para commando force, under the command of Colonel

[60] *Indonesia,* no. 1 (April 1966), 188–89.
[61] Hughes, pp. 132–37.
[62] *Ibid.,* pp. 137–40; Dommen, pp. 152–53.

Sarwo Edhie, was ordered into Central Java to "clean up" the deeply divided province, in view of the reported unreliability of a great part of the Diponegoro Division. A ruthless campaign of extermination of Communists and alleged Communists was inaugurated in Central Java and quickly spread to East Java and other provinces. Most accounts agree that the army triggered the massacres that took place in Indonesia in the following months, but in most places it enlisted the aid of Moslem and other anti-Communist youth groups, who probably accounted for the greater part of the death toll.[63]

Varying assessments of the number of people killed in the anti-Communist hurricane have been made, but actual figures will probably never be known.[64] As time has passed, however, the tendency has been to enlarge rather than lower the estimates, so that at present there is a disposition among Western scholars to accept a figure of between half a million and one million. It is generally agreed that, particularly in East Java and Bali where, in proportion to the population, the death toll appears to have been heaviest, communal tensions exacerbated by the land reform conflicts of 1964–65 and other political feuds go far to explain the scale of the slaughter. Until studies of the episode are made at the village and small town levels, however, the nature of what was involved will not be fully understood.

As the wave of violence swept the country, the Communists remained largely passive and quiescent; only in a few isolated instances did stalwarts in PKI strongholds try to establish some kind of resistance.[65] A dispersed and shattered leadership seems to have lost all capacity to rally the party or cope with the decimation of its ranks. Sticking to the last to the hope that Sukarno would pull their irons out of the fire, the leaders went into hiding and became to all intents and purposes deactivated. Illustrative of the paralysis that afflicted the cadre forces of the party is the following account by a PKI member

---

[63] Hughes, pp. 149–61; Dommen, pp. 150–51; Bunnell, "Indonesia's Quasi-Military Regime," pp. 23–24.

[64] See Hughes, pp. 184–94.

[65] Nugroho Notosusanto and Ismail Saleh, *The Coup Attempt of the "September 30 Movement" in Indonesia* (Djakarta, 1968), pp. 64–65. This semi-official Indonesian account of the coup minimizes PKI resistance; it is similar in vein to those of Hughes, pp. 150–51, and Dommen, p. 150. The account by Arnold Brackman, *Indonesia: The Gestapu Affair* (New York, 1969), pp. 31–32, uses more highly colored language but the substance is not very different.

and wife of a Central Committee functionary of the way she and her husband reacted in the weeks and months following the coup:

> After September 30, we went on with our work for some days in the normal manner, but no one with whom we came in contact was able to inform us as to what had happened or what we were expected to do. As the atmosphere in Djakarta grew worse, we just sat at home and waited for instructions. My husband had been given no guidance about what to do in such an eventuality. We did not expect things to turn out so badly; we thought there would be a setback for the party but that eventually it would be sorted out by Sukarno.
>
> That is why the party disintegrated so rapidly. There were no orders, and no one knew who to turn to or who to trust, since arrests had started and we knew there had been betrayals. . . . [Party leaders] sent word just to wait, and I know that a party leader's wife was sent to see Sukarno.
>
> The arrests started in the second week of October, but we were not touched at that time. My husband was finally arrested on December 20. The circumstances were that ———'s hiding place was betrayed and he came to my husband, who took him somewhere else, but this fact too was betrayed and the reason given for my husband's arrest was that he failed to inform on ———.
>
> Previous to this, we had heard of killings in the provinces, but we had no idea of their extent.[66]

Aidit himself was arrested and summarily executed by the army in Central Java, probably on or about November 22.[67] Njoto and Lukman were taken and slain in the following months. By the end of 1966 all members of the Politburo had been killed or taken prisoner except Adjitorop, who had the good fortune to be in China at the time of the coup attempt and now leads the expatriate PKI group resident in that country.

When, in March 1966, Sukarno lost his stubborn rearguard action against the army and the anti-Communist student groups, who, in the wake of the coup, became the new arbiters of street politics, the PKI was formally banned, along with its affiliates.[68] But the act had little

---

[66] Interview with "X," Nov. 1968.

[67] The exact circumstances and date of Aidit's death are matters of dispute, and no official statement on the matter has ever been made. See the circumstantial account given by Hughes, pp. 162–72.

[68] On the struggle for power between Sukarno, the army, and the students,

more than formal significance—the organization had already been decimated and underground attempts to resuscitate it, repeatedly frustrated by army vigilance and remorselessness, failed to make significant headway.[69]

THE PKI AND THE COUP

The voluminous documentation and literature that have appeared on the October 1 affair are concerned above all with the PKI's role in the affair. The interpretations that have been offered fall into two categories: those that accept the present Indonesian government's case that the coup was masterminded and executed by the PKI leadership, and those that consider the charges against the PKI to be either unproven or plainly misconceived. An evaluation of these interpretations and the evidence offered for each is set out in Appendix B. The conclusion arrived at, on the basis of the available facts, is that the official Indonesian case is suspect and that the genesis of the September 30 Movement is to be sought in the activities of a group of dissident officers of the Diponegoro Division from Central Java. If there was any degree of PKI involvement, a matter about which there is suggestive but far from conclusive evidence, then it was very limited and probably peripheral to the main conspiracy.

This view of the event, based on an analysis of the trial materials that have been released by the Indonesian government and other facts brought to light by independent researchers, is admittedly tentative and does not explain all aspects of the affair. It accords best, however, with the implications to be derived from the ideology and strategy of the PKI as delineated in this study. In the absence of proof one way or the other with regard to the PKI's role in the coup, inductive reasoning based on these considerations is, it is suggested, just as important in arriving at an assessment as the deductions that can be made from the plethora of evidence (frequently inconsistent or contradictory) adduced at the trials.

---

see Donald Hindley, "Indonesian Politics, 1966–67: The September 30 Movement and the Fall of Sukarno," *The World Today*, XXIV, no. 8 (August 1968), 345–56.

[69] For a review of underground PKI activity since 1965, based heavily on official sources but discounting their reliability to some extent, see J. M. Van der Kroef, "Indonesian Communism since the 1965 Coup," *Pacific Affairs*, XLIII, no. 1 (Spring 1970), 34–60.

It has been a constant theme of this book that the PKI sought a peaceful road to power in Indonesia and that this was an aim from which the Aidit leadership never deviated and in pursuit of which it was prepared to exhibit great patience, flexibility, and a willingness to compromise significant elements of orthodox Communist strategic principle. Animated by a nationalist and accommodating spirit, and conscious both of the strength of its foes and the weakness of its own position, the party resolved to stick like a leech to Sukarno and, by a combination of ingratiation and carefully staged pressure, to insert itself into his power structure.

Nothing occurred in 1965 to indicate that the PKI intended to abandon this long-established and trusted strategy. On the contrary, with Sukarno's more decided backing, the party began to move against its opposition in ways that had full presidential and governmental approval. In particular, attempts to break the army's monopoly of the instruments of violence were carefully devised to avoid giving the army leadership any legitimate excuse for resorting to the one form of contest in which it would enjoy an overwhelming advantage over the Communists.

In these circumstances, it seems inconceivable that the PKI should have deliberately chosen to challenge the army on its own ground, especially since the armed units on which the party might hope to rely were immeasurably inferior to those available to the army command. The only circumstance in which such a course would make sense from the PKI's point of view would be if the leadership believed that the army was about to launch a full–scale crackdown against it.[70] The case advanced by the present Indonesian government denies that there was any such imminent threat to the party, and the story put out by the September 30 Movement alleging a planned coup by a "general's council" lacks substance. Still, Aidit *may* have believed the reports of such a plot—may even have been inveigled into believing them—and he may as a consequence have obtained from the PKI Politburo a blank check to encourage or acquiesce in the countermeasures being prepared by rebel units in the armed forces. (This is

---

[70] Sukarno's much discussed illness in early August may be discounted as a serious motivating factor, since he had recovered in ample time for the PKI to adjust its plans.

a possible interpretation of the evidence offered by Sudisman at his trial; see Appendix B.)

The argument is not convincing, however. In view of the PKI's close relations with Sukarno by this time, it is hard to believe that, if Aidit had had what appeared to him good grounds for suspecting the existence of an army conspiracy to strike down the party, he would have failed to seek the president's protection or that, if sought, such protection would not have been forthcoming. It would have been a comparatively simple matter for Sukarno to immobilize the army by placing its leaders under close arrest, retailing to the nation in his inimitable style the basis for his action and stringing out the resolution of the affair while he reorganized the service more to his liking. On past performance, the president would have had relatively little difficulty in winning support for his actions from enough senior officers to ensure success.

There is an alternative hypothesis not entirely inconsistent with Sukarno's style. If Aidit should have informed him not only of the threat posed by the generals' council but also of the officers' cabal to foil it, Sukarno might have decided to let the events come to him, as he had been known to do on previous occasions, counting on his authority to handle the situation and preserving the maximum number of options in any possible outcome. In other words, he could conceivably have told Aidit to keep an eye on events, especially from the rebel angle, take no action to prevent them coming to a head, and leave it to him to gather the strings together at the right moment. Such an explanation would be consistent with Aidit's relationship with the president and also with the purported discretion accorded Aidit by his Politburo. Sukarno would not have been likely to anticipate that his task would be greatly complicated by the summary execution of the captured generals. If some such version of events is credible, it still leaves the role of the PKI as marginal to the coup itself.

In the absence of much more acceptable evidence linking the PKI with the October 1 affair, the conclusions that can be drawn from the basic ideology and strategy of the party, which required above all that it fortify its relationship with the president and keep open the peaceful road that relationship symbolized, remain the most reliable guide to its actions at that time.

THE REPUDIATION OF "AIDITISM"

The debacle suffered by the PKI in the wake of the October 1 affair broke the spell that the party's progress under the Aidit line had cast over the PKI for fifteen years; there followed bitter criticism from survivors inside and outside Indonesia, which had been absent or muted while the organization was profiting from the dexterity of the slain leaders. Two ideological streams became discernible within the remnants of the PKI during 1966 and 1967. The first was represented in Indonesia by a group styling itself the Political Committee of the PKI and reputedly headed, until his arrest in December 1966, by Sudisman, a Politburo member; this group had its counterpart among the expatriates in China led by Politburo member Adjitorop. The second stream, which called itself the Marxist-Leninist Group of the Communist Party of Indonesia, was centered in Moscow and seems to have had little if any organized following inside Indonesia itself. Although the critique of the Aidit period put out by the Moscow-based group followed that of the Sudisman group, it will be more convenient for the purposes of exposition to consider it first.

Given its initial public airing in March 1967,[71] the "Moscow statement" takes its stand on the analysis and strategy outlined by the PKI at its fifth congress in 1954 and, in particular, endorses the concept of the united national front as expounded at the congress. In the course of time, the statement asserts, the PKI diverged from the correct program drawn up at that congress in such a way as to weaken the independent class spirit of the Indonesian Communist movement. It distinguishes as the cardinal theoretical sin of the Aidit leadership the thesis that in the conditions of the Indonesian revolution it was necessary to "subordinate class interests to national interests," a notion which it interprets as substituting a nonclass "Nasakom unity" for the united national front based primarily upon the alliance of the workers and peasants. From this approach flowed the playing down of class struggles, the elevation of the peasant question above that of working class hegemony, and dependence on the national bourgeoisie and its aspirations.

[71] In the pro-Soviet Indian Communist journal *Mainstream* on March 11 and 18.

The document makes much of the ideological degeneration in the PKI that followed its adoption of erroneous theories. It speaks of the leadership of primary party organizations and peasant mass organizations as having been in the hands of rich peasants and nonpeasants; of complacency and lack of vigilance toward the party's enemies; of the party's financial dependence on bourgeois elements; and of mass actions being replaced by negotiation and lawsuits. The leaders are accused of having stifled criticism and initiative from the rank-and-file, practised a personality cult, and allowed decisions to be flouted with impunity. Crucially, it argues that the PKI's dependence on Sukarno and its reliance on nationalist rather than class issues for support, prevented it from combating the rise of the new class of bureaucratic capitalists effectively. In the crisis atmosphere of 1965, the leaders' nerves had failed them and they took "a rash decision to begin preparation for playing the role of 'savior,' with or without President Sukarno and other democratic forces." In this oblique reference to the October 1 affair, the PKI leaders are accused of "muddleheadedness" and "adventuristic fantasies."

The "Moscow statement" is basically correct in defining the main evolution of PKI ideology under Aidit in terms of a shift away from class-based action to nationalist dynamics. Its depiction of the effects on the party, although exaggerated and one-sided, also contains a substantial amount of truth. And in pointing to the dilemma faced by the organization in 1965, when crisis developments threatened to undo the patient work of fourteen years, it is doing no more than emphasizing an obvious fact. But its critique does little justice to the complexity of the problems faced by the Aidit leadership or the dexterity with which the leadership sought to resolve those problems. Still less does it offer a credible alternative to the policies pursued by the Aidit group.

Presumably the Moscow-based critics would argue that the PKI should have continued to follow faithfully the guidelines laid down in 1954. But they ignore the fact that the 1954 program already enshrined the ambivalence regarding the relative importance of the workers and peasants on the one hand, and the national bourgeoisie on the other, in the united national front, and that it failed to provide any clear guidance on the critical issue of how the PKI was to gain hegemony in the front. It is easy to assert that the party should simultaneously have safeguarded its independence, fanned the class struggle, and maintained an alliance with Sukarno and other progressive elements in the national bourgeoisie, if the social and political history of the period is assumed, without analysis, to have permitted this course; such is the case with this document. As the Aidit leadership saw the problem, however, the downgrading of class struggle was demanded by the logic of the party's position, after experiments with industrial agitation in the urban centers had shown such action to be too costly and too threatening to their alliance with Sukarno to be continued. They tried another approach to the same problem with the land reform actions in 1964 (an episode which the document slurs over), only to be beaten back once more. Without a consideration of these experiences, and the environment in which they occurred, the statement merely constitutes a doctrinaire recapitulation of the united national front concept in the form favored by Soviet exegesis.

Until September 1966, much the same comments could be made about the critique of the other surviving PKI group. In fact, in statements issued from Central Java and Albania as late as August 1966,[72] both the PKI underground in Indonesia headed by Sudisman and the Peking expatriates also treated the analysis and prescriptions contained in the 1954 program as valid. They too pointed to a theoretical innovation that epitomized the Aidit leadership's deviation from Marxism-Leninism, but in their case the thesis selected for special castigation was Aidit's concept of the state with two aspects. As the Central Java document puts it,

According to this "two-aspect theory" a miracle could happen in Indonesia. Namely, the state could cease to be an instrument of the ruling oppressor classes to subjugate other classes, but could be made the instrument shared by both the oppressor classes and the oppressed classes. And the fundamental change in state power, that is to say, the birth of a people's power, could be peacefully accomplished by developing the "pro-people" aspect and gradually liquidating the "anti-people aspect."

Again, in strict terms of Marxian theory, the criticism is right to the point, but it offers little insight into the social and political reality the

---

[72] Both statements appear in *Indonesian Tribune* (Tirana), vol. I, no. 1 (Nov. 1966).

PKI had to grapple with. Aidit, it will be recalled, advanced the concept of the state with two aspects only in 1963, and the notion followed on from a whole series of ideological propositions that had been elaborated during the preceding years. It is difficult in these circumstances to regard it as in any way crucial for an understanding of the alternatives available to the party in opening up the road to power.

In the documents of the Sudisman-Peking stream, the baneful influence which had led the PKI on to the wrong path is equated with "modern revisionism," the same charge leveled by the CPC against the CPSU and its attendant Communist parties. Under this influence, the Albanian statement contends, the PKI was steadily transformed into a petty bourgeois body. Leaders and cadres became "bourgeoisified" by their relations with the national bourgeoisie and their positions in governmental and semigovernmental bodies. The party was thrown open to the most diffuse elements in an attempt to impress the national bourgeoisie. Little or no ideological training was given to the party's members. Great concessions were made to nationalist ideology, as formulated by Sukarno, and the party watered down its own theory to conform with this official ideology, in the end arguing that Marxism and Sukarnoism were identical and both could become the property of the whole nation. The organization became bogged down in legalistic and parliamentary forms of struggle.

The itemization of sins is familiar and, allowing once more for the partiality of focus, not too wide of the mark. But the abstract quality of the analysis and its grounding in the 1954 program provide no more of an alternative strategic concept than does the Moscow statement.

From September 1966, however, the Peking expatriates and (as far as can be judged from the paucity of material available) the main centers of PKI underground activity in Indonesia have broken decisively with the fundamental tenets of the Aidit line and gone over to a Maoist strategy based on the necessity under all circumstances to wage armed agrarian revolution. In that month, a statement by the underground roundly denounced Aidit's whole policy as based on parliamentarianism, capitulation to the national bourgeoisie and Sukarno, denial of the class struggle, legalism, and the adoption of a peaceful path to socialism.[73] The nationalist emphases of the Aidit leadership were rejected outright, the document stating that the international struggle against imperialism had ceased to be the main contradiction in Indonesia after the end of the war with the Dutch and had been succeeded by the conflict of interests between the workers-peasants and the compradores, bureaucratic capitalists, and landlords. The PKI should have prepared for and led armed peasant struggle, relying not on an adulterated Indonesianized version of Marxism-Leninism, but on the thought of Mao Tse-tung.

This standpoint at least has the merit of presenting a real alternative to the Aidit ideology. Whether it would have proved any more successful than his strategy in the given conditions is another question. There is no guaranteed invincibility about guerrilla warfare, as the history of the insurrections in Malaya and the Philippines demonstrates. The reasons advanced by Aidit for eschewing such a strategy in Indonesia have a solid ring to them, however the situation may appear in retrospect to persecuted Communists who lack any legal channels of struggle.

It is hard to avoid the impression that the attacks on the Aidit leadership's policies reflect more a psychological reaction to defeat, and the sense of betrayal that goes with a fall so drastic and traumatic, than a considered reappraisal of the leadership's ideology and policies. It is natural, too, that the hunted or exiled Communists should look to one or other of the major founts of their movement's authority for explanations of the debacle and remedies for the future. Given the history of Indonesian Communism, however, this stage of acute ideological dependency is likely to be transcended if and when the PKI manages to regain any semblance of its former organized strength.

[73] "Build the PKI Along the Marxist-Leninist Line to Lead the People's Democratic Revolution in Indonesia," *Indonesian Tribune,* vol. I, no. 3 (Jan. 1967).

Conclusion

Ingenuity and flexibility were the hallmarks of PKI ideology in the period surveyed. These were the cardinal qualities required in circumstances posing formidable problems for the Communists in their quest for survival and political advance; at the same time, the experiences and dispositions of the party's leaders well fitted them to display just these qualities. If the constraints upon the PKI leaders derived essentially from the domestic socio-political framework, so the transcendence of these constraints, in so far as it was achieved, was the product of an uninhibited freedom in adapting Communist ideas to Indonesian conditions.

Once having assumed the leadership of the party, the Aidit group quickly recognized the social and political handicaps they faced in realizing their objectives. They were well aware that, by failing to win the struggle for supremacy during the national revolutionary war, the PKI had not only lost the initiative to the civil and military elites that dominated the postindependence scene but had also suffered debilitation, obliquy, and demoralization. There was no immediate possibility of the party's challenging those in government by root-and-branch opposition, either through industrial-political warfare or armed peasant struggle. Even limited urban militancy was shown to be counterproductive by the experience of August 1951, and the weak links between the party and the peasantry meant that there was no prospect, in the short term, that a base for violent social revolution could be built in the villages.

Having satisfied themselves of their inability to operate successfully outside the bounds of the postindependence political framework, the party's leaders had little choice but to come to terms with both the existing political system and the dominant cultural patterns influencing politics and to work for their transformation from within. What sustained them, and soon gave them an important political opening at the elite level, was their fervent belief that those in power had betrayed the national revolution by failing to eradicate imperialist and feudal influences and that they, the Communists, alone possessed the vision, the program, and the dedication to the goals of complete independence and popular welfare to realize these aims. This belief was based on the leaders' experiences both as national revolutionaries and as Communists and was buttressed by their knowledge that disillusionment with the fruits of independence and frustration over the experience of generating political unity and economic development were leading elements among the political public and the radical nationalist elite to find the Communist outlook attractive. In such circumstances the leadership was ready to take the long view and subordinate the direct struggle for paramountcy to a circuitous strategy with a strongly populist flavor.

Initially, the accent on nationalism was not seen as ruling out class appeals and actions. The PKI leaders viewed the worker-peasant alliance as the cornerstone of their strategy and the strengthening of class consciousness among these strata as essential to the achievement of ultimate political hegemony. But this strengthening had to be achieved slowly and delicately, and in such a way as not to breach the relationship established between the PKI and the PNI, and later between the PKI and the president.

Meanwhile, the main thrust of PKI ideology and activity fortified the party's reliance on nationalism to increase its strength and influence. The implications of this policy, including the supporters won and influence established in pursuing it, made any sharp break with the approach of accommodating and reconciling the "progressive" wing of the elite virtually unthinkable. This was already true by the later stages of the parliamentary period. The demise of that system, and the introduction of the steps leading to Guided Democracy, threw the party's dilemma into stark relief. The prospect of a regime in which army power in the political sphere would be greatly augmented and officially legitimized and in which the PKI's fate would necessarily depend to a large extent on the favor of a willful and unpredictable president shook the confidence of the Communist leaders and provoked the strongest signs of disquiet ever to appear within the higher echelons of the party.

Hardheaded political judgment convinced Aidit and his colleagues, however, that their options were so circumscribed as to be negligible. Sandwiched between the overwhelming Sukarno-army combination on the one side and the anti-Communist rebels on the other, haunted by the recollection of Madiun, and conscious of the dubious reliability of their followers in a crunch for which they had not been prepared by the ideological emphasis of the leadership, they saw no alternative but to adapt to the new distribution of power and recommence the process of probing and penetration that they had undertaken so skillfully in the previous period.

At first, the portents were dismal for the Communists: Sukarno could not fulfill his promise of a *gotong rojong* cabinet; the government swung to the right in 1959, after the substantial defeat of the Outer Islands rebellion; and the army pursued its vendetta against the parties, and above all the PKI, with indefatigable zeal. The leadership felt compelled to try to make the party's presence felt by demonstrations of political opposition and industrial militancy, but the July 1960 showdown faced it with army obduracy and presidential ambivalence such that it was obliged to back down.

Once again the nationalist cause, espoused now with renewed vigor by Sukarno, provided the way out. Just as it had supplied the cement for the PKI-PNI alliance in the fifties and promoted the ousting of the other main political elite grouping, the Masjumi-PSI, so now the cause of nationalism served as the means both of establishing Sukarno's primacy under Guided Democracy and solidifying his relations with the PKI at the expense of the army leaders.

With steadily increasing self-confidence and comprehension of the terms of the political contest, the PKI leaders advanced a set of ideas that oriented the organization behind the nationalist perspective and provided it with specific action directives for expanding the party's strength and influence within this framework. By an adroit exploitation of the formal objectives of the regime, they were able to introduce issues of welfare and economic progress into the ambit of the nationalist crusade and to demonstrate their problem-solving expertise in ways that enhanced their appeal both to the workers and peasants and to elite groups sympathetic to Sukarno. By the latter part of

1963, the party had thrown off the restrictions imposed upon it by the army in the earlier years of Guided Democracy, placed itself in the forefront of the mass movement supporting "Sukarnoism," and laid the basis for a political offensive designed to bring it at least a substantial share in governmental power.

The price exacted by the policies the party had followed in order to reach this position had been considerable. The PKI had been obliged to emphasize the concordance between its objectives and those of Sukarno and to play down its independent role and aims. It had had to mobilize its following within National Front guidelines, avoiding class lines of action and the promotion of class consciousness. It had been compelled to reinforce the pretensions and play down the shortcomings of the "progressive" members of the national elite in the greater interest of avoiding isolation. Even against anti-Communists its agitation had largely had to be confined to issues and limits which its allies would sanction; in the case of the army it had been restricted to oblique and muffled criticism.

So long as the Communists operated within the dominant values set by the society and the regime—nationalist perspectives, consensus politics, and *aliran* forms of representation—their energy paid steady dividends. But after 1963 the party began to move outside these bounds in order to break the deadlock that kept it in the position of junior partner to the elite. Although the radical offensive was cast in nationalist terms and directed toward antiprogressive targets, the PKI's vehemence and new-found militancy indicated to the governing groups that the squeeze was being put on them; their reactions polarized according to their estimates of the intentions of Sukarno and the relative strengths of the major contending factions, the PKI and the army. For their part, the Communists found that their attempt to move beyond National Front and *aliran* politics through stimulation of unilateral peasant actions brought them the same kind of setback as they had suffered earlier, in 1960, when they had sought to use union discontent as a political lever.

Aidit's solution to the problem of gaining access to key power positions, epitomized in the concept of the state with two aspects, was designed to take utmost advantage of the PKI's assets—its formidable resources for mass-mobilization and its close working relationship with Sukarno—and to negate its weaknesses—crucially, the inferiority of its independent resources to those of its opponents, typified by the unsuitability of its following for use as a fighting force and the strength of the army as a counterforce.

The flaw in the strategy lay in the fact that it depended on the will and controlling role of the president. While he remained in command of events and was disposed to use his power to force acceptance of the PKI as a full partner in government, there was always a possibility that the party would gain office. Whether, in these circumstances, office would have been equivalent to power, or capable of being converted into power, is another question. There is no guarantee that, even if Aidit's formula had worked, the PKI would have been able to escape being loaded with a share of governmental responsibility for a failing system while still being subject to the countervailing forces of the army and the politico-bureaucratic incumbents. Office without power would not have been a novel experience for a Communist party, as the early postwar governments of Italy and France and some of the arrangements sponsored by Batista in Cuba serve to recall.

As it was, the matter never came to the test. The underlying premise of Aidit's strategy—that Sukarno's stature would keep political conflict within stable bounds while the PKI pressed its attack on its opponents—proved faulty. It was a considerable gamble, considering the state of the nation in 1965 and the predictable response of the party's opponents to its move to raise the political stakes; and it did not come off. One sudden and presumably unanticipated event was sufficient to bring down the whole ideological construction like a house of cards and expose the PKI's vulnerability to a change in the political balance. Once Sukarno, the lynchpin, was loosened in his place, the independent resources of the PKI were shown to be woefully inadequate to cope with a situation of threat.

Every political strategy, and certainly every revolutionary strategy, requires its fair share of fortune at crucial stages if it is to succeed. And even the most carefully laid plans and calculations are liable to be set at nought by an unpredictable event. If the Aidit program was peculiarly vulnerable, it is by no means clear that it could have been otherwise. In retrospect, the odds seem always to have been against the Communists, even when they were making their greatest advances; that they reached as far as they did, rather than that they failed to grasp their objective, may well be the more significant fact when the capabilities of the party's leaders during this period are assessed.

The destruction of the once vast and omnipresent Communist organization in Indonesia and the ousting of the powerful president who had acted as its patron could not fail to bring about a drastic realignment in Indonesian politics, the scope and implications of which lie outside the ambit of this book. But it is hardly to be expected that a party which in its heyday claimed some twenty million followers and attuned its policies so closely to the climate of the time would not have had a lasting impact, in terms of changed perceptions and attitudes, even though, so far as much of the party's actual membership was concerned, the Communist imprint was probably light and poorly distinguished from the official state ideology. To gauge this impact with any confidence would demand much new research and require a solution to the problem of estimating to what extent and in what ways the long term legacy of Communism would be likely to express itself over time within a substantially altered political environment. Some tentative suggestions may be offered, however, on the basis of the attributes of Communism in Indonesia in the recent past than have been disclosed in the course of our discussion.

One of the principal objects of this book has been to analyze the sources and nature of the very considerable attraction that Communism of the Aidit style had for large numbers of Indonesians during the era of Guided Democracy. The approach has been to investigate the nature of PKI ideology, and it has become abundantly clear in the course of examining these ideas and their implications for action that the meaning they had for those who formulated, received, and acted upon them can only be understood by relating them to the total political process in Indonesia and beyond that to the underlying socio-cultural orientations that moulded this process.

The interaction between PKI ideology and the dominant thrust of Sukarno-style nationalism has been treated in dynamic and dialectical terms to demonstrate the manner in which each reacted upon and transformed the other in the course of an association of some length and intimacy. The PKI's relationship to its cultural environment, however, has been discussed somewhat one-sidedly, with the stress being on the influence that Javanese values in particular exerted on

Communist concepts and perceptions. It is appropriate now, therefore, to examine the value-transforming role of PKI ideology.

The PKI leaders, it has been emphasized, were children of the Japanese occupation and the national revolution that followed it, and for them the tenets of Communism represented not a substitute for the nationalism that fired the struggle for Indonesia's emancipation and self-assertion but the most genuine and advanced form of that nationalism. The personal search for codes of symbolic meaning in an age of flux and social disruption which animated the whole *pemuda* generation was inextricably bound up with a commitment to the revolution and the nation. The future Communist leaders were no exception, as their continuing involvement in the revolutionary nationalist mystique testified. As their acquaintance with and dedication to Communism deepened and took on more disciplined ideological form, and as they assumed the responsibilities of party leadership, they found a solution to the twin problems of individual identity and national destiny in a set of interconnected and role-determining goal orientations, which in turn influenced the outlook of their followers.

Communism appeared to the PKI leaders to offer the most thoroughgoing and satisfying blueprint for the modernization of their society. The major reason Communism attracted them was that it unambiguously repudiated all compromise with the imperialist enemy that they blamed for their national degradation, economic backwardness, and personal frustrations and sufferings. It had moreover given salutory proof of its capacity to transform weak and dependent states into strong and independent ones, particularly in the cases of the U.S.S.R. and China. The young, energetic PKI leaders, unlike many of their older and higher-status nationalist competitors, felt little in the way of attachment to the *djaman normal* of the years before 1942, a period which many nationalists looked back on half-longingly as one of law and order and "standards," as well as of humiliating racist practice, but which the PKI leaders saw exclusively in terms of oppression, degradation, and the stifling of the nation's capacities. Toughminded, practical people that they were, Aidit and his colleagues had concluded from their experience of Dutch and Japanese rule that modern techniques and modern organization spelt strength, while their absence defined weakness. They were scornful of the compromises with imperialism embodied in the 1949 independence settlement and the restorationist policies of early postindependence governments that left power safely in the hands of the men of high Western education who were also the scions of good families. At the party's fifth congress in 1954 they outlined a program that closely followed the current Communist prescriptions for modernization: expulsion of the foreign owner and his influence, industrialization, social revolution and technological development in the countryside, radical renovation of political structures, and obliteration of all forms of backwardness and superstitution.

In later years the PKI leaders considerably modified their approach to the problems of modernization. In place of the Soviet model that had inspired their early programs, they substituted in the period of Guided Democracy concepts that placed greater emphasis on the acquisition of national strength through anti-imperialist resolve and fidelity to the "Indonesian identity." This evolution, as we have seen, coincided with the increasing reliance placed by both Sukarno and the PKI on radical nationalist symbols and campaigns in their struggle for supremacy over rival aspirants to power.

In the course of this reformulation of its political precepts, the PKI's message acquired a more pronounced traditionalist tone, especially in its *abangan* heartland of Central and East Java, where the party had from the outset displayed an accommodating sensitivity toward customary ways. Nevertheless, in comparison with the styles of Sukarno and the political elite, the PKI's ideas retained a decidedly modernist thrust stemming from received Communist doctrine. During the Guided Democracy period (and, arguably, earlier), the PKI could justly be described as the most modern of Indonesian organizations. Alone in the Indonesian political constellation, the Communist leaders combined an expressive politics, imbued with a strong sense of history and progress, with a markedly practical and pragmatic approach to immediate issues. As Harry Benda tentatively suggested in 1964, they combined "the appeals of solidarity-making with the skills (alleged or real) of problem-solving in an Indonesian historical context."[1] They continued to display a more pronounced and detailed concern for problems of economic development than did Sukarno or the other political parties. Their party alone sought, to a considerable

[1] "Democracy in Indonesia," *The Journal of Asian Studies,* XXIII, no. 3 (May 1964), 455, n. 19.

degree successfully, to transcend the *aliran* base of politics[2] and to transmit in its propaganda modern notions of the state, citizenship, and the political process.

The party sought to induct the masses into politics in an active way and to break down the barriers to national awareness posed by local, ethnic, and religious loyalties and cleavages. Again, it strove to imbue the workers with modern-style trade union consciousness and called for both a technological and social revolution in the villages. In 1964, when its political accommodation to Sukarno's neotradition-alist style was most marked, it intensified its efforts to eradicate "mysticism and superstition" in the villages by launching a "new culture movement," one of whose aims was to establish people's science centers.[3]

Perhaps the most notable contribution made by the PKI to the modernizing of Indonesian life was in the sphere of organization. Japanese occupation techniques and the national revolution had given impetus to the development and spread of mass organizations, and the PKI was not alone in carrying them forward into the postindependence era. But it was not only the most successful practitioner of the art of organization-building; in addition, the organizations under its banner were more efficient then those of any of the party's competitors and more closely approached the criteria by which modern organizations are distinguished from their traditional or transitional predecessors: universal standards of recruitment, promotion by merit, specificity of roles, and a recognized hierarchy of authority applying uniform rules of control and checking.[4]

Many overseas observers were struck by the relatively businesslike attitudes of PKI cadres and the high standards of performance they aspired to in carrying out their tasks in the organization. Guy Pauker, for instance, a close and critical observer of Indonesian Communist

[2] Lev, *The Transition to Guided Democracy*, p. 10. See also Donald Hindley, "Political Power and the October Coup in Indonesia," *Journal of Asian Studies*, XXVI, no. 2 (Feb. 1967), 238–39.

[3] See the article by Aidit in *Review of Indonesia*, XI (May–June–July 1964), 31.

[4] For a stimulating analysis of the different operational principles under-lying organizations in traditional, modern, and what he terms "prismatic" (neither traditional nor modern) settings, see Fred W. Riggs, *Administration in Developing Countries* (Boston, 1964), pp. 164–73.

activity, was impressed by "the intellectual rigor and shrewdness" of the party's leaders and the manner in which they had "motivated and inspired dedicated cadres," and by the presence in party circles of "an intellectual ferment which is lacking elsewhere"; he paid tribute to the "honesty, integrity and dedication" of the leaders and cadres, and the "skill, realism, imagination and boldness" shown by the leadership.[5] Similarly, the party was notable for the fidelity with which its local committees applied the decisions of the central directing bodies. The practical political emphasis in *Harian Rakjat,* in comparison with the other Djakarta dailies, was also noted by Pauker as a feature of the party.[6]

With the rapid expansion of the PKI into the villages after 1954, the character of peasant political and social life was strongly affected by these modes of political organization and action. The effects, involving the politicization, and thereby the intensification, of many longstanding bases of socio-cultural cleavage, may not have been entirely beneficial, but they marked the beginning of an entirely new stage of political participation on the part of the peasant. Njoto claimed in 1965, "We are the men who are modernizing life in the villages; we are the men introducing the twentieth century."[7] It was an overstatement, but one not without a substantial foundation in fact.

Fundamental to the Communist vision of the future, which the PKI upheld, was the role that the workers and peasants were called on to play in effecting their own emancipation from exploitation and oppression and the salvation of the nation as a whole. Once again, it is not surprising that the strongest advocates of a social revolutionary and egalitarian ethic should have emerged from among the radical *pemuda* of the forties' generation. The Communist leaders, who came mainly from families of relatively low status (but not from the working class or peasantry), had high aspirations but were convinced that, while they and their kind had set the revolution going in 1945 and had upheld its ideals most unswervingly, the fruits of independence had gone to a compromising older generation whose claims to prestige and power rested disproportionately on their higher traditional status

[5] "Indonesia: The PKI's Road to Power," pp. 258–60, 276.

[6] *Ibid.,* p. 276.

[7] Interview with the Dutch journalist Huib Hendrikse; from field notes kindly made available by Mr. Hendrikse.

and the higher Western education they had obtained by virtue of their parents' favored social position.

The diffuse utopianism that characterized the radical *pemuda* was, in the case of the young Communists, transformed into a coherent theory of social revolution that could be realized by mobilizing the untapped potential of the workers and peasants. Communism reached out to the masses by catering to their interests and at the same time reformulating their long traditions of messianism and utopianism in a modern idiom. The Communists described a beckoning future to the have-nots, and assured them of their ability to attain it by their own efforts, using the PKI's formula of organization.

As in other respects, so too in its efforts to defend and improve the conditions of the workers and peasants was the PKI forced to compromise for the sake of its alliance strategy. It maintained the tempo of its welfare and bargaining efforts on behalf of the masses, but these had little tangible effect in a period of rapid inflation and economic deterioration. When in 1965 Njoto listed the important gains made by the workers under Communist leadership, he could pinpoint only two substantial material improvements—the introduction of the seven-hour working day and the proclamation of May 1 as a national holiday—both secured during the fifties. He was quick to add that the greatest victories won in revolutionary struggle were "mental and ideological victories, namely that the Indonesian people rely on their own efforts."[8] There is a suggestion of political casuistry about this statement, but it nonetheless contains within it a significant element of truth. The PKI, by stimulating and assuaging to some degree the needs and yearnings of the propertyless and poverty-stricken millions who followed it and by sowing among them the seeds of self-consciousness and self-activity, did provide for them a spiritual satisfaction that goes far to explain the party's immense support.

As far as individual party activists were concerned, the modern character of the PKI as an organization made successful achievement-oriented activity possible for thousands of talented people who might otherwise have had no socially acceptable opportunity to exercise their skills. Through the party's powerful organization, these individ-

[8] *Harian Rakjat,* April 30, 1965.

uals found scope for the employment of their capacities either directly in party and mass organization affairs or in official posts allocated to the PKI at the national and local levels. The high proportion of well-to-do or ambitious individuals—teachers, skilled workers, peasant proprietors, and the occasional small enterprise manager—among PKI sponsors and functionaries in the towns and villages suggests that the party provided an important vehicle for merit-based advancement and prestige and the prospect of still greater openings for the talented.[9] To this extent the Communist movement may be seen as offering an escape from ascription-based patterns of social stratification similar to that provided for other groups by reforming Islam or Christianity.[10]

Of this Communist heritage in Indonesia, part may well become absorbed without great hindrance into the new political arrangements created following the PKI's destruction and the ousting of Sukarno. The Suharto Government and the dominant ideologues of the 1970's have their own concepts of modernization, which may well provide certain groups with an ethic relevant to the tasks of transforming society. But there is no indication that this ethic has the kind of mass appeal that Communism generated, or that it caters for the aspirations of the *abangan*. It has still to be demonstrated that it can channel the energies of the talented coming up against class and ascription barriers. This lack may prove an enduring source of instability and discontent.

The PKI, without doubt, was considerably more than a particular manifestation of an international ideology and political movement. It was an undeniably Indonesian phenomenon, driving deep roots into a society in the throes of transformation and making itself at home within the lifeways of a great part of the population. Its immolation left a vacuum at the base of Indonesian society which has yet to be filled.

[9] See Van der Kroef, *The Communist Party of Indonesia*, p. 302.

[10] Harry Benda made the analogous point that, "It is not inconceivable that in Asia (as elsewhere) Communist movements as such provide a substitute for decayed or vanishing social institutions"; "Reflections on Asian Communism," *The Yale Review*, LVI, no. 1 (Oct. 1966), 12–13.

Appendix A:
The October 1 Affair

The first word that most Indonesians, and the outside world, received of the coup affair came in a broadcast over Djakarta radio at 7.15 A.M. on the morning of October 1, 1965. The announcement stated that, as a result of "a military move within the army in the capital city of Djakarta which was aided by troops from other branches of the armed forces," a body styling itself the September 30 Movement and led by Lieutenant-Colonel Untung, commandant of a batallion of Sukarno's personal bodyguard, the Tjakrabirawa Regiment, had arrested a number of generals belonging to "the self-styled Generals' Council," seized important installations in the capital, and placed the president and other prominent leaders under its protection. These actions, it was stated, had been taken in order to prevent a planned coup by the generals' council, sponsored by the United States Central Intelligence Agency and scheduled to take place prior to October 5 (Armed Forces Day). The announcement added that the Djakarta initiative would be "followed by actions throughout Indonesia against agents and sympathizers of the Council of Generals" and foreshadowed the formation of an Indonesian Revolution Council to uphold the government's policies. Finally, it denounced "power-mad generals and officers who have neglected the lot of their men, and . . . lived in luxury, led a gay life, insulted our women, and wasted Government funds."[1]

The confused events of the night of September 30 and the whole of October 1 are the subject of an already considerable body of literature,[2] and it is intended here to give no more than a brief résumé

[1] From the translation published in *Indonesia*, no. 1 (April 1966), 134–35.
[2] A range of available references is contained in the bibliography. A useful summary of the main coup events, setting out the sources of conflicting accounts, is contained in Van Langenberg.

of the salient facts and inferences. It would appear that during the night of September 30 there assembled at Halim air force base, on the outskirts of Djakarta, a force consisting of one battalion each from the Tjakrabirawa Regiment, the Diponegoro Division stationed in Central Java, and the Brawidjaja Division from East Java, the latter two having been brought into the capital for the Armed Forces Day celebrations. Under the command of several junior army and air force officers, these units were dispatched in the early hours of the morning to the homes of seven top generals, including the defense minister, General Nasution, and the army commander, General Jani, with orders to secure them and bring them to Halim. General Nasution eluded his captors, but the remaining six generals were seized, three of them being killed in the ensuing struggle; the survivors were put to death at a place called Lubang Buaja (the Crocodile's Hole) within the Halim perimeter.

Simultaneously with the seizure of the six generals, units of the coup forces occupied a number of key points in the capital, including the telecommunications building, Djakarta radio, and the approaches to the presidential palace. These actions substantially completed the military phase of the operation in Djakarta. The conspirators had clearly set themselves limited objectives in this respect, and they now concentrated on securing a political solution favorable to their goals through President Sukarno.

The president arrived at Halim about 9 A.M., but it has not been established whether he went there on his own initiative after learning of the early morning broadcast, as he later claimed, or whether he was persuaded to go to the airfield under escort by coup representatives.[3] Two other prominent national figures were already there: Air Force Commander Omar Dhani, who is alleged to have given the coup group permission to operate out of Halim the previous day, and who thereafter cooperated with it, and PKI Chairman Aidit. How Aidit came to be there is, again, unclear,[4] but he appears to have been lodged in a house some distance away from the place where the president took up quarters and to have taken no part in the discussions initiated by Sukarno.

It is reasonable to assume that Sukarno (whether he approved the

[3] See Van Langenberg, pp. 7–9.
[4] *Ibid.,* p. 21.

conspirators' actions or not) was mainly concerned to restore his political authority and take such profit from the new situation as he could. He was not a man to act precipitately, however, and before he could sanction what had taken place he had to be reasonably sure that he could effect changes that would reflect a weakening of the army's position. In this respect two serious obstacles must have given him pause. First, Defense Minister Nasution had escaped and might already be moving to suppress the coup. Secondly, when the president summoned his available ministers and advisers to Halim for consultations he discovered that Generals Umar and Pranoto were at the headquarters of Kostrad, the army's strategic command, and that Major General Suharto, the Kostrad commander, had taken charge there and had refused to allow the two generals to leave for Halim; the blunt terms in which Suharto interdicted the president's summons to the generals indicated that he intended to take counter action against the intended coup.[5] Sukarno therefore faced a situation in which on one side stood a small force led by a group of junior officers seeking to gain his approval for actions that served his political objectives, while on the other side was ranged the bulk of the army, with some 60,000 troops positioned in and around the capital, under the command of an experienced and authoritative senior officer.

In the circumstances, it is not surprising that he declined to give public approval to the coup group's aims; in all probability, he realized by late morning that the Djakarta throw was doomed and that the most he could hope to accomplish was a political compromise. With this in mind he announced early in the afternoon the appointment of General Pranoto (perhaps the most Sukarno-minded of the top officers of the General Staff) as caretaker commander of the army in succession to the murdered General Jani.[6] But Suharto, by this time well advanced with his plans for crushing the coup, simply ignored the president's decision and proceeded with his operations.

The coup group, still seeking to attract support and stiffen the resolve of their associates in Central Java, broadcast again over Djakarta radio at 2 P.M. A decree was pronounced on the formation of the Indonesian Revolution Council, and, after a recapitulation of the

[5] See Suharto's account of this episode in a speech made on Oct. 15, 1965; *Indonesia,* no. 1 (April 1966), 171.
[6] Van Langenberg, pp. 15–16.

motives and aims of the September 30 Movement, it was specifically prescribed that the Revolution Council would assume the role of the government in place of the existing cabinet. The names of forty-five members of the council were announced, among them the key members of the coup group and an assortment of political and military figures.[7]

By late afternoon General Suharto had secured the defection of Brawidjaja Battalion 530, and not long afterwards the capital was cleared of coup forces without casualties. Suharto then sent word to Halim that he was in command of the capital and intended to assault the air force base unless the September 30 Movement abandoned it.[8] At Halim itself, attempts were apparently made to persuade President Sukarno to accompany the rebels to Central Java, there to make a stand against the army. Sukarno rejected the proposal, however, and at about 10 P.M. departed by car for his palace at Bogor.[9] The rest of the company scattered to various locations; Aidit flew to Central Java about midnight in an air force plane shared with Omar Dhani.[10]

Following the early morning broadcast of October 1 on Djakarta radio, supporting actions were taken in Central Java by army groups in Semarang, Jogjakarta, Salatiga, Magelang, and Solo.[11] Where these were not quickly foiled, as in Semarang and Salatiga, they collapsed during the next few days in the wake of the news that the coup had fallen through.

Public comments on the coup while it was still in progress were minimal, most newspapers and political party representatives either maintaining silence or confining themselves to neutral statements. There were notable exceptions, however. At 9.30 A.M. on October 1, Air Force Commander Omar Dhani issued an order of the day in which the September 30 Movement was characterized as "a movement to secure and safeguard the Revolution and the Great Leader of the Revolution against CIA subversion." With reference to the

---

[7] For the terms of the announcement and the composition of the Revolution Council, see *Indonesia*, no. 1 (April 1966), 136–39.

[8] Suharto's October 15 speech describes his operations that day in some detail; *ibid.*, pp. 160–78.

[9] Van Langenberg, pp. 19–20.

[10] *Ibid.*, p. 21.

[11] For accounts of the coup actions in Central Java, see particularly Notosusanto and Saleh, pp. 41–65, and Van Langenberg, pp. 23–38.

actions taken by the coup group, Dhani stated that, "The body of the Army has been purged of those elements who are manipulated by foreign subversives and who endanger the Indonesian Revolution." The air force, he stated, would "always and continuously support and uphold any progressive revolutionary movement." Dhani's order of the day was broadcast by the plotters at 3.30 P.M. the same day, presumably in an attempt to bluff Suharto out of taking military action against them.[12]

The Central Leadership Council of the PNI met at an undetermined time the same day and issued a statement, of which two conflicting versions exist.[13] Both, however, express what can reasonably be described as guarded approval of the September 30 Movement, in that each makes known the Council's "deep appreciation to soldiers who have shown their loyalty in safeguarding" Sukarno and declares a readiness "to support every action taken to purge the apparatus of the revolution of bogus elements and those who would undermine [Sukarno's] authority."

Finally, and ultimately of greatest significance, an editorial appeared in the PKI daily, *Harian Rakjat,* on October 2. This issue went to press in the late afternoon of October 1, so presumably the editorial was written some time in the early afternoon. It expressed undisguised support for the "patriotic movement" led by Untung in its "measures . . . to safeguard President Sukarno and the Republic of Indonesia from a coup by a socalled Council of Generals." While describing the events of the day as "an internal army affair," *Harian Rakjat* at the same time declared that "we the People . . . are convinced of the correctness of the action taken by the September 30 Movement [which has] the sympathy and support of the People."[14] The only other PKI body known to have made a comment on the coup in similar terms was the East Java Pemuda Rakjat leadership.[15]

[12] *Indonesia,* no. 1 (April 1966), 143–44.
[13] Both versions are set out in full in *ibid.,* pp. 198–200.
[14] *Ibid.,* p. 184.
[15] *Ibid.,* p. 185.

Appendix B:
Interpreting the Coup

In the four years following the attempted coup, some 200 alleged participants were tried in Djakarta and a number of provincial capitals. They included, among the armed forces plotters, Lieutenant-Colonel Untung, Brigadier-General Supardjo, and Air Force Major Sujono; from the PKI, Politburo members Njono and Sudisman and the alleged leader of the Special Bureau, Kamarusaman bin Ahmed Mubaidah, alias "Sjam" or "Sam"; and, from Sukarno's palace circle, former Foreign Minister Subandrio, former Air Force Commander Omar Dhani, and the ex-governor of the Central Bank, Jusuf Muda Dalam. The overwhelming majority were sentenced to death, though as of 1973 not all sentences had been carried out.

The trials lent support to, and filled out, the army's claim that the October 1 coup was masterminded by the PKI. On the basis of interrogations and evidence taken up to mid-1967 a semiofficial account of the coup plot was published in Djakarta,[1] the key points of which may be summarized as follows:

> The September 30 Movement was a creature of the PKI, brought into being by the machinations of a *Biro Chusus,* or Special Bureau, of the party headed by two men known as "Sjam" and "Pono," who worked directly under the instructions of Aidit. The secret Biro Chusus had been established in November 1964 to direct members of the armed forces who had been recruited by the PKI or had shown pronounced sympathy for the party. All major participants in the coup attempt were clients of the Biro and had acted in accordance with its directives.

[1] Notosusanto and Saleh, *The Coup Attempt.* Both authors are closely connected with the Indonesian army.

When Aidit returned from abroad early in August 1965 he convened a series of Politburo meetings at which he outlined the critical problems facing the PKI as a result of the deteriorating health of President Sukarno. He informed the Politburo that he had reliable information about the existence of a generals' council and its plans to launch a coup to overthrow Sukarno and crush the PKI. At the same time he reported that a group of "progressive officers" within the army was ready to forestall the council of generals. Aidit spoke in favor of pre-emptive action against the army and won the Politburo's approval of his taking charge of measures to secure this end. It was agreed that "they would have to secure President Sukarno's support for the 'movement.' "[2]

The PKI's aim was not to seize political power for itself but to "prevent the army from eliminating the Party after Sukarno's death."[3] It was in effect seeking "time to develop its power in a peaceful manner according to Aidit's strategy" in a situation where "both sides began calculating their chances in the post-Sukarno era."[4]

The generals' council was in fact a PKI fiction, and the progressive officers were direct agents of the PKI's secret apparatus. Upon instructions from Aidit, the Biro Chusus called meetings of the key coup officers in the capital during August and September and worked out plans for the strike. It also took steps, through its branches in the provinces, to prepare supporting actions in favorable regions. Several leading party functionaries, including Njono, Sudisman, and Peris Pardede (the first two members of the Politburo, the third a candidate member), were also given the task of alerting selected party cadres, particularly in the capital, to mobilize party activists once the coup had been successfully carried out.

On the eve of the coup, the conspirators obtained the blessing and cooperation of Air Force Commander Omar Dhani to use the facilities of Halim air force base for their headquarters. In

[2] *Ibid.,* p. 9.
[3] *Ibid.*
[4] *Ibid.,* pp. 6–7.

addition, a few days before the coup, it was decided to recall PKI volunteers who had received weapons training at Halim under the aegis of the air force and to use them to fill the gaps in the coup forces.

After publication of the account by Notosusanto and Saleh, one trial in particular, that of "Sjam," added details implicating Aidit still more deeply. According to Sjam's evidence, Aidit was responsible for the entire direction of the coup operation, even down to writing the decrees concerning the Revolution Council and its composition that were broadcast over Djakarta radio.[5]

The official version of the coup attempt has not been publicly challenged in Indonesia (except in occasional innuendos in the gossip columns of left-leaning dailies), and any effort to do so systematically would be likely to be construed as pro-Communist intervention and to invite reprisals. The legitimacy of the Suharto government rests strongly upon acceptance by the political public of its case that the PKI committed treason against the state by attempting to overthrow the political system by force and that, by encouraging the Communists and trying to shelter them even after their treason, Sukarno forfeited his right to lead the nation. Psychologically, there are bound to be great inhibitions about negating a thesis in the name of which such an enormous amount of blood was shed, deep social divisions laid bare, and the overpowering figure and ideology of the president overthrown. Although Indonesians active in public life hold differing opinions regarding the desirability of the army's prominent role in the new regime, there is a common disposition to accept the aftermath of the coup as an inescapable, if regrettable, resolution of an insupportable political impasse. Finally, from the army's point of view, had the accent not been placed on the PKI's role Sukarno might well have regained the political initiative and negated the advantages gained by the military as a result of the coup.

Outside Indonesia, however, there has been considerable debate concerning the circumstances of the coup, and especially the role of the PKI. While some writers have endorsed the general substance of the

---

[5] Mahkamah Militer Luar Biasa, *Keputusan Perkara Kamarusaman bin Ahmad Mubaidah (Sjam)* (Djakarta, 1968); mimeo), especially pp. 17–19, 55–60, 69–72.

government's case,[6] and in a few cases gone further in attributing larger ambitions to the PKI,[7] others have expressed varying degrees of doubt about the fact, and still more the degree, of the PKI's involvement in the September 30 Movement.[8]

The trials have not been subjected to systematic analysis, in part because of the amount of evidence involved, the time spread over which the trials have been held, and the difficulty of obtaining access to all trial records. (Some of the evidence has been taken in secret, and other trial testimony had not been released as of 1973). There are a number of grounds, however, on which objections might be raised to the results of the trials and the case built upon them: the nature of the trials and the circumstances in which they were held; the inadequacy and dubious quality of the evidence presented; and the inherent unlikelihood of the cases presented.

The very fact that these were political trials invites scepticism regarding their impartiality and scrupulousness. Army investigators and tribunals had the major role in the preparation and conduct of the trials, and the army's interest in indicting the PKI was, on any count, very considerable. Because it was in a position to select the testimony, and because most of the defendants and witnesses, being incarcerated for long periods before giving their accounts, were subject to various inducements and pressures, the army has been open to the charge of presenting a victor's version of the facts.[9] The fact that the trials

[6] See, for example, Dommen; Justus M. Van der Kroef, "'Gestapu' in Indonesia," *Orbis,* IX, no. 2 (Summer 1966), 458–87; John O. Sutter, "Two Faces of Konfrontasi: 'Crush Malaysia' and the Gestapu," *Asian Survey,* VI, no. 10 (Oct. 1966), 523–46; Tarzie Vittachi, *The Fall of Sukarno* (New York, 1967); Guy J. Pauker, "Indonesia: The Year of Transition," *Asian Survey,* VII, no. 2 (Feb. 1967), 138–50.

[7] See in particular, Arnold Brackman, *The Communist Collapse in Indonesia* (New York, 1969).

[8] For example, Lev, "Indonesia 1965, The Year of the Coup," Wertheim, "Indonesia Before and After the Untung Coup"; Lucien Rey, "Dossier of the Indonesian Drama," *New Left Review,* no. 36 (March–April 1966), 26–40; Hughes; McVey, "Indonesian Communism and China," pp. 378–88; Roger K. Paget, "The Military in Indonesian Politics: The Burden of Power," *Pacific Affairs,* XL, nos. 3–4 (Fall and Winter, 1967–68), 294–314.

[9] Allegations of torture and other forms of intimidation were made by some accused, and conditions in the prisons and detention camps were and are bad enough to offer conceivable inducements for cooperating with the authorities.

proceeded during what can only be described as a witch hunting crusade directed against the PKI does nothing to dispel these misgivings; it was hardly an atmosphere in which anybody would be likely to volunteer evidence favorable to the party or to resist strongly inducements to add to the official case against it. More specifically, the execution without trial of the three top leaders of the PKI and other alleged participants in the coup who might have contributed to our knowledge of the events of October 1, 1965 (in particular all the divisional staff members of the Diponegoro Division responsible for the coup actions in Semarang), removed from the scene people who might have cast a different light on matters.

The version of the coup presented by Notosusanto and Saleh has some general features that are noteworthy. Although it calls the PKI as a whole to account for the coup, it by no means makes clear the extent of the involvement even of the top leaders, let alone the cadres or ordinary party members. Indeed, their presentation of the trial evidence leaves open the possibility that Aidit alone concocted the coup conspiracy and that such approval and cooperation as he obtained from other leaders was based on his assurances to them that a seizure of power was planned by the generals' council and that a group of progressive officers had taken the initiative in opposing such a move. But even the case against Aidit is ambiguous. Although the official account describes the generals' council as "mere fiction, intentionally established to stir up political and social contradictions which were part of [the PKI's] tactics to achieve political power,"[10] it is not convincingly demonstrated either that Aidit, or the other PKI leaders, invented the generals' council or that the party leadership did not in fact believe in its existence and alleged plans.

Unlike early postcoup accusations against the PKI, the trials did not focus on the *Harian Rakjat* editorial of October 2 and other slight public evidences of PKI support for the coup. The reason may be that such public pronouncements conflicted somewhat with the *dalang,* or behind-the-scenes manipulator, role being attributed to the PKI; in any case, it seems safe to regard these instances as of little relevance in determining the PKI's involvement. On the one hand,

[10] Notosusanto and Saleh, p. 143.

there is little doubt that the party would have welcomed a successful coup of the kind attempted by Untung and his accomplices; on the other hand, the general position of the PKI on the day of the coup seems to have been one of understandable caution, and perhaps confusion. From neither aspect do we obtain any indication of the Communists' role in the conspiracy.

The issue of China's part in the coup has not been pursued by the Indonesian government with any vigor either; although there were reports of Chinese arms having been smuggled into the country, a connection with the coup was not established, and allegations that Chinese leaders had advance knowledge of the coup also tended to fade out.[11] Notosusanto and Saleh do not even refer to the question of China's role.

The trials were noticeably reticent about President Sukarno's part in the affair. Some evidence was advanced to the effect that he had prior knowledge of at least the September 30 Movement,[12] but the matter has never been thoroughly pursued. Political considerations were clearly an important factor here: while New Order radicals pushed hard for nearly two years to have Sukarno indicted for complicity in the coup, the government, mindful of the divisive effects that arresting the president would have, resisted the pressures. The former first minister, Subandrio, fared less fortunately; as the chief official scapegoat for Sukarno's policies and pro-PKI sympathies, he was tried and sentenced to death, largely on the rather flimsy grounds

[11] On the issue of possible Chinese involvement, see R. P. L. Howie, "China and the Gestapu Affair in Indonesia: Accomplice or Scapegoat?" (paper delivered to the Australasian Political Studies Association Conference, Canberra, August 1970).   ,

[12] See Notosusanto and Saleh, p. 37. In a book published in 1973, Antonie A. C. Dake, a Dutch writer, attributes the prime moving role in the coup attempt to Sukarno. Dake bases his analysis largely on a restricted document held by the Indonesian authorities, containing a record of the interrogation in 1970 of former Sukarno aide Colonel Bambang Widjanarko. However, Dake's book does not reproduce any part of the Widjanarko statement that came into his possession, and its reliability as evidence cannot therefore be evaluated. On other crucial aspects of the coup, Dake draws uncritically on parts of the trial proceedings and interviews with New Order officials to arrive at conclusions which the present author is unable to accept. Antonie A. C. Dake, *In The Spirit of the Red Banteng: Indonesian Communists Between Moscow and Peking,* The Hague, 1973, pp. 377–423.

that he had foreknowledge of the coup and failed to take preventive measures against it.[13]

The caliber and credibility of crucial trial evidence may be tested by looking at three key issues relating to the question of PKI complicity in the coup: the role of the volunteers at Halim; Aidit's part in preparing the proclamations of the September 30 Movement; and the management of the coup leaders by the Biro Chusus. On none of these is the official position compelling.

Early versions of the coup plot presented the training of PKI-leaning volunteers at Halim as a calculated part of the secret coup preparations. Subsequently, however, there has been a tendency to accept the fact that this training was initiated early in July 1965, before the coup plot was formulated, and that it represented a contribution by the air force to the setting up of a fifth armed force. Emphasis in the trials, accordingly, shifted to the assertion that the volunteers were recalled to Halim a few days before the coup, with the knowledge and cooperation of the PKI, for the purpose of swelling the coup forces.[14] According to these accounts, the volunteers took part in every phase of the military activities associated with the coup attempt, beginning with the kidnaping of the generals and the occupation of key points in the capital.[15]

There are a number of reasons for questioning this account. According to Air Force Major Sujono, one of the accused, who was in charge of volunteer training at Halim, the volunteers present on the night of the coup included members of Perti and Partindo as well as of Pemuda Rakjat. The presence of non-PKI youth was confirmed by the prosecutor in Untung's trial, who stated that Pemuda Marhaenis were at Lubang Buaja at the time of the coup. Other volunteers, including members of both Pemuda Marhaenis and the strongly anti-Communist G. P. Ansor, were expected to arrive on October 1. This makes it unlikely that the PKI-affiliated youth were specifically recalled for a secret operation. An alternative explanation—that an unusually large number of volunteers was present at Halim in prepa-

[13] *Ibid.,* p. 136.
[14] *Ibid.,* pp. 27–28.
[15] *Ibid.,* pp. 20–22, 27–33.

ration for the Armed Forces Day celebrations—seems much more probable.

It appears similarly unlikely that the PKI volunteers were used in the military operations carried out by the coup group. As Ruth McVey has noted,

At Untung's trial there took place an exchange between him and the Prosecutor in which the latter sought to gain an admission from Untung that it was not ideological reasons but military ones which decided the coup group *not* to employ the volunteers in kidnapping the generals. It developed that when the coup group had proved unable to secure the co-operation of the cavalry battalion, Air Force Major Sujono had suggested that they make use of the volunteers currently training at Halim, but that this had been rejected by the others as impractical. . . . It was not, it appears, until the fading moments of the coup, when it was necessary to provide cover for the troops at Medan Merdeka who were about to retreat to Halim, that a use was found for the volunteers at the airfield. They were then given arms . . . and were sent to Medan Merdaka to act as decoys for the retiring troops, which, apparently in considerable bewilderment, they did.[16]

These queries in relation to the official account are of considerable importance, since they put in doubt a good deal of the evidence implicating Njono and other PKI figures in preparations for the coup.

On the face of things, the pronouncements of the September 30 Movement on the day of the coup seem unlikely to have been directly inspired by Aidit or other PKI leaders, as was alleged particularly by "Sjam." The statements concentrated on service grievances and were markedly lacking in the political sophistication and style characteristic of PKI documents and speeches. In at least one respect, they even fell short of the requirements for a Sukarnoist stance, since the call for the maintenance of Indonesia's "free and active" foreign policy revived a political slogan long since abandoned in favor of Sukarno's confrontation, New Emerging Forces, and Peking axis

[16] Private communication to the author. Cf. the Untung trial record, Pusat Pendidikan Kehakiman A. D., "Gerakan 30 September": *Dihadapan Mahmillub di Djakarta, 2. Perkara Untung* (Djakarta, 1966), pp. 46–49. See also the account of evidence given at Njono's trial by air force officers who armed the volunteers; *Berita Yudha*, Aug. 13, 1966.

strategies.[17] Nor did the composition of the Revolution Council measure up to the Nasakom standards advocated by the PKI in either the representativeness or the political standing of those chosen. The council was, as PKI Politburo member Sudisman said at his trial, a body of "lightweight Nasakom notables";[18] a noted Western authority on Indonesian politics has remarked of it, with equal validity, that it "lacked coherence or political sense."[19] The large number of armed services representatives on the council (nineteen out of forty-five) was out of character with PKI attitudes, and consideration of the backgrounds and mutual connections of these officers suggests that service alignments rather than political sympathies with the PKI constituted the criterion for selection.[20]

It could be argued, of course, that Aidit (alone or in collaboration with Sjam) deliberately composed the decrees and announcements in such a way as to support a fiction that they emanated from an autonomous group of military conspirators. If so, one can only admire the skill with which he conveyed the flavor of small-town military politics but remain puzzled by the fact that he felt it necessary to give the decrees such a politically naive character. For reasons which will be discussed below, a more straightforward explanation is to be preferred.

The official case that the PKI masterminded the coup may fairly be regarded as hinging on the evidence that the principal military participants were PKI members or sympathizers who acted under direct instructions from the party's Biro Chusus. PKI *complicity* may be demonstrated in other ways, but the connection between the officers and the Biro is vital to establishing the PKI as the *dalang* of the operation.

There is little reason to doubt that the PKI had a secret apparatus that cultivated armed services contacts; but, despite the evidence assembled and presented in the trials, the thesis that the coup plotters

[17] See McVey, "Indonesian Communism and China," pp. 379–80.
[18] Typescript of Sudisman's trial plea, kindly made available to me by Benedict R. O'G. Anderson.
[19] Lev, "Indonesia 1965: The Year of the Coup." p. 107.
[20] Ruth McVey has kindly given me data on this point, which she plans to use in a future publication.

acted as its conscious instruments remains difficult to accept. What can be gleaned from public sources concerning the careers and views of these men either contradicts the official case or makes it highly unlikely. In a number of instances, statements linking the conspirators with the PKI are simply wrong, as is the case, for example, with the charge that Untung and Lieutenant Ngadiman (Battalion 530) fought on the Communist side in the 1948 Madiun affair.[21]

A brief résumé of the known facts about the careers and views of the four principal coup leaders will indicate why the charge that they acted as creatures of the PKI lacks credibiilty.[22]

Lieutenant-Colonel Untung. Untung served in Battalion 454 of the Diponegoro Division from about 1954 to 1965. In 1963 he headed one of two detachments dropped into West Irian to carry on commando warfare and returned as a hero after the campaign was concluded. Interviewed in May 1963 in connection with his Irian exploits, he concluded his remarks to the newspaper reporter by saying the he hoped the families of all those who had died in the campaign would place their trust in the Almighty, keep the Faith, and remain grateful to the One God.[23] When he was married, in 1964, General Suharto appears to have thought highly enough of him to travel to Central Java to be present at the wedding.[24]

In February 1965, Untung was promoted and transferred to his battalion command in the Tjakrabirawa Regiment; since this was a highly sensitive post, both the army and the palace would have had good reason to check its incumbent thoroughly from the security standpoint. He is said to have consulted frequently in this period with a well known holy man in Central Java, Kjai Hahfud, from whom he obtained various charms including one for invulnerability.[25]

---

[21] Ruth McVey, who has heard Untung's taped confession, informs me that he stated that he was insufficiently politically conscious at the time of Madiun to appreciate the PKI's position and followed the orders of his anti-Communist superiors. Ngadiman refuted allegations made against him by declaring that one of the eight medals he had earned as a soldier had been for fighting against the Communists in 1948; see *Antara,* April 2, 1966.

[22] I am indebted to Ruth McVey for much of the following biographical information.

[23] *Kedaulatan Rakjat,* May 7–10, 1963.

[24] *Ibid.,* April 29, 1964.

[25] *Berita Yudha,* Jan. 13, 1966.

In his confession, Untung admitted to have been controlled by the PKI since 1950 and to having received extensive indoctrination at the hands of the party. But, according to Ruth McVey, the confession reveals a marked lack of dexterity with elementary PKI jargon (for example, it refers continually to "Marxism and Leninism" instead of "Marxism-Leninism") and attributes to the party terms never previously found in its vocabulary.

Brigadier-General Supardjo. The highest ranking officer actively associated with the coup, Supardjo, had had a long and distinguished record of service in the Siliwangi Division stationed in West Java that had included action against the Darul Islam, the regional rebels, and Malaysian forces along the Kalimantan border. In 1963 he underwent training at Fort Bragg in the United States, as assignment that would have entailed careful vetting by Indonesian and American army security agencies. On his return to Indonesia in mid-1963 he was given charge of all training and indoctrination of Siliwangi troops, a highly responsible and trusted position in the army's premier division.[26] Ruth McVey writes that "A knowledgeable informant who knew Supardjo in this capacity described him as bright, nonpolitical, but talked much about how the civic mission, in which he was active, must be developed further to help the country's advancement and prevent the PKI from further infiltrating the villages."[27] Two years later he was appointed commander of a brigade in West Kalimantan and promoted to Brigadier-General.

Colonel A. Latief. At the time of the coup Latief was commander of Brigade I of the Djakarta garrison, elements of which took part in the military action in the capital on October 1. Brigade I had formerly been attached to the Diponegoro Division, stationed at Srondol in Central Java, but in November 1963 it was transferred to Djakarta to strengthen the capital's defenses and security. It is most unlikely that Latief would have been appointed to such a critical post if there had been serious grounds for suspecting him of close PKI affinities.

Colonel Sahirman. Head of Section I (Intelligence) of the

---

[26] *Pikiran Rakjat,* June 25, 1963.

[27] Private communication to the author. Supardjo, however, may well have been more benevolently disposed toward the PKI than this account suggests, since he appears to have been a solid Sukarnoist.

Diponegoro staff at Semarang, Sahirman was the principal leader of the Semarang coup group and was named by General Suharto on October 2, 1965, as one of the chief plotters, along with Untung and Supardjo. Ruth McVey's comments regarding Sahirman are pertinent:

Given PKI strength in Central Java, that territory was naturally considered critical for army intelligence; the fact that Sahirman was appointed to head it, and by [General] Sarbini, whose pre-coup reputation was strongly anti-Communist, would indicate there was no thought of any untoward connections on his part. Moreover, his acceptance for training at Fort Leavenworth, the Army Staff and Command School, the highest for which foreign students are accepted in the U.S. (from which he graduated *cum laude* not long before the coup) would mean that he had passed review by CIA observers, who would have been interested in him anyway as head of Central Java military intelligence. All officers proposed for U.S. training were so reviewed, and every year four or five were turned down because there had been some feeling that they had leftist or other undesirable connections.[28]

After the coup, acquaintances expressed surprise at his complicity, for he had been thought too worldly to be a Communist; he was fond of parties and a good time.[29]

While the data presented above on the key figures in the coup suggests that they were unlikely to have been members of the PKI or conscious agents of it, it does not of course conclusively rule out this possibility; it does, however, tend strongly to support what Sudisman is alleged to have told fellow Politburo member Pardede shortly before the coup, "that the 'progressive officers' were not as strong as the PKI because they had never had any party education."[30] Later we shall give some consideration to other facets of their biographies which, it will be argued, provide a more plausible explanation of their actions and connections than any alleged links with the PKI. At present, however, we are concerned with the relationship, if any, between overt coup participants and the PKI. The reliability of trial evidence regarding the Biro Chusus is also relevant to this question. At the Djakarta trials it was revealed, according to Notosusanto and Saleh, that there existed a

[28] Private communication to the writer.
[29] *Pikiran Rakjat,* Dec. 17, 1965.
[30] Notosusanto and Saleh, pp. 121–22.

secret *Biro Chusus* (Special Bureau) which was directly under Aidit as head of the Organisation Department of the Central Committee [of the PKI]. Sjam and Pono, the main *pembinas* [managers] of the coup officers in Djakarta, were members or even leaders of the Central *Biro Chusus,* while in Central Java the coup officers were "managed" by members of the Regional *Biro Chusus.*[31]

The writers then discuss in some detail the structure of the Biro, from which we gather that it was a tightly knit organization with branches in all major provincial centers, headed at all levels by trusted party cadres and applying a uniform pattern of operations.

There are two major grounds for questioning whether the Biro Chusus existed and worked in the manner described. The first concerns the role of Sjam, who at his trial emerged as Aidit's most trusted secret agent and head of the Biro. The man's political history invites more than a little suspicion regarding the claims made for and by him. He is believed to have been born in Tuban, Bodjonegoro, and to have been aged forty-three at the time of the coup attempt. It is said that during the national revolution he was a member of Battalion X in Jogjakarta, which at that time was led by the present Indonesian head of state, General Suharto. During the same period, until 1947, he is described as having been active in the BTI in Jogjakarta; he is supposed to have made Aidit's acquaintance at that time.[32] He then went to Djakarta and worked for SOBSI, becoming editor of the magazine *Buruh,* secretary of SOBSI's Djakarta branch, and an official of the sailors' and dockworkers' unions.[33]

One source claims that he became an active member of the PKI in 1949,[34] but so far as can be ascertained there is no public record of his association with the party or its mass organizations after 1950. He may have become a secret party operator from early 1951, as was claimed at his trial, but this would imply a degree of confidence in him on the part of Aidit, newly established as PKI leader and faced with a very confused situation in the organization, that would take some explaining.

On the other hand, there is evidence of Sjam's affiliation with quite

[31] *Ibid.,* pp. 10–11.
[32] *Sinar Harapan,* March 13, 1967.
[33] Information supplied by Ruth McVey.
[34] *Sinar Harapan,* March 13, 1967.

a different political grouping at this time. On May 1, 1951, the PSI daily, *Suara Sosialis,* listed him (under the name of Kamaruzaman) as one of twenty-nine selected members undergoing intensive party training in Djakarta. He appears to have remained a well regarded member of the PSI until at least the end of 1955,[35] a fact of some significance considering that party's selective recruiting habits and its good connections with various branches of the intelligence services.

Further light was shed on Sjam's career by the army officer who arrested him in March 1967, who stated in a newspaper interview that Sjam had acted as an informant for Section I (Intelligence) of the Greater Djakarta Regiment from 1955 onwards. (The Greater Djakarta Regiment formed part of the Siliwangi Division until 1960.) The officer further claimed that Sjam had managed to elude capture for eighteen months after the October 1 affair because he had been protected by his former army superiors.[36]

These facts can be interpreted in any number of ways. Perhaps the most plausible explanation is that Sjam was one of those not unfamiliar figures in Djakarta circles who lived by retailing inside information to various interested groups. It is quite possible that all the bodies with whom he had dealings were prepared to use him; it is more doubtful that any of them would have appointed him head of its secret apparatus.

The second basis for caution in accepting the official account of the functioning of the Biro Chusus concerns that body's regional activities. In two cases where it has been possible to check on its operations outside the capital, by reference to provincial trials in Jogjakarta and Medan, the picture that emerges does not conform to the model outlined in the Djakarta proceedings. In Jogjakarta, where the biggest series of provincial trials was held, the plot, according to Notosusanto and Saleh, was planned as follows:

The orders for the launching of the "September 30 Movement" and for the creation of the "Revolutionary Councils" came from Regional Committee boss Sudijono who conveyed them to Wirjomartono, of the Central Java *Biro Chusus,* who was the chief "manager" for the Jogjakarta military. It was Wirjomartono who dictated the steps to be taken by the

---

[35] According to an Australian colleague who interviewed a high-ranking PSI man in 1967.

[36] *Sinar Harapan,* March 13, 1967.

officers stationed in Jogjakarta. The trials of Wirjomartono and ex-Major Muljono revealed that most of the officers and non-commissioned officers involved in the "September 30 Movement" were ex-PKI members or PKI sympathisers who had been "managed" by Wirjomartono for some time.[37]

Now, bearing in mind that the PKI Politburo is alleged to have decided in early August to support the progressive officers in preventing a coup by the generals' council, and that the Djakarta coup group began their meetings some time before August 17, we would expect that key regional personnel of the Biro Chusus would at least have been alerted to the menace of the generals' council at about this time. Yet, according to the account of the Jogjakarta conspiracy given by Notosusanto and Saleh, Wirjomartono, a member of the Central Java Biro Chusus and its key operative in Jogjakarta, was only told of the existence of the generals' council and of a group of younger officers hostile to it on September 25, and then by a fellow party member who was not even a member of the Biro. Later the same day he was visited by his Biro "boss," Sudarmo, and instructed to obtain the support of his army contacts for the September 30 Movement. This he did on September 27, four days prior to the Djakarta action.[38] Assuming the tight management that Notosusanto and Saleh postulate, it is difficult to explain why the Jogjakarta initiative only got off the ground, ideologically as well as militarily, at that late stage.

There is another peculiar and unsatisfactory feature of the Jogjakarta coup account. Wirjomartono is alleged to have told his army contacts on September 27 that "it was necessary to remove the Commander of the 72nd Military Zone, Colonel Katamso, from his position"; and Katamso and his deputy were in fact the only commanding officers murdered by coup forces in the provinces during the first days of October.[39] What is odd about this episode is that Colonel Katamso, during his term of duty in Jogjakarta, had shown himself to be more than ordinarily willing to go along with the PKI or at least to give the impression of doing so. He had, for example, attended the PKI's nineteenth anniversary celebration in Jogjakarta in May 1964, the only non-PKI official of rank to do so, and this, moreover,

[37] Notosusanto and Saleh, pp. 11–12.
[38] *Ibid.*, p. 46.
[39] *Ibid.*, pp. 46, 48–49.

before the PKI had become fashionable. His speeches had a decided Nasakom flavor to them, and it was also said of him that he had hidden the Jogjakarta PKI leader, Sudijono, during the anti-Communist campaign that followed the Madiun affair.[40] Considering that Sudijono was one of the two PKI officials alleged to have given Wirjomartono his instructions on September 25,[41] the singling out of Colonel Katamso for destruction seems decidedly perverse.

The Medan trials produced a different account again of secret PKI activities. Although they had quite a different notion of the composition of the generals' council from that of the Djakarta plotters, and although they were not well informed on events in the capital on October 1, at least some of the officers tried in Medan do appear to have been PKI sympathizers. In their case, however, the PKI control apparatus was known as the *Biro Hubungan,* or Contact Bureau, and its principals were armed forces veterans who were PKI adherents. This system, as Ruth McVey has observed, "would be more congruent with usual PKI organizational practice" and accords better with what little was known before the coup of PKI methods of approaching the army. It does, however, rather destroy the picture of a monolithic secret apparatus of PKI cadres spanning the country. It should perhaps be added that those tried in Medan denied any connection with the Djakarta plotters; certainly they took no overt action to support the coup.[42]

If there are difficulties about accepting the present Indonesian government's explanation of the events of October 1, 1965, is there a more plausible alternative? Those who carried out the coup operations in Djakarta, it will be recalled, claimed that it was "an internal army affair," a view also put forward at the time by the PKI. This claim has been emphatically rejected by the military government and also treated caustically by some of those writers who identify with the government's position. As a complete explanation, it seems no more adequate than does the view that the PKI masterminded the coup; but this does not justify ignoring or minimizing the common orienta-

[40] From press items noted by Ruth McVey. References to Katamso's speeches may be found in *Nasional,* Dec. 31, 1963; *Kedaulatan Rakjat,* Dec. 31, 1964, Feb. 9 and 26, and March 9, 1965.
[41] Notosusanto and Saleh, p. 46.
[42] Private communication to the writer.

tions and mutual relations of the major actors in the coup, as the trials and other accounts which concentrate on the issue of PKI responsibility have tended to do. By taking fully into account the obvious indicators of an intra-army conspiracy in the coup, we may be able to arrive at a convincing theory of its genesis and development, without at the same time dismissing its equally salient whole polity aspects.

The task of unraveling the threads of a military conspiracy has not been made easier by the Indonesian army authorities' apparent attempt (for reasons that have already been suggested) to suppress evidence of conflict within and between the armed services. The summary execution of the Diponegoro staff officers involved in the coup may have been motivated by such considerations. Similarly, the trials were confined to army and air force dissidents, although the extensive purges that took place in the police force and navy in 1966 and subsequently indicate that these services were not the only ones with loyalty problems. Just how these conflicts were related to the coup, if at all, is impossible to establish in the circumstances, but, even if attention is confined to the army and the air force, then some highly suggestive considerations emerge.

It would appear from the service backgrounds of the leaders of the coup and from the support evidenced for the September 30 Movement in Central Java that rebel sentiment against the army staff command was centered in the Diponegoro Division and that it there enjoyed extensive support from officers just below the command levels. The two other army units most closely involved in the coup— Battalion 530 of the Brawidjaja Division and Battalion 328 of the Siliwangi Division—had enjoyed particularly close relations with Untung's old battalion, Diponegoro Battalion 354. All were raider battalions attached to Kostrad, the army strategic command, and designated as shock units in operational undertakings. Units from the three battalions had trained together as paracommandos and seen service together in West Irian.

There were any number of sources for grievance within the army of particular relevance to the units with which we are most concerned. Economic dissatisfaction, which was emphasized in the pronouncements of the September 30 Movement and also in the statements issued by the Jogjakarta conspirators,[43] had increased following cuts in the army budget in 1963 and the simultaneous rise in the price of key commodities under the IMF-sponsored economic reform program. In a speech at that time, General Sarbini urged the army to remain united in the face of unavoidable economic difficulties, and he referred specifically to the rise in public transport fares and the decrease in the army ration (which meant that the soldiers no longer got free sugar, margarine, and cigarettes).[44] Ruth McVey comments:

Although the military enjoyed a relatively privileged position vis-a-vis the rest of the population, and even compared with its civilian counterparts in rank, the economic position of the officer corps by early 1965 was not entirely enviable. If an officer was not stationed in a locality where he had relatives or roots, if he had no access to economic power by virtue of his position, office, or his associate officers, and if his post was not so independent that he could devote himself to several businesses in addition to his regular duties, then his family's life could be quite hard.[45]

In these circumstances, resentment was more than likely to be directed at those more fortunate (or unscrupulous) officers who had access to considerable spoils as a consequence of their positions. An obvious target in this respect was the army staff command, many of whose members were notorious for the style of life they enjoyed in the capital. It is not necessary to look far for an explanation of the September 30 Movement's denunciations of "power-mad generals and officers who have neglected the lot of their men, and who above the accumulated sufferings of their men have lived in luxury, led a gay life, insulted our women, and wasted government funds."

Men like Latief, Supardjo, and Untung were well situated to share and express the grievances of the disadvantaged officers and fighting men. They were line officers, only recently posted to the capital, and therefore lacked experience of Djakarta's peculiar political trafficking and had no ready access to the spoils available to their better placed colleagues. It would have been easy for them to conclude that their

[43] *Kedaulatan Rakjat*, Nov. 8, 1965.
[44] *Ibid.*, June 19, 1963.
[45] Private communication to the author.

grievances could be set right by purging the service of rogues in high places and restoring the revolutionary virtues.

Untung, Supardjo, and others among the conspirators may have had cause to damn the generals' "neglect of their men" from an additional standpoint. They were, as has been stated, front line officers with considerable combat experience. Untung had seen service as a paracommando leader in the difficult West Irian campaign, where casualties were high and the privations suffered by the soldiers and volunteers acute. After the ceasefire, the surviving troops remained in Irian for six months or more and, on the basis of press accounts of the time, seem to have been well and truly "left for dead" by the general staff, lacking regular pay and supplies and occupying an uneasy and unpopular position between the Irian population and the United Nations forces. This history may help to account for the fact that no less than three of the four senior army men who saw service in West Irian joined the September 30 Movement.[46]

Supardjo, on the other hand, was dispatched in mid-1965 to the command of confrontation forces in West Kalimantan. If he had not been aware of the fact before he left, he could not have been there long before realizing that, so far as the general staff was concerned, the Malaysia campaign was militarily defunct and the air force was being left to carry the burden of the action. If Supardjo took Sukarno's patriotic rhetoric seriously (and, as we shall see, there is reason to believe that he did) this experience would not have been calculated to strengthen his loyalty to his high command.

The army participants in coup actions were overwhelmingly of ethnic Javanese origin and shared a cultural ethos at odds with the cosmopolitan spirit of the capital elite. There are strong echoes of an intensely nativistic genus in the pronouncements of the September 30 Movement, with their emphasis on the foreign inspiration behind the generals' council, which had "stained the name of the army," and their calls for the support of the nationalistic policies and slogans of Sukarno, based, as we have seen, on an appeal to "Indonesian identity." Of Supardjo, it was specifically alleged by a fellow participant in the coup, Air Force Lieutenant-Colonel Heruatmodjo, that

---

[46] Untung, Captain Bambang Supeno of Battalion 530, Brawidjaja Division, and Captain Kartawi of Battalion 454, Diponegoro Division.

he "disliked the senior officers for flirting with foreigners";[47] even in the absence of direct knowledge of such a kind about the other conspirators, it is probably true to say that they shared his general view in this regard. They could not have been ignorant, especially in the months preceding the coup, of the deepening conflict between the president and the general staff officers, and it is not difficult to estimate where their sympathies and emotional loyalties would have lain.

Enough has been said earlier about the grounds for air force conflict with the army to make further elaboration of likely reasons for the complicity of senior air force officers in the coup attempt unnecessary. As we have seen, the rivalry between the two services had a long history, in the course of which the air force had aligned itself with the president and his policies in order to secure his backing for their claims to parity with the army. During 1965, relations between the two services had deteriorated markedly, owing especially to conflicts over the conduct of confrontation and the fifth force proposal. Given the opportunity, and reasonable assurances of presidential blessing, it would not have been hard to obtain air force support for a plot against the group currently controlling the army's general staff.

That there were opportunities for liaison, at least between the key conspirators, is sufficiently well established to explain their engaging in joint action. The principal army participants all knew each other well enough, through service in the Diponegoro Division or the Rangers, to make their coming together explicable. Those with para-commando training would also have come into sufficiently close contact with air force officers to be aware of their sentiments about the general staff and the possibility of their participation in the coup plot. Among some leaders of the coup relations appear to have gone beyond those of mere service contact. Untung, for example, is said to have been a close friend of Sahirman, the intelligence officer of the Diponegoro Division,[48] and there is also evidence that he was closely acquainted with Latief.[49] The necessary liaison between the Djakarta

[47] *Antara,* July 29, 1966.

[48] *Berita Yudha,* Oct. 23, 1965.

[49] Untung is said to have confessed that the idea for the precoup conferences came from Latief and himself and that they fled together after the collapse of the coup; *Berita Yudha,* Feb. 24, 1966; *Pikiran Rakjat,* Oct. 19, 1965.

coup group and their allies in the Diponegoro Division could have been provided by a trip Untung made to Central Java some time in late August 1965, ostensibly to collect objects and make arrangements in connection with the Armed Forces Day celebrations, in which Untung was to have had a prominent part.[50]

If it is accepted that the major actors in the coup attempt had sufficiently compelling reasons to act against the generals, that they had the opportunity and the cohesion to act together as a conspiratorial group, and that the evidence of their being PKI members or agents lacks conviction, then the conclusion should probably be that they did form a cabal of "progressive officers" as claimed by the PKI. The question of PKI complicity would then turn, not upon its manipulation of dependent agents, but upon its relations with a relatively autonomous group of plotters.

Evidence that Aidit at least had some connection with the conspirators is at least suggestive. Of all the statements made at the trials on this issue, the testimony of the Politburo member Sudisman is the most compelling, particularly given the impression of credibility his trial demeanor made on foreign observers who were present. His account of the party's Politburo meetings bears out the essentials of the account given by Notosusanto and Saleh.[51] Furthermore, a clandestine document distributed by the underground PKI in 1966, and attributed to Sudisman, charged Aidit with having engaged in the "adventure" after obtaining the Politburo's sanction to counter what Aidit had presented as a threatened coup by a generals' council.[52]

Other circumstantial evidence is provided by the fact that after 1965 the two émigré factions of the PKI, bearing allegiance respectively to Moscow and Peking, agreed on Aidit's complicity if on no other aspect of the PKI's previous activities.[53] Finally, Roger Paget has noted that the fact of PKI involvement in the coup was not denied by any of the PKI members whom he interviewed in 1965 and

[50] McVey, "Indonesian Communism and China," p. 386, n. 39.

[51] Typescript in the author's possession.

[52] See Rex Mortimer, "Indonesia: Emigre Post-mortems on the PKI," *Australian Outlook*, XXII, no. 3 (Dec. 1968), 347–59.

[53] *Ibid.*

1966.[54] The present writer had the same experience with émigré PKI members in Europe.

The circumstances of Aidit's presence at Halim on the day of the coup, however, have never been satisfactorily explained. Quite apart from the question of how he came to be there, it has never been claimed that Sukarno and Aidit came together at any stage while the issue of the coup was in doubt; and Njoto, the president's favorite among the PKI leaders, had been permitted to accompany Subandrio on a trip to North Sumatra. It seems extraordinary that if Aidit had any connection with the plot he should have allowed it to collapse without once seeking Sukarno's advice or attempting to influence him throughout the crucial hours of October 1.

Viewing this evidence in the light of the conclusions already drawn with respect to the coup, it is reasonable to suppose that Aidit suggested to his fellow PKI leaders in early August or thereabouts that, in view of Sukarno's failing health and the threat of a coup by the generals' council, they should encourage an initiative contemplated by a group of progressive officers to pre-empt the generals and should attempt to gain the president's approval for the contemplated action. Having been persuaded by Aidit's report, the Politburo presumably authorized him to proceed, and several members, including Sudisman, became marginally involved in Aidit's planning.

We do not know how Aidit may have come to know of the progressive officers' movement; conceivably he was told either by the party's underground apparatus in the armed forces or by the mysterious Sjam. (If the latter, the possibility that Sjam was acting as a provocateur cannot be discounted.) The question of whether, on this hypothesis, Aidit himself believed the reports of an impending army coup must also remain open, although it would appear that the answer would have to be positive to make political sense of his actions. Finally, for reasons already explained, we are ignorant of the degree of Sukarno's prior knowledge of and reaction to the coup plot.

Carrying the assumption of Aidit's involvement further, it would seem that only a very few leading members of the PKI were drawn into preparatory work for the coup and that possibly none of them

[54] Paget, p. 298.

except Aidit had any detailed knowledge of what was to occur. Aidit presumably must have known, however; it is hard to believe that a seasoned political leader of his acuteness would have gone along with such a gambit unless he was (or believed he was) fully apprised of what was in store. In fact, the most likely explanation of why he would have continued to associate with the plot after Sukarno's recovery is that he wanted to be sure it did not go off half-cocked in a way that would give the army a pretext for a general crackdown on the left (with which enough of the military plotters were linked to make such a reaction possible). Again, it is conceivable that he was systematically misled in his calculations by Sjam.

Construing this interpretation at its worst, then, the PKI leaders appear as the manipulated rather than the manipulators. Drawn into something they could not control (and in most cases did not even know enough about to make careful estimates), and more deeply implicated than they had anticipated by the use made of their volunteers by the plotters, they were eventually placed at the mercy of the enemy they had so long striven to fend off. The party's apparent lack of control over the conspirators once more highlighted the perennial problem faced by the Communists: that, in a political situation where arms were the final arbiters, those with the guns dictated the terms.

The writer readily concedes that the preferred interpretation of the October 1 affair leaves many gaps. In addition to those already admitted, it has not been possible to give any coherent picture of the likely decision-making structure of the plot or to identify the key leader among the military conspirators. The most that is claimed for this account is that it accords best with what is now known concerning the coup attempt and with the political logic of the time.

How close the October 1 affair came to success will remain a matter of controversy, as will the prospects that a successful outcome would have opened up for the PKI. Argument will continue over the question of whether, if General Nasution had shared the fate of his fellow generals, Sukarno would have taken a more determined stand in support of the conspiracy. And the issue of what would have happened if Sukarno had appointed Suharto instead of Pranoto as caretaker commander of the army on October 1 will attract further specu-

lation. Would Suharto have been amenable to an accommodation
with the changed balance of forces, or does his decisive and defiantly
anti-Sukarno action very early on that day indicate that his solidarity
was firmly with the anti-Communists?[55]

[55] In this regard, it should be mentioned that queries and suggestions have
been raised regarding General Suharto's role in the coup itself, some sources
arguing that he may have played a more devious part in the affair than has
been generally recognized. To support this hypothesis, emphasis has been laid
on his close service and (in some cases) personal relations with the most
prominent army conspirators; the fact that he paid a visit to Supardjo's
Kalimantan headquarters in August 1965; and certain curious features of the
coup, notably that Suharto was not on the list of generals to be eliminated
and that, although the coup forces on October 1 occupied three sides of
Merdeka Square in Djakarta, they left unguarded the vital Kostrad headquarters from which Suharto was able to organize his *contraprise*. Most recently, it has been revealed by General Suharto himself that between 11 P.M.
and midnight on the eve of the coup, he was visited at the hospital, where he
was attending his sick child, by Latief, one of the key coup leaders. On these
various aspects, see Paget, pp. 298–99; McVey, "Indonesian Communism and
China," p. 385, n. 38; and W. F. Wertheim, "Suharto and the Untung Coup—
The Missing Link," *Journal of Contemporary Asia,* I, no. 2 (Winter 1970),
50–51. Professor Wertheim in particular strongly suggests that the coup
episode was a provocation involving Suharto aimed at liquidating both the
army command and the PKI.

Select Bibliography

The works cited below comprise only those which were of most direct and important assistance to me. With respect to PKI material, I have confined the bibliography almost exclusively to the period following July 1959, since full bibliographies for earlier periods may be found in other works. Publication of PKI periodicals was suspended between October 1960 and mid-1963. I have not cited the following periodicals of which I was able to obtain only a few scattered numbers: *Bendera Buruh, Berita Wanita, Ilmu Marxis, PKI dan Perwakilan.*

BOOKS AND PAMPHLETS

Adams, Cindy. *Sukarno: An Autobiography.* Indianapolis, 1965.
Adamy, Thaib. *Atjeh Mendakwa.* Atjeh, 1964.
Adjitorop, Jusuf. *Peranan dan Tugas-tugas Hukum Nasional dalam Alam Manipol.* Djakarta, 1963.
Aidit, D. N. *Aidit Membela Pantjasila.* Djakata, 1964.
——. *Anti-Imperialisme dan Front Nasional.* Djakarta, 1962.
——. *Dare, Dare and Dare Again!* Peking, 1963.
——. *Dekon dalam Udjian.* Djakarta, 1963.
——. *Djalan ke Demokrasi Rakjat bagi Indonesia.* Djakarta, 1954.
——. *Hajo, Ringkus dan Ganjang Kontrarevolusi.* Djakarta, 1963.
——. *The Indonesian Revolution and the Immediate Tasks of the Communist Party of Indonesia.* Peking, 1964.
——. *The International Communist Movement and the Southeast Asian Revolution.* Djakarta, 1963(?). Mimeo.
——. *Kaum Tani Mengganjang Setan-setan Desa.* Djakarta, 1964.
——. *Kibarkan Tinggi Pandji Revolusi.* Djakarta, 1964.
——. *Langit Takkan Runtuh.* Djakarta, 1963.
——. *Marxisme dan Pembinaan Nasion Indonesia.* Djakarta, 1964.
——. *Menempuh Djalan Rakjat.* Djakarta, 1952.
——. *Menempuh Tahun 1959.* Djakarta, 1959.

——. *Pemetjahan Masalah Ekonomi dan Ilmu Ekonomi Indonesia Dewasa Ini.* Djakarta, 1964.

——. *Pengantar Etika dan Moril Komunis.* Djakarta, 1962.

——. *Peranan Koperasi Dewasa Ini.* Djakarta, 1963.

——. *Pilihan Tulisan.* 2 vols., Djakarta, 1959–1960.

——. *PKI dan ALRI.* Djakarta, 1963.

——. *PKI dan AURI.* Djakarta, 1963.

——. *PKI dan Polisi.* Djakarta, 1963.

——. *Politik Luarnegeri dan Revolusi Indonesia.* Djakarta, 1965.

——. *Problems of the Indonesian Revolution.* Bandung, 1963.

——. *Revolusi, Angkatan Bersendjata dan PKI.* Djakarta, 1964.

——. *Revolusi Indonesia, Latarbelakang, Sedjarah dan Haridepannja.* Djakarta, 1964.

——. *Set Afire the Banteng Spirit! Ever Forward, No Retreat!* Peking, 1964.

——. *Socialisme Indonesia dan Sjarat-sjarat Pelaksanaannja.* Djakarta, 1962.

——. *Strengthen National Unity and Communist Unity.* Djakarta, 1962(?).

——. *Tentang Sastra dan Seni jang Berkepribadian Nasional Mengabdi Buruh, Tani dan Pradjurit.* Djakarta, 1964.

Akademi Ilmu Sosial Aliarcham. *Sedikit Tentang Riwajat dan Perdjuangannja.* Djakarta, 1964.

Anderson, Benedict R. O'G. "The Idea of Power in Javanese Culture," in Claire Holt, ed., *Culture and Politics in Indonesia.* Ithaca, N.Y., 1972.

——. "Japan: 'The Light of Asia,' " in Josef Silverstein, ed., *Southeast Asia in World War II: Four Essays.* New Haven, Conn., 1966.

——. *Java in a Time of Revolution: Occupation and Resistance, 1944–1946.* Ithaca, N.Y., 1972.

——. *Mythology and the Tolerance of the Javanese.* Ithaca, N.Y., 1965.

——. *Some Aspects of Indonesian Politics under the Japanese Occupation: 1944–1945.* Ithaca, N.Y., 1961.

——, and Ruth T. McVey. *A Preliminary Analysis of the October 1, 1965 Coup in Indonesia.* Ithaca, N.Y., 1971.

Asmu. *Djadikan Tavip Sendjata Ditangan Kaum Tani.* Djakarta, 1964.

——. *Masalah-masalah Landreform.* 2 vols., Djakarta, 1964.

Barisan Tani Indonesia. *Untuk Demokrasi, Tanah Produksi dan Irian Barat.* Djakarta, 1962.

Benda, Harry J. *The Crescent and the Rising Sun.* The Hague and Bandung, 1958.

Bone, Robert, Jr. *The Dynamics of the Western New Guinea (Irian Barat) Problem.* Ithaca. N.Y., 1958.

Bracken, Arnold. *The Communist Collapse in Indonesia.* New York, 1969.

——. *Indonesia: The Gestapu Affair.* New York, 1969.

——. *Indonesian Communism: A History.* New York, 1963.

——. *Southeast Asia's Second Front: The Power Struggle in the Malay Archipelego.* New York, 1966.

Brimmell, J. H. *Communism in Southeast Asia.* London, 1958.

Castles, Lance. *Religion, Politics and Economic Behavior in Java: The Kudus Cigarette Industry.* New Haven, Conn., 1967.

Dahm, Bernard. *Sukarno and the Struggle for Indonesian Independence.* Ithaca, N.Y., 1969.

d'Encausse, Hélène Carrère, and Stuart Schramm. *Marxism and Asia: An Introduction with Readings.* London, 1969.

Djokosudjono. *Dengan Semangat Komunis Jang Tinggi Sukseskan Plan 4 Tahun dan Kikis Habis Segala Kelemahan.* Djakarta, 1964.

Feith, Herbert. *The Decline of Constitutional Democracy in Indonesia.* Ithaca, N.Y., 1962.

——. "Dynamics of Guided Democracy," in Ruth T. McVey, ed., *Indonesia.* New Haven, Conn., 1963.

——. "Indonesia," in George McT. Kahin, ed., *Governments and Politics of Southeast Asia.* 2d ed., Ithaca, N.Y., 1963.

Geertz, Clifford. *Agricultural Involution: The Process of Ecological Change in Indonesia.* Berkeley and Los Angeles, 1963.

——. *The Development of the Javanese Economy: A Socio-Cultural Approach.* Cambridge, Mass., 1956.

——. "Primordial Societies and Civil Politics in the New States: The Integrative Revolution," in Geertz, ed., *Old Societies and New States.* Glencoe, Ill., 1963.

——. *The Religion of Java.* Glencoe, Ill., 1960.

——. *The Social History of an Indonesian Town.* Chicago, 1965.

Gordon, Bernard K. *The Dimensions of Conflict in Southeast Asia.* New York, 1966.

Grant, Bruce. *Indonesia.* Melbourne, 1967.

Griffith, William E. *Sino-Soviet Relations, 1964–65.* Cambridge, Mass., 1967.

——. *The Sino-Soviet Rift.* Cambridge, Mass., 1964.

Hanna, Willard A. *Bung Karno's Indonesia.* New York, 1960.

Harian Rakjat. *Polemik Merdeka-Harian Rakjat.* Djakarta, 1964.

Hawkins, Everett D. "Labor in Transition," in Ruth T. McVey, ed., *Indonesia*. New Haven, Conn., 1963.

Hindley, Donald. *The Communist Party of Indonesia, 1951–1963*. Berkeley and Los Angeles, 1964.

Hughes, John. *The End of Sukarno*. London, 1968.

Jaspan, M. A. *Aspects of Indonesian Political Sociology in the Late Sukarno Era*. Perth, Australia, 1967.

———. *Social Stratification and Social Mobility in Indonesia*. Djakarta, 1960.

Jay, Robert. *Religion and Politics in Rural Central Java*. New Haven, Conn., 1964.

Kahin, George McT. *Nationalism and Revolution in Indonesia*. Ithaca, N.Y., 1952.

Kautsky, John H. *Communism and the Politics of Development*. New York, 1968.

———, ed. *Political Change in Underdeveloped Countries: Nationalism and Communism*. New York, 1962.

Legge, John D. *Central Authority and Regional Autonomy in Indonesia: A Study in Local Administration*. Ithaca, N.Y., 1961.

Lenin, V. I. *Selected Works*. 2 vols., Moscow, 1947.

Lev, Daniel S. *The Transition to Guided Democracy: Indonesian Politics, 1957–1959*. Ithaca, N.Y., 1966.

Lowenthal, Richard. *World Communism: The Disintegration of a Secular Faith*. New York, 1966.

Lukman, M. H., *Adjakan PKI kepada Kaum Pengusaha Nasional*. Djakarta. 1963.

———. *Tentang Front Persatuan Nasional*. Djakarta, 1963.

———. *Untuk Perbaikan Pekerdjaan dalam Front Persatuan Nasional*. Djakarta, 1964.

McEwan, Keith. *Once a Jolly Comrade*. Brisbane, 1966.

Mackie, J. A. C. *Problems of the Indonesian Inflation*. Ithaca, N.Y., 1967.

McLane, Charles B. *Soviet Strategies in Southeast Asia: An Exploration of Eastern Policies under Lenin and Stalin*. Princeton, N.J., 1966.

McVey, Ruth T. "Indonesian Communism and China," in Tang Tsou, ed., *China in Crisis*. 2 vols., Chicago, 1968, vol. II.

———. "Indonesian Communism and the Transition to Guided Democracy," in A. Doak Barnett, ed., *Communist Strategies in Asia*. London, 1963.

———. *The Rise of Indonesian Communism*. Ithaca, N.Y., 1965.

———. *The Soviet View of the Indonesian Revolution*. Ithaca, N.Y., 1957.

Mahkamah Militer Luar Biasa. *Keputusan Perkara Kamarusaman bin Ahmad Mubaidah (Sjam)*. Djakarta, 1968.

Mao Tse-tung. *Selected Works.* 4 vols., London, 1954.

Modelski, George. *The New Emerging Forces: Documents on the Ideology of Indonesian Foreign Policy.* Canberra, 1963.

Mortimer, Rex. *The Indonesian Communist Party and Land Reform, 1959–1965.* Melbourne, 1972.

Mozingo, D. P. *Sino-Indonesian Relations: An Overview, 1955–1965.* Santa Barbara, Cal., 1965.

Munir, Mohammed. *Atasi Krisis Sandang Pangan. Tjiptakan Iklim Politik Ke-Gotong Rojongan Nasional.* Djakarta, n.d.

Njono. *Biar Andjing Menggonggong Hajo Madju Terus.* Djakarta, n.d.

Njoto. *Marxisme Ilmu dan Amalnja.* Djakarta, 1962.

——. *Strive for the Victory of the Indonesian Revolution with the Weapon of Dialectical and Historical Materialism.* Peking, 1965.

Notosusanto, Nugroho, and Ismail Saleh. *The Coup Attempt of the "September 30 Movement" in Indonesia.* Djakarta, 1968.

Paauw, Douglas. "From Colonial to Guided Economy," in Ruth T. McVey, ed., *Indonesia.* New Haven, Conn., 1963.

Partai Komunis Indonesia. *ABC Revolusi Indonesia.* Djakarta, 1962.

——. *Bagaimana Masjarakat Berkembang.* Djakarta, 1964.

——. *Basmi Penjakit Puasdiri.* Djakarta, 1964.

——. *Deklarasi Moskow 1957 dan Pernjataan Moskow 1960.* Djakarta, 1965.

——. *Djalan Baru Untuk Republik Indonesia.* Djakarta, 1953.

——. *Dokumen-dokumen Kongres Nasional ke-VI PKI.* Djakarta, 1960.

——. *Keputusan-keputusan Sidang Pleno ke-III CC PKI.* Djakarta, 1963.

——. *Kita Tjinta Damai, Tetapi Lebih Tjinta Kemerdekaan.* Djakarta, 1962.

——. *Madju Terus! Dokumen-dokumen Kongres Nasional ke-VII (Luarbiasa) PKI.* Djakarta, 1963.

——. *Melawan Revisionisme.* Djakarta, 1964.

——. *Memerangi Liberalisme.* Djakarta, 1961.

——. *Memerangi Subjektivisme.* Djakarta, 1963.

——. *Menanggulangi Kesulitan-kesulitan Ekonomi dengan Semangat Trikora.* Djakarta, 1962.

——. *Program PKI.* Djakarta, 1953.

——. *Putusan-putusan Sidang Pleno CC PKI.* Djakarta, 1953.

——. *Resolusi-resolusi Sidang Pleno ke-I CC PKI.* Djakarta, 1963.

——. *Seminar Nasional Wanita Tani.* Djakarta, 1964.

——. *Serba-serbi Dokumen Partai 1961.* Djakarta, 1962.

——. *Serba-serbi Dokumen Partai 1962.* Djakarta, 1964.

——. *Socialisme Hariini dan Hariesok Bangsa-bangsa.* Djakarta, 1963.

——. *Tuntutan untuk Bekerdja Dikalangan Kaum Tani.* Djakarta, 1955.

Pauker, Guy J. *Communist Prospects in Indonesia.* Santa Barbara, Cal., 1964.

——. "Indonesia: The PKI's Road to Power," in Robert A. Scalapino, ed., *The Communist Revolution in Asia.* Englewood Cliffs, N.J., 1965.

——. *The Rise and Fall of the Communist Party of Indonesia.* Santa Barbara, Cal., 1969.

——. "The Role of the Military in Indonesia," in J. J. Johnson, ed., *The Role of the Military in Underdeveloped Countries.* Princeton, N.J., 1962.

Peltzer, Karl J. "The Agricultural Foundation," in Ruth T. McVey, ed., *Indonesia.* New Haven, Conn., 1963.

Pusat Pendidikan Kehakiman A.D. *"Gerakan 30 September": Dihadapan Mahmillub I di Djakarta. Perkara Njono.* Djakarta, 1966.

——. *"Gerakan 30 September": Dihadapan Mahmillub II di Djakarta. Perkara Untung.* Djakarta, 1966.

Runturambi. *Pendemokrasian Pembangunan Nasional.* Djakarta, 1961.

Sakirman. *Kembali ke Dekon. Laksanakan Konsekwen Patriotisme Ekonomi.* Djakarta, 1964.

Schlesinger, Arthur M., Jr. *A Thousand Days: John F. Kennedy in the White House.* Boston, 1965.

Schramm, Stuart, *Mao Tse-tung.* London, 1967.

Selosoemardjan. *Social Change in Jogjakarta.* Ithaca, N.Y., 1962.

Simon, Sheldon W. *The Broken Triangle: Peking, Djakarta, and the PKI.* Baltimore, 1969.

Skinner, G. W., ed., *Local, Ethnic, and National Loyalties in Village Indonesia.* New Haven, Conn., 1959.

Sentral Organisasi Buruh Seluruh Indonesia. *Mempertahankan dan Memperluas Hak-hak Kaum Buruh.* Djakarta, 1959.

——. *Peranan Buruh Wanita dalam Pembangunan.* Djakarta, 1961.

——. *Peranan dan Tugas Dewan Perusahaan.* Djakarta, 1963.

——. *Untuk Memperkuat dan Memperbesar SOBSI Seluruh Negeri.* Djakarta, 1962.

——. *Untuk Mempertinggi Produksi dan Melantjarkan Distribusi Pangan.* Djakarta, 1962.

Sudisman. *43 Tahun Menempu Kesabaran, Ketjintaan dan Kegemasan Revolusioner.* Djakarta, 1964.

——. *43 Tahun PKI.* Djakarta, 1964.

——. *Konsolidasi Kerapian dan Militansi Organisasi Partai.* Djakarta, 1964.

Sukarno. *Dibawah Bendera Revolusi.* 2 vols., Djakarta, 1963.

——. *Go Ahead, PKI!* Djakarta, 1965.

——. *Indonesia Leaves the United Nations.* Djakarta, 1965.

——. *Lahirnja Pantjasila.* Bandung, 1961.

——. *Like an Angel that Strikes from the Skies: The March of our Revolution.* Djakarta, 1960.

——. *Marhaen and Proletarian.* Ithaca, N.Y., 1960.

——. *Reach for the Stars!* Djakarta, 1965.

——. *Revolusi, Sosialisme Indonesia, Pimpinan Nasional.* Djakarta, 1961.

——. *Sarinah: Kewadjiban Wanita dalam Perdjuangan Republik Indonesia.* Djakarta, 1963.

——. *Tahun "Vivere Pericoloso."* Djakarta, 1964.

Sutter, John O. *Indonesianisasi: Politics in a Changing Economy, 1940–1955.* 4 vols., Ithaca, N.Y., 1959.

Tan, T. K., ed. *Sukarno's Guided Indonesia.* Brisbane, 1967.

Tjugito. *Untuk Memperbaikan Pengorganisasian Buruh Agraria.* Djakarta, 1961.

Universitas Rakjat. *UNRA: Gaja Baru.* Djakarta, 1964.

Van-der Kroef, Justus M. *The Communist Party of Indonesia.* Vancouver, 1965.

——. *The West New Guinea Dispute.* New York, 1958.

Vittachi, Tarzie. *The Fall of Sukarno.* New York, 1967.

Weatherbee, Donald E. *Ideology in Indonesia: Sukarno's Indonesian Revolution.* New Haven, Conn., 1966.

Wertheim, W. F. *Indonesian Society in Transition.* Brussels, 1959.

Willner, Ann Ruth. *The Neotraditional Accommodation to Independence: The Case of Indonesia.* Princeton, N.J., 1966.

Worsley, Peter. *The Third World.* London, 1967.

Zagoria, Donald. *The Sino-Soviet Conflict, 1956–1961.* Princeton, N.J., 1962.

PERIODICAL AND NEWSPAPER ARTICLES AND OCCASIONAL PAPERS

Adjitorop, Jusuf. "Peranan Inteligentsia dalam Revolusi Indonesia," *Harian Rakjat,* Oct. 19, 1963.

Aidit, D. N. "Beberapa Masalah Politik dan Pertahanan," *Harian Rakjat,* July 19, 1963.

————. "Dengan Semangat Banteng Merah Mengkonsolidasi Organisasi Komunis jang Besar," *Harian Rakjat*, July 6, 1964.

————. "Djadilah Komunis Jang Baik dan Lebih Baik Lagi," *Harian Rakjat*, June 11–12, 1964.

————. "For National Unity," *World Marxist Review*, Feb. 1960.

————. "Ganjang Setan-setan Desa dan Perkuat Persatuan Nasional," *Harian Rakjat*, May 4, 1964.

————. "Kalau Imperialis Mengagresi Indonesia, diseluruh Asia Tenggara akan Berkobar Api Revolusi," *Harian Rakjat*, Sept. 11, 1964.

————. "Kaum Tani Djawa Barat Mengganjang Setan-setan Desa," *Harian Rakjat*, May 11–16, 1964.

————. "Kembali ke UUD 1945 untuk Perubahan dalam Politik dan Penghidupan," *Bintang Merah*, XV, July–Aug. 1959.

————. "Laksanakan 6 Baik," *Harian Rakjat*, July 17, 1961.

————. "Launch a New Culture Movement in Our Villages," *Review of Indonesia*, XI, May–July 1964.

————. "Madju Terus Menggempur Imperialisme dan Feodalisme," *Harian Rakjat*, Jan. 2, 1961.

————. "Marxisme-Leninisme dan Pengindonesiannja," *Harian Rakjat*, Feb. 25, 1964.

————. "Masalah Pengerahan Dana dan Tenaga untuk Pembangunan," *Harian Rakjat*, Jan. 10, 1964.

————. "Mengganjang 'Malaysia' dan Revisionisme adalah Tugas Nasional," *Harian Rakjat*, Nov. 1, 1963.

————. "Patriotisme dan Internationalisme," *Harian Rakjat*, Nov. 12, 1962.

————. "Pemetjahan Masalah Ekonomi dan Ilmu Ekonomi Indonesia," *Harian Rakjat*, July 10, 1964.

————. "Perhebat Ofensif Revolusioner disegala Bidang," *Harian Rakjat*, May 12–14, 1965.

————. "Pertahanan Nasional harus Tunduk pada Strategi Umum Revolusi Indonesia," *Harian Rakjat*, June 29, 1963.

————. "Revolusi Kalimantan Utara Bantuan Besar bagi Indonesia," *Harian Rakjat*, Dec. 18, 1962.

————. "Some Questions of the Indonesian Revolution and the PKI," *Peking Review*, Sept. 13, 1963.

————. "Tak Mungkin Membangun Sosialisme Indonesia djika Imperialisme-Feodalisme Masih Ada," *Harian Rakjat*, Aug. 28–29, 1961.

————. "Tanpa Kaum Komunis tak Bisa Masalah-masalah Penting dan Pokok Dipetjahkan," *Bintang Merah*, XVI, Feb. 1960.

——. "Tentang Rentjana Malaysia," *Harian Rakjat,* Feb. 1, 1963.

——. "The Sixth National Congress of the Communist Party of Indonesia," *Review of Indonesia,* VI, Nov.–Dec. 1959.

——. "Untuk Pelaksanaan jang Lebih Konsekwen dari Manifesto Politik," *Bintang Merah,* XVI, July–Aug. 1960.

——. "Utamakan Persamaan Dikalangan Kaum Revolusioner," *Bintang Merah,* XVI, Sept. 1960.

Asmu. "BTI Berdjuang untuk Demokrasi Tanah-Produksi dan Irian Barat," *Suara Tani,* Nov.–Dec. 1962.

——. "Masalah Landreform," *Bintang Merah,* XVI, Jan. 1960.

——. "Pertinggi Produksi, Selamatkan Dekon dan Ganjang 'Malaysia,' " *Suara Tani,* May–Aug. 1963.

——. "The People Can Crush 'Malaysia' and Simultaneously Overcome Food Difficulties," *Review of Indonesia,* XI, Jan.–Feb. 1964.

——. "The Question of Land Reform," *Review of Indonesia,* VII, July 1960.

Bakri, Ismail. "Dengan Berani terus Melawan Kaum Penghisap Besar Didesa," *Harian Rakjat,* Feb. 19, 1963.

——. "Madju terus Mengintegrasikan PKI dengan Kaum Tani," *Harian Rakjat,* Jan. 13, 1964.

Barisan Tani Indonesia. "Pelaksanaan setjara Konsekwen UUPA dan UUPBH Membantu Suksesnja Program Pemerintah," *Harian Rakjat,* Jan. 7, 1964.

Benda, Harry J. "Decolonization in Indonesia: The Problem of Continuity and Change," *American Historical Review,* LXX, no. 4 (July 1965), 1,058–1,073.

——. "Democracy in Indonesia," *The Journal of Asian Studies,* XXIII, no. 3 (May 1964), 449–456.

——. "Reflections on Asian Communism," *The Yale Review,* LVI, no. 1 (Oct. 1966), 1–16.

Brackman, Arnold. "Communist Strategy in Post-Gestapu Indonesia," *Asia,* no. 14 (Spring 1969), 32–50.

Bunnell, Frederick P. "Guided Democracy Foreign Policy, 1960–1965," *Indonesia,* no. 2 (Oct. 1966), 37–76.

——. "Indonesia's Quasi-Military Regime," *Current History,* LII, no. 305 (Jan. 1967), 22–28.

Burchett, W. G. "The Story Behind Indonesia's Coup," *Labour Monthly,* Jan. 1966.

Castles, Lance. "Coup and Counter-coup in Indonesia," *Australia's Neighbors,* 4th series, nos. 29–30 (Nov.–Dec. 1965), 5–7.

——. "Notes on the Islamic School at Gontor," *Indonesia,* no. 1 (April 1966), 30–45.

——. "Socialism and Private Business: The Latest Phase," *Bulletin of Indonesian Economic Studies,* I, no. 1 (June 1965), 13–45.

Curtis, Robert. "Malaysia and Indonesia," *New Left Review,* no. 28 (Nov.–Dec. 1964), 5–32.

Derkach, Nadia. "The Soviet Policy Towards Indonesia in the West Irian and Malaysian Disputes," *Asian Survey,* V, no. 11 (Nov. 1965), 566–71.

Dommen, Arthur J. "The Attempted Coup in Indonesia," *The China Quarterly,* no. 25 (Jan.–March 1966), 144–70.

Feith, Herbert. "Indonesia's Political Symbols and their Wielders," *World Politics,* XVI, no. 1 (Oct. 1963), 79–97.

——. "President Sukarno, the Army, and the Communists: The Triangle Changes Shape," *Asian Survey,* IV, no. 8 (Aug. 1964), 969–80.

——. "Some Political Dilemmas of Indonesia's Intellectuals," Paper presented to the Australasian Political Studies Association, August 1964.

Glassburner, Bruce. "Economic Policy-making in Indonesia, 1950–1957," *Economic Development and Cultural Change,* X, no. 2 (Jan. 1962), 113–33.

——, and Kenneth D. Thomas. "The Swing of the Hoe: Retooling Begins in the Indonesian Economy," *Asian Survey,* I, no. 4 (June 1961), 3–12.

Graham, Stuart L. "Assessments of the PKI," *Australia's Neighbours,* 4th series, nos. 31–32 (Jan.–Feb. 1966), 4–7.

Harahap, Banda. "Beberapa Masalah Kebudajaan dan Pendidikan Ideologi bagi Pekerdja Kebudajaan Komunis," *Harian Rakjat,* March 9, 1965.

Hindley, Donald. "The Indonesian Communist Party and the Conflict in the International Communist Movement," *The China Quarterly,* no. 19 (July–Sept. 1964), 99–119.

——. "The Indonesian Communists and the CPSU Twenty-second Congress," *Asian Survey,* II, no. 1 (March 1962), 20–27.

——. "Indonesian Politics, 1965–67: The September 30 Movement and the Fall of Sukarno," *The World Today,* XXIV, no. 8 (Aug. 1968), 345–56.

——. "Indonesia's Confrontation of Malaysia: The Search for Motives," *Asian Survey,* IV, no. 6 (June 1964), 904–13.

——. "Political Power and the October 1965 Coup in Indonesia," *Journal of Asian Studies,* XXVI, no. 2 (Feb. 1967), 237–49.

——. "President Sukarno and the Communists: The Politics of Domestication," *American Political Science Review,* LVI, no. 4 (Dec. 1962), 915–26.

Howie, R. P. L. "China and the Gestapu Affair in Indonesia: Accomplice or Scapegoat?" Paper delivered at the Australasian Political Studies Association Conference, August 1970.

Hutapea, B. O. "Beberapa Peladjaran dari Konferensi Nasional Tani Pertama PKI," *Bintang Merah,* XV, April 1959.

Kahin, George McT. "Malaysia and Indonesia," *Pacific Affairs,* XXXVII, no. 3 (Fall 1964), 253–70.

Legge, John D. "Indonesia After West Irian," *Australian Outlook,* XVII, no. 1 (April 1963), 5–20.

Lembaga Kebudajan Rakjat. "Djebol Kebudajaan Imperialisme AS, Bangun Kebudajaan Nasional, Kobarkan Kebangkitan Tani," *Harian Rakjat,* March 1, 1964.

Lev, Daniel S. "Indonesia 1965: The Year of the Coup," *Asian Survey,* VI, no. 2 (Feb. 1966), 103–10.

——. "Political Parties in Indonesia," *Journal of Southeast Asian History,* VIII, no. 1, (March 1967), 52–67.

Lukman, M. H. "Apa harus Kelakukan djika Hendak Menganggulangi Keadaan Ekonomi Sekarang," *Harian Rakjat,* June 23–24, 1965.

——. "A Correct Party Policy Guarantees a Strong United Front," *World Marxist Review,* Aug. 1959.

Mackie, J. A. C. "Indonesian Politics under Guided Democracy," *Australian Outlook,* XV, no. 3 (Dec. 1961), 260–79.

——. "Indonesia's Government Estates and their Masters," *Pacific Affairs,* XXXIV, no. 4 (Winter 1961–62), 337–60.

——. "Inflation and Confrontation in Indonesia," *Australian Outlook,* XVIII, no. 3 (Dec. 1964), 278–98.

——. "The Political Economy of Guided Democracy," *Australian Outlook,* XIII, no. 4 (Dec. 1959), 285–92.

——. "Recent Developments in Indonesia," *Australia's Neighbours,* 3rd series, nos. 108–9 (July–Aug. 1960), 1–4.

McVey, Ruth T. "An Early Account of the Independence Movement (Semaun)," *Indonesia,* no. 1 (April 1966), 46–75.

——. "The Strategic Triangle: Indonesia," *Survey,* no. 54 (Jan. 1965), 113–22.

Mitchell, David. "Communists, Mystics and Sukarnoism," *Dissent* (Melbourne), no. 22 (Autumn 1968), 28–32.

Mortimer, Rex. "Class, Social Cleavage and Indonesian Communism," *Indonesia,* no. 8 (Oct. 1969), 1–20.

———. "Indonesia: Emigre Post-mortems on the PKI," *Australian Outlook,* XXII, no. 3 (Dec. 1968), 347–59.

Njoto, "Perdjuangan PKI untuk Kemerdekaan Nasional jang Penuh, Demokrasi dan Perdamaian," *Bintang Merah, XV,* July–Aug. 1959.

———. "Persatuan Kita lebih Kuat dari Bom Atom," *Harian Rakjat,* July 5, 1962.

Paget, Roger K. "The Military in Indonesian Politics: The Burden of Power," *Pacific Affairs,* XL, nos. 3–4 (Fall and Winter 1967–68), 294–314.

Partai Komunis Indonesia. "Consolidate Unity to Defend Democracy and Struggle for an Improvement in the Living Conditions of the People," *Review of Indonesia,* VII, Jan. 1960.

———. "Djadikan 1965 Tahun Mengganjang Kapitalis Birokrat dan Melakasanakan Dekon untuk Memenangkan Dwikora," *Harian Rakjat,* Jan. 1, 1965.

———. "Enter 1964 with the Banteng Spirit," *Review of Indonesia,* XI, Jan.–Feb. 1964.

———. "Madju Terus dengan Semangat Trikora Menganggulangi Soal Ekonomi," *Harian Rakjat,* Oct. 12, 1962.

———. "Mari Bebaskan Irian Barat dengan Djalan Apapun," *Harian Rakjat,* Sept. 30, 1961.

———. "Penghapusan Keadan Bahaja untuk Mengganjang Kaum Kontra-revolusi dibidang Politik dan Ekonomi," *Harian Rakjat,* May 1, 1963.

———. "PKI Melantjarkan 'Gerakan 1001,'" *Harian Rakjat,* Feb. 9, 1962.

———. "Resolusi Politbiro CC PKI Mengenai Pekerdjaan Delegasi PKI ke-Kongres ke-XXII CPSU," *Harian Rakjat,* Dec. 16, 1961.

———. "Theses on the 44th Anniversary of the Communist Party of Indonesia," *Review of Indonesia,* XV, May–July 1964.

Pauker, Ewa T. "Ganefo I: Sports and Politics in Djakarta," *Asian Survey,* V, no. 4 (April 1965), 171–85.

Pauker, Guy J. "Current Communist Tactics in Indonesia," *Asian Survey,* I, no. 3 (May 1961), 26–35.

———. "General Nasution's Mission to Moscow," *Asian Survey,* I, no. 1 (March 1961), 13–22.

———. "Indonesia: Internal Development or External Expansion?" *Asian Survey,* III, no. 2 (Feb. 1963), 69–75.

——. "Indonesia in 1964: Towards a People's Democracy?" *Asian Survey*, V, no. 2 (Feb. 1965), 88–97.

——. "Indonesia's Eight-year Overall Development Plan," *Pacific Affairs*, XXXIV, no. 2 (Summer 1961), 115–30.

Ra'anan, Uri. "The Coup that Failed," *Problems of Communism*, XV, no. 2 (March–April 1966), 37–43.

Rey, Lucien, "Dossier of the Indonesian Drama," *New Left Review*, no. 36 (March–April 1966), 26–40.

Sakirman. "Arti-arti Sokongan PKI kepada UUD 1945 dan Demokrasi Terpimpin," *Bintang Merah*, XVI, May–June 1960.

——. "Back to the Dekon for Consistent Implementation of Economic Patriotism," *Review of Indonesia*, XI, Jan.–Feb. 1964.

——. "Lawan Neo-kolonialisme dan Bentuk Kabinet Front Persatuan dengan Poros Nasakom," *Harian Rakjat*, March 11, 1963.

Schmeits, Eric. "The '30th September Affair' in Indonesia," *France-Asie*, XX, no. 2 (184, Winter 1965–66), 209–38.

Schmitt, Hans O. "Foreign Capital and Social Conflict in Indonesia," *Economic Development and Cultural Change*, X, no. 3 (1962), 284–93.

——. "Post-Colonial Politics: A Suggested Interpretation of the Indonesian Experience, 1950–1958," *The Australian Journal of Politics and History*, IX, no. 2 (Nov. 1963), 176–83.

Selosoemardjan. "Land Reform in Indonesia," *Asian Survey*, I, no. 2, (Feb. 1962), 23–30.

Sentral Organisasi Buruh Seluruh Indonesia. "Program Tuntutan Sosial-ekonomi SOBSI," *Harian Rakjat*, May 3, 1961.

Sudisman. "Songsong Kemenangan Sosialisme dengan Optimisme," *Harian Rakjat*, Oct. 29, 1963.

Sutter, John O. "Two Faces of Konfrontasi: 'Crush Malaysia' and the Gestapu," *Asian Survey*, VI, no. 10 (Oct. 1966), 523–46.

Thomas, Kenneth D. "Recent Developments in Indonesia," *Australia's Neighbours*, 4th series, nos. 11–12 (Jan.–Feb. 1964), pp. 6–8.

——, and Bruce Glassburner. "Abrogation, Takeover and Nationalisation: The Elimination of Dutch Economic Dominance from the Republic of Indonesia," *Australian Outlook*, XIX, no. 2 (Aug. 1965), 158–79.

Utrecht, Ernst. "Land Reform," *Bulletin of Indonesian Economic Studies*, V, no. 3 (Nov. 1969), 71–88.

Van der Kroef, Justus M. "Agrarian Reform and the Communist Party of Indonesia," *Far Eastern Survey*, XXIX, no. 1 (Jan. 1960), 5–13.

——. "Dilemmas of Indonesian Communism," *Pacific Affairs,* XXXV, no. 2 (Summer 1962), 141–59.

——. "Gestapu in Indonesia," *Orbis,* IX, no. 2 (Summer 1966), 458–87.

——. "Indonesia, Malaysia and the North Borneo Crisis," *Asian Survey,* III, no. 4 (April 1963), 173–81.

——. "Indonesian Communism and the Changing Balance of Power," *Pacific Affairs,* XXXVII, no. 4 (Winter 1964–65), 357–83.

——. "Indonesian Communism's Expansionist Role in Southeast Asia," *International Journal,* XX, no. 2 (Spring 1965), 189–205.

——. "Indonesian Communism Since the 1965 Coup," *Pacific Affairs,* XLIII, no. 1 (Spring 1970), 34–60.

——. "Indonesian Communism's 'Revolutionary Gymnastics,'" *Asian Survey,* V, no. 5 (May 1965), 217–32.

——. "Indonesia's New Parliament," *Eastern World,* Sept. 1960.

——. "Javanese Messianic Expectations: Their Origin and Cultural Context," *Comparative Studies in Society and History,* I, no. 4 (1959), 299–323.

——. "Land Reform and Social Structure in Rural Java," *Rural Sociology,* XXV, no. 4 (Dec. 1960), 414–30.

——. "The West New Guinea Settlement: Its Origins and Implications," *Orbis,* VII, no. 1 (Spring 1963), 120–49.

Weinstein, Franklin B. "The Second Afro-Asian Conference: Preliminary Bouts," *Asian Survey,* V, no. 7, (July 1965), 359–73.

Wertheim, W. F. "Communist Views of State Capitalism, with Special Reference to South and Southeast Asia," Paper delivered at a seminar of the Centre for Southeast Asian Studies, University of Hull, June 1968.

——. "From Aliran towards Class Struggle in the Countryside of Java," Paper delivered at the International Conference on Asian History, Kuala Lumpur, August 1968.

——. "Indonesia Before and After the Untung Coup," *Pacific Affairs,* XXXIX, nos. 1 and 2 (Spring and Summer 1966), 115–27.

THESES

Anderson, Benedict R. O'G. "The Pemuda Revolution: Indonesian Politics, 1945–46." Ph.D. dissertation, Cornell University, 1967.

Bunnell, Frederick P. "The Kennedy Initiatives in Indonesia, 1962–1963." Ph.D. dissertation, Cornell University, 1969.

Polomka, Peter. "The Indonesian Army and Confrontation." M.A. thesis, Melbourne University, 1969.

Smith, A. E. D. "The Ideology of Sukarno and the Tradition of Java." M.A. preliminary thesis, Monash University, 1967.

Van Langenburg, Michael. "The September 30 Movement: The Contradictions." B.A. Honours thesis, Sydney University, 1967.

NEWSPAPERS, PERIODICALS

Bintang Merah, Jan. 1959–June 1965.

Ekonomi dan Masjarakat, March 1959–Dec. 1964.

Harian Rakjat, Jan. 1959–Oct. 1965.

Indonesian Tribune (Tirana), 1966–68.

Peking Review, 1963–65.

Review of Indonesia, Dec. 1957–Jan. 1965.

Suara Tani, Jan. 1959–Feb. 1965.

World Marxist Review (Prague), 1958–1965.

Index

Abdulgani, Ruslan, 245
Adams, Cindy, 82n
Adjie, Ibrahim, 386
Adjitorop, Jusuf, 391, 395
Aidit, 20, 29, 33–38, 41 43, 75, 87,
95, 99, 101, 115, 126, 190, 223,
246, 313, 332, 370–71, 377, 395
Biography, 20, 29, 30, 33, 34–38,
41; leadership of PKI, *see under*
Partai Komunis Indonesia; and
Sukarno, 36–37, 79, 87, 88–89, 121
123, 135–36
Congress reports: 5th (1954), 43–
65 *passim*, 75, 182–83, 276, 334;
6th (1959), 72, 182, 183, 184n,
257, 260, 334, 338; 7th (1962),
92–93, 108, 131, 210, 258, 263,
295
On armed forces, 108, 109, 110–
11, 114–16, 125, 371–72; on civil
service, 128, 130; on class structure,
45–48, 62–64, 75, 97–99, 135–36,
142–69 *passim*, 164, 397, 399; and
coup attempt, 381, 385, 388, 391,
394, 414, 416, 418–26 *passim*, 430,
438–40; on economic policy, 256–
63 *passim*, 264, 266n, 269–73; on
Guided Democracy, 108, 123–24,
205; on imperialism, 44–45, 47, 51,
52, 55–57, 96–97, 134, 142–44,
161, 205, 210–11, 227–35, 246,
272, 301, 312, 316, 329, 358; on
international Communist movement, 330–44 *passim*, 347n, 352–
57, 358–62 *passim;* on international
politics, 182–86, 210–11, 226–39,
348, 349; on land reform, 44–47,
276, 281–85, 287–96, 303–7, 309–
28; on Malaysia, 201–2, 210–11,
217, 219, 220–21, 222, 227, 231–
34, 240–41, 242–46, 381; on

Manipol, 94–99; on National Front,
100–2; on nationalism, 30, 33–34,
52, 53, 202, 277, 336, 396; on
Pantja Sila, 92–95; on parliamentary system, 48, 68–76 *passim*, 77–
79, 88, 99–100, 101, 110–11, 117–
20, 122, 123–26; on peasantry, 45–
47, 49, 63, 146–47, 276–77, 279–
82, 294, 295, 297–304, 306–9,
311-12, 315–16, 321, 324–26; on
police, 113; on regional government,
130–32; on religion, 92–95, 99,
115; on socialism, 65, 170, 171,
172–73, 356; theory of state, 61–
62, 132–40 *passim*, 397–98, 403;
on united national front policy,
46–48, 51, 58–59, 62–63, 67–69,
84, 159, 325; on West Irian, 165,
190, 192, 232, 234
Ali, *see* Sastroamidjojo, Ali
Ali, S. M., 172n
Aliarcham Academy, 162, 256
Anderson, Benedict R. O'G., 31, 31n,
33n, 34n, 35, 36n, 38n, 194n,
426
Angkatan Muda, 35
Angkatan Pemuda Indonesia, 37
Ansor, G. P., 317, 424
Apter, David E., 22n
Armed forces, 113–14, 115, 371–72,
382–83; *see also* Army
Army, 114, 187, 196, 198, 203, 242–
43, 250, 251, 265, 322, 361,
374–75, 404; and confrontation,
79, 109, 207, 209, 242–43, 245,
374, 381, 436; coup, 387–92,
393, 394, 415, 416, 420, 421,
433–34; extramilitary activity,
65, 66, 68, 109–12; under Guided
Democracy, 105, 109–10, 120,
168, 402, 403; and Sukarno, 69–